Simon J. Ortiz

D1736132

Simon J. Ortiz

A Poetic Legacy of Indigenous Continuance

Edited by Susan Berry Brill de Ramírez
and Evelina Zuni Lucero

University of New Mexico Press | Albuquerque

© 2009 by the University of New Mexico Press
All rights reserved. Published 2009
Printed in the United States of America

LIBRARY OF CONGRESS CATALOGING-IN-PUBLICATION DATA
Simon J. Ortiz : a poetic legacy of indigenous continuance /
    edited by Susan Berry Brill de Ramírez and Evelina Zuni Lucero.
        p. cm.
    Includes bibliographical references and index.
    ISBN 978-0-8263-3988-1 (PBK. : ALK. PAPER)
1. Ortiz, Simon J., 1941– —Criticism and interpretation.
I. Brill de Ramírez, Susan Berry, 1955–
II. Lucero, Evelina Zuni, 1953–
PS3565.R77Z87 2009
818'.5409—dc22

                    2008052978

Book design and type composition by Kathleen Sparkes.
This book was composed using Warnock Pro OT 10.5/13.5, 26P.
Display type is Warnock Pro family as well.

CONTENTS

《

《

FOREWORD

Thank You, Simon

Greg Cajete

I first met Simon as a teacher at the Institute of American Indian Arts in Santa Fe, New Mexico, where we both taught in the mid-1970s. I was the new high school science teacher and Simon was teaching creative writing. In our roles as teachers, we initiated our relationship and responsibility for passing on our knowledge to the next generation. Since then, Simon has continued to pass on his knowledge of creative writing and Native life in various institutions in the United States, Canada, and around the world, spreading his wealth of knowledge about Indigenous consciousness and places through his teaching and his gift of poetry.

Simon's work and his personal contribution to Native studies programs in general and specifically to the University of New Mexico's program has been significant since its early years. First as a former faculty member of the University of New Mexico Native American Studies program and as an articulate advocate for Indigenous rights and issues, Simon has personally influenced several generations of students. In addition, his writing is consistently used in Native American studies programs and courses throughout the United States and Canada.

I.

"That's the place that Indian people talk about" is a phrase that Simon has used to describe where he comes from in the writing of his poetry. The specific poem of this title points to Paiute sacred places at Oso Springs, but as he does here and elsewhere in his writing, Simon stories the ancestral lands that are sacred to Indigenous America, sharing the deep feelings that we have for our homelands, using poetry and storytelling to convey this more broadly to all his readers. As Simon reminds us, sacred place is at once a place of spirit, of his home of Acoma, of his consciousness as a poet and an Indigenous man, and about his personal journey through the Indigenous landscape and his own inner landscape of mind and spirit.

Through his extensive reflections as a poet, teacher, and human being, Simon teaches all of us, through the power of the orality of the spoken word, that the world, especially the Indigenous world, is a multifaceted, multicontextual world. Through his poetry, he makes us see, feel, and hear our worlds anew. He helps us "remember to remember" where we come from, our places of origin, and our possible destinies.[1]

Because he is a Pueblo man, an Acoma man, a descendant of the generations of the Pueblo Revolt, Simon's work has given contemporary Pueblo people a perspective of ourselves that is invaluable as a frame of reference for our contemporary lives and for the ongoing development of Pueblo identity.

It is important to remember that Simon is first and foremost a contemporary Pueblo Storyteller. In this role, Simon perpetuates the Pueblo tradition of storytelling. As explained in my book on Indigenous education, elders, grandmothers and grandfathers, great aunts and great uncles, hold the stories of their families and their people. It is they who give the stories, the words of good thought and action, to the next generation. . . . They tell us what it means to be one of the People. They tell us about our relationship with one another and to all things that are a part of our world. They tell us about the nature of respect, responsibility and care for one another and our community. So it goes, giving and receiving, giving and receiving stories—helping us all to remember that the story of our community is really the story of ourselves (169). Simon is a Pueblo Storyteller!

II.

Simon's work as a poet, storyteller, and teacher spans centuries of tribal history and memory and his own experiences as a reflective soul, engaging his own inner world, all in relation to his outer world as an Acoma man, an Indigenous man living in a modern world. He shares this inner dialogue with us through his poetry, through his example, and through his teaching.

Simon carries forward the oral tradition of Indigenous America that has always been an essential aspect of traditional teaching. In Indigenous consciousness, poems are first and foremost *teachings*, the foundation of Indigenous songs, prayers, and stories which articulate our most cherished relationships, our philosophy, our history, and our visions. In this sense, Simon's work becomes a source of content and methodology for exploring the nuances of Indigenous community life and place. In these times when Indigenous communities span reservations and urban settings, communal and personal spaces, Simon stories a sense for our place in the world. Story allows individual life, community life, and the life and processes of the natural world to transmit Indigenous thought. In turn, he conveys how the vitality of Indigenous thought is dependent upon and contributes to the lives of those individuals who, in turn, are in relationship with the places, the history, and the lives (past, present, and into the future) of Indigenous people.

Indigenous community is a Story that is a collection of individual stories, ever unfolding in the lives of the people who are part of that tribe, that family. Indigenous community is a living entity whose story is vitalized when it is nourished through the attention of its tellers and its listeners. Ideally, the listeners learn and become ever more integrated as persons and as community members. When a story finds that special circumstance, when its message is fully received, it induces a direct and powerful understanding. It then becomes a real teaching. This is the essence of what Simon achieves through his poetry, his fiction, and his nonfiction.[2]

Collectively, Indian people must address the inherent challenge of finding ways to live their guiding stories in contemporary life. The challenge is difficult, but the stories we live by define us as a tribal people, and when these defining stories cease to live through us, we become truly image without substance. Alienated from the roots of our primal stories, we drift in the ocean of contemporary mass society, continually trying to define ourselves through prepackaged images and distorted stories that are not our own.

There is a symbiotic relationship between the storyteller, the story, and the listener. If listeners nourish the story through their spirit, it can tell them something useful about their lives that they can hear and apply. Living our personal myths through a contemporary form of Indigenous *storying* ensures that we remain connected to the guiding stories that have given us life, so that, as Simon reflects, we can come to "the place that Indian people talk about." Simon helps us realize that if we are looking for something on which to build our lives, we should look not just to the facts of the world, but also to our own stories, spirit, and imagination. Simon continues to show us ways to do this through his writing and his teaching.

May the good spirits guide and keep us always as we journey to "the place that Indian people talk about." Let us all Be With Life! *Beh-Wo-Wah Nhee Nee!*

NOTES

1. Gregory Cajete, *Look to the Mountain: An Ecology of Indigenous Education* (Durango, Colorado: Kivaki Press, 1994), 169.

2. In this paragraph, Cajete reemphasizes concepts that are here reprinted from his earlier book, *Look to the Mountain*. In this context, he articulates the importance of these ideas in relation to Oritz (169).

WORK CITED

Cajete, Gregory. *Look to the Mountain: An Ecology of Indigenous Education.* Durango, Colorado: Kivaki Press, 1994.

ACKNOWLEDGMENTS

This volume has been a project three years in the making and indeed has been a labor of love. The process has involved intensive collaboration with co-editor Susan Brill Berry de Ramirez, whose careful and insightful editing I have learned much from. Susan first proposed the project in 2005, following the publication of the special *Studies in American Indian Literatures* (*SAIL*) issue she edited that focused on Simon. Our first collaboration involved pitching the book idea to Luther Wilson at the University of New Mexico Press and then crafting a book proposal, thus establishing a successful pattern of give and take in formulating the book idea, editing, and structuring. I thank all contributors to this volume for their careful scholarship and creative endeavors in bringing to the forefront Ortiz's place in Native American, American, and world literature; I thank my family for their patience and encouragement during the process. I also thank the Institute of American Indian Arts for their support of this project. It was during my year of sabbatical that the final stage of the project was accomplished. Were it not for the time granted me for creative and scholarly endeavors, as well as funding for travel to conferences, completion of the project would have been set back. Special thanks go to Ann Filemyr, Dean of the Center for Arts and Cultural Studies, and my creative writing colleague, Jon Davis, for this support. Finally, I would like to thank Simon Ortiz for his words, both spoken and written, that have been an inspiration and at times, an utter amazement. *Her-kem* to all.

I, too, would like to thank each of the contributors for their words, their insights, their vision. Through the co-editorial course of researching, reading, and writing for this volume, I have learned much about the literary achievements of Simon J. Ortiz. The Association for the Study of American Indian Literatures (ASAIL), the Modern Language

Association's division on American Indian Literatures, and the journal *SAIL* all provided the initial impetus for the focus on Simon Ortiz's work with a special session at the New Orleans Modern Language Association annual conference in 2001 and the special *SAIL* issue 16.4 (Winter 2004). Thanks go to many, but centrally to the Director of the University of New Mexico Press Luther Wilson who championed this volume from the start. Lisa Pacheco, Acquisitions Editor, Maya Allen-Gallegos, Managing Editor, and Suzanne G. Fox, copy editor, have been invaluable in their guidance and improvements. Bradley University, the Intercultural Activities Committee, and English Department Chairs Peter Dusenbery and Robert Prescott supported much of the work of the volume, including bringing Simon to Peoria for a reading and time with classes and myself, thereby making possible my interview with him. English Department secretaries Carolyn Rosser and, later, Shelley Walker, and graduate assistant Rasheité Radcliff have served in invaluable ways through various stages of the project.

Especial thanks go to my husband Antonio and son Jose, who bore with a wife's and mother's busyness, but most important is my thanks to my co-editor Evelina Zuni Lucero, who provided the needed structure, organization, and creativity that helped to produce a volume that I am continuing to learn from. Insuring the crucial Indigenous and Pueblo grounding for the project, Professor Lucero consistently pushed me to deeper levels of critical inquiry; for example, the introductory sections that are focused specifically on Ortiz's Keres language use and his poetics, developed and written last, would not have been produced were it not for Lucero's insight, encouragement, and support, even though it required lengthening an already long introduction.

So many joys occurred throughout the process of this collection, one of which I feel important to share. During the spring of 2008, our son Jose needed to give a report about a famous American to his fourth grade class; he chose Simon Ortiz, whom he had met the year before. The students were to dress up as their important people, so Jose chose to wear a nice button-down shirt and his father's bolo tie. Jose began his report to his class at St. Mark School in Peoria, Illinois, "I am Simon J. Ortiz, an important American writer!" In this way, Jose honored the man and the writer. So, too, do I want to thank and honor Simon J. Ortiz for his extraordinary accomplishments. Yes, thank you all.

Photo by David Burckhalter. © David Burckhalter.

INTRODUCTION

Simon J. Ortiz

*A Poetic Legacy of Indigenous Continuance,
Belonging, and Commitment*

Susan Berry Brill de Ramírez and
Evelina Zuni Lucero

We are honored to bring out the first edited collection of essays and creative pieces about Native American writer Simon J. Ortiz.[1] This volume directly builds on the special issue of *Studies in American Indian Literatures* (16.4) that was devoted to Ortiz's work. *SAIL* is to be commended for encouraging the experimental scholarly shift that welcomed the new directions of subjective scholarship and testimony, including a powerfully dialogic mix of critical essays, expressive pieces of creative nonfiction, interviews, and poetic illustrations of Ortiz's contributions to Native American, Indigenous, American, and world literatures. Accordingly, this volume, too, draws on diverse communication styles to present the depth and range of Ortiz's contribution. Since he is unquestionably regarded as one of the literary giants of the twentieth and twenty-first centuries, it is indeed time for a book-length collection devoted to Ortiz. Such a volume permits scholars and creative writers to respond to his literary contributions, which began in the early 1970s and extend to the present day. Having published more than two dozen volumes of poetry, prose fiction, children's literature, and nonfiction work, Ortiz has seen his writing widely anthologized around the world.

Native writers active during 1970s, such as Ortiz, N. Scott Momaday, James Welch, Leslie Marmon Silko, and Gerald Vizenor, have each served pivotal roles in developing contemporary Native American literatures and, more broadly, globally Indigenous literatures. The larger literary contributions of each of these writers are such that the very concept of literature has been forever changed. The tribal and communal imperatives that underlie their crafts and their commitments to transformative aesthetics categorically call into question any notions of literature for literature's sake.[2] Ortiz, Momaday, Welch, Silko, Vizenor, and so many other Native American and Indigenous writers worldwide are firmly committed to helping create an accessible and engaged literature that serves the wellbeing of persons and communities, despite contemporary poststructural privilegings of the text at the presumed expense of story. In a proffering to the nation whose imperial expansionism has perpetuated the prior European colonization of Native peoples and Native lands, Ortiz concludes his introduction to his collection *Woven Stone* thus: "The United States will not be able to survive unless it comes to know and truly accept its indigenous reality and this is its continuance. Through our poetry, prose, and other written works that evoke love, respect, and responsibility, Native Americans may be able to help the United States of America to go beyond survival" (32–33).

I

Voice of Experience, Vision of Continuance

Evelina Zuni Lucero

Beginnings are often small, like the trickle of snowmelt in spring that becomes the headwaters of a mighty river. In Simon J. Ortiz's case, an analogous watershed moment in his life came when as an impressionable young man he discovered the Beat poets, in particular Allen Ginsberg and Gary Snyder. Noting that their writing was about experience, "writing from and about experience and writing as experience," he was struck with a surprising revelation: "And the revelation that was brought to light for me was that as an Acoma person I also had something important, unique to say" ("Introduction," *Woven Stone*, 19). At eighteen, Ortiz could not know that thirty years after the publication of his first book in 1977 he would be hailed by Native literary critics Jace Weaver, Craig S. Womack, and Robert Warrior as one of Native literature's "major statesmen" (Weaver, Womack, Warrior, *Literary Nationalism*, xvi). Nor could he know he would gain a stature and place in world literature. Over the span of his writing career, Ortiz has written poetry that is layered and dense with meaning and moves in multiple directions, essays that confront colonization in the Americas head on, stories that reveal political and social realities in the everyday worlds, actions, and struggles of ordinary people. His voice has rung strong and clear, cutting when he relates Pueblo and Native historical truths, compassionate when he speaks out of the Pueblo philosophy of life that permeates his thinking. Telling his-story conjoined with the stories of Pueblo and all of the Indigenous Peoples in the Americas, he has, in fact, "had something important, unique to say." Telling his-story conjoined with the stories of Pueblo and all of the Indigenous Peoples in the Americas, he has been "writing from and about experience and [living] writing as experience" to the point that one writer observed, "[O]ne does not easily separate the man from his writings" (Weaver, Womack, Warrior, *Literary Nationalism*, xvi).

Journey on the Road of Life
In his essays, Ortiz has written extensively of the development of his voice. His writings taken as whole mark his journey on the *heeyyaanih*, the road of life, and like Ortiz himself, are grounded in the oral tradition and all it encompasses.[3] More than just a theme or dominant motif in his writing, journey is an evocation of his life and literary experiences. The subjects he addresses—language, continuance, interdependence of land, people, and the natural world, and human struggles against adversity—grow out of the oral tradition of Ortiz's Acoma Pueblo, and thus are intertwined concepts constitutive of Ortiz's life and writing.

Ortiz attributes his "native dzheni," the Acoma Keres language, his first language, as a sustaining force in his life. Though he has spoken and written primarily in English throughout his life, he writes in the introduction to *Woven Stone* (1992) that "This early language from birth to six years of age in the Acoma family and community was the basis and source of all I would do later in poetry, short fiction, essay and other works as a storyteller and teacher. . . ." (6). Simon's native language, one of the ancient Indigenous languages of the Americas, forms and informs his sense of self as an Acoma, as does each aspect of his people's culture, land, and history. Language, Story, People, Place, Home—all comprise the knowledge of who he is and of which he has written throughout his career. In his early work, Simon explicitly expresses how story and storyteller emerge from the same place, and form and inform one another in the telling; this can be seen in the sentence-length title of a poem, "Like myself, the source of these narratives is my home. Sometimes my father tells them, sometimes my mother, sometimes even the storyteller himself tells them" (*A Good Journey* in *Woven Stone*, 168). As the title indicates, the poem itself consists of three stories, the first told by his father, presumably the second by his mother, and the third by Ortiz as "storyteller."

In the preface of his 1999 volume of collected short stories, *Men on the Moon*, Ortiz reiterates the relationship between place and story and an Indigenous consciousness: "My identity as a Native American is based on the knowledge of myself as a person from Acoma Pueblo, a cultural and geographical place, and this knowledge has its sources as 'story'" (ix). Some years later, in his poem "Hindruutsi, In The Way of My Own Language That Is My Name," Ortiz again asserts his grounding in his Indigenous identity and consciousness:

> Hindruutsi, I am of the Eagle People.
> Aacqu is my home.
> I am of the Acoma people.
> That is the way therefore I regard myself.
> I cannot be any other way or person
> You must learn this well.
> That is the way therefore you will recognize me.
>   (*Out There Somewhere*, 95)

The body of prayer, song, ritual drama, ceremony, and stories comprising the Pueblo oral tradition conveys, relates, and celebrates culture, social values, history, beliefs, and customs, all of which ground individuals in a Pueblo worldview.[4] Immersed as Ortiz was as a child in the stories of his world and people—traditional narratives of prayer, song, ritual drama and ceremony, historical accounts, family stories, and community gossip—he developed a love for the poetry of language and story that has always been integral to Acoma and Pueblo culture and that still endures. For Ortiz, understanding the full import of the oral tradition came with time. He writes,

> [A]ll [these stories] were interesting and vitally important to me, because though I could not explain it then, they tied me into the

communal body of my people and heritage. I could never hear enough of the stories. Consequently, when I learned to read and write, I believe I felt those stories continued somehow in the new language and use of the new language, and they would never be lost, forgotten, and finally gone. They would always continue. ("Introduction," *Woven Stone*, 9)

A complex social system of customs and beliefs integrates an individual from birth into Pueblo society and, ideally, serves to form a secure sense of being, belonging, and commitment to the community, although as Santa Clara Pueblo scholar Greg Cajete points out, it is "an ideal whose depth of expression is almost never achieved in contemporary communities of today" (*Look to the Mountain: An Ecology of Indigenous Education*, 172). As expressed by Pueblos, it is a process of becoming human,[5] of becoming complete.[6] As a teenager, though not yet able to express it, Ortiz realizes that his "heritage and culture and how they were expressed were the basis of who [he] was and how [he] came into being as a human being" (*Woven Stone*, 18).

Ortiz understands and believes that the oral tradition weaves the Native community together, emphasizing that it encompasses more than just the "verbal-vocal manifestations" of storytelling, songs, and other forms of the oral tradition—extending to include the relationships engendered in the telling, the underlying belief system, and the lifeways that the oral tradition sustains and maintains ("Introduction," *Woven Stone*, 7). In *Look to the Mountain: An Ecology of Indigenous Education*, Cajete develops the idea of the oral tradition as a source of content and methodology for Indigenous community education, explaining that "Indigenous cultures are extensions of the story of the natural community of a place, and they evolve according to ecological dynamics and natural relationships" (169). Pueblos don't just live in communities; they live Community. Participation in community on some level—familial, social, governmental, ceremonial—in different servitor roles assumed over time and in varying degrees nurtures relationships that in turn strengthen and maintain community and bonding to homeland, and a spirit of resistance to outside assaults. Cajete elaborates on the instruction, guidance, and personal and collective history that is passed on in the intimacy of family and close relationships and to be lived out in community participation, the core strength of Pueblos:

In Indigenous communities, the elders, the grandmothers and grandfathers hold the stories of their families and their people. It is they who give the stories, the words of good thought and action to the children. They tell the children how the world and their people came to be. They tell the children of their experiences, their life. They tell them what it means to be one of the People. They tell them about their relationship to each other and to all things that are part of their world. They tell them about respect—just as their grandparents told them when they were children. So it goes, giving and receiving, giving and receiving stories—helping children remember to remember that the story of their community is really the story of themselves! (*Look to the Mountain*, 169)

In fact, since colonization began, the oral tradition in its many forms (song, ceremony, ritual drama, as well as story) has especially been a cohesive continuum of stories. In his landmark 1981 essay, "Towards A National Indian Literature: Cultural Authenticity in Nationalism,"[7] Ortiz writes, "Indeed through the past five centuries the oral tradition has been the most reliable method by which Indian culture and community integrity have been maintained" (256). Making the necessary and crucial point that the oral tradition in all its forms is an ongoing process, incorporating "foreign ritual, ideas, and material in [the people's] own terms," using the "newer languages" of conquest and hybrid continuance (Spanish, French, and English), their Story, including the event and impact of colonization, is remembered, signified, and expressed, most importantly, "on their own terms" (256–57). The oral tradition relates the people's Story, the collective journey through time that they continue to live out in spirit, practice, and belief, and reenact in story in ways that draw them together as a people.

According to our emergence story, Pueblo people emerged from the underworld at Shipapu in the north. The people of the current nineteen Pueblos, autonomous communities with details of the emergence story specific to each people, journeyed to their present locations along and west of the Rio Grande. Laguna Pueblo writer Leslie Marmon Silko points out that although each of the Pueblos specifies its place of emergence, usually associated with a body of water, "it is clear the Pueblo people do not view any single location or natural springs as the one and only true Emergence Place. Each Pueblo group recounts stories connected with Creation, Emergence, and Migration, although it is believed that all human beings, with all the animals and plants, emerged at the same place and at the same time" ("Interior and Exterior Landscapes: The Pueblo Migration Stories," 36). It is from these stories of journey that Pueblo people form their Indigenous concepts of themselves, journeys made since time immemorial in a series of migrations, journeys that are personal, collective, historical, and spiritual, exterior and interior,[8] reenacted in reverent story, song, ritual dance and mime, and ceremony. Of his own people, Ortiz writes, "Acoma Pueblo people believe they came into Existence as a human culture and community at Shipapu, which they know as a sacred mythic place of origin. Shipapu and a belief in Shipapu, therefore and thereafter, is the mythic source of their Existence" ("Introduction," *Speaking for the Generations: Native Writers on Writing*, xiii–xiv). When he describes his Pueblo's migration, Ortiz uses the Keres language to place his community and name his people, as well as assert the people's cultural sovereignty:

> Aacqumeh hanoh's name for the local community . . . is
> Deetseyamah—The North Door. Looking northward from Aacqu
> [the old pueblo] and the tall rock monolith on which the mother
> pueblo sits, there is an opening, like a gateway between two
> mesas. . . . Aacqumeh hanoh came to their valley from a direction
> spoken of as the northwest. The place they came to had been
> prepared for them, and the name Aacqu, therefore means that:
> Which Is Prepared. . . . Their journey had been long and difficult
> from the northwest through vast experience, trials, and crises.
> Kaashkatruti, that's where we lived before, the people say in
> their oral tradition, pointing northwestward ("Our Homeland, a
> National Sacrifice Area," *Woven Stone*, 337–38).

Pueblo homelands are infused with a sense of the sacred in the land: specific mountains, mesas, rivers, lakes, and springs designated as sacred sites and places of power, home to spirits, and plant and animal helpers. As recorded in oral narratives, the ancestral Pueblo homeland that was given to the People by the Creator included Colorado, northwest New Mexico, and west central New Mexico, northeast Arizona and east central Arizona (Sando, *Pueblo Nations: Eight Centuries of Pueblo Indian History*, 22), aboriginal territory later "claimed" by Spanish explorers for the Spanish Crown in 1540 and later "acquired" by the United States from Mexico through war.[9]

Since 1539, the People's story is layered with the colonial legacy of successive Spanish, Mexican, and American governments which has been incorporated into collective memory. Beginning in 1539, the Spaniards undertook a series of expeditions to explore, missionize, and colonize with the initial aim of securing riches, laying claim to the land, and subduing our Native populations, actions that prompted Ortiz in "Our Homeland, A National Sacrifice Area" to refer to the conquistadors as "mercenaries, errand boys, and mystics" (*Woven Stone*, 341). The ninety-three Pueblo settlements (Dunbar-Ortiz, *Roots of Resistance: A History of Land Tenure in New Mexico*, 11) viewed the initial expeditions as intrusions and responded to them with armed resistance.

The first expedition in 1539 led by Franciscan friar Marcos de Niza was launched in search of the fabled Seven Cities of Cibola. The Moorish slave Esteban sent ahead of Niza was killed when he angered Hawikuh (Zuni Pueblo) with his threatening demands for women and gifts. Without entering the pueblo, Niza erected a cross and laid claim to the land for Spain; upon his return to Mexico, he substantiated the existence of Cibola. One year later, in 1540, Francisco Vasquez de Coronado set out on a second expedition in search of the Seven Cities of Gold. First angered by the rape of a woman and later by the imprisonment of Pueblo leaders during the Spaniards' quest for gold, the Pueblos rose up against the Spaniards and were forcibly quelled. After scouting the land and finding it suitable for colonies but lacking in gold and wealth, the expeditionary force returned south with an injured Coronado. In 1581, Augustine Rodriguez led a third expedition, this time an ill-fated missionary effort. Several expeditions later in 1598, Don Juan de Oñate established a colony in New Mexico, founding its capital in northern New Mexico across the river from present day Ohkay Owingeh Pueblo (formerly referred to as San Juan Pueblo). The capital later moved to Santa Fe. The Spaniards imposed an autocratic civil and church rule upon the Pueblos. Under the *encomienda* and *repartimiento* systems, soldiers and colonists were given land grants of Pueblo lands through which civil and religious leaders could extract Pueblo labor and taxes of produce, clothing, and hides. The conflicted legacy of this history is such that even as Coronado and Oñate are venerated as founding fathers by New Mexican Hispanos, they are regarded as figures of brutal and horrific infamy by Pueblos.

The Pueblos chafed under the repressive, corrupt, and exploitative economic and religious system, with its imposed Christian practices and intolerance of Pueblo sacred beliefs manifested in the harassment of religious leaders, whippings, and forbidding of Pueblo religious activities. The Pueblo Revolt of 1680, a concerted resistance by Pueblos with their allies, Navajos, Apaches, *genizaros* of mixed Indigenous descent, mestizos, and mulattos, drove out the Spaniards for twelve years. In 1692, the Spanish colonists and military under Diego de Vargas returned, their mission now to hold a northern frontier. Open resistance continued for a few years afterward, though it lacked the full-scale unity of the Pueblo Revolt. Eventually, the resistance lessened as the colonists and Pueblos gradually accommodated one another, though the Pueblos did not stop resenting the Spanish civil and religious systems. As a result, the Pueblo religion was taken underground to preserve its integrity.[10]

Following Mexico's successful revolution against Spain in 1823, colonization by Spaniards in the Rio Grande valley gave way to short-lived Mexican control of the northern frontier. Because of other critical matters facing the new government and its distance from central Mexico, the northern territory was largely ignored, during which time the Pueblos suffered further land losses. The newly formed Mexican government had granted Indians all rights of citizenship, including the right to buy and sell property. By taking advantage of the preoccupied central government, officials in the northern frontier obtained Pueblo land by falsifying documents and titles to the land. Then in 1849, the United States acquired the Southwest, including New Mexico west of the Rio Grande and north of the Gadsden Purchase of 1853, as part of the Guadalupe-Hidalgo treaty that ended the Mexican-American War. The Gadsden Purchase later added southern portions of New Mexico and Arizona to the U.S. holdings.

A new era of struggle for cultural and political sovereignty began for the Pueblos. The U.S. territorial government recognized the unique standing granted the Pueblos by the Spanish and Mexicans, but did not officially recognize the Pueblos as Indians with the same protections of their land and resources as other U.S. tribes until 1913. In the intervening years, the Pueblos filed a series of lawsuits to protect their land and resources. In 1876, the Supreme Court ruled in a case detrimental to the Pueblos, *United States v. Joseph*, that Pueblo lands were not federally protected and the Pueblos, as "civilized Indians" who were not federal wards, could sell their lands to non-Indians. By the early 1900s, a significant number of Hispanos and Anglos had obtained title to Indian land-grant holdings through purchase or squatting. In a 1913 reversal of the *Joseph* ruling, the Supreme Court in *United States v. Sandoval* found that the Pueblos "were entitled to the same federal protection as other tribes—including protection against their land being sold to or settled by non-Indians" (Wegner 382), jeopardizing non-Indian claims to ancestral Pueblo land. New Mexico's response was a congressional bill introduced in 1922 by New Mexico Senator Holm O. Bursum, which effectively provided non-Indians a way to obtain title to Indian lands and water rights. The Council of All the New Mexico Pueblos decried the bill as a simultaneous assault on Pueblo land, culture, and sovereignty, since it also awarded the state jurisdiction over civil and criminal matters in the Pueblos (Wenger, "Land, Culture, and Sovereignty in the Pueblo Dance Controversy," 383). An organized and massive outcry by Native and non-Native organizations led to the bill's defeat. The Pueblo Land Act of 1924 established a lands board to clear the claims to some 60,000 acres of Pueblo lands by non-Indians that arose out of the 1876 Supreme Court ruling. Most of the lands board's findings, however, favored non-Indians, and Pueblos did not receive adequate compensation for lost titles and no compensation for titles the board extinguished.[11]

Acquisition of New Mexico by Anglo-Americans brought dramatic changes to the Pueblo rhythm of life, and land and water use. The building of the railroad, introduction of wage economy, mining, education, and attacks on Pueblo religion necessitated a continued struggle for sovereignty and protection of aboriginal land and water rights, which were unrecognized by the United States. More recent battles waged by the Pueblos include the Taos Blue Lake controversy, which resulted in the lake being returned to Taos Pueblo in 1970, and the legislative battle with the state over casino compacts in the 1990s. In a state that touts its tricultural heritage (Hispanic, Native, and Anglo-American) to encourage tourism, the Pueblos also faced a series of controversial celebrations of conquest: the three hundredth anniversary of the reconquest of the Pueblos by Diego de Vargas in 1692; the "Cuarto Centenario," or the four hundredth anniversary of Don Juan de Oñate's colonization of New Mexico in 1598 and erection of an Oñate monument at Alcalde, New Mexico; and the three hundredth anniversary of the founding of Albuquerque in 1706.[12]

Seeking to expose this dark legacy of five centuries of colonization, Ortiz gives voice to our struggles and active resistance to colonizing forces. In "Our Homeland: A National Sacrifice Area," Ortiz covers the span of Pueblo oral history from time immemorial to the 1980s, highlighting changes to the Pueblo way of life and beliefs, and the continual exploitation, oppression, and environmental degradation that resulted from centuries of colonialism, the American expansionist agenda, and capitalist impulse. Ortiz notes the People sometimes dwell on stories of past good times when grass, rain, and food were abundant and the people secure, but they do so not out of a wistful reminiscence, but to set the context for the struggles they faced when change inevitably came and times became hard:

> In the oral tradition, war, crisis, and famine are spoken about. The people had to cope with eras when catastrophe came suddenly, inevitably, and perhaps necessarily when the people had not paid careful heed to their responsibilities. They speak about dissension among clans and within families. They note the loss of good leadership, due to ineptitude and corruption and bad judgment. The oral tradition does not ignore bad times and mistakes that people have made throughout their history. And it is told in mythic proportion in order to impress upon those hearing that there are important lessons, values, and principles to be learned. ("Our Homeland: A National Sacrifice Area," 345)

During precolonial times of hardship, the people relied on Indigenous knowledge to address challenges. Pueblo oral tradition, however, records a time of change that the people were inadequately equipped to deal with—"a change that was bent upon a kind of destruction that was total and undeterred and over which they seemed to have no control" ("Our Homeland: A National Sacrifice Area," 346). That change, of course, was the coming of European and, later, American military, political, religious, and economic systems. Yet the people never gave in, never ceased resisting colonization whether through armed resistance, legal and political recourse, or maintaining their cultural integrity in the face of forcible pressures to assimilate. As Ortiz articulates in "Towards a National Indian Literature," the oral tradition has been at once a creative response to colonization and one of resistance, including the crucial role of oral tradition in lands rights litigations, resistance to cultural assimilation, and affirmations of tribal sovereignty. Drawing on an extended example of the incorporation of a specific Catholic ritual into an Aacqumeh ceremony, Ortiz makes the point that the celebration is, nevertheless, distinctly Acoma, notwithstanding its adoption of Spanish names and the Christian practice of celebrating saints' days: "[T]his celebration speaks of the creative ability of Indian people to gather in many forms of the socio-political colonizing force which beset them and to make these forms meaningful *in their own terms*" (254, emphasis added), an intentional act of refusal to succumb to the myths of conquest and to forsake cultural ways of expression. Ortiz uses a second example of a ritual drama reenacting the Aacquma hanoh's encounter with the Spaniards[13] to illustrate how the oral tradition "speaks crucially about the experience of colonization" (256), again an act of resistance in its determination to tell of their experience. The essay is itself an act of resistance against entrapment of the "Indian" in cultural and representational stasis and is an assertion of indigeneity in Native terms. Ortiz writes, "It has been this resistance—political, armed, spiritual—which has been carried out by the oral tradition. The continued use of the oral tradition today is evidence that the resistance is on-going. Its use, in fact, is what has given rise to the surge of literature created by contemporary Indian authors" (257). In these ways, Ortiz teaches us to embrace the vitality and necessity of orality, stories, and literature.

The Flow of Life

More strongly than any other Native writer, Ortiz articulates and demonstrates the oral tradition as a dynamic lifeway to resist, teach, integrate, guide, and map one's way, most particularly in navigating the treacherous minefields of colonialism laid upon the Indigenous landscape, all the while maintaining an Indigenous consciousness. With the fullness of his traditional background to draw upon, Ortiz is able to bring the continuance of the oral tradition into his written literature in ways that few other Native writers can, a gift that he offers as a responsibility to and from his people. Ortiz writes of his teen years, "I became aware that I was living in a time and place that was the result of change in which Native American people had a role. . . . Though I didn't understand exactly how this role worked or could work, I felt it was there and nothing could change it. Therefore it was important to remember the past so that I could learn from it what there was to do in the present" ("Introduction," *Woven Stone*, 17). This thought is expressed in the collective in the poem "This is the Way Still We Shall Go On":

> It is necessary to look back to the past.
> Gazing we will see how our peoples in the past lived,
> how they were guided, how they lived well,
> We who are living today, that is how we are to be guided by.
> That is the way of living that will be correct and good for us
> (*Out There Somewhere*, 92).

In "It Is No Longer the Same As It Was in the Olden Days," Ortiz articulates the sense of continuity conveyed in the oral tradition. "Yes, although it is no longer like the past days were, / still necessarily toward the future we must look. / That is the way still we must keep on going" (*Out There Somewhere*, 98). "The way still we must keep on going" conveys the urgency and necessity of continuance with which the oral tradition strengthens the People through vexing and changing times. In poetic tribute to the resilience the oral tradition makes possible, his poem "Right of Way" addresses the difficulty the speaker has in explaining to elders yet another request by the state for a right of way on the People's land. Rather than remain disempowered in a silence "that is no way to continue / and you want to continue"—the speaker tells stories about the birth and growth and struggles of his People and children, "You tell that kind of history, / and you pray and be humble. / With strength, it will continue that way. / That is the only way. / That is the only way" (*Fight Back* in *Woven Stone*, 260).

His early work, *Going for the Rain* (narrative poems based on the oral tradition), and *A Good Journey* (with journey as the narrative thread), was initially compiled into one manuscript and then later separated for publication. In these books, Ortiz states he sought to "instill that sense of continuity essential to the poetry and stories in the books, essential to Native American life in fact. . . . This quality of continuity or continuance I believe must be included and respected in every aspect of Native life and outlook" ("Introduction," *Woven Stone*, 9). He explains that continuance is living one's life fully and responsibly in the time, circumstances, and place into which one is born, and with a conscious awareness of one's lived and inherited past:

I have often heard Native American elders repeat, "We must always remember," referring to grandmothers and grandfathers, heritage, and the past with a sense of something more than memory or remembering at stake. *It is knowing present place and time, being present in the here and now essentially,* just as past generations knew place and time whether they were Acoma, Lakota, or Mayan people. *Continuance, in this sense, is life itself* ("Introduction," *Woven Stone*, 9–10, emphasis added).

Here Ortiz conveys that oral history is not simply a preservation of the past as a static historical record, but an ongoing, living history, a flow of time, event, and experience to be lived fully in the "here and now," the act of which carries the past into the present, into the future. In this way, Ortiz reminds us that our identity as Native people is a function of where we come from, historically, tribally, geographically. As Pueblo people, our presence, our present, is a gift from the struggles of our ancestors through time, surviving beyond the horrors of conquest and the challenges of our tribes' continuance to the present day. In turn, our presence, our present, is our gift to the future.

In "Four Years Ago," from Ortiz's early poetry collection *Going for the Rain*, in which he stories his journeys throughout the United States, he expresses how this sense of Indigenous continuity on these lands attains meaning only in the passage of reflective time and lived existence. The Indigenous speaker of the poem, en route home, experiences uncertainty, an ahistorical moment, while "somewhere" in Wisconsin "four years ago." Ortiz shows us how language and story and an accompanying perspective reground the speaker in time and place:

> I wondered
> in what period of history
> I was then.
>
> I wonder that now.
>
> Yesterday,
> I told my wife,
> "You must see me
> in the perspective
> of my whole life."

It all adds
Ups and downs
(*Woven Stone*, 95–96).

The poem suggests that life, history, a person, becomes knowable when set in perspective. Meaning or significance only comes in retrospect and reflection. In the prologue to *A Good Journey*, Ortiz explicitly observes that understanding of self, of life, comes only with the experience of life, with its accompanying despair and tragedy, beauty and joy, moments of confusion and clarity: "It is all part of the traveling that is a prayer. There are things he [a man] must go through before he can bring back what he seeks, before he can return to himself" (38). Upon return, the man's prayers bring the blessing of rain, and more: "The man returns to the strength that his selfhood is, his home, his people, his language, the knowledge of who he is. The cycle has been traveled; life has beauty and meaning, and it will continue because life has no end" (*Woven Stone*, 38).

Formed and informed as he was in his Indigenous self by his community, language, culture, and history in his early years, Ortiz nonetheless had to withstand assaults on his sense of self as he grew older, eventually finding that strength spoken of in *Journey's* prologue, which came to him with maturity, life experience, and reflection. As a teen, watching changes wrought by the intrusions of the larger, outside white American world into the Acoma world, Ortiz states, "With astonishment, amazement, and occasional bewilderment, I noticed these things, and I thought about them seriously as a young Native American saw an older world change under his feet" ("Introduction," *Woven Stone*, 16). Being able to articulate these changes and what they meant to his Native sense of self, however, was also part of his development as a writer. Making note of the powerful force the dominant American culture can exert on colonized people, he writes of his own early struggle for a Native voice: "Just as it claimed land and sovereignty, American society and culture can claim your soul. . . . [W]hile I knew myself as an Acoma and was inspired by an emerging ethnic cultural nationalism, I did not write about being Native American" (*Woven Stone*, 20). This awareness and the effect on his evolving craft as a poet and prose writer is evident throughout his writing. After his initial suppression of a Native identity, Ortiz does not flinch from the harsh realities of the Native experience in his own life, or that which has occurred historically and in the Western hemisphere.

"A San Diego Poem: January to February 1973" aptly illustrates Ortiz's journey to voice. Consisting of four poems about an airplane journey, it beautifully demonstrates the power of story, of the oral tradition, to help us make our way through the confusion and uncertainty of modern times. The first poem, titled "The Journey Begins," starts with traditional prayer; in the second poem "Shuddering," as the plane lifts off, the speaker longs to find among the "bland" expressions assumed by his fellow travelers a face demonstrating "a stark history," no matter what that might be—murder or angst; in flight, increasingly agitated, the speaker seeks in vain to orient himself to the earth below, an act that could ground, comfort, and calm him in this uncertain venture: "I recite the cardinal points of my Acoma life, / the mountains, the radiance coming / from those sacred points, gathering / into the center." Lacking the sense of direction, however, he is unable to center himself, nor can he find comfort in reciting rote Catholic prayers. Furthermore, the speaker states, "The prayers of my Native selfhood / have been strangled in my throat" (*A Good Journey*, in *Woven Stone*, 166), a poetic statement of the struggles of the subaltern to speak, to articulate self and world.

The third of the San Diego poems, "Under L.A. International Airport," turns to the speaker's experience of being lost in the tunnels under the airport, evoking the deeply ironic image of the Native as an alien immigrant lost in the underbelly of the American system, unable to navigate his way in a foreign world superimposed upon Native lands:

> Even with a clear head, I've never been good
> at finding my way out of American labyrinths.
> They all look alike to me. . . .
> I am somewhat educated, I can read and use a compass;
> yet the knowledge of where I am is useless.
> Instead, it is a sad, disheartening burden.
> I am a poor, tired wretch in this maze (167).

The fourth poem, "Survival This Way," marks the way through the confusion. It is an affirmation of continuance and the role played by language in that process. Here and always, Ortiz's words demonstrate the strength that has been crucial to Pueblo culture and continuance. Ortiz writes of the assurance of survival for Indigenous people in America through story:

We traveled this way,
gauged our distances by stories
and loved our children.
We taught them
to love their births.
We told ourselves over and over
again,
"We shall survive this way" (168).

His poetry and short stories of the late '60s to the early '80s were complied into *Woven Stone* in 1992 and *Men on the Moon* in 1998. Ortiz's focus on journey[14] and oral tradition in his early work is brought together to a focus on maps in subsequent poems. He writes his way from the Acoma Pueblo of his childhood through the realities of late twentieth century and early twenty-first-century American racism and colonization. *After and Before the Lightning*, his 1994 collection of poems written during a winter on the prairies of South Dakota on the Rosebud Indian reservation, consists of poems recording observations, story, memory, a season ("a reality that could not be denied"), and addresses the literal and metaphorical winters of his life. In the preface, Ortiz states the volume was written to give meaning (a map) to his existence, to locate himself not only physically on the "endless snowy sweep of the prairie," but in the cosmos:

On a daily basis and in a moment-to-moment way, I found
this poetry reconnecting my life to all Existence with a sense
of wonder and awe. . . . When the poems came about and I
wrote them, I felt like I was putting together a map of where I
was in the cosmos. I'm not certain that "map" is the correct term,
and I'm not certain if, as a writer and poet, I was even successful
in noting and expressing what I wanted and need most of all:
reassurance that by facing reality—winter and my life—I was
doing the right thing. Yet I believe now I'm doing the right thing
and I will stand by that (xiii–xiv).

In many ways, Ortiz's poetic maps serve the important similar function of geographic familiarization found in our Pueblo oral hunting stories. Not only do these stories mark an event and provide useful knowledge about hunting (or, in Ortiz's poetry, about the experiences of one man and those he has known), but both the hunting stories and the poetry also literally serve as maps to assist others who travel similar pathways. Silko has explained that hunting stories in the oral tradition held more than mere entertainment value. They also conveyed necessary information about the behavior and migration patterns of mule deer, along with details of geography, descriptions of landmarks, and locations of fresh water: "Thus, a deer-hunt story might also serve as a map," which later saved people who lost their way but found their bearings after spotting landmarks described in the story (Silko, "Interior and Exterior Landscapes," 32).

Such mapping also serves well as a metaphor for the guidance and orientation that stories can provide to travelers on the road of life. Even more specifically, in traditional and even in many contemporary hunting stories, much as in Ortiz's poems, markers and directions guide listeners and readers beyond the more literal details of the hunts or their respective geographies. In "Across the Prairie," Ortiz writes of the *haitsee*, a hoop made of oak with cotton string marking the four directions and the center. Explaining the larger significance of the haitsee, the speaker says,

> It's a map of the sky-universe,
> my father said. You make one
> when you prepare to travel.
> So you will always know
> where you are, to where to return.
> Haitsee, a map of the universe
> > (*After and Before the Lightning*, 21–22).

The poem speaks to centering, connection, and guidance through orientation in the cosmos along the axis points, internal and external grounding, on a large scale of destiny, memory, and time, what Brill de Ramírez terms a "geography of belonging" that is affirmed and strengthened through Ortiz's use of relational language and story ("A Geography of Belonging: Ortiz's Poetic, Lived, and Storied Indigenous Ecology, 25–26").[15]

Similarly, in another poem from the collection, "Long Roads," that sense of connection and distance in the perspective of the long roads of South Dakota "from here / into the blue snow distance. / Cosmic lines drawn forth" in the first stanza is set against a larger scale of destiny, and time and distance of the cosmos in the second. Ortiz uses the collective "we" to write comparatively of the collective memory/journey across the cosmos, across the reaches of time: "Long roads are our history. / And the dream's songs / are imbedded in blood-memory" (21). With the connotations inherent in "blood" as life, as flow, as ancestry, the imagery in "blood-memory" invokes continuance of the People and the People's story since the primal mists of time immemorial. Travelers on long roads we are all, embarking on individual and collective journeys, "gaug[ing] our distances by stories" as Ortiz writes in "Survival This Way." Noting that his poems are marking his path, Ortiz states, "Living and writing evolve as I continue to live and write. I am most conscious of my life as a journey, and what I write is a map that comes about every moment for me. Every day is like that and that's my certainty, a memory of how my journey has been till now" (*After and Before the Lightning*, xvi).

In *Out There Somewhere*, published in 2002, he places himself "out there somewhere in America," physically away from his Aacqumeh homeland, but not "in any absolute way" ("Preface," not paginated). Asserting an Indigenous identity in the vastly changed circumstances and shifting demographics in which Native people find themselves in the twenty-first century, Ortiz identifies with other Native people similarly away from Native homeland, culture, and community, stating, "We also continue to be absolutely connected socially and culturally to our Native identity" ("Preface," not paginated). Poems in this volume address connection to land, culture, language in the face of debilitating addictions, jailings, racism, and an identity imposed upon Native people by others, which results "in the loss of a sense of a centered human self and the weakening and loss of Indigenous cultural identity" (*Out There Somewhere*, 45). A number of poems in this volume are written in the Keres language with English translations. Ortiz alludes to the directive power of the oral tradition to point the way through harsh realities and challenges to survivance and life. "No Weather Map," referring to Ortiz's mapping of his life's journey through writing, begins, "Poems are not weather reports. / No data, no radar pictures. Yet / somehow my sense of things / and the way I map my way requires / a clear design that I can look at" (120). The poem continues with the speaker looking outside, checking and appreciating the natural elements, all of which represent "poetic data in its purest form." Ortiz concludes the poem by saying, "My weather is in the living margin / open to me, the place where I stand / and the place I see;

this is poetry / and the design my journey needs" (120). Poems, of course, are not forecasts of the weather or events, but are part of the continuing, evolving body of the oral tradition that can mark a path in the here and now, a pattern to reveal significance, meaning, guidance.

Vision of Continuance

For Ortiz, there is only one response to ongoing onslaughts on Indigenous wellbeing. He writes "In the Moment Before," "[W]e must think as we pray: / always one with our struggle, hope, and continuance, / always for the sake of the land, culture, and community" (21). It is the message he has consistently conveyed. As people who, according to our origin stories, emerged from the earth, Pueblos hold a close and special relationship to the land, a worldview infused with spirituality that integrates our peoples with our lands—homelands that nourish human, plant, and animal life in a reciprocal relationship of respect; earthen clay that forms our pottery vessels and the architecture of our ornos (outdoor ovens), homes, and kivas, and earthen plazas that center us within our mother villages; the rich valley soils that brings forth crops in our outlying fields; and the waters of the rivers, lakes and springs, and precious rainfall that sustain all life. The landscape itself tells us who we are, reminding us of the stories of our journeys and history and orienting us in all directions, including our connection to the cosmos. In "The People and the Land ARE Inseparable," Silko points out, "To be a people, to be part of a village, is the dimension of human identity that anthropology understands least, because this sense of home, of the people one comes from, is an intangible quality, not easily understood by American-born Europeans. . . . This is where [our] power as a people, as a culture lies: with this shared consciousness of being part of a living community that continues on and on. . . ." (90). Over four and a half centuries of struggle (physical, legal, socioeconomic, political, psychological), we have fought for our homeland, our lives, our way of life. Thus, the phrase "for the sake of the people, the sake of the land" resonates in the whole of Ortiz's work, arising out of the Pueblo and Native concepts of reciprocity with its inherent responsibilities of the people to the land and water that nourish them.

Two works directly address the topic: *Fight Back: For the Sake of the People, the Sake of the Land* (1980), written as a political statement about the environmental damage caused by the mining industry in the

Acoma-Grants-Laguna area, and Ortiz's 1998 introduction to *Speaking for the Generations, Native Writers on Writing*, "Wah Nuhtyuh-Yuu Dyu Neetah Tyahstih (Now It is My Turn to Stand)." "As an influence—in fact, as an essential element—in the development of my writing, my Native voice has come from the concept of the necessary and essential relationship of land and people, and it is my hope and wish that this voice will have Continuance as the land and people continue to have Existence," he writes (xviii). In "We Have Been Told Many Things but We Know This to Be True" from *Fight Back*, Ortiz states this concept directly and simply: "The land. The people. / They are in relation to each other. / We are in a family with each other. / The land has worked with us. / And the people have worked with it" (*Woven Stone*, 324).

For Indigenous peoples of the Americas, the land, the Earth, is regarded as mother, a loving, nurturing, life-giving source. For Pueblos, our origin, our birth, as a people is of the Earth, and marks an intimate, sacred relationship. Leslie Marmon Silko writes, "The landscape sits in the center of Pueblo belief and identity. . . . For this reason, the Pueblo people have always been extremely reluctant to relinquish their land for dams or highways" (Silko, "Interior and Exterior Landscapes," 43). She adds that the earth-scarring open-pit mining of uranium deposits north of Laguna,[16] which Ortiz addresses in *Fight Back*, had "a powerful psychological impact upon the Laguna people" and that "from now on, it, too will be included in the vast body of narratives that makes up the history of the Laguna people and the Pueblo landscape. And the description of what the landscape looked like *before* the uranium mining began will always carry considerable impact" (44). Indeed, the legacy of the uranium mining continues to take its toll on the health of Pueblo members. Because of all such traumatic changes to the Native landscape impacting culture, Ortiz understands that as a member of an Indigenous community, it is imperative to advocate environmental causes:

> Speaking for the sake of the land and the people means speaking
> for the inextricable relationship and interconnection between
> them. Land and people are interdependent. In fact, they are one
> and the same essential matter of Existence. . . . If anything is
> most vital, essential and absolutely important in Native cultural
> philosophy, it is this concept of interdependence: the fact that
> without land there is no life, and without a responsible social and

cultural outlook by humans, no life-sustaining land is possible. . . . [W]e are living today only because the generations before us—our ancestors—provided for us by the manner of their responsible living ("Introduction," xii).

Responsibility and advocacy by Native writers are important components of Ortiz's vision for Native American literature. He strongly articulates in his essay "Towards a National Indian Literature" that the "inspiration and course for contemporary Indian literature" comes not only from the oral tradition but also from Indigenous writers recognizing their responsibility to advocate for the sake of the people, the sake of the land. He lists several issues that Native writers need to address: "self-government, sovereignty, and control of land and natural resources; . . . racism, political and economic oppression, sexism, supremacism, and the needless and wasteful exploitation of land and people, especially in the U.S." (259). The assumption of responsibility and advocacy by Native writers contributes to developing nationalism in Native literature, which, he states, "indeed it should have" (259).

In this 1981 essay, Ortiz addresses issues he has articulated in other writings: Native people's appropriation of English and other languages for their own uses[17]; the oral tradition as a dynamic body of continuing stories with transformative power to maintain an Indigenous cultural consciousness in the face of overwhelming change; the nationalistic character inherent in Native writers' advocacy for their communities and cultures; rejection of non-Native ideas of cultural purity and the stasis implied therein; and the people's creative response to and continuing resistance against outside dominance. More than twenty-five years later, the ideas still resonating, Ortiz's essay served as the seed for ideas and discussion on nationalism and Native literary criticism in the recently published *American Indian Literary Nationalism*, which includes a foreword by Ortiz.[18] The authors, Jace Weaver, Craig S. Womack, and Robert Warrior, note in the preface that Ortiz's "exemplary humanism is evident everywhere in his stories and equally so in his life . . . [and his] compassion extends across many lines of gender, race and class. . . . He is our best example that a nationalist is not the same thing as an isolationist" (xvii).

His "exemplary humanism" becomes evident in words such as these: "As an Aacqumeh hahtrudzai and a writer, I believe that being real in a real world is loving and respecting myself. This I believe has always been the true and real vision of Indigenous People of the Americas: to love, respect, and be responsible to ourselves and others, and to behold with passion and awe the wonders and bounty and beauty of creation and the world around us" (*Woven Stone*, 32). Ortiz further exemplifies this in his careful attention to terms for Native people, preferring those that are broadly inclusive of Indigenous persons of the Americas, insisting on terms that recognize the humanity of Indigenous people, and eschewing any that would deny their political and cultural sovereignty to name themselves.

Expounding on the ideas in "Towards a National Indian Literature" in his introduction to *Woven Stone* (1992), Ortiz addresses his concerns about Native literature and extends his vision to the entire Western Hemisphere: "We need to insist on Native American self-sufficiency, our heritage of cultural resistance, and advocacy for a role in international Third World de-colonizing struggles, including recognizing and unifying with our indigenous sisters and brothers in the Americas of the Western Hemisphere" (27). In 2001, a volume appeared that spoke of the struggles of the Indigenous Mayan people of southern Mexico. One of Ortiz's many efforts in support of his fellow Indigenous Americans includes penning an essay in the book *Questions and Swords: Folktales of the Zapatista Revolution*, in which he affirms the common hemispheric experiences of five centuries of colonization, of the socioeconomic inequities that have increased due to the North American Free Trade Agreement (NAFTA), and the increasing need for Native peoples to articulate their realities to the world. Inviting readers to consider the implications of Indigenous demands for justice, Ortiz raises the issue of the wholesale theft of homelands, continents, and a hemisphere: "Think of it: What if Indians throughout the Americas rose in united force to seek the return of their land, culture, and community? Think of it!" (*"Haah ah, mah eemah: Yes, it's the very truth,"* 59).

Ortiz sees Indigenous intellectuals and writers playing a crucial role in developing a unified Indigenous vision. Just as he continually experienced a coming into being as an Aacqumeh hanoh with an Indigenous consciousness that continued in English and would never be lost or subsumed, he sees the potential for a similar collective fulfillment for the Indigenous People of the Americas that must be guarded and nurtured. Ortiz believes a unified vision is essential for Indigenous continuance and depends on full acceptance of one another on all levels of human interaction ("Introduction," *Woven Stone*, 31).

Yet there is much to do to fulfill that vision. Ortiz states that since the 1960s, Native writers "to some extent" have been "advocating ethnic cultural expression, describing Native American ways and thought, analyzing and criticizing Western civilization, and promoting indigenous heritage and language" ("Introduction," *Woven Stone*, 27). To successfully carry on the struggle against colonization and internalized oppression, however, he believes analysis and criticism should be directed inwardly as well. Ortiz's evaluation of the state of Native literary affairs in the 1990s is direct: "We [Native writers] have not yet thoroughly and honestly focused on critical issues that are directly related to our identity and existence as human beings who are Native Americans, citizens of the United States, carriers of a unique cultural heritage, and who are faced with ethnocentrism among ourselves and racism. . . . [I]t is critical to deal with these issues" ("Introduction," *Woven Stone*, 28). Ortiz points the way out of the mire by calling for a critical examination of the hegemonic nature of racism and its byproduct, ethnocentrism or tribalism. Decrying ethnocentrism as ultimately a self-destructive, unproductive means of seeking to (re)assert control over our lives, Ortiz sees its danger in that its inward preoccupation works against hemispheric unity.

Ortiz also sees the need to cast off victimhood, which debilitates and causes fear. With their feet firmly planted in the present reality, neither looking back with nostalgia or forward with romanticized illusions, Native writers, he states, "must have an individual and communally unified commitment to their art and its relationship to their indigenous culture and people, especially with regard to social, cultural, political-economic health and to progressive development" ("Introduction," *Woven Stone*, 32). In so doing, Native writers demonstrate their kinship with social and political activist literary greats Pablo Neruda, Meridel LeSueur, Ernesto Cardenal, and Nazim Hikmet, whose writing comes out of love for their communities, the very quality necessary for Indigenous continuance. Furthermore, he sees the survival and continuance of the United States inextricably bound to acknowledgment of "its indigenous past"; it is the clear, strong, committed voices of Indigenous writers who will tell the story the nation needs to hear "to go beyond survival" ("Introduction," *Woven Stone*, 33). In his most recent writing on the topic in the foreword to *American Indian Literary Nationalism*, Ortiz speaks simply and straightforwardly of the challenge before Native writers and scholars to address the many serious issues of representation and advocacy: "We have to; there is not much choice" (xiii). Drawing on the strength and inspiration provided by the unity of the Pueblos during the Pueblo Revolt and the resistance, persistence, and resilience born of struggles against annihilation and colonization, Ortiz as writer, educator, and elder points us ever toward survivance and continuance. We have our roles to play in our time, just as our ancestors did in theirs.

II

A Geography of Belonging: Ortiz's Poetic, Lived, and Storied Indigenous Ecology

Susan Berry Brill de Ramírez

Simon J. Ortiz's poetry bespeaks an aesthetics of belonging and survivance deeply rooted in his ancestral ties to his Acoma Pueblo people and their respective tribal homelands. As Evelina Zuni Lucero affirms, the convergence of the genetic and experiential, the tribal and the global, has defined and formed Ortiz's worldview and voice. When he reiterates his emphasis on the welfare of "the people and the land," he very deliberately points to the specificity of his tribal community and his Indigenous ancestral homelands, while also inclusively embracing the entirety of Indigenous peoples, the scope of global environmental concern, and the sum of humankind. Ortiz's remarkable poetic lens is very consciously grounded in his Acoma Pueblo traditions of storied and participative orality and ethics. The conjunctive call of the oral and the ethical come together in a fascinating and intricate aesthetics of belonging that are manifested in the following aspects of Ortiz's work, each delineated and briefly discussed in the subsequent sections of this introductory essay:

- Native American indigeneity as an Acoma Pueblo man determines Ortiz's rootedness in a community, a place, a culture, and the language that interweaves all three;

- the transformative power of language and story is brought to bear in a twenty-first century globally inclusive aesthetic;

- his deeply held connections to ancestral lands are manifested

in expansive ecological orientations that are rooted in
reciprocities of inclusion and belonging;

- his conscious commitments to Indigenous connections that
  cut across tribal affiliations and global geographies invite
  readers to consider the complexities of Indigenous lives and
  histories, contending with the larger forces of colonization
  and its consequent diasporic exigencies;

- Ortiz's sophisticated critique of the literary as fundamentally
  distinct from the oral realms of storytelling produces vibrant
  texts with intricately episodic and associational structures
  that imbue their writing with conversive (intersubjectively
  conversative and personally transformative) meaning
  and free the texts from the more superficial and limiting
  organizations of topic, chronology, or self;

- and his masterful craft brings to bear the skills of the oral
  storyteller and the literary writer, a remarkable poetics that
  invites readers as listener-readers into a literarily complex, yet
  eminently accessible, body of literature.

Indigenous Acoma Pueblo Roots

Simon J. Ortiz's first language was the Acoma language of his family and
his ancestors. He learned to speak with the words and stories that emerged
within the scope of his people's origins in the Americas. To approach his
work, it is crucial to recognize that his first words, the words that determined his identity and his connections to family, tribe, and land, are words
rooted in the history and landscape of the American Southwest. All writers are shaped by their early experiences with literature. For Ortiz, his love
for language and writing emerged out of a distinctive fusion of Indigenous
tribal stories and written literature: "As early on I associated reading with
oral stories, . . . my real interest and love of reading had to do with stories.
I'd heard stories all my life, ranging from the very traditional to the history
of Acoma-Mericano relations to current gossip" (*Woven Stone*, 9). Ortiz is
of a generation whose first language, the Indigenous tongue, was still lin-
guistically dominant, but the diverse languages that were constitutive of
his development as a writer reflect the very colonialist legacy of his people
and lands. The originating language for his writing was English, which he

largely learned in schools,[19] a practice designed to force Native students to assimilate, and one common in most schools open to Native students throughout much of the twentieth century, including Bureau of Indian Affairs run boarding schools, church run boarding and day schools, and nearby public schools. Notwithstanding the Manifest geopolitical histories of Europrimacy as it played out around the globe, Ortiz makes it profoundly clear that he, his people, and the Indigenous peoples of the world have refused to be conquered by the patent simplicity of the narratives of conquest, whether colonial or postcolonial. Much as Ortiz's Acoma and fellow Indigenous Pueblo, *mestizo, genízaro,* Diné, and Apache ancestors affirmed their rights to self-determination and rule when they successfully defeated the Spaniards in the Pueblo Revolt of 1680 (*Woven Stone,* 347), Ortiz affirms his tribal affiliation, his cultural heritage, his geographic center, and his personal, familial, tribal, and Indigenous history in a literary voice that speaks an a priori indigeneity via the colonial language of English and regardless of the indoctrinating weight of the west's institutionalized education systems.

While it is English that was Ortiz's first written language and that, thereby, wields a literary primacy of language, it is significant that English was nevertheless his second spoken language and thereby a language whose firstness is definitially qualified and decentered before the fundamental primacy of his Native tongue. His love of stories originated in his Acoma language, which served to identify his person within a community, within a landscape, within a history. Indeed, even in his public presentations, Ortiz often begins and ends in his Native language, with a traditional introduction that presents him in terms of his tribal and clan affiliations and concluding with a poem or story that is read or recited in both Acoma and its more broadly accessible English language versions. By inserting the language of his people and his ancestry in his oral presentations and his writing before audiences and readers who are, by and large, unfamiliar with any of the Pueblo languages, Ortiz takes a bold linguistic turn that categorically calls into question the primacy of English as the language of the United States and as *the* language of American letters. Even in a volume whose geographic center is set in the Lakota homelands of South Dakota, Ortiz uses his own tribal language and geography to articulate the stories of an Acoma man living through the harsh winter on the northern plains. His poetry collection *After and Before the Lightning* is oriented calendrically, with the poems, stories, and other prose sections organized as journal entries throughout a winter season: namely the period after the last rainstorm (and the final lightning of the fall), through the first thunderstorm of the spring.

The very first journal entry from November 18 orients the volume through Ortiz's own ancestral landscape in a poetic prose story about Antelope Father-Elder who goes out in the winter weather offering his prayers at places sacred to the Acoma people. Ortiz first references him within his linguistic home as Kuutse-hanoh Naisdeeyah, offering the English language name second in a subsequent sentence (4). After providing his name as "Antelope Elder," then to ensure his readers' comprehension, Ortiz makes a further bold move, sharing part of the elder's personal prayers and songs. In doing so, he affirms for his readers the firstness of indigeneity and the attendant primal relationships of those deeply connected to their sacred ancestral geographies, for Ortiz presents the Antelope Elder's words in the utterance of an old Acoma man: "Hahdhishra Haaweh-shthih Shiwana? Hahdhi-shra Haaweh-shthih Shiwana?" (4). Instead of translating these lines for his readers, Ortiz follows them with the blank space of a line and paragraph break, inviting his readers to consider the orality and significance of the Acoma words, including their very presence within an English language text. The stanza break provides the emphatic space that underscores the reality of indigeneity, the continuance of ancestral roots that must, nevertheless, emerge within American letters, and, in a powerfully Indigenous deconstructive move, a presence that decenters the linguistic and literary sovereignty of conquest.

In the next stanza, Ortiz continues the story of the elder's wintertime prayers, noting the "thick snow clouds" and the "deep snow" that ominously covered the trails and water holes (4). It is only after this that Ortiz provides a translation of the prior prayer songs, but he does so in a particularly interesting way. After relating that the elder went outside to offer his prayers to the winter spirits, Ortiz first shares his song in the Keresan language of the Acoma Pueblo people. Then, after describing the winter weather conditions and the snow, he shares the song again in a way that conveys the ongoing events of the story, namely the elder's spiritual communion and journey: "He sang: 'Where are you, Snow Shiwana? Where are you, Snow Shiwana?'" (4). The translation is not an editorial intrusion, but rather the continued singing of the old man. Analogous to the prior line and paragraph break, after the continuation of his prayerful song, Ortiz provides another blank line so that his readers can absorb what has just been related. Then the story continues to its ultimate cosmic grounding and communal climax.

Ortiz's intertribal diary takes place in the Lakota homelands, where he taught for a year at Sinte Gleska College on the Rosebud reservation, but the volume's early linguistic, geographic, and storied indigenization is firmly rooted in Ortiz's own Acoma tribal world. The hybridity that is consequent to Spanish colonial rule and the subsequent colonization by an expanding United States is evidenced in a traditional story about Caballo Pinto (a spotted horse), Aliyosho (a young boy), and the rey (the king) and his pueblo, whose various versions are interwoven throughout the volume (33–34, 82–84, 95–96). A story traditional to the Pueblo, Mexican, and Spanish world is related in English with Spanish language terms, along with a reference to the king's "pueblo"—a term that could indicate a colonial Spanish primacy in the story, but when placed within the poetic lens of an indigenous "Pueblo" writer, even this one term "pueblo" becomes indigenized. Furthermore, the volume's Pueblo rootedness is underscored because this traditional story is the one story in the volume given an emphatic primacy in its different versions and iterations, which are strategically interspersed at different places in the volume and throughout the cold season (December 4, February 2 and 9).

As spring comes closer, Ortiz's linguistic indigeneity, too, returns, here in a poem about the buffalo of the northern plains that invoke remembrance of the buffalo of Ortiz's own ancestral memory. Offering a prayer poem to the buffalo, Ortiz speaks his own tribal and ecological geography in a way that embraces diverse tribes, places and times: the Lakota and the Acoma, South Dakota and New Mexico, the present and the remembered past. His poetic entry for February 14 describes a herd of buffalo first seen in the distance. In a nominal personification that recognizes the interwoven mythical and actual subjectivity of the animals, they are named first in Ortiz's tongue: "I can feel there are buffalo about— / . . . / The spirit of Muushaitrah" (102).[20] At mid-February, the sun is returning, but it is still the middle of winter with the continuing bitter cold weather. "A great shadow of winter hovers / has for weeks, months / . . . / there is no sun but only the light. / It is Muushaitrah though, the song / of its spirit, the Sun" ("February 14," 102). Both Buffalo and Sun are personified, are engaged in intersubjective relations by the Indigenous singer in the poem who speaks directly to Buffalo while also affirming Sun's subjectivity and song. In the next stanza, the singer offers the Sun's welcome song to Muushaitrah. The English language version is an iterative emphatic that continues the singer's song:

> Muushaitrah,
> weh dzuutroh
> weh truhpoh
> weh tchiahtsastih.
> Dawaa-eh, Aneh eh
> meh-yuunah shrah,
> meh yuunah niieshruu.
> Staidzee, niieshru.
> Staidzee, niieghu.
>
> Daa-ah emih, Oshratrah
> Kqaihyuh, Kqooyoutih tah.
> Muushaitrah, dzih-yuutih-tahnih.
> Muushaitrah, stihyuutih-tahnih. . . .
> Buffalo,
> you have come to us,
> you have come in,
> you come about and around.
> Thank you, it is beautiful,
> you are still alive,
> you will always live.
> In everything, living.
> Everything will live.
>
> This is the way, Sun,
> its Song, Singing it is.
> Buffalo, it is singing for it.
> Buffalo, I am singing for it (102).

The Indigenous language version of the prayer song reflects the intricacy of its orally informed poetics that, in very few lines, include a masterful combination of repetition, alliteration, and rhyme (both within and at the end of lines). The poem "Buffalo Light Now" as a whole demonstrates a masterful interweaving of worlds (actual and mythical), times (present, past, and future: "you are still alive"), and two very different languages, all in a relatively short six stanzas (seven if the prose paragraph at the end is included as part of the poem itself).[21] Additionally, Ortiz wields changes in pace (evidenced in the line and stanza breaks, in the length of lines and stanzas, and metre, changes in tone (narrative, reportorial, and prayerful), and changes in syntax, grammar, and metre, each of which is required by the different registers of poetic narrative and prayer song and, also, by the very different languages. The poem's subtly complex poetics serve the crucial purpose of accessibility by providing sufficient introductory entry for listener-readers to engage the poignancy of a contemporary sacred presence of buffalo in the northern plains to an Acoma man whose ancestors storied their experiences with buffalo prior to the eradication of the animal in the southern plains. Albeit probably unintentional, it is nevertheless significant (and not surprising) to find, in a Valentine's Day poetic journal entry crafted by a man like Ortiz, a prayer song of love offered to the buffalo in their very real presence in the plains, in their remembered Acoma past when buffalo still roamed the outer ranges where the Pueblo men hunted them, and as a poignant sign of the wholeness of creation, both in the compromised horrors of conquest (of people and the land, with buffalo as a sign for both) and in the resilience of creation and her creatures to endure. Using various relational tools of linguistic familiarization,[22] Ortiz makes a distant land and experience part of his own world and story. He invites his listener-readers, too, to engage those poetic stories.

The prayer song to the buffalo, to Muushaitrah, depicts a poetic craft that deftly indigenizes diverse stories, peoples, times, and places while striving to insure a broad poetic accessibility. Ortiz explains that much of his own development as a writer stems from the varied stories that surrounded him in his tribal community as a child and which his creative writing remembers: "Stories were told about people of the Aacqumeh community, our relatives, both living and long ago, and there were stories of mythic people and beings who were wondrous and heroic and even magical. . . . Consequently, when I learned to read and write, I believe I felt those stories continued somehow in the new language and use of the new language and they would never be lost, forgotten, and finally gone. They would always continue" (*Woven Stone*, 9). As a contemporary poet, Ortiz has remained faithful to his Indigenous origins regardless of the directions taken by his craft. Being acutely aware of the integral role played by storytelling in the interwoven fabric of his Acoma community, he states that "they tied me into the communal body of my people and heritage" (*Woven Stone*, 9). Accordingly, Ortiz's holistic commitment to his Indigenous community and voice manifests itself in tribal poetry and stories that embrace other tribes, other lands, other languages, and, indeed, all creation.

Transformative, Globally Inclusive Aesthetics

The transformative power of language and story evident in Ortiz's work comes from an ancestral legacy that dates back millennia; its integrity is based on an "oral tradition [that] is inclusive; it is the actions, behavior, relationships, practices throughout the whole social, economic, and spiritual life process of people. In this respect, the oral tradition is the consciousness of the people" (*Woven Stone*, 7). Words come from persons and cultures and times. As Ortiz makes patently clear, one's words also bear great responsibility forward as the utterance and its effect spread outward towards others. An inherent ethical and political imperative throughout Ortiz's work that embraces the whole earth as our larger community or πόλις (polis, or city-state)[23] extends the boundaries of community worldwide. In implicit and explicit critiques of the intertwined histories of Manifest empire-building and nation-state development, Ortiz translates his ancestral communalism beyond the limits of the Platonic state and into globally-minded twentieth- and twenty-first-century perceptual inclusiveness—the very "worldliness" that postcolonial critic Edward Said clarifies as "the opposite of separatism, and also the reverse of exclusivism" ("The Politics of Knowledge," 28).

At the outset of *Out There Somewhere*, Ortiz takes up his concerns with worldwide Indigenous conditions. In "Headlands Journal," the geographic specificity of an elite arts retreat is immediately expanded on the first page as Ortiz in the persona he adopts and two artists (one from Mexico and one from Nigeria) talk about the sociological and psychological conditions that influence the incarceration rates in their respective lands. What Ortiz chooses to include from that conversation is telling in that it is not specific to his own Acoma Pueblo, nor even regionally based in the American Southwest, but instead is more broadly inclusive, taking a northern turn to Alaska (not unlike Silko's similar turns in *Storyteller* and *Almanac of the Dead*). The speaker comments to the two artists at the Headlands Center for the Arts: "Alaska has a 17 percent Native population in the state and a 70 percent Native inmate population in its state prison" (3). In very few words, Ortiz relates the larger hemispheric stories of American racism and colonization, and the catastrophic legacy of both upon the Indigenous peoples of North America. In a move away from comparable stories of his own tribe and cultural geography, Ortiz speaks the Indigenous statistics of a different place and people and, thereby, the broader truths and realities of contemporary (and past) America. Here and elsewhere, Ortiz conveys that to speak poetically in deeply meaningful ways is to speak truths grounded in the lived exigencies of people whose stories bear relevant witness to most, if not all, readers.[24]

Noting the relevance of bearing witness as a powerful tool for the Indigenous peoples of the United States and elsewhere, Spokane writer Gloria Bird addresses the personal story as a political act of witnessing:

> To me as a writer, everything is politically motivated. Indeed, being Indian in the United States is inherently political. . . . In light of this, I see my personal story as bearing witness to colonization and my writing as a testimony aimed at undoing those processes that attempt to keep us in the grips of the colonizer's mental bondage. . . . What is understood is that our positions within a system that is designed to deny us is tenuous and continually threatened and that there is truly strength in the number of witnesses who can carry our stories outward ("Breaking the Silence, Writing as 'Witness,'" 28–29).

It is not surprising that Bird's essay appears in the significant collection of essays that Ortiz brought together, in which various Native writers describe the challenges and responsibilities for writers deeply informed by their respective tribal commitments that extend beyond the personal and the self, and which require the outward lens and voice of their Indigenously inclusive, global ethic. In this collection and throughout his own prose and poetry, Ortiz demonstrates an aesthetic articulation that consistently transforms alterity into vocalized subjectivity, absence into presence, and insignificance into meaningfulness—whether of Ortiz's own experiences or those of his fellow tribal members, of other Indigenous people, of other persons regardless of their Indigenous or diasporic history, or of other aspects of creation that Ortiz broadly references as "the land."

"Headlands Journal" begins with the interaction of a group of artists at the arts center. In the poetic retelling, Ortiz poignantly notes the patent invisibility of many aspects of the world to storytellers, artists, and singers, those whose traditional roles centrally involved community wellbeing, but who all too often forget those roles. While grounding our perceptions in the experiential specificity of time and place, "Headlands Journal" nevertheless extends its boundaries outward, reminding its listener-readers of the traditional power of song and prayer and speech, of their relevance in orienting ourselves within creation, and that the placefulness that matters is a geography of belonging broadly inclusive of the entirety of the cosmos:

> The moon,
> > the moon,
> my voice in song.
> To say
> > to say
> what I really mean to say.
> Moon,
> > moon song,
> singing moon song.
>
> Sitting outside the dining hall smoking. Anica, Emily, others. Emily offers a roll-your-own, which I decline.
>
> I say, "In jail I've seen roll-your-owns so well made they're rolled better than machine-rolled ones." Nobody pays any mind (3).

In these few lines, the holistic connectedness that conjoins one lone human being with the moon and, thereby, all of creation, a person who then articulates that relationship in song, "singing moon song" ("Headlands Journal," 3), is sharply contrasted in the following lines, which show members of the arts center community who are disconnected even from those with whom they sit. The artists are disengaged, disassociated, disinterested. One oddly offers a cigarette to a nonsmoker, whose responding raw rejoinder about jailhouse experiences is categorically ignored.

The poem suggests here that connecting deeply with an aside about jailhouse "roll-your-owns" is inextricably related to the placefulness that permits the crafting and singing of a moon song. To be part of any place is to be placed as part of creation and in relation to and with each other in time and history. Jean Comaroff emphasizes the moral imperative underlying the processes by which persons become deeply connected with each other and within geographies of belonging, whether with the inclusive breadth that Ortiz invokes or in the narrower spans of locality and temporality. She explains that the interrelational process "reaches into diverse realms of collective being-in-the-world: into the struggle to construct a meaningful sense of belonging—and, hence, of moral and material community" ("The End of History, Again?: Pursuing the Past in the Postcolony," 129). In Ortiz's poem, the speaker's seemingly offhand comment about what he has seen in jail offers the grounding gift of story to his fellow writers and artists—interconnected, personal grounds that Ortiz knows and stories as crucial to the wellbeing of life in the world. Had the fellow artists inquired regarding the jailhouse "roll-your-owns," they would have shown their interest in the speaker's experiences and, too, in the realities of Native America in which the jails and prisons incarcerate much higher percentages of Native peoples than the demographics of the land would suggest. In the artists' silent disinterest, Ortiz invites his readers to hear again, more deeply, the implied stories of conquest, racism, Manifest elitism, and interpersonal isolation which, at that moment, the artists neither hear nor value. The relational proximity to the moon that precipitates the song resonates in the distances between nearby fellow artists and the resulting loneliness that comes from disconnection.

There is a cost that comes from the lost opportunities of story, a cost not only to the individual, but, even more importantly, to communities and to the planet as a whole. The aesthetics of stories make possible deep understandings and meaningfulness that are simultaneously inwardly and outwardly directed. Psychologists Peter Harper and Mary Gray explain that "The creation and telling of stories [have] been used universally by cultures, communities and individuals to provide hope, meaning, purpose and understanding in life. . . . [Stories] are a vehicle through which people are able to develop understanding and coherence in their worlds" (42). Even the very articulation of such conversive language conveys a potentially transformative power that is part of the warp and woof of everyday life, not solely relegated to the realm of myth and imagination. Native writer and scholar Kimberly Blaeser (Anishinaabe) affirms this, stating explicitly that in "Native belief systems and literary accounts, the creative power of words and thought is not confined to mythic time. Past and present, words and thought are believed to have a certain power . . ." (*Vizenor*, 19–20). Indeed, John Attinasi and Paul Friedrich note that deeply relational converse can "catalyze or somehow create a realignment or a reinforcement that is fundamental in the point of view, even the depths of the imagination," effecting potential and actual personal and community transformations through, what they term, "conversion conversations" or "life-changing dialogues" ("Dialogic Breakthrough: Catalysis and Synthesis in Life-Changing Dialogue," 45, 43). In "It is No Longer the Same as It Was in the Olden Days," placed later in the volume, Ortiz affirms that struggles to change oneself and the world must be not against, but rather toward, connection and continuance: "How and what is it today we shall do? / This is the way you must be thinking. / We must continue to be. / It is necessary. / With courage . . ." (*Out There Somewhere*, 98). By using the second-person pronoun, the narrator speaks directly to the reader, and use of the open-ended, inclusive first-person plural underscores the fact that the ways forward require personal and collective continuance. Storytelling, poetry, song— all are ways by which language facilitates interpersonal connections within, across, and even beyond time and place that, in turn, present their transformational capabilities. As Ortiz reminds us, we are at once becoming and being.

Indigenous Ecologies of Community

Regardless of whether Ortiz's poetry and prose are explicitly oriented within his own tribal community, as in his earlier collections *Going for the Rain, A Good Journey*, or *Fight Back: For the Sake of the People, for the Sake of the Land* (all collected in *Woven Stone*), or directed more outwardly as in *Out There Somewhere, from Sand Creek*, and *After and Before the Lightning*, invariably his writing is defined by an indigenously grounded holism that envisions community in broad environmental terms. In this way, he reminds his readers that human life is inextricably intertwined with the surrounding biotic communities. Any concern for the people must, Ortiz urges, include concern for the land. Indeed, he begins his edited volume *Speaking for the Generations: Native Writers on Writing* by stating that his "own writing comes from a similar dynamic of reciprocity shared by the land, water, and human culture" ("Introduction," xv). As an Acoma Pueblo man, Ortiz understands the deep connections that a people can feel and live towards the Earth. Ortiz speaks a global ecology of belonging with integrity, authenticity, and humility that is deeply informed by the traditional architecture of the Pueblo homes and villages; the people's contact with the Earth during their ceremonial dances; in the Pueblo earthen ovens and farming lifestyles; in the ancient Pueblo homelands with sites and structures, the sacredness of which preceded the arrival of Coronado and throughout the subsequent waves of Spanish and later Euro-American colonizers; and in the more contemporary struggles against cancer, poverty, and landscapes horrifically desecrated and poisoned by the deadly infamy of the Grants Uranium Belt. In their heyday, more than forty working mines spewed radioactive waste and chemicals into the air, ground, and water in a region known for its high winds, just upstream from several Acoma Pueblo communities, including Deetseyamah (McCarty's) where Ortiz grew up.[25]

Aldo Leopold's articulation of a "land ethic" that includes "soils, waters, plants, and animals, or collectively: the land" (*A Sand County Almanac and Sketches Here and There*, 204) echoes the oral tradition's storied conscience of the people. It is the traditional way of life that has defined Pueblo people's commitment to their ancestral geography. It is a traditional way of life with ecological relevance that is increasingly critical to a globally warming planet. In his poetry and stories, Ortiz invites his readers to take lexical steps into an aesthetics centered in the actualities of people's everyday lives and infused with the sacred reach of creation. Grounding his words in physicality, Ortiz conveys the deeply rooted connections to a landscape, a home, and a community in his ode to a wall that surrounds the community's graveyard and much of its lived and storied history. Sharing the touch of the earthen walls of the people's homes, Ortiz invites his readers to poetically experience the tactile connections that literally and symbolically bind persons and communities together. Whether it is in the lasting interwoven stones in "A Story of How a Wall Stands" (*Woven Stone*, 145) or the ways by which each person finds their own place in creation, the importance of "fit" and belonging is vital: "Essentially, it is how you fit / into that space which is yourself, / how well and appropriately" (*Woven Stone*, 129). Far from a self-oriented concern with personal fulfillment or ego, Ortiz expresses that personal identification and fit that are inextricably interconnected with "the land, rivers, the mountains, plants, animals, / all life that is around us / that we are included with, / . . . Standing again, within, among all things . . ." (*Woven Stone*, 289–90). It is a deep placefulness and "sense of presence" that is defined by a person's grounded outward orientation. The wall of "Woven Stone" is not a wall for its own sake; it is a "support" for the "hundreds of tons of dirt and bones . . . [of] a graveyard built on a steep incline" (128, 145). In Ortiz's "Four Deetseyamah Poems," the conjunctive title points to its geography of belonging, a conversation between the speaker and Joy as they affirm that "presence . . . has to do / with a sense of worth, dignity, / and how you fit with occasion, place, / people, and time" (128).

Ines Hernandez-Avila and Stephano Varese emphasize the centering placefulness that has helped to define Indigenous peoples' senses of belonging: "In the best of circumstances, indigenous peoples have nurtured, sustained, and reproduced a core identity that encompasses traditional wisdom, a spiritual rootedness to the land (as cultural geocenter and as hemisphere), and the complex of expressions that comprise the oral tradition" ("Indigenous Intellectual Sovereignties: A Hemispheric Convocation. An Overview and Reflections on a United States/Mexico Binational Two-Part Conference," 86).[26] Ortiz's poetry is a contemporary continuation in literary form of this ancestral, tribal, regional, and global tradition as well—whether literary or oral. This holistic ecological orientation emphasizes hemispheric and global realities while maintaining its ancestral and historical grounds in the cultures and lands of Acoma Pueblo and the U.S. Southwest.

Of his literary and lived struggles against the tragic environmental injustice that has turned ancestral lands and sacred places into Superfund sites, Ortiz states: "We must understand the experience of the oppressed, especially the racial and ethnic minorities, of this nation, by this nation and its economic interests" ("Our Homeland, A National Sacrifice Area," *Woven Stone*, 337–63). Regional and global ecopolitics notwithstanding, Ortiz makes it clear that his environmental commitment is categorically an Indigenous ecology of place and community: "It is an absolute sense of an Indigenous cultural community that involves the inter-related elements of the human, natural, and spiritual environment" ("Haah-ah," 58). Laguna Pueblo writer Leslie Marmon Silko places such a geography of belonging firmly within the historical trajectory of personal and community survival in the face of the natural climatic and unnatural colonialist forces that have threatened their peoples. "Survival depended upon harmony and cooperation not only among human beings, but among all things . . . the land, the sky, and all that is within them . . ." (Silko, "Landscape, History, and the Pueblo Imagination," 85). Even more broadly inclusive of the lands and peoples of the region, Ortiz crafts a conversation in a series of poems from Many Farms on the Diné (Navajo) reservation northwest of Acoma, underscoring the importance of ecosystemic sensibilities: "'What would you say that the main theme / of your poetry is?' / 'To put it as simply as possible, / I say it this way: to recognize / the relationships I share with everything'" (*Woven Stone*, 68). In another poem, he reiterates this reciprocity that is part and parcel of communal relationship:

We Have Been Told Many Things but We Know This to Be True

The land. The people.
They are in relation to each other.
We are in family with each other
        (*Woven Stone*, 324–25).

The Junctive Postcoloniality of Indigeneity and Diaspora

Combining the affiliative complexities embodied in a colonized indigeneity and an acknowledged identity as an American (nationally and hemispherically), Ortiz's life and writing demonstrate the extent to which people distanced either physically or psychically from their Native or ancestral homelands can find and make meaningful connections to particular places and times, whether actual or mythic, to live interdependent lives consciously as parts of creation. The historical legacies of the past 500 years of Manifest Destiny have genocided, brutalized, marginalized, and otherwise relocated and dislocated persons and communities. Ortiz comes from a people who have suffered the brunt of such savagery stemming backward to the earliest years of Spanish conquest, and yet who have survived today and into the future. In a recent interview, Ortiz comments on the very dislocative effects of colonization and the continuing struggles of Indigenous peoples, whose geopolitical conditions are still largely controlled by the dominance of Euroamerica:

> What is really taking place is that, when the land was lost from our control, a break severed us people from the land, a break created a barrier between the land and us so that we no longer had access in terms of our identity to the land.
>
> Because our systems of knowledge are connected with the land, how we saw ourselves, that function of knowledge of ourselves was lost. . . .
>
> The loss of language, the decrease of fluent language use is a part of that loss. So we found ourselves suddenly doubtful. We had less sense of being tribally identified if we couldn't speak the language or did not know ceremonial knowledge or lost the language terms for relatives—mothers, fathers, aunts, uncles, cousins and all that—you know, how we addressed each other.
>
> Then the community systems, the community in terms of sovereignty and self-government, that was lost. And now we sometimes don't know who we are. Am I a real Indian if I don't know these things?
>
> Colonialism really has devastated us a lot because of those things (Ortiz in Brill de Ramírez, "Burden," (120–21).

As a U.S. Army veteran who has taught and lived in Canada and different parts of the United States, and as an Acoma Pueblo man whose Indigenous roots extend backward at least a millennium on Pueblo lands and much further throughout his people's history in the Americas, Ortiz stories the experiences of the disenfranchised and disconnected and the struggles and efforts requisite toward survivance, dignity, and sovereignty on all levels—cultural, intellectual, and political. Ortiz well understands the efficacy of shared stories as a potent means for individual and community integration and health, especially in light of the appalling prolongation of Indigenous marginalization and invisibility in the United States.

In a reminder of Aimé Césaire's powerful mathematical equation about the colonialist processes that objectified peoples to conditions of subalterity—"colonization = 'thingification'" (*Discourse on Colonialism*, 21)—Ortiz's poetic rendering of his journal from his time at the Arts Center delineates everyday experiences with fellow artists and writers whose creative sensibilities are often clouded by cultural blinders that obscure their recognition of past and contemporary American imperialism, even when the evidence is right in front of them. In one poem, Ortiz stories the all too common experience of Native Americans whose cultures are viewed as alien. In an interaction at the Arts Center, a Euro-American artist romanticizes and exoticizes Indigenous America, telling the Indigenous speaker of the poem, "It's good for them to hear you speak in a foreign language. . . ." (*Out There Somewhere*, 11). Providing an emphatic line break in the prose poem, Ortiz invites his readers to consider the attribution of Native America as *foreign* within the scope of its ancestral lands. After the comment has been made, Ortiz writes, "I didn't know what to say, so I didn't say anything right away" (11). The pause underscores the appalling irony of the ignorance of a dominant culture America, that characterizes Indigenous America as "foreign" to national "melting pot" or "salad bowl" representations that define "American" as either uniformly Euro-American or as diversely immigrant. Regardless of the essentialist emphases on "melting pot" uniformity or "salad bowl" diversity, it is the liminality of the indigene whose centripetal invisibility ruptures the territorial assumptions about a geography the fundamental placefulness of which reflects an a priori belonging in the Americas.

As Ortiz knows well, the realities of placefulness and belonging are far more complex than former modernist claims to and postmodern critiques of subjectivity have addressed. Indeed, Daniel and Jonathan Boyarin affirm the hybridity that has been part and parcel of the world's cultures throughout time, noting that "Diasporic cultural identity teaches us that cultures are not preserved by being protected from 'mixing' but probably can only continue to exist as a product of such mixing. Cultures, as well as identities, are constantly being remade" ("Diaspora: Generational Ground of Jewish Identity," 721). The complexity of diasporic hybridity is such that ecocritic Lawrence Buell notes that "Diaspora can feel wrenching and liberatory by turns" (232). The Pueblo peoples' survivance through the virtually incessant onslaught of Spanish, Mexican, and American conquest came because of their capacities to accommodate, evolve, and re-invent. The integrity of the tribes endured beyond inquisitional brutality, geographic enclosures, and melting pot assimilationism. Skills of inclusive creativity and adaptability were brought to bear where strategic elasticity enabled continuance. As Silko states, "Pueblo cultures seek to include rather than exclude. The Pueblo impulse is to accept and incorporate what works" ("The Indian With a Camera," 6).[27]

Whereas the majority of the world's peoples have always been in contact with other peoples, the intermixing of cultures through conquest, trade, or other forms of contact (whether friendly, competitive, or aggressive) has defined and infused peoples and cultures diversely. For the Pueblos, that has meant cataclysmic upheavals in what Barbara Kirshenblatt-Gimblett terms a "convergence of diasporas" ("Spaces of Dispersal," 342). Each of the extant Pueblo tribes has demonstrated interwoven processes of continuance and adaptation that have successfully navigated through ancestral memories of distant migrations and arrivals, stages of emergence, more recent diasporas that brought waves of outsiders onto Pueblo lands (Spanish conquistadors, missionaries, and Ladinos and other hidden *conversos* forced out of inquisitional Spain; subsequent colonialist arrivals of *hispano* and indigenous Mexicans; and the later Euro-Americans pushing westward and reifying the expansionist claims of an empire-building America), consequent diasporic pressures that left many pueblos abandoned and surviving community members taking refuge among other communities and tribes, and the legacies of the United States' governmental onslaught upon the tribes whether through boarding school, child removal, relocation, or other comparably disastrous policies.

This history underlies each embedded pause as the speaker of the poem considers how to respond to explicit comments about the foreignness of an Indigenous language—comments that serve to further diasporize Native Americans through an orientalizing gaze[28] that perceives indigeneity as alien to its very ancestral lands. In a subsequent pause further in the poem, Ortiz invites his readers, too, to hear the actual awkward silence, finally broken with the Indigenous response: "You mean the Acoma Pueblo language I was speaking." / "Yeah," he said from the backseat. "That language. The foreign one" (*Out There Somewhere*, 11). The re-asserted perception of indigeneity as fundamentally foreign to America, like salt in a wound, re-emphasizes the remembered and experiential pain of disenfranchisement as manifested in centuries of genocide, cultural destruction, abuse, displacement, alcoholism, and marginalization, leading Ortiz's Indigenous narrator to despair, "Sometimes I feel like killing somebody" (11). In a Veteran's Day poem, he writes, "I am a veteran of at least 30,000 years":

> Caught now, in the midst of wars
> against foreign disease, missionaries,
> canned food, Dick & Jane textbooks, IBM cards,
> Western philosophies, General Electric,
> I am talking about how we have been able
> To survive insignificance
>   (*Woven Stone*, 108).

Ortiz understands profoundly the processes and consequences of internal and geographic dislocation. For all of the Indigenous peoples of the Americas, diasporic pressures forced the relocation of individuals, families, and tribes. In many cases, tribes were divided between the geographically diasporized and those who found ways to remain on or near tribal homelands, such as the Cherokee who are still in North Carolina, the Choctaw in Mississippi, and the Mesquakie in Iowa. Even for those tribes that, like many of the Pueblo tribes, remained on their ancestral lands, the extensive trade networks that spanned the western hemisphere were disrupted and tribes and communities who had maintained long-standing contact became strangers. As Hernandez-Avila and Varese well note, "Historically, the colonially engendered fragmentation of indigenous peoples created a corollary fragmentation of indigenous knowledge systems and a rupturing of hemispheric information networks that were in place before contact" ("Indigenous Intellectual Sovereignties," 85). Ortiz responds to the challenges of past and ongoing attempts at cultural eradication by turning to the power of language as a means of creative and restorative stitching, storying the fabric of humanity back into coherent form and aesthetic power. In this way, Ortiz demonstrates the "deeper seismological shift . . . [toward] the decolonization of Eurocentric power structures and epistemologies" articulated by postcolonial scholars Robert Stam and Ella Shohat ("Traveling Multiculturalism: A Trinational Debate in Translation," 296).

In his poem "For the Children," Ortiz tells the story of the Acoma Pueblo children who were taken away to Mexico as payment for the church bells. For more than 400 years, the Acoma people have told and retold the story of the stolen children. The very walls of the pueblo on the south side by the graveyard contain a well maintained hole that is to remember the lost children, a small hole that is nevertheless "big enough / for a little boy or a little girl to climb through" (*Out There*, 70). In this way, the children remain part of their people; as the stones of the wall are overlaid into and upon each other, so are the children held and interwoven into the hearts and minds of the Pueblo. As Ortiz tells us about the hole in the wall (the very wall whose construction is described in "A Story of How a Wall Stands" [*Woven Stone*, 145]):

> It is a door, the round hole, for the children
> To climb through when they return
> When they return to Acoma one day.
>
> Still today the people wait (70).

Through the stories about the children, the people remember them and, more broadly, the tribe's struggles and survivance through waves of outside colonization. Thus important connections are made across times and lands as the Acoma people remember and honor their ancestors, finding strength and encouragement in those stories despite great sadness and loss, and finding hope, too, for their descendants. In this poem, Ortiz broadens the reach of the children's story, sharing the story "out there somewhere" to all readers of the book, inviting them to consider poetically and deeply the history of his people, the consequences of history upon children, families, and communities, and the power of lived re-membrance. Noting that any move is both a leaving and an arriving, "both a flow and a space, both a process of deterritorialization and a mode of reterritorialization," Vilashini Coopan reminds us that directionality may point away from home and sacred space, but that it also invariably points forward to the future and backward to the past in holistic temporal and geographic embrace, even when that forward or backward is invested with devastating consequents ("The Ruins of Empire: The National and Global Politics of America's Return to Rome," 87).

Whether it is in the economically forced relocation of Acoma men seeking work in California—a leaving redefined in Acoma terms as the men sing their way: "Kaalrrahuul-rre-neeyaa-ah/Kaalrrahuul-rre-neeyaa-ah-ah"[29] (*Out There*, 59) or in his volume *from Sand Creek*, which shares the history of the United States' massacre of Cheyenne and Arapaho women, children, and elders, Ortiz demonstrates for us the power of language, story, and poetry to weave together the torn fabric of humankind towards integration and patched wholeness—a storied means of reconnection or re-membering, of reterritorialization. As Sophia Lehmann notes, language has the capacity "to define and to create this sense of commonality between people who share history and experience" ("In Search of a Mother Tongue: Locating Home in Diaspora," 103). Through story, Ortiz shows us how we can live shared experiences via an "aesthetics of rupture and connection" that reaches across geographies and facilitates an engaged placefulness regardless of time, genetic history, or locative orientation (Glissant, 151).

Conversive Intricacies and Intimacies

Ortiz and fellow regional writers such as Silko, Momaday, Luci Tapahonso, and Ofelia Zepeda have consciously worked to inform their literature with the dynamic orality of their respective tribal storytelling voices. As Ortiz states explicitly in the preface to his early collection *A Good Journey*, "There is a certain power that is compelling in the narrative of a storyteller simply because the spoken word is so immediate and intimate. It was the desire to translate that power into printed words that led me to write *A Good Journey*. I wanted to show that the narrative and technique of oral tradition could be expressed as written narrative and that it would have the same participatory force and validity as words spoken and listened to" (*Woven Stone*, 151). In all cultures prior to the advent of their respective written literatures, what would later become known as poetry, drama, prose fiction, and the other literary forms and genres were all part and parcel of one oral medium that served the larger purposes of community and individual integration. As Silko has explained regarding her Laguna Pueblo culture, stories were told "co-creatively" with the storyteller pulling the story out of the listeners,[30] much like the collaborative unfolding of conversations, a process that Ortiz writes is requisite for storytellers' and writers' words to cohere into meaningful concept: "A story is not only told but it is also listened to; it becomes whole in its expression and perception" ("Always the Stories," 57).

Writers like Ortiz bring a conscious recognition of the conversive intricacies possible in written literature. Ortiz crafts much of his poetry and prose with a clear sense of the traditional unifying effect of the conversive (which literally means "to turn with")—the words, the language, the story serve the larger ends of interpersonal relations.[31] Specific conversive tools evident in Ortiz's writing include strategic voice shifts (to the second-person direct address and the first person plural inclusive); defamiliarization of the exoticized indigene (as Edward Said did in his correction of "orientalism") couched within a process of demystification and familiarization that collectively re-orients the listener-reader[32] to an Indigenous perspective; a sense of storied placefulness that welcomes listener-readers into diverse geographies of belonging; interwoven worlds that include the everyday familiar with the imagined and historical extraordinary; the recognition of the regionally eco-systemic that attributes intentionality and personhood across species and beings, making possible intersubjective relations between humans and nonhumans[33]; a descriptive minimalism that requires the listener-reader to flesh out what is sketched; repetition for emphatic and empathic understanding; and a narrative emphasis on the story as a whole, so that the characters do not receive an undue primacy that would impede listener-reader engagement and involvement in the unfolding story.

The conversive rhetorics Ortiz wields facilitate experiential connections through the power of story—language as a realizing means even towards the physicality of sense perception. As he says of Acoma oral traditions, "It is basically a way to understand and appreciate your relationship to all things. The song as language is a way of touching" (*Song, Poetry and Language*, 9). Without literally touching the woven stone of the Acoma walls, Ortiz stories the tactile experience for his readers through a reenactment of his father's words:

> He tells me these things
> the story of them worked with his fingers, in the palm
> of his hand, working the stone
> and the mud until they become
> the wall that stands a long, long time
> (*Woven Stone*, 145).

In "That's the Place Indians Talk About," he invites his listener-readers to join him in hearing about and, thereby, experiencing through story a place that is sacred to the Shoshonean peoples that is now enclosed within a United States military facility. To bring his readers into the storytelling circle, he crafts the poem in the voice of a Paiute elder about the Coso Hot Springs:

> That's the place Indians talk about.
> Listen,
> that's the way you hear.
> Pretty soon, you can hear it,
> coming far away
> deep in the ground, deep down there coming,
> closer and closer.
> . . .
> Hearing,
> that's the way you listen.
> The People talking,
> telling the power to come to them
> . . .
> the moving power of the voice,
> the moving power of the earth
> the moving power of the People
> (*Woven Stone*, 324).

Through the extra indentations before the words "Listen" and "Hearing," which stand alone on their respective lines, Ortiz conveys the emphatic and empathic silence prior to each of these words as the Paiute elder invites us all to focused attention and close listening. In this way, all people, including Ortiz and his listener-readers, whether Shoshonean or not, whether Indigenous or diasporic, are brought into community within the inclusive sphere of the conversive. Learned in English language literary technique, Ortiz deliberately imbues his literary craft with the conversive power of orality. Refusing to accept the pat delineations between the written and the spoken, the textual and the oral, Ortiz has touched the transformative power of language in song, chant, prayer, and story.

The Elegant Poetics of Woven Words and Worlds
There is an elegance to a poetics whose intricacies draw upon the conversive artistry of the oral storyteller and the textual rhetorics and forms of

written poetry. Accordingly, appreciations of Ortiz's craft would do well to consider the construction of the 400-year-old wall at Acoma Pueblo that, Ortiz writes, "supports hundreds of tons of dirt and bones" in the community graveyard (*Woven Stone*, 145). An apparently simple poem that delineates the structure and its construction is, in fact, a profoundly beautiful reflection on the sacredness of life and the survivance of a people whose ancestors are remembered and cared for through the centuries—a reverie that brings to mind similarly poetic lines by Sir Thomas Browne,[34] which bespeak the sacred discovery of an ancient burial site in his own England:

> Now since these dead bones have already out-lasted the living
> ones of *Methuselah*, and in a yard under ground, and thin
> walls of clay, out-worn all the strong and specious buildings
> above it; and quietly rested under the drums and tramplings
> of three conquests; What Prince can promise such diuturnity
> unto his Reliques, or might not gladly say, "*Sic ego componi*
> *versus in ossa velim*" [So may I lie when turned to dust]
> ("Hydriotaphia: Urne-Burial," 148).[35]

In 1658, during the period when, across the Atlantic, the Pueblo people suffered the horrors of early Spanish colonization, the ancient and sacred urn burial site becomes, for Browne, a vehicle for remembering when his own people were conquered by foreign invaders. In Ortiz's poem, he gives tribute to his people's history, their lives and their deaths, and the importance of remembrance.

As Roger Dunsmore touches upon in his essay in this volume, "In these descriptions of his father carving, singing, talking about language or explaining how a stone wall stands, Simon Ortiz has suggested a Pueblo Poetics" (211). In this section of the introduction, I want to honor the ancestry behind Ortiz's craft by delineating some of the distinctive features of his Pueblo poetics, including rhythm, rhyme, and repetition. It is important to affirm Ortiz's emphasis that the meaningfulness of language is in its use, in its completeness, even as that wholeness is made up of its respective elements, as a wall in its wholeness is made of many stones.[36]

In the prose epigraph that introduces the poem "A Story of How A Wall Stands," Ortiz points out that the wall "looks like it's about to fall

down the incline [behind it] but will not for a long time" (145). The Acoma
speaker describes his father's stone work, in which stone and mud come
together in an interweaving that produces "the wall that stands a long,
long time" (145). In a demonstration of the wall's intricate woven pattern
and its making, he interlaces his fingers and hands, much as the rhythm of
the poem, its feet and metre, too, reflect the overlaid interconnections:

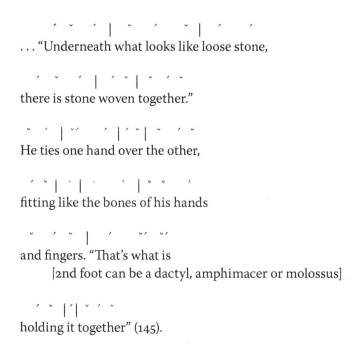

... "Underneath what looks like loose stone,

there is stone woven together."

He ties one hand over the other,

fitting like the bones of his hands

and fingers. "That's what is
        [2nd foot can be a dactyl, amphimacer or molossus]

holding it together" (145).

The three stanzas of the twenty-four line poem demonstrate many of
the creative tools of Ortiz's literary and storytelling experience and skill.
The metre, punctuation, line breaks, caesura within lines, and the divi-
sions between stanzas determine much of the pace of the poem, as well as
providing the textual space and reading pauses for emphasis and consideration. The majority of lines either end with emphatic iambs and amphi-
macers ("... wĭth stóne/... yŏu sée" and "... stóne ănd múd" [ll. 1, 2, 5]),
slow solemn spondees ("... loóse stóne/"; "... lóng tíme." [ll. 6, 18/24]), or
understated trisyllabics ending on an unstressed syllable ("... tŏgéthĕr/";
"... cárefŭllў/"; "pátiĕntlў/" [ll. 7, 12, 14]) that lead to interlinear enjambe-
ment and also, in a number of cases, subsequent understated trochees that
end sentences and clauses in the middle of lines.

Rhyme, para-rhyme, alliteration, and assonance draw especial attention to the semantic interrelatedness of the poem that reflects the intricacy of the woven stone: "stone," "one," and "bones"; "woven together" and "over the other" (with a double para-rhyme in "woven"/"over" and "together"/"the other"); fitting, holding, and working. Parallel phrases ("like loose stone" and "like the bones"; "Underneath" and "over the other") and the repetition of words ("stone" [ll. 1, 3, 5, 6, 17, 22], "hand" [5, 8, 9, 16, 22], "mud" [5, 13, 23], "fingers" [10, 15, 21], "long, long time" [18, 24, and in the prose epigraph]) bring together the stone and mud, wall and graveyard, the remains of ancestors and contemporary literary craft, the voices of history and the sonority of one poem.

Words, phrases, and even clauses draw back onto each other after the fashion of the interwoven stone. There are four parts of the poem in which the father is presented as the grammatical and syntactic subject, but it is important to note that it is the wall that is always the subject of the poem—the craft of its construction, and the metaphoric endurance of the wall's people. The father's subjectivity and that of the speaker of the poem serve as transitional vehicles that help readers move towards the larger story.

> My father, . . .
> says, "That's just the part you see" [ll. 1–2],
>
> He ties one hand over the other [1. 8]
>
> "It is built that carefully,"
> he says, . . . [ll. 12–3]
>
> He tells me those things, the story . . . [ll. 19–20].

Even though the father's orientation is towards the wall and his crafting of it, three of the four verbs that give him syntactic subjectivity point to his role as storyteller, as the one who "says," who "tells," a semantic emphasis which is also manifested in the iambs ("He ties"; "he says") and amphibrach ("He tells me") that lay rhythmic stress on the verb. In this way, the father's oral teaching is paralleled with the storytelling poetic craft of the poem and its own Acoma father poet, Ortiz. This is further emphasized in the father's greater presence and specificity in the first two stanzas. By the final stanza, Ortiz pulls the father back, remembering his guidance in the third person ("He tells me those things, the story . . . ,") while underscoring the father's role as storyteller (145).

By this point, the reader has been gradually transitioned towards the sacred strength of the wall and its precious remains. While the wall is named in the poem's title, it does not wholly appear in nominal mention until the final line of the poem, as the entire poem is a reflection on the efforts, skill, and care involved in its creation and endurance, and that as a profound metaphor for a people and their ancestors who are supported by the wall. As the Tewa/Hopi elder Albert Yava explained to the ethnographer Harold Courlander, the Pueblo perspective encourages focusing on the larger story, not on the person:

> If I seem to say a lot about myself, it is really my times that I am thinking about. I am merely the person who happened to be there at a particular time. It is hard to put down something with myself as a center of interest—that is, to say I did this or that. It makes me out as important, which isn't the way I see it. We Tewas and Hopis don't think of ourselves that way (Courlander, *Big Falling Snow: A Tewa-Hopi Indians Life and Times and the History and Traditions of His People*, 4).

Much as Albert Yava affirms the larger importance of the stories of existence and creation, Ortiz's poetic and prose oeuvre draws extensively on his own life experiences, but this does not reflect a self-referential focus. Rather, Ortiz relates poetic story-worlds made accessible through his own mapped Indigenous loci of experience and framed by a prosody that, in so many ways, elicits a poignantly evocative beauty of "expression and perception."[37]

The craft evident in this and the vast majority of Ortiz's other poetic work can be further seen in his remarkable ability for effective pace, tone, rhythm, metre, symbolism, ambiguity, irony, and mood. His Keres language poetry is distinctive in its conversive tools of parallelism, assonance, and repetition of terms, images, and stories, as in "For the Children" (70), a poem that returns to the graveyard wall to commemorate the loss of the children taken away to pay for the church bells. Here he remembers the wall's history and that of the Acoma people, as evidenced in a hole in the wall that has been carefully maintained—a hole that is sufficiently large for a returning child to fit through. Ortiz's skilled poetics not only interweave words, but also stories and realities within poems, between poems, and across his many published volumes to develop meaning diversely and effectively. Much can be learned from Ortiz's craft and poetics, which draw on the combined richness of his Acoma Pueblo storytelling culture and traditions and his literary training. New studies may show significant family resemblances to the work of other Pueblo writers, perhaps to other regional Native writers, perhaps more broadly even to Indigenous writers continentally and globally. Beyond indigeneity, meaningful family resemblances may be found across times and oceans in the oral rhetorics of the *Iliad* and Sophocles, *Beowulf* and Chaucer, and even the work of the great Persian poets Rumi, Saadi, and Hafiz. Scholars need to explore the richness of Ortiz's poetry and prose in new and daring ways, including extensive studies of his poetics.

III

Ortiz's Literary Legacy

Susan Berry Brill de Ramírez and Evelina Zuni Lucero

In this collection, we want to pay tribute to Ortiz's craft and literary legacy. To do this, it is important to begin by acknowledging that his gift is an offering that, in turn, comes from his parents and his family, from his clan and his tribe, from his home and ancestral lands, from the interwoven and, all too often, knotted history of colonization and empire building. Accordingly, we honor Ortiz and all those participative along his creative path, many of whom are mentioned in the interviews in this volume. To articulate the larger story of Ortiz's writing and his role in the development of Native American literatures, we incorporate both critical essays and creative pieces. At the center of the study of Native American literatures is the profound understanding of the importance of telling the whole of a story honestly and completely; this often involves incorporating not only diverse voices, but also diverse ways of telling the story (through poetry, story, drama, song, chant, etc.). With that idea in mind, we include a wide ranging collection of writing by academic scholars, Native writers, and Simon Ortiz himself: personal essays and creative pieces, interviews, reviews, and literary critical essays. Ortiz's personal story is an important part of the larger story of the development of Native American literatures, and can't be separated from it. Rather, his life and writings, his politics and philosophies, his struggles and achievements through almost a half century of active writing become the lens to focus the larger historical picture. As Ortiz tells us, "The words, the language of my experience, come from how I understand, how I relate to the world around me, and how I know language as perception. That language allows me vision to see with and by which to know myself" (*Song, Poetry and Language*, 12).

All together, these writings establish a full context that will help readers understand the early history and ongoing development of the contemporary Native American literary outpouring often referred to as the "Native American Literary Renaissance," which began in the 1960s and of which Simon Ortiz is an integral part. The multitude of voices and variety of formats articulate Ortiz's impact on the broader development of Native American literatures. Through the voices of Native writers who Ortiz affected in some significant measure, the volume shows his active engagement in the development of cultural studies and Native American literatures on a number of fronts, and in ways that have rippled out in widening circles from individuals to tribal, regional, national, hemispheric, and global levels of awareness and appreciation. The volume also illuminates the historical, cultural, and political factors that shaped Native writers and launched the literary outpouring that followed. By offering a historical perspective that allows readers a heightened understanding of Ortiz's literary craft and importance, we hope this volume will contribute to substantive critical approaches to Native American literatures in keeping with Native thought and philosophy. Additionally, as many of the pieces in this volume express directly, the insights and aesthetics of Ortiz's Indigenous point of view are invaluable contributions to literary studies that turn to the postcolonial, the ecocritical, the globally Indigenous, and the globally comparative as geographies of belonging in an aesthetics of inclusion and authenticity.

The collection begins with a preface by Gregory Cajete (Santa Clara Pueblo), Director of Native American Studies at the University of New Mexico. Cajete speaks powerfully about the challenges now facing Indian people, pointing to the crucial role that Ortiz's words play in assisting his fellow Pueblo and Indigenous peoples in finding their moorings in life and in community. Noting the traditional place that stories have held throughout time among the Indigenous peoples of the world, Cajete especially emphasizes the contemporary need for visionary storytellers like Ortiz. "And in these times, Indigenous communities span reservations and urban settings, communal and personal spaces, Simon's poetry stories a sense for our place in the world. . . . Simon helps us realize that if we are looking for something to build our lives on, that we should look not just to the facts of the world, but also to our own stories, spirit and imagination" (ix-xii).

The first section of the book begins with Ortiz's own words and life story. Two seminal essays by Ortiz are reprinted herein: his early essay "Song, Poetry and Language: Expression and Perception" (originally published as a separate booklet by Navajo Community Press) and his more recent "Native Heritage: A Tradition of Participation." These are followed by three interviews with Ortiz. An earlier interview with University of New Mexico (UNM) Professor David Dunaway and our subsequent interviews with Simon offer comprehensive overviews of his life and craft, providing a regional and historical lens pointed toward Acoma Pueblo, the larger intertribal Pueblo region, and Albuquerque and the University of New Mexico. All three of the interviewers have enduring ties to the region and UNM—whether tribally and ancestrally, professionally, and/or scholastically. "Simon J. Ortiz: The Writing the Southwest Interview," Dunaway's early interview from 1988 (a section of which was published in the special Ortiz issue of Studies in American Literature [16.4]), spans Ortiz's life and his emergence as a major literary figure. Brill de Ramírez's interview, "The Burden of Images and the Importance of Land, Culture, and Community," looks at Ortiz's years at the University of Toronto, the development of aboriginal studies there, and the literary trajectory of his writing. Evelina Zuni Lucero's interview "In His Own Words" was conducted at Ortiz's home in Deetseyamah and in Albuquerque and Santa Fe. This interview deeply grounds Ortiz's insights about his life and his writing within a Pueblo frame that speaks of the very particular history and legacy of his, their, people. Whereas Ortiz speaks comfortably within a regional focus with Dunaway and Brill de Ramírez, with Lucero he opens up wholly, speaking in the voice of an elder Pueblo writer and educator. The poetic epigraph for this section, Ralph Salisbury's "For Simon Ortiz," grounds Simon's words at their origin: Sky City (Acoma Pueblo). In motion evoking the cycle of rain and the offering of prayer, Ortiz's words, "circle the world," melting lies "frozen so hard / they seemed Truth," blessing the earth across times and geographies (72).

The second section of the book includes essays by Native writers and scholars whose work has been directly influenced by Simon Ortiz's pioneering craft. The enormity of Ortiz's legacy is extensively global, generationally enduring, and tangibly affective and effective. The brief creative nonfiction pieces and the longer personally infused scholarly essays of this section speak to Ortiz's impact on the writing and lives of Indigenous scholars and writers in very personal and concrete ways. Building on the information, expression, history, and insight in the interviews, there is a precious specificity articulated in this centering section that strictly critical scholarship often points to, but rarely touches. This section begins with an epigraphic poem by Kimberly Roppolo (Cherokee, Choctaw, Creek descent) that speaks to Simon's literary legacy to the younger generations of Native writers. In Roppolo's "Morning Star Song," she speaks of the transformative power of a poetry that has "case[d] the hardness in the eyes of tomorrow" and which "maps trails" forward for "our Aunties and Uncles, / writers from many tribes" (168-69).

In "The Same Family of Stories," Ortiz's contemporary Leslie Marmon Silko (Laguna Pueblo) speaks of the shared stories, conversations, and letters that formed much of her literary relationship with Ortiz and that played a crucial role in her development as a writer: "When I wrote my short stories, I wanted them to belong to the same family of stories Simon wrote" (175). The essay "Generosity in Continuance: The Gifts of Simon J. Ortiz" by Gwen Westerman Griffin (Sisseton Wahpeton Dakota) speaks about the accessibility of Ortiz's work to a broad range of readers even as his Indigenous voice strongly speaks for Native communities and serves as a mentor for many emergent and established Native writers. In reprints from the *SAIL* issue, Joy Harjo (Muscogee Creek), Evelina Zuni Lucero (Isleta/Ohkay Owingeh Pueblo), and Laura Tohe (Diné) speak of how Ortiz's work entered their lives at pivotal points in the 1970s and directly influenced and inspired their own work. In "Poetry Can Be All This," Harjo relates her exhilarating realization of "how a kernel of meaning, and sound condensed to one page could stagger the world with meaning" (184). In "The Stories He Lives By," Lucero expresses "the amazing discovery [through Ortiz] . . . that Indians could be authors," and sees Ortiz as making a way for all Native writers who followed (187–88). In "It Was That Indian," Tohe speaks of how, upon hearing Ortiz read for the first time, "a little revolution exploded in [her] mind" as he powerfully addressed the very social and political issues affecting her own Diné people and lands, a revolution that later translated to her own work (190–91).

"Simon Ortiz, 'Cored Tightly' in Prayer, Song, and Protest," Kathryn W. Shanley's (Assiniboine) essay, speaks very directly about the ravages of humans colonized to the subaltern margins of fractured selves and the enormous efforts to emerge beyond the tow of alcohol. Referencing the Nakoda term *unshiga*, which she explains is "related to trickster philosophy, a paradoxical state of power and failure and the recognition of an innate insignificance," Shanley points to Ortiz's personal and literary survivance that articulate "visions of dignity in the face of difficulty" (196, 199). We would like to especially note that, of the contributors to this volume, many of the Native women writers and scholars chose to contribute in the more intersubjective forms of poetry and creative nonfiction essays. Even in the critical essays that follow (and our own introduction and interviews), a distinctively female voice resonates. It is heard in the essays by Kimberly Blaeser, Sophia Cantave, Elizabeth Ammons, Debbie Reese, and Elizabeth Archuleta, finding a welcome place in the inclusively grounded ethic of Ortiz's Indigenous Acoma poetics. Traditionally, women readers have more readily found a place within female authored texts. Ortiz's Indigenous ethic demonstrates the inclusive accessibility of a literature grounded in a tribal and historical specificity that speaks realities and experiences relevant to all peoples within their own respective geographies of belonging.

The larger section (Part III) of the book consists of longer critical essays that explore Ortiz's work in diverse directions, drawing on a range of literary critical tools and methods. Esther Belin's (Diné) poem "No Mistaking the Boundaries" serves as the poetic epigraph for this third section. In a tribute to Ortiz acknowledging his assertions of Indigenous continuance, Belin speaks of the futility of imposed boundaries to contain the land, the people, to separate them, to silence them, reminding us of what Ortiz articulates: "The land, the people." The critical essays begin with one of the two longer essays reprinted from the special *SAIL* issue. Roger Dunsmore's "Simon Ortiz and the Lyricism of Continuance: 'For the Sake of the People, For the Sake of the Land'" originated as a presentation at the Modern Language Association session in San Francisco that provided the initial impetus for a collection devoted to Ortiz. In an essay that looks closely at familial relations as expressed in Ortiz's poetry, Dunsmore makes the stunning claim that "Simon Ortiz is the most important poet writing in America today," pointing to Ortiz's remarkable poetic combination of the "prayerful," the "ferociousness" of endurance through colonization, and the poetic aesthetics of what Dunsmore terms "motion/emotion" (211–12). Kimberly M. Blaeser (White Earth Anishinaabe) develops further a critical aesthetics that articulates the craft of Ortiz's poetry. In "Sacred Journey, Poetic Journey: Ortiz Re-turning and Re-telling from the Colonized Spaces of America," Blaeser recrafts work from two previously published pieces into a longer examination of the interwoven "literary and cultural continuance" and "political awareness and activism" as exemplified in Ortiz's work. Echoing the distinctive combination of Ortiz's Indigenous inclusivity which, while rooted in his tribal geography and history, is expansively global, Blaeser concludes her essay thus: "His stance is ever that of one who resides in occupied territories, in the colonized spaces of America. The poetic gesture he makes points us beyond" (213, 230).

David L. Moore's essay "'The story goes its own way': Ortiz, Nationalism, and the Oral Poetics of Power," like the Dunsmore piece, is a reprint from the *SAIL* issue and one of the originating papers presented at the MLA Ortiz session. Choosing an effective minimalist position that gives Ortiz's own words primacy, Moore's critical voice serves as a sparse yet clearly directive guide that coheres insights regarding an "aesthetic of openness," "ethics of power," and an "affirmation of dynamic cultural authenticity" demonstrated in Ortiz's poetry (234–35). In "Reading Simon Ortiz and Black Diasporic Literature of the Americas," Sophia Cantave demonstrates Ortiz's hemispheric and global reach, drawing on his poetic vision as a critical tool for delineating the processes by which diasporized persons indigenize themselves to become part of distant and alien geographies. Looking at the work of black Caribbean writers Jacques Stephen Alexis, Michelle Cliff, and Mayra Montero, Cantave explains that Ortiz's poetic vision "prompted this subtle, yet profound, difference in my understanding about the ways people of African descent lay claim to their new environments, the conflicting nature of those claims, and the struggle for black American continuity within the fact of white hegemony" (248). Regional and cross-tribal relevance and authenticity are explored and expanded in Jeff Berglund's "'They should look in the space that is in here': Developing an Ethics of Reading American Indian Literature." Berglund points to the literary accessibility that comes from the personal and ancestral authenticity of knowledge, evidenced by allied scholars accepting the "decolonizing tactic" that requires "giving up mastery of a text." As Berglund explains, "Such a reorientation of the academic pursuit of mastery of content, and an emphasis on contextually appropriate and ethical methodologies, I believe, gives greater emphasis to cultural ownership of material and reminds outsiders of privileges and responsibilities of the initiated and of the protocols cultural outsiders should be aware of" (278).

Explicitly turning to Ortiz's holistic commitments to "the people and the land" at Acoma Pueblo and elsewhere, Elizabeth Ammons presents an ecocritical approach to Ortiz's prose fiction in *"Men on the Moon* and the Fight for Environmental Justice." Orienting her essay through Ortiz's Keres language origins and the ancestral lands of Acoma Pueblo, Ammons demonstrates Ortiz's subtle yet constant voice that demythologizes the "colonial ethic of unlimited conquest and consumption," noting that his work draws crucial attention to the "hugely disproportionate and often catastrophic environmental threats to [indigenous people's] health, lives, economic survival, and cultural and religious well-being because of governmental and corporate policies and practices that target them" (290). This history underlies the risks that Ortiz and his people have lived with and the risks that Ortiz articulates as fundamental to caring and engaged lives. Sean Kicummah Teuton (Cherokee) addresses the importance of human and "mutual ecological vulnerability" for living meaningful and empathic lives which, he argues, are as necessary in the academy as they are within tribal communities. "In Open Daring: Risk and Vulnerability in the Poetry of Simon J. Ortiz," Teuton presents Ortiz's work as a model of actual and articulative risk, stating that only when literary scholars accept and shoulder real risk will their work, like Ortiz's, have effect "defending the shared planetary lives at stake" (321).

Expanding the range of critical attention, Debbie Reese (Nambe Pueblo) turns to Ortiz's commitment to the education of children: Acoma, Pueblo, Indigenous, worldwide. Her essay "Simon Ortiz: The Importance of Childhood" introduces his children's literature, including bilingual Keres/English books, one regionally trilingual Keres/English/Spanish volume, and his other English language volumes for children.

As Reese makes patently clear, Ortiz, like many other Indigenous writers, carries his tribally inclusive communal ethic forward in his writing, in this case in his continual reminder of the importance of the children, the future generations. Elizabeth Archuleta (Yaqui), too, addresses issues of ethics and engages the very existential questions of personhood that Ortiz raises throughout his work. Her essay "Learning to be Human: An Indigenous System of Ethics in the Writing of Simon Ortiz" points to the importance of Indigenous epistemologies as a means of access to the inclusively relational ethical imperative that runs throughout Ortiz's writing.

Geary Hobson (Cherokee-Quapaw/Chickasaw) also writes about Ortiz's commitment to exposing continuing colonialist injustices Indigenous people face worldwide, reminding us that, the virtues of postcolonial theory notwithstanding, the temporal "post-" in postcolonial ignores Native peoples who are "still living under the yoke of the Euro-American colonization of Indian lands and nations" (366). Hobson's review of "Simon J. Ortiz's Powerful Poetic Resistance: A Review Essay of *A Good Journey* and *Fight Back: For the Sake of the People, For the Sake of the Land*," written over two decades ago, communicates the excitement that Ortiz's early publications generated as Native people read poetry that spoke the realities of their worlds, lives, and histories. We have chosen to end the essays by reprinting Lawrence Evers' groundbreaking essay, "The Killing of a State Trooper." In this essay, Evers engages the poetics and the history of Ortiz's story while communicating to the broad literary establishment the importance of Ortiz's work, as well as the legitimacy of literary scholars turning to the burgeoning body of Native literatures. Evers examines Ortiz's "The Killing of a State Cop" "to see the role of the individual imagination to the creation of fiction" as Ortiz renders an adept turn of "that small line segment of history into circles of form" (367–68).

The volume concludes with an epilogue by Osage writer and scholar Robert Warrior, currently Director of Native American Studies at the University of Illinois. Warrior begins by thinking back to his peoples' own songs and dances and his own struggles to learn his ancestral Osage language. In those efforts, he relates that "No other intellectual encouraged me in my studies of wazhazhe i-e more than Simon, and his published work on the importance of Indigenous languages helped me crystalize my own sense of how and why what I was learning was important" (389).

In his summary, Warrior articulates the enormous influence that Ortiz has had on the writers he has mentored, the readers he has moved, the students he has taught. In summing up the contributions in this volume, Warrior emphasizes that his ending is a beginning, a call for future study and appreciation of Ortiz's tremendous gifts to us all. He concludes by saying, "Beyond all these things that Simon has written, there's so much more, and my hope for his readers in the future is that they glimpse in his work all the different ways he has participated in the complex and changing Indigenous world" (393).

This collection of work, which is focused on Simon J. Ortiz, his remarkable craft and life that have straddled so many worlds and lifetimes in one, is indeed a gift to us all. Each of the contributions in this volume says such important things about literature and the world, how these two are integrally interwoven, and how it is Ortiz who in so many ways helps us to understand these interconnections more deeply and more comprehensively.

NOTES

1. To date, Andrew Wiget's early volume about Ortiz's work, various critical essays scattered in diverse publications, and the special issue of *Studies in American Indian Literatures* devoted to Ortiz are the sum total of the focused critical attention on Ortiz.

2. The phrase "literature for literature's sake" points back to the "art for art's sake" ideology that presumed that art could be created bereft of politics. In fact, for much of the twentieth century and its New Critical and deconstructive influences, textual craft was privileged with the concomitant devaluation of politicized literature. Tendencies toward the apolitical can be found in many cultures' art and literature (e.g., the relativism of classical Athens's Sophists, the development of the lyric poem from Sappho and Ovid through to much contemporary poetry, and contemporary hypertextual literary experiments). Clear expressions of the "Art for Art's Sake" movement can be seen in Edgar Allan Poe's essay "The Poetic Principle," http://www.eapoe.org/works/essays/poetprnd.htm (accessed October 28, 2008), and Oscar Wilde's essay "The Decay of Lying," http://www.online-literature.com/wilde/1307/ (accessed October 28, 2008).

3. Ortiz addresses the concept of the road of life as it applies in his life and writing in Evelina Zuni Lucero, "Simon J. Ortiz: In His Own Words," in this volume (140–41, 157, 160).

4. While the Pueblo oral tradition transmits sacred knowledge, Laguna

Pueblo writer Leslie Marmon Silko explains that it also encompasses the whole of life's events:

> Pueblo oral tradition necessarily embraced all levels of human experience. Otherwise the collective knowledge and beliefs comprising ancient Pueblo culture would have been incomplete.... [T]he Pueblo Oral tradition knew no boundaries. Accounts of the appearance of the first Europeans (Spanish) in Pueblo country or of the tragic encounters between Pueblo people and Apache raiders were no more and no less important than stories about the biggest mule deer ever taken or adulterous couples surprised in cornfields and chicken coops. Whatever happened, the ancient people instinctively sorted events and details into a loose narrative structure. Everything became a story ("Interior and Exterior Landscapes," 31).

5. For a discussion on this topic, see Elizabeth Archuleta, "Learning to be Human: An Indigenous System of Ethics in the Writing of Simon Ortiz," in this volume (339–60).

6. Pueblo scholar Gregory Cajete in *Look to the Mountain: An Ecology of Indigenous Education* writes,

> Indian community is the primary context for traditional education. Community is the context in which the affective dimension of education unfolds. It is the place where one comes to know what it is to be related. It is the place of sharing life through everyday acts, through song, dance, story and celebration. It is the place of teaching, learning, making art, and sharing thoughts, feelings, joy, and grief. It is the place for feeling and being connected. The community is the place where each person can, metaphorically speaking, *become complete* and express the fullness of their life. Community is "that place that Indian people talk about" [quoting Ortiz], it is the place through which Indian people express their highest thought (emphasis added, 164–65).

7. Originally published in *MELUS* 8, no. 2 (Summer 1981): 7–11 and reprinted in Jace Weaver, Craig S. Womack, and Robert Warrior, *American Indian Literary Nationalism*, 251–60. All quotations are from the reprinted essay.

8. Silko distinguishes between the "exterior" geographical formations that evoke the stories of the journey of the emergence, and the "ritual circuit or path" that speaks of her Laguna people's "interior" journey:

> a journey of awareness and imagination in which they emerged from being in the earth and all-included in the earth to the culture and people they became ... The narratives linked with prominent features of the landscape ... delineate the complexities of the relationships that human beings must maintain with the surrounding natural world if they hope to survive in this place. Thus, the journey was an interior process of the imagination, a

growing awareness that being human is somehow different from all other life—plant, animal, and inanimate. Yet, we are all from the same source: awareness never deteriorated into Cartesian duality, cutting off the human from the natural world ("Interior and Exterior Landscapes," 37).

9. Roxanne Dunbar-Ortiz notes that in precolonial times, the Pueblos were "part of a larger socioeconomic context," consisting of large settlements designated by anthropologists as the "Mogollon" (probably the ancestors of the Pima and Tohono O'odham peoples in Arizona), "Anasazi" (Pueblo ancestral culture group that climaxed in the eleventh century in the Four Corners area of Colorado, Utah, Arizona, and New Mexico), and "Hohokam" (probably related to Hopi and Zuni Pueblo), civilizations to the west and southwest of the northern Rio Grande Valley, most of which were forsaken in the 1200s as the people migrated to the Rio Grande Valley.

The larger political and economic area of these previous communities extended south to the valley of México and included the present northern interior of México. Encompassing the area from the Pacific Ocean to the Great Plains, as far east as the present state of Kansas, the total area included 170,520,470 square miles of territory and was considered the northern frontier of central México by precolonial Mesoamericans and later by the Spanish colonialists (*Roots of Resistance: A History of Land Tenure in New Mexico*, 18–19).

Dunbar-Ortiz cites Charles DiPeso's use of "Gran Chichimeca" to refer to the northern territory, so called by precolonial Mesoamericans and later by Spaniards; the area was also called "Aztlan" in precolonial times by those in the south (176n3).

10. Joe S. Sando, *Pueblo Nations, Eight Centuries of Pueblo Indian History* (Santa Fe: Clear Light Publishers, 1992), chapter 3; Roxanne Dunbar-Ortiz, *Roots of Resistance: A History of Land Tenure in New Mexico*, 3–35.

11. Sando, *Pueblo Nations*, chapter 4; Tisa Wenger, "Land, Culture, and Sovereignty in the Pueblo Dance Controversy," 381–412; See also Nell Jessup Newton, et al., eds. *Cohen's Handbook of Federal Indian Law*, 319–36.

12. Dunbar-Ortiz, *Roots of Resistence*, 156–59. For the Pueblo response to the celebrations, see also Brenda Norrell, "Pueblos Decry War Criminals," *Indian County Today*, June 6, 2005, http://www.indiancountry.com/content. cfm?id=1096411133 (accessed March 18, 2008); Brenda Norrell, "Pueblos Protest Albuquerque Tricentennial," *Indian Country Today*, April 25, 2005, http://www. indiancountry.com/content.cfm?id=1096410806 (accessed March 18, 2008).

13. In retaliation for the death of two Spanish soldiers at the hands of Acomas, Don Juan de Oñate sent a large force to Acoma in January 1599. After a three-day battle, over 800 Acoma men, women, and children were killed.

Harsh punishment was meted out to the survivors: One foot of males over the age of twenty-five was severed, and they were sentenced to slavery along with males and females between the ages of twelve and twenty-five. Children were taken away and never returned (Dunbar-Ortiz, *Roots of Resistance*, xvi; Norrell, "Pueblos Decry War Criminals").

14. For a discussion on this topic, see Kimberly M. Blaeser, "Sacred Journey, Poetic Journey: Ortiz Re-turning and Re-telling from the Colonized Spaces of America," in this volume (213–31).

15. For a full discussion of "a geography of belonging" see Susan Brill de Ramirez, "A Geography of Belonging: Ortiz's Poetic, Lived, and Storied Indigenous Ecology" in the second part of the introduction in this volume (25–52).

16. In 1953, Anaconda began open-pit mining of uranium deposits north of Laguna Pueblo near the village of Paguate. The Anaconda Jackpile mine was part of the largest known United States uranium ore deposit in the Grants Mineral Belt in New Mexico, which ran under the Navajo, Acoma, and Laguna Indian reservations. From 1953 to March 1982, twenty-four million tons of ore was mined in a round-the-clock, year round operation. Following closure of the mine, the uranium tailings lay exposed, blown by the wind, until land reclamation began in 1989. See testimony by Manuel Pino in *Poison Fire, Sacred Earth: testimonies, lectures, and conclusions* (Munich: The World Uranium Hearing, 1993). http://www.ratical.org/radiation/WorldUraniumHearing/ (accessed May 12, 2008); "Laguna and Acoma Pueblos," *Voices from the Earth* 8, no. 2 (Summer 2007). http://www.sric.org/voices/2007/v8n2/laguna_and_ acome_pueblos.html (accessed May 12, 2008).

17. See Ortiz's foreword, "Speaking-Writing Indigenous Literary Sovereignty" in Jace Weaver, Craig S. Womack, and Robert Warrior, *American Indian Literary Nationalism*, vii–xiv. In it, Ortiz elaborates on his ideas on Native use of the English language, stating, "[W]e must determine for ourselves how English is to be a part of our lives socially, culturally, and politically. . . . Although we have to make sure we do not compromise ourselves by inadvertently speaking-writing what we don't want to mean (because English carries a lot of Western social-cultural baggage), English language writing can work to our advantage when we write with a sense of Indigenous consciousness" (xiv).

18. The volume, co-authored by Native literary critics Jace Weaver, Craig S. Womack, and Robert Warrior, seeks to "enliven discussions of what nationalism can and should mean within contemporary scholarship on Native literature" (Weaver, Womack, and Warrior, *American Indian Literary Nationalism*, xv).

19. Louis Althusser implicated the educational systems as powerfully manipulative tools of the state—terming those Ideological State Apparatuses

(ISAs). Althusser's essay "Ideology and Ideological State Apparatuses" is reprinted in the collection *The Critical Tradition: Classic Texts and Contemporary Trends*, David H. Richter, ed. (Boston: Bedford/St. Martin's, 2007), 1263–72 (reprinted from Althusser's *Lenin and Philosophy and Other Essays*, Ben Brewster, trans. [London: New Left Books, 1971]).

20. See chapter X of my earlier volume *Contemporary American Indian Literatures and the Oral Tradition* for a discussion of the subjectivity of animals in Native American and other literatures (117–26).

21. Future scholars who are conversant in both the Keres and English languages will be able to discuss the intricacies of Ortiz's poetry in both registers. Analogously, there is much work to be done in exploring the Indigenous poetics of those writers who craft their literary work wholly or partially in their respective Indigenous languages.

22. Here the term "familiarization" is being used with the converse of Shklovsky's use of the term "defamiliarisation" wherein he signified the literary craft that transformed the everyday and the ordinary into the unfamiliar, the new, the notable. As the converse, familiarization is one of the more common tools of traditional oral storytelling across cultures worldwide in which the unusual, the mythic, the ancient, the distant, and the imagined are conveyed in ways that make them readily connective, easily engaged, and comprehensible to listeners. A good collection of Victor Shklovsky's literary analyses is his *Theory of Prose*, Benjamin Sher, trans., with an introduction by Gerald L. Bruns (Elmwood Park, IL: Daltrey Archive Press, 1991).

23. The term πολις is used here to indicate the "family resemblances" (in the Wittgensteinian sense) between the classical Greek city-states and the Pueblo communities. I remember teaching the essay "The Polis" from H. D. Kitto's volume *The Greeks* in freshman composition classes at the University of New Mexico (Chicago: Aldine Pub., 1964). The Greek city-state structure and culture seemed alien to many of my students, but the Pueblo students recognized a familiar world, although distant in time and place.

24. The phrase "bear witness" is used quite deliberately to draw the connections between Ortiz's writing and the *testimonios* of Latin America. It is important to remember that Ortiz's Pueblo peoples lived throughout an extensive region that included much of the current American Southwest and also extended down into what is currently northern Mexico. Accordingly, it is not surprising that Native American writers who are Pueblo would be particularly aware of and focused on border, Mexican and Central American, and hemispheric issues. Ortiz was involved in a project to bring the concerns of the Indigenous peoples of southern Mexico to the attention of Americans, contributing an essay titled *"Haah-ah, mah-eemah*: Yes, it's the very truth" to the volume *Questions and Swords: Folktales of the Zapatista Revolution*, 50–59. In this essay, which is

analogous to testimonial works of creative nonfiction like *I, Rigoberta Menchú*, and throughout his work, Ortiz bears powerful witness to his life and times and to the lives and times that he has come to know tribally, genetically, ancestrally, familially, regionally, geographically, experientially, and literarily.

25. In a powerfully moving work of creative nonfiction titled "Our Homeland, A National Sacrifice Area" that combines prose and poetry, Ortiz details the history of his Acoma people and their lands that have been under continuous assault since 1540 C.E. (*Fight Back* in *Woven Stone*, 337–63).

26. Ecocritic Joni Adamson notes that Native peoples have articulated their life experiences in ecosystemic ways, even in relation to the catastrophic experiences of colonization: "However, just as they always had before, the people went out into the changing world and incorporated into their oral traditions the understanding they were gaining of both social and environmental changes. They linked stories of the tall grass, abundant harvests, and clear, fast-running water with stories of oppression and loss—not out of a sense of nostalgia, but because they were making connections" (*American Indian Literature, Environmental Justice, and Ecocriticism*, 60–61).

27. Indeed, Samir Dayal states pithily that "To resist the homogenizing tendencies of 'diversity talk' one must recognize the constitutive heterogeneity of diasporic positionalities and affiliations, and the shifting (self)-identifications and unpredictable alliances of the diasporic transnational" ("Diaspora and Double Consciousness," 50).

28. As Edward Said explains in the afterword of his seminal volume *Orientalism*, "as a system of thought Orientalism approaches a heterogeneous, dynamic, and complex human reality from an uncritically essentialist standpoint" (333). "In the discourse of modern Orientalism and its counterparts in similar knowledges constructed for Native Americans and Africans [there is] a chronic tendency to deny, suppress, or distort the cultural context of such systems of thought in order to maintain the fiction of its scholarly disinterest" (345).

29. Here Ortiz writes the Acoma inflection of the name of the state of California: "Kaalrrahuul-rre-neeyaa."

30. In her essay "Language and Literature from a Pueblo Indian Perspective," Silko explains that "The storytelling always includes the audience and the listeners, and, in fact, a great deal of the story is believed to be inside the listener, and the storytellers' role is to draw the story out of the listeners" (57). Noting the relational aspect of storytelling, ecocritic C. A. Bowers notes the active responsibility of story-listeners: "in order for an elder to tell a coherent story the listener must know how to participate in the relationship" (*Educating for an Ecologically Sustainable Culture: Rethinking Moral Education, Creativity, Intelligence, and Other Modern Orthodoxies*, 176–77).

31. Conversive communications present the inverse of discourse (etymologically signifying "to run to and fro"). In the former, language serves as the means towards the larger ends of interpersonal and intercommunity relationship building and restoration; the latter utilizes persons as the means towards the discursive ends of signification, logic, argument, and op/positionality.

32. The term "listener-reader" is used to communicate the conversive role of readers as distinct from a more distanced discursive interaction. Ortiz used this term years ago in emphasizing the interrelationality of storytelling, whether oral or written: "With *A Good Journey* I try to show that the listener-reader has as much responsibility and commitment to poetic effect as the poet" (*Woven Stone*, 151).

33. It is important to clarify that this attribution of personhood broadly throughout creation is in no wise an anthropomorphic view that posits human qualities in non-human beings (e.g., animals, plants, rocks). Personhood is an attribution of intentionality within the level of existence of particular creatures. In his essay "The Status of Persons or Who Was that Masked Metaphor," descriptive psychologist James R. Holmes states explicitly that "paradigmatically, a person is an individual whose history is a history of deliberate action. . . . There is however, nothing about the concept of a person that requires persons to be human beings" ("The Status of Persons or Who Was That Masked Metaphor?" 30). For a more developed discussion of interpersonal relationality across species, also see my earlier volume *Contemporary American Indian Literatures and the Oral Tradition*.

34. Browne demonstrates the oral sonority of language in his prose work which bears noticeable relation to some of Ortiz's poetics. The voice and tone of Browne's "Hydriotaphia: Urne-Burial or, a Brief Discourse of the Sepulchrall Urnes Lately Found in Norfolk" also bears a strong family resemblance (in the Wittgensteinian sense) to the Ortiz poem, albeit with the crucial difference that Ortiz reflects upon his own ancestors' remains, while the Browne piece turns to the burial site of his ancestors' conquerors, the Romans.

35. The Latin lines come from the poetry of Tibullus, "Elegia II," line 26, page 81 of *Albii Tibulli*, Liber Tertius (book three) from the compilation *Catulli Tibulli Propertii: Poemata Selecta*, A. H. Wratislaw and F. N. Sutton, eds. (London: George Bell & Sons, 1891). Translation of Latin line by A. B. Chambers.

36. "And I meant that a word is not spoken in any *separate parts*, that is, with reference to linguistic structure, technique of diction, nuance or sound, tonal quality, inflection, etc. Words are spoken as complete words" (Ortiz, *Song, Poetry and Language* in this volume) (76).

37. This reference to "expression and perception" in Ortiz's work is discussed in his essay "Song, Poetry and Language: Expression and Perception" in this volume (75–85).

WORKS CITED

Adamson, Joni. *American Indian Literature, Environmental Justice, and Ecocriticism: The Middle Place.* Tucson: The University of Arizona Press, 2001.

Attinasi, John and Paul Friedrich. "Dialogic Breakthrough: Catalysis and Synthesis in Life-Changing Dialogue." In *The Dialogic Emergence of Culture,* edited by Dennis Tedlock and Bruce Mannheim, 33–53. Urbana: University of Illinois Press, 1995.

Bird, Gloria. "Breaking the Silence, Writing as 'Witness.'" In *Speaking for the Generations,* edited by Simon J. Ortiz, 28–29.

Blaeser, Kimberly M. *Gerald Vizenor: Writing in the Oral Tradition.* Norman: University of Oklahoma Press, 1996.

Bowers, C. A. *Educating for an Ecologically Sustainable Culture: Rethinking Moral Education, Creativity, Intelligence, and Other Modern Orthodoxies.* Albany: State University of New York Press, 1995.

Boyarin, Daniel, and Jonathan Boyarin. "Diaspora: Generational Ground of Jewish Identity." *Critical Inquiry* 19, no. 4 (1993): 693–725.

Brill de Ramírez, Susan Berry. *Contemporary American Indian Literatures and the Oral Tradition.* Tucson: University of Arizona Press, 1999.

Brill de Ramírez, Susan Berry, and Edith Baker. "'There are balances and harmonies always shifting; always necessary to maintain': Leslie Marmon Silko's Vision of Global Environmental Justice for the People and the Land." *Journal of Organization and the Environment* 18, no. 2 (June 2005): 213–28.

Browne, Sir Thomas. *Selected Writings.* Edited by Sir Geoffrey Keynes. Chicago: The University of Chicago Press, 1968.

Buell, Lawrence. "Ecoglobalist Effects: The Emergence of U.S. Environmental Imagination on a Planetary Scale." In *Shades of the Planet,* edited by Wai Chee Dimock and Lawrence Buell, 227–48. Princeton: Princeton University Press, 2007.

Cajete, Gregory. *Look to the Mountain: An Ecology of Indigenous Education.* Durango, Colorado: Kivaki Press, 1994.

Césaire, Aimé. *Discourse on Colonialism.* New York: Monthly Review Press, 1972.

Comaroff, Jean. "The End of History, Again?: Pursuing the Past in the Postcolony." In *Postcolonial Studies and Beyond,* edited by Ania Loomba, Suvir Kaul, Matti Bunzl, Antoinette Burton, and Jed Esty, 125–44. Durham, NC: Duke University Press, 2005.

Cooppan, Vilashini. "The Ruins of Empire: The National and Global Politics of America's Return to Rome." In *Postcolonial Studies and Beyond*, edited by Ania Loomba, Suvir Kaul, Matti Bunzl, Antoinette Burton, and Jed Esty, 80–100. Durham, NC: Duke University Press, 2005.

Dayal, Samir. "Diaspora and Double Consciousness." *The Journal of the Midwest Modern Language Association* 29, no. 1 (Spring 1996): 46–62.

Dimock, Wai Chee, and Lawrence Buell, eds. *Shades of the Planet: American Literature as World Literature*. Princeton: Princeton University Press, 2007.

Dunbar-Ortiz, Roxanne. *Roots of Resistance: A History of Land Tenure in New Mexico*. Norman: University of Oklahoma Press, 2007.

Glissant, Édouard. *Poetics of Relation*. Translated by Betsy Wing. Ann Arbor: University of Michigan Press, 1997.

Harper, Peter, and Mary Gray. "Maps and Meaning in Life and Healing." In *The Therapeutic Use of Stories*, edited by Kedar Nath Dwivedi, 42–63. London: Routledge, 1997.

Hernandez-Avila, Ines, and Stefano Varese. "Indigenous Intellectual Sovereignties: A Hemispheric Convocation. An Overview and Reflections on a United States/Mexico Binational Two-Part Conference." *Wicazo Sa Review* 14, no. 2 "Emergent Ideas in Native American Studies" (Autumn 1999): 77–91.

Holmes, James R. "The Status of Persons or Who Was That Masked Metaphor?" *Advances in Descriptive Psychology* 6 (1991): 15–35.

Kirshenblatt-Gimblett, Barbara. "Spaces of Dispersal." *Cultural Anthropology* 9, no. 3 "Further Inflections: Toward Ethnographies of the Future" (August 1994): 339–44.

"Laguna and Acoma Pueblos." *Voices from the Earth* 8, no. 2 (Summer 2007). http://www.sric.org/voices/2007/v8n2/laguna_and_acome_pueblos.html (accessed May 12, 2008).

Lehmann, Sophia. "In Search of a Mother Tongue: Locating Home in Diaspora." *MELUS* 23, no. 4 "Theory, Culture and Criticism" (Winter 1998): 101–18.

Leopold, Aldo. *A Sand County Almanac and Sketches Here and There*. Oxford: Oxford University Press, 1949.

Loomba, Ania, Suvir Kaul, Matti Bunzl, Antoinette Burton, and Jed Esty, eds. *Postcolonial Studies and Beyond*. Durham, NC: Duke University Press, 2005.

Newton, Nell Jessup, et al., eds. *Cohen's Handbook of Federal Indian Law*, 319–36. Newark: LexisNexis, 2005.

Norrell, Brenda. "Pueblos Decry War Criminals." *Indian Country Today,*
June 6, 2005. http://www.indiancountry.com/content.cfm?id=1096411133
(accessed March 18, 2008).

———. "Pueblos Protest Albuquerque Tricentennial." *Indian Country Today,*
April 25, 2005. http://www.indiancountry.com/content.cfm?id=1096410806
(accessed March 18, 2008).

Ortiz, Simon J. *After and Before the Lightning.* Tucson: The University of
Arizona Press, 1994.

———. "Always the Stories: A Brief History and Thoughts on My Writing."
In *Coyote Was Here: Essays on Contemporary Native American Literary
and Political Mobilization,* edited by Bo Schöler, 57–69. Aarhus, Denmark:
SEKLOS/University of Aarhus, 1984.

———. *FIGHT BACK: For the Sake of the People/For the Sake of the Land.*
INAD Literary Journal 1, no. 1 Albuquerque: Institute for Native American
Development, Native American Studies—University of New Mexico, 1980.

———. *from Sand Creek: Rising in this Heart which is Our America.* Tucson:
The University of Arizona Press, 1981.

———. *Going for the Rain.* Berkeley: Turtle Island Foundation, 1977.

———. *A Good Journey.* Tucson: University of Arizona Press, 1984, 1977.

———. *"Haah-ah, mah-eemah:* Yes, it's the very truth." In *Questions and
Swords: Folktales of the Zapatista Revolution* by Subcomandante Marcos,
50–59. El Paso: Cinco Puntos Press, 2001.

———. "Introduction: *Wah nuhtyuh-yuu dyu neetah tyahstih* (Now It Is My
Turn to Stand)." In *Speaking for the Generations: Native Writers on Writing,*
edited by Simon J. Ortiz, xi–xix. Tucson: University of Arizona Press, 1997.

———. *Out There Somewhere.* Tucson: University of Arizona Press, 2002.

———. "Preface." In *Men on the Moon.* Tucson: University of Arizona
Press, 1992.

———. *Song, Poetry and Language—Expression and Perception.* Tsaile, AZ:
Navajo Community College Press, 1978.

———. "Speaking-Writing Indigenous Literary Sovereignty." Foreword to
American Indian Literary Nationalism, by Jace Weaver, Craig S. Womack,
and Robert Warrior, vii–xiv. Albuquerque: University of New Mexico Press,
2007.

———. "Towards a National Indian Literature: Cultural Authenticity in
Nationalism." *MELUS* 8, no. 2 (Summer 1981): 7–11. Reprinted in *American
Indian Literary Nationalism,* by Jace Weaver, Craig S. Womack, and Robert
Warrior, 251–60. Albuquerque: University of New Mexico Press, 2007.

———. *Woven Stone*. Tucson: The University of Arizona Press, 1992.

Poe, Edgar Allan. "The Poetic Principle." Edgar Allan Poe Society of Baltimore. http://www.aepoe.org/works/essays/poetsprnd.htm (accessed October 28, 2008).

Poison Fire, Sacred Earth: Testimonies, Lectures, Conclusions. The World Uranium Hearing. Salzburg, Munich: World Uranium Hearing, 1993. http://www.ratical.org/radiation/WorldUraniumHearing/ (accessed May 12, 2008).

Said, Edward W. *Orientalism*. New York: Vintage Books, 1979; afterword, 1994.

———. "The Politics of Knowledge." *Raritan* 1 (Summer 1991): 18–31.

Sando, Joe S. *Pueblo Nations: Eight Centuries of Pueblo Indian History*. Santa Fe: Clear Light Publishers, 1992.

Silko, Leslie Marmon. "The Indian With a Camera." In *A Circle of Nations: Voices and Visions of American Indians/North American Native Writers and Photographers*, edited by John Gattuso, 4–7. Hillsboro, OR: Beyond Words, 1993.

———. "Interior and Exterior Landscapes: The Pueblo Migration Stories." In *Yellow Woman and a Beauty of the Spirit: Essays on Native American Life Today*, 25–47. New York: Simon and Schuster, 1996.

———. "Landscape, History, and the Pueblo Imagination." In *On Nature: Nature, Landscape, and Natural History*, edited by Daniel Halpern, 83–94. San Francisco: North Point, 1987.

———. "Language and Literature from a Pueblo Indian Perspective." In *English Literature: Opening Up the Canon*, edited by Leslie A. Fiedler and Houston A. Baker Jr., 54–72. Baltimore: Johns Hopkins University Press, 1981.

———. "The People and the Land ARE Inseparable." In *Yellow Woman and a Beauty of the Spirit: Essays on Native American Life Today*, 85–91. New York: Simon and Schuster, 1996.

Stam, Robert, and Ella Shohat. "Traveling Multiculturalism: A Trinational Debate in Translation." *Postcolonial Studies and Beyond*, edited by Ania Loomba, Suvir Kaul, Matti Bunzl, Antoinette Burton, and Jed Esty, 293–316. Durham, NC: Duke University Press, 2005.

Weaver, Jace, Craig S. Womack, and Robert Warrior. Preface to *American Indian Literary Nationalism*, xv–xxii. Albuquerque: University of New Mexico Press, 2007.

Wenger, Tisa. "Land, Culture, and Sovereignty in the Pueblo Dance Controversy." *Journal of the Southwest* (22 June 2004): 381–412.

Wilde, Oscar. "The Decay of Lying." The Literature Network. http://www. online-literature.com/wilde/1307/ (accessed October 28, 2008).

Yava, Albert. *Big Falling Snow: A Tewa-Hopi Indian's Life and Times and the History and Traditions of His People.* Edited by Harold Courlander. Albuquerque: University of New Mexico Press, 1978.

Simon J. Ortiz on the campus of the Albuquerque Indian School in July 1978. Photo by Evelina Zuni Lucero.

PART I

Essays by and Interviews with Ortiz

For Simon Ortiz

Ralph Salisbury

Engine eager, creators' ancestors sensing kin,
migrated generations ago—
and, yet,
my small Asian car could only get
half way up the road
a movie crew had left,
to twist like a rattlesnake's sloughed skin, beneath Sky
City, where Simon Ortiz remains
always at home,
while his words circle the world,
suns warming North Pole
and South at the same time,
and lies,
frozen so hard
they seemed Truth,
melt,
ascending, becoming
Sky City's neighbors in sky
then falling, slaked growth blessing earth's
centuries of people, Simon's
and ours, again.

Song, Poetry and Language

Expression and Perception, A Statement on Poetics and Language

Simon Ortiz

My father is a small man, in fact, almost tiny. I think it must be the way that the Pueblo people were built when they lived at Mesa Verde and Pueblo Bonito. That's a long time ago, around 800–1200 A.D. One thousand years ago—this man? He's very wiry, and his actions are wiry. Smooth, almost tight motions, but like currents in creek water or an oak branch in a mild mountain wind. His face is even formed like that. Rivulets from the sides of his forehead, squints of his eyes, down his angular face and under his jaw. He usually wears a dark blue wool cap. His hair is turning a bit gray, but it's still mostly black, the color of distant lava cliffs. He wears glasses sometimes if he's reading or looking closely at the grain swirls of wood he is working with.

My father carves, dancers usually. What he does is find the motion of Deer, Buffalo, Eagle dancing in the form and substance of wood. Cottonwood, pine, aspen, juniper which has the gentle strains of mild chartreuse in its central grains—and his sinewed hands touch the wood very surely and carefully, searching and knowing. He has been a welder for the ATSFRY railroad and is a good carpenter, and he sits down to work at a table which has an orderly clutter of carving tools, paints, an ashtray, transistor radio, and a couple of Reader's Digests.

His movements are very deliberate. He holds the Buffalo Dancer in the piece of cottonwood poised on the edge of his knee, and he traces—almost caresses—the motion of the Dancer's crook of the right elbow, the way it

---

Originally published as a booklet (Tsaile, AZ: Navajo Community College Press, 1977).

*is held just below midchest, and flicks a cut with the razor-edged carving
knife. And he does it again. He knows exactly how it is at that point in a
Buffalo Dance Song, the motion of elbow, arm, body and mind.*

*He clears his throat a bit and he sings, and the song comes from that
motion of his carving, his sitting, the sinews in his hands and face and the
song itself. His voice in full-tones and wealthy, all the variety and nuance
of motion in the sounds and phrases of the words are active in it; there is
just a bit of tremble from his thin chest.*

I listen.

> *Stah wah maiyanih, Muukai-tra Shahyaika,*
> *duuwahsteh duumahsthee Dyahnie guuyyoutseh mah-ah.*
> *Wahyuuhuunah wahyuuhuu huu nai ah.*

Recently, I was talking with a friend who is enrolled in a Navajo language
course. She is Navajo, but she does not know how to speak Navajo. That
is the story at present with quite a number of Indian young people who
use English as the language with which they express themselves. English
is the main language in which they experience the meaning and the uses
of language.

She made a comment about not being able easily to learn Navajo as a
course of instruction. She said, "I can't seem to hear the parts of it," referring to inflections and nuances of spoken sentences and words.

I referred to a remark I made sometime before, "The way that language
is spoken at home—Acu. The tribal people and community from whom I
come—is with a sense of completeness. That is, when a word is spoken, it is
spoken as a complete word. There are no separate parts or elements to it."
And I meant that a word is not spoken in any *separate parts*, that is, with
reference to linguistic structure, technique of diction, nuance of sound,
tonal quality, inflection, etc. Words are spoken as complete words.

For example, when my father has said a word—in speech or song—
and I ask him, "What does that word break down to? I mean breaking
it down to the syllables of sound or phrases of sound, what do each of
these parts mean?" And he has looked at me with exasperated—slightly
pained—expression on his face, wondering what I mean. And he tells me,
"It doesn't break down into anything."

For him, the word does not break down into any of the separate elements that I expect. The word he has said is complete.

The word is there, complete in its entity of meaning and usage. But I, with my years of formal American education and some linguistic training, having learned and experienced English as a language—having learned to recognize the parts of a sentence, speech, the etymology of words, that words are separable into letters and sounds and syllables of vowels and consonants—I have learned to be aware that a word does break down into basic parts or elements. Like that Navajo friend who is taking the Navajo language course, I have on occasion come to expect—even demand—that I hear and perceive the separated elements of Indian spoken words.

But, as my father has said, a word does not break down into separate elements. A word is complete.

In the same way, a song really does not break down into separate elements. In the minds and views of the people singing it at my home or in a Navajo religious ceremony, for whatever purpose that a song is meant and used, whether it be for prayer, a dancing event, or as part of a story, the song does not break down. It is part of the complete voice of a person.

Language, when it is regarded not only as expression but is realized as experience as well, works in and *is* of that manner. Language is perception of experience as well as expression.

Technically, language can be disassembled according to linguistic function which mainly deals with the expression part of it. You can derive—subsequently define—how a language is formed, how and for what purpose it is used, and its development in a context. But when the totality is considered, language as experience and expression, it doesn't break down so easily and conveniently. And there is no need to break it down and define its parts.

Language as expression and perception—that is at the core of what a song is. It relates to how my father teaches and sings a song and how a poet teaches and speaks a poem.

There is a steel vise at one end of the table my father works at. He clamps a handlong piece of wood in it. This pine is the torso of an Eagle Dancer. The Dancer is slim and his chest is kind of concave. The eagle is about to fly aloft, and my father files a bit of the hard upper belly with a rasp. Later, he will paint the dancing Eagle man who has emerged out of the wood.

My father built the small house in which we sit. The sandstone was quarried near Shuutuh Tasigaiyamishrouh, on the plateau uplift south of here, towards Acu. This is his workshop. It has a couple of windows and a

*handmade door because he couldn't find the right size door at the lumber-
yard in Grants where he trades. The single room is very secure and warm
when he has a fire built on cold days in the woodstove which is one of those
that looks like a low-slung hog.*

*There are a couple of chairs on which we sit and the table with his
work and a bed in the corner. There is a stack of shelves against the eastern
wall. My mother stores her pottery there. The pottery is covered with some
cloth which formerly used to sack flour. I think there is a box of carpentry
tools on the floor below the lowest shelf. Against another wall is a bookcase
which doesn't hold books. Mainly there are pieces of wood that my father is
carving—some he started and didn't feel right about or had broken and he
has laid aside—and a couple of sheep vertebra he said he is going to make
into bolo ties but hasn't gotten around to yet. And a couple of small boxes,
one of them a shoe box, and the other a homemade one of thin plyboard in
which are contained the items he uses for his duties as a cacique.*

*He is one of the elders of the Antelope people who are in charge of all
the spiritual practice and philosophy of our people, the Acumeh. He and
his uncles are responsible that things continue in the manner that they
have since time began for us, and in this sense he is indeed a 1,000 year old
man. In the box are the necessary items which go with prayer: the feathers,
pollen, precious bits of stone and shell, cotton string, earth paints, cornmeal, tobacco, other things. The feathers of various birds are wrapped in
several years ago newspaper to keep the feathers smoothed. It is his duty to
insure that the prayer songs of the many and various religious ceremonies
survive and continue.*

My father sings, and I listen.

Song at the very beginning was experience. There was no division
between experience and expression. Even now, I don't think there is
much of a division except arbitrary. Take a child, for example, when he
makes a song at his play, especially when he is alone. In his song, he tells
about the experience of the sensations he is feeling at the moment with
his body and mind. And the song comes about as words and sounds—
expression. But essentially, in those moments, that song that he is singing is what he is experiencing. The child's song is both perception of that
experience and his expression of it.

The meaning that comes from the song as expression and perception
comes out of and is what the song is.

Stah wah maiyanih, Muukai-tra Shahyaika,
duumahsteh duumahsthee Dyahnie guuhyoutseh mah-ah.
Wahyuuhuunah wahyuuhuu huu nai ah.

This is a hunting song which occurs to me because it is around deer hunting season. I look around the countryside here, the piñon and the mountains nearby, and feel that I might go hunting soon, in November. The meaning the song has for me is in the context of what I am thinking, of what I want and perhaps will do. The words are translatable into English and they are,

> My helping guide, Mountain Lion Hunting Spirit Friend,
> In this direction, to this point bring the Deer to me.
> Wahyuuhuunah wahyuuhuu huu nai ah.

The latter part of the song is a chanted phrase that is included with all hunting songs. The meaning—the song for the hunt, asking for guidance and help—is conveyed in English as well. There is no problem in deciphering the original meaning, and I don't think there ever really is when a song is taken to be both expression and perception.

The meaning that is has for me is that I recognize myself as a person in an active relationship—the hunting act—with Mountain Lion, the spirit friend and guide, and Deer. It is a prayer. A prayer song. The meaning that it has, further, is that things will return unto me if I do things well in a manner that is possible, if I use myself and whatever power I have appropriately. The purpose of the song is first of all to do things well, the way that they're supposed to be done, part of it being the singing and performing of the song, and that I receive, again well and properly, the things that are meant to be returned unto me. I express myself as well as realize the experience.

There is also something in a song that is actually substantial. Then you talk or sing with words that are just words—or seem to be mere words—you sometimes feel that they are too ethereal, even fleeting. But when you realize the significance of what something means to you, then they are very tangible. You value the meaning of the song for its motion in the dance and the expression and perception it allows you. You realize its inherent quality by the feeling that a song gives you. You become aware of the quietness that comes upon you when you sing or hear a song of quiet quality. You not only feel it—you know. The substance is emotional, but beyond that, spiritual, and it's real and you are present in and part of it. The act of the song which you are experiencing is real, and the reality is its substance.

A song is made substantial by its context—that is its reality, both that which is there and what is brought about by the song. The context in which the song is sung or that a prayer song makes possible is what makes a song substantial, gives it that quality of realness. The emotional, cultural, spiritual context in which we thrive—in that, the song is meaningful. The context has to do not only with your being physically present, but it has to do also with the context of the mind, how receptive it is and that usually means familiarity with the culture in which the song is sung.

The context of a song can be anything or can focus through a specific event or act but it includes all things. This is very important to realize when you are trying to understand and learn more than just the words or the technical facility of words in a song or poem. That means that one has to recognize that language is more than just a group of words and more than just the technical relationship between sounds and words. Language is more than just a functional mechanism. It is spiritual energy that is available to all. It includes all of us and is not exclusively in the power of human beings—we are part of that power as human beings.

Oftentimes, I think we become convinced of the efficiency of our use of language. We begin to read language too casually, thereby taking it for granted, and we forget the sacredness of it. Losing this regard, we become quite careless with how we use and perceive with language. We forget that language beyond the mechanics of it is a spiritual force.

When you regard the sacred nature of language, then you realize that you are part of it and it is part of you, and you are not necessarily in control of it, and that if you do control some of it, it is not in your exclusive control. Upon this realization, I think there are all possibilities of expression and perception which become available.

This morning my father said to my mother and me, "On Saturday, I am going to go hunting. I am telling you now. I will begin to work on Tuesday for it." He means that he will begin preparations for it. He explained that my brother-in-law will come for him on Friday, and they are going to hunt in Arizona. This is part of it, I know, the proper explanation of intention and purpose. I have heard him say that since I was a boy.

The preparations are always done with a sense of excitement and enjoyment. Stories are remembered.

Page was a good storyteller. I don't know why he was called Page—I suppose there is a story behind his name but I don't know it. Page was getting older when this happened. He couldn't see very well anymore, but he was taken along with a group of other hunters. "I was to be the kuusteenhruu," he said. The camp cook sticks around the camp, sings songs and makes prayers for the men out hunting, and waits, and fixes the food. Page got tired of doing that. He said, "I decided that it wouldn't hurt if I just went out of camp a little ways. I was sort of getting tired of sticking around. And so I did; I wasn't that blind."

He walked a ways out of their camp, you know, looking around, searching the ground for tracks. And he found some, great big ones. He said, "It must be my good fortune that I am to get a big one. I guess I'm living right," and he reached into his cornfood bag and got some meal and sprinkled it with some precious stones and beads and pollen into the big tracks. He said, "Thank you for leaving your tracks, and now I ask you to wait for me, I am right behind you." And putting his mind in order, he followed the tracks, looking up once in a while to see if the large deer he could already see in his mind was up ahead.

"I was sure in a good mood," Page said, and he would smile real big. "Every once in a while I sprinkled cornfood and precious things in the tracks. They were big," he said and he would hold out his large hand to show you how big, "and I would sing under my breath." He followed along, kind of slow you know because he was an old man and because of his eyes, until he came down this slope that wasn't too steep. There was an oak brush thicket at the bottom of it. He put his fingers upon the tracks to let it know that he was right behind, and the tracks felt very warm.

He said, "Ah haiee, there you will be in the thicket. There is where we will meet," and he prayed one more time and concluded his song and set his mind right and checked to make sure his gun was ready—I don't know what kind of rifle he had but it was probably an old one too. And he made his way to the thicket very carefully, very quietly, slightly bent down to see under the branches of the oak. And then he heard it moving around in the thicket, and he said quietly, "Ah haiee, I can hear that you're a big one. Come to me now, it is time, and I think we are both ready," just to make sure that his spirit was exactly right. And he crouched down to look and there it was some yards *into the thicket and he put his rifle to his shoulder and searched for a vital spot, and then it turned to him and it was a **pig**.*

"Kohjeeno!" Page said, his breath exhaling. He lowered his rifle, cussed a bit, and then he raised his rifle and said, "Kohjeeno, I guess you'll have to be my kquuyaitih today," and shot the pig. He cut the pig's throat to let the blood and then on the way back to camp he tried to find all the precious stones he had dropped in the tracks of the pig.

After that, until he went back North—passed away—his nephews and grandsons would say to him, "Uncle, tell us about the time the kohjeeno was your kquuyaitih." And Page would frown indignant a bit, and then he would smile and say, "Keehamaa dzee, we went hunting to Brushy Mountain . . ."

The song is basic to all vocal expression. The song as expression is an opening from inside of yourself to outside and from outside of yourself to inside but not in the sense that there are separate states of yourself. Instead, it is a joining and an opening together. Song is the experience of that opening or road if you prefer, and there is no separation of parts, no division between that within you and that without you, as there is no division between expression and perception.

I think that is what has oftentimes happened with our use of English. We think of English as a very definitive language, useful in defining things—which means setting limits. But that's not supposed to be what language is. Language is not definition; language is all-expansive. We, thinking ourselves capable of the task, assign rules and roles to language unnecessarily. Therefore, we limit our words, our language, and we limit our perception, our understanding, our knowledge.

Children don't limit their words until they learn how, until they're told that it's better if they use definitive words. This is what happens to most everyone in a formal educational situation. Education defines you. It makes you see with and within very definitive limits. Unless you teach and learn language in such a way as to permit it to remain or for it to become all-expansive—and truly visionary—your expressiveness and perceptions will be limited and even divided.

My father teaches that the song is part of the way you're supposed to recognize everything, that the singing of it is a way of recognizing this all-inclusiveness because it is a way of expressing yourself and perceiving. It is basically a way to understand and appreciate your relationship to all things.

The song as language is a way of touching. This is the way that my father attempts to teach a song, and I try to listen, feel, know and learn that way.

When my father sings a song, he tries to instill a sense of awareness about us. Although he may remark upon the progressive steps in a song, he does not separate the steps or components of the song. The completeness of the song is the important thing, how a person comes to know and appreciate it, not to especially mark the separate parts of it but to know the whole experience of the song.

He may mention that a particular song was sung sometime before or had been made for a special occasion but he remembers only in reference to the overall meaning and purpose. It may be an old, old song that he doesn't know the history of or it may be one he has made himself. He makes me aware of these things because it is important, not only for the song itself, but because it is coming from the core of who my father is and he is talking about how it is for him in relationship with all things. I am especially aware of its part in our lives and that all these things are a part of that song's life. And when he sings the song, I am aware that it comes from not only his expression but from his perception as well.

I listen carefully, but I listen for more than just the sound, listen for more than just the words and phrases, for more than the various parts of the song. I try to perceive the context, meaning, purpose—all of these items not in their separate parts but as a whole—and I think it comes completely like that.

A song, a poem, becomes real in that manner. You learn its completeness; you learn the various parts of it but not as separate parts. You learn a song in the way that you are supposed to learn a language, as expression and as experience.

I think it is possible to teach song and poetry in a classroom so that language is a real way of teaching and learning. The effort will have to be with conveying the importance and significance of not only the words and sounds but the realness of the song in terms of oneself, context, the particular language used, community, the totality of what is around.

Yesterday morning, my father went over to Diabuukaiyah to get oak limbs for the Haadramahni—the Prayer Sticks. After he got back he said, "The Haadramahni for hunting are all of hardwoods, like the hahpaani." The oak grows up the canons which come out of the lava rock of Horace Mesa.

And at this worktable, he shows me. "This is a Haitsee—a Shield if you want to call it that—and it is used as a guide." It is a thin, splitted strip of hahpaani made into a circle which will fit into the palm of your hand. "There is a star in the center—I will make it out of string tied to the edges of the circle. This is a guide to find your way, to know directions by. It is round because the moon is round. It is the night sky which is a circle all around in which the stars and moon sit. It's a circle, that's why. This is part of it, to know the directions you are going, to know where you are at."

He shows me a stick about the thickness of his thumb. The stick is an oak limb split in half, and he runs the edge of his thumbnail along the core of the wood, the dark streak at the very center of the wood. The streak does not run completely straight, but it flows very definitely from one end to the other. And my father says, "This is the Heeyahmani. This is to return you safely. This is so you will know the points on your return back, the straight and safe way. So you will be definite and true on your return course. It is placed at the beginning point of your journey. This line here is that, a true road."

And then he explains, "I haven't gotten this other stick formed yet, and it is of oak also. It is pointed on both ends, and it is stout, strong." He holds up his right hand, his fingers clutched around the stout oak limb. "It's for strength and courage, manliness. So that in any danger you will be able to overcome the danger. So that you will have the stamina to endure hardship. It is to allow you to know and realize yourself as a man. It is necessary to have also."

He tells me these things, and I listen. He says, "Later, we will sing some songs for the hunt. There is a lot to it, not just a few. There are any numbers of prayer. There are all those things you have to do in preparation, before you begin to hunt, and they are all meant to be done not only because they have been done in the past but because they are the way that things, good things, will come about for you. That is the way that you will truly prepare yourself, to be able to go out and find the deer, so that the deer will find you. You do those things in the proper way so that you will know the way things are, what's out there, what you must think in approaching them, how you must respond—all those things. They are all part of it—you just don't go and hunt. A person has to be aware of what is around him, and in this way, the preparation, these things that I have here, you will know."

My father tells me, "This song is a hunting song, listen." He sings and I listen. He may sing it again, and I hear it again. The feeling that I perceive is not only contained in the words but there is something surrounding those words, surrounding the song, and it includes us. It is the relationship that we share with each other and with everything else. And that's the feeling that makes the song real and meaningful and which makes his singing and my listening more than just a teaching and learning situation.

It is that experience—that perception of it—that I mention at the very beginning which makes it meaningful. You perceive by expressing yourself therefore. This is the way that my father teaches a song. And this is the way I try to learn a song. This is the way I try to teach poetry, and this is the way I try to have people learn from me.

One time my father was singing a song, and this is the instance in which this—perception by/expression of—became very apparent for me. He was singing this song, and I didn't catch the words offhand. I asked him, and he explained, "This song, I really like it for this old man." And he said, "This old man used to like to sing, and he danced like this," motioning like the old man's hands, arms, shoulders, and he repeated, "This song, I really like it for this old man."

That's what the song was about, I realized. It was both his explanation and the meaning of the song. It was about this old man who danced that way with whom my father had shared a good feeling. My father liked the old man, who was probably a mentor of some sort, and in my father's mind during the process of making the song and when he sang it subsequent times afterwards, he was reaffirming the affection he had for the old guy, the way "he danced like this."

My father was expressing to me the experience of that affection, the perceptions of the feeling he had. Indeed, the song was the road from outside of himself to inside—which is perception—and from inside of himself to outside—which is expression. That's the process and the product of the song, the experience and the vision that a song gives you.

The words, the language of my experience, come from how I understand, how I relate to the world around me, and how I know language as perception. That language allows me vision to see with and by which to know myself.

Native Heritage

A Tradition of Participation

Simon Ortiz

*In honor of Thomas Banyaca, Hopi revered elder
and cultural statesman, a voice for all of us, who
passed into eternal life, February 6, 1999*

Storytelling is an event. The storyteller doesn't just tell about the characters in the story, what they did or said, what happens in the story and so on. The storyteller participates in the story with the listeners, who are also taking part by listening. The story is not simply a narrative being told or listened to—it's occurring; it's happening.

Some time ago, when my father said in our Acoma language, 'Yaaka Hano naitra guh,' I suddenly didn't know what he was talking about. I grew up speaking our native language and I have heard that announcement countless times. But I've also acquired some formal education in Western cultural philosophy and linguistics and other strange practices, and so for a moment I didn't know what my father was saying.

You see 'Yaaka Hano naitra guh' literally translates into 'Corn People will occur.' Or happen, come about, come into being. In a conversational sense, it's an announcement that means 'The people of the Corn Clan will be putting on a dancing event.' That's what my father said and meant, but what he also meant literally was that the 'Corn People will occur.' Or happen or come about or come into being. Yaaka Hano naitra guh.

The Corn Hano will bring that event about. The dancing will be

This essay was originally published in *Legacy and Prosperity*, a special issue of the journal *Whole Terrain: Reflective Environmental Practice* (Volume 8, 1999–2000): 64–69.

happening. The people will take part in the dancing event. In a meta-phorical sense, they will come into being as Corn People in that event. In a philosophical sense, they will give it life and by so doing they will give themselves life. They, therefore, as Corn People, will come into being.

My formal white American education and its insistence on objectifi-cation removed me from the context of my father speaking to me within the indigenous cultural world of the Acoma people. I was listening to and hearing what he said but not "participating" in the event of him speaking with me.

The main task for an oral storyteller is to make a story happen or come about in which the listeners participate. For a writer it's to encourage the participation of the reader in the event of the writing. This joined endeavor of writer-storyteller and reader-listener is when the story is most effective or believable. And as teller and listener participants in the story event, they come into being like the Corn Hano come into being in the Corn Dance event. In a sense, the story affirms them as writer and reader (or teller and listener) by joining them as a story that brings them about.

Idealistically, the writer's goal always is to convey a story he believes in. Conversely, he ingests likewise. The stories that come from my Acoma Pueblo cultural experience, both traditional and contemporary, are numerous, but I remember certain ones because they seem to particu-larly communicate the critical element of participation I refer to.

My mother, who is deceased, told us of the time, once, as a little girl, she and a younger sister and a woman went to roast piñons. "Stuuwahmeeskuh-nahtee-ih," she said. That means to pick green unopened cones off piñon trees and roast them in a hole or pit dug in the ground. "We walked to the mesa east of Aacqu," she said, pointing with her hand in that direction as she talked.

"We climbed to the higher part of the mesa where there were lots of piñons that year. We got a lot of them, the higher ones we had to use a long stick to reach on the upper branches. Then we dug a pit in the ground and built a fire in it and let it burn down to coals. And then the woman and me and my sister—we were just little then—put the piñon cones in the pit, and on top of them we put some green piñon tree branches and then covered everything with a layer of sand. After that, we built a fire on top of the sand, and then we waited."

With her words in the Acoma language, my mother made my family vividly see the "story" of roasting piñon cones many years ago. By evoking for us the experience in terms of time, place, and circumstance, making us see, in other words, we believed the story.

She went on. "It smelled good from the smoke and steam rising from the roasted piñons when we uncovered them. The cones had opened and the piñon nuts inside were cooked from the coals in the pit. They were hot to touch too, and we had to be careful with them as we ate some. After the cones cooled down, we put them in gunny sacks to carry them on our shoulders and backs.

"When we started walking across the wide valley toward Aacqu, it was already late in the day. After walking for a long time, we got to a place where the Maashahdruuwee lives in a deep cave in a hillside. The woman stopped walking, and she said to me and my little sister, 'When you get here, where the Maashadruuwee lives, you are to holler. So holler.' She hollered, and my sister and I hollered too. And then the woman said, 'Gaimeh-eh, Maashahdruwee, please, bring Aacqu just a little closer to us poor little girls who are so tired.'

"We were all so tired, and it was getting late in the day. By the time we got to the mesa foot of Aacqu, it was dark, and the woman's husband had come looking for us. And as we were by the church my father had come looking for us too. That was that time, a long time ago, when I was a little girl, but I remember it very clearly."

I remember—very clearly too—my mother telling the story of that time in her childhood which was, she said, about 1910 or so. She was probably sitting at the kitchen table after we had gotten through eating. Or maybe she was sitting on the little bench beside the low wooden table where she always sat while she worked on her pottery. It was in a home setting very familiar, very ordinary, and natural, and she would have been involved in an activity that was "her." Setting or place and activity with which one can identify are major features within my mother's story, as well as the moment in which she told the story so that her story is in a real sense a reenactment of my mother's personal being and presence.

And to bring the story to mind now as my mother told it and to recall the act and moment of her telling, it is to participate in that reenactment.

My father, also deceased, told the following story to me at least once. He may have told it more times than that, but I remember it for some reason as only being told once, which perhaps has to do with how momentous and profound the story and the occasion of the storytelling were.

"It was cold, so cold that winter, freezing for days. Snow lay deep and piled hard. Everyone at Acoma and Deetseyaamah was having a hard time, had been for a long time, years it felt like."

As he spoke, the expression on my father's face was distant, his eyes looking away from the present. "My father and mother were dead. So just my baby sister and I were left at home. We were alone."

I recall the palms of his hands were held upward as if to receive what fate had in store, and there was the hint of a resigned shrug of his thin shoulders. "My older brother had gone away too. He was in the Army during World War One. So my sister and I were all alone."

The tone of my father's voice was husky and low and soft, his words were almost whispered although distinctly phrased. And I had to listen very carefully.

He seemed to not want to talk about that difficult time, like he did not want to remember certain details, but grittily he went on. "Many of the Acoma people were sick. They were dying from a severe sickness. An epidemic. There seemed to be nothing we could do about it, nothing that anybody could do.

"There were burials all the time. So people just stayed up at Acoma, taking care of the sick and dying, burying the dead. That's where everyone was when my baby sister got sick. Very sick for days. I felt helpless. There was nothing that anyone could do. There was no one around. I was nine years old. It was bitter cold, those winter days."

Those years in the early decades of this century were dark and desperate, hopeless years for Indians. When my father spoke about that time, I felt the dreary weight of his words, not wanting to hear them yet knowing it was important that I do so, that I listen and hear, so I could remember them.

"When my baby sister died, I didn't know what to do except what was necessary. Wrapping her in a blanket, holding her in my arms, we began walking on the road up to Acoma."

My father's voice would drift away as if finally his words were inadequate to express his feelings about that time, like he was unable to explain and describe the sickness that had overcome the Acoma people and their world, like he was still burdened by the helplessness of a nine-year-old Indian boy alone in the world.

I was a teenager, maybe fourteen or fifteen, when my father told that story. Maybe we had stopped during a hot afternoon to rest from hoeing weeds at our garden, and something had triggered his memory. I don't recall the particular activity of the moment because what was most prominent was the mood, the emotion evoked by his tone of voice, his choice of words, and his body language and facial expressions, all of these showing his deep personal feelings and thoughts.

Although my father usually told stories along with and as part of what he was doing, whether it was working in the garden or carving a buffalo dancer from a piece of wood, with certain stories he would stop what he was doing and just speak. This story occasion was such a time.

A moment like that was a signal for me also to be held within the quiet and focused attention needed to listen and hear—and to learn and remember the story—and to be aware of the profound and momentous nature of the story.

Participation as a listener in this story for me has to do with realizing how emotionally important my father's words (and the memories they provoked) were to him personally and to Indian people who were faced, at the time he spoke about, by dark and desperate years and circumstances. And the need for participation by me, the listener (as a teenage boy), was communicated to me by my father who stopped whatever activity he was doing to "just speak." So that I would realize and accept the responsibility to listen, see, and hear my father's words, telling me about himself as a 9-year-old boy, telling me about a necessary decision he made when his baby sister died, telling me about what it was like for Indian people then, urging upon me the responsibility to learn and remember.

To *participate* in a story has to do with accepting the responsibility for a story, I believe. And this has to do with the importance of appropriate translation from one language to another. I do not have the professional education and training in linguistic and cultural theory to define "appropriate translation" but I do realize and appreciate the need to convey meaningfulness from one language and cultural context to another.

Not too long ago, I had a visit one morning from an elder of Acoma Pueblo, my native community. I was in the utility room at my sister's house putting dirty clothes in the washer when I heard Joe Cool, my other sister's family dog, barking. Taking a brief, quick look out the kitchen window, I didn't see what Joe Cool was barking at. But a short while later, there was a light knock on the door.

Going to the door, I hollered, "Come in," and opened the door to find an elder man standing there, who I didn't recognize.

"Guwaadze, Naishtiyah. Deetyah oopuh," I said to the Acoma elder in the proper respectful way, inviting him to come in and sit down on the couch in the living room.

"Dawaah eh," he responded, thanking me and shaking my hand which I held out in greeting. And then I was suddenly lost for words because I had no idea who the Acoma elder was.

The man seemed to be in his late 80's or early 90's, and I could tell he couldn't hear very well since he leaned and tilted his head towards me when I spoke to him. And I think his eyesight was poor although his dark brown eyes were clear and bright. The old man had a peaceful, soothing smile and a firm voice, and I was immediately comfortable with him. But I was vastly intrigued, and somewhat mystified, by his sudden appearance at my door.

I told him who I was by introducing myself. "Simon Ortiz stuuhdah. Mericano kadzeh-nih shiyah emeh eh, eh steh. Hihdruutsee, dah aah shihyah etyuuh eh steh," I said, identifying myself by my American name and my Acoma name. And indicating the distinctions by referring to two different language contexts, i.e., American English and Acoma.

When I told him the names of my deceased parents and explained that I was their eldest son, he said, "Stahmah ahkah Myrna stieutah-nih. Where is her house?" And then at this point I began to get a faint idea of who the old man was.

"As you may know," he said, "Myrna is the daughter of my brother. My brother who went back to the earth long ago is the father of Myrna and her sisters."

"Hah uh," I said, and I added, "Linda and Rachel and Myrna, all of them are my older sisters. I did not know their father, of course, since my mother Mamie married my father, Dzaillrai-shahtah, after my sisters' father passed on."

"Eh mee," the Acoma elder said, smiling and chuckling in recognition of this knowledge. When I told him my sister Myrna was not at her house, to which I pointed out the window, that she was at work at Wingate Indian Boarding School, the old man seemed disappointed, and he grew quiet.

Finally, however, I could not contain my curiosity about who he was, and I wanted to ascertain his identity. So I said, "Naishtiyah, amoo-uh, I have to ask you your name, because I truly don't recognize you. I may not know you, for which I have to apologize for my inadequate knowledge."

Since I was sort of embarrassed, my remark was kind of halting and hesitant. The Acoma elder looked at me with a slightly puzzled expression on his face, probably because I had been talking with him so familiarly up to that point, as if I knew him very well. And then his deeply wrinkled brown face broke into a beautiful warm smile.

Laughing gently, he said, "Wah-yuuh-tyai, stuu dah," and his direct easy manner put me completely at ease again. "Dawaah eh, amoo-uh naishtiyah," I said, thanking him, "for telling me your name. However, I still don't recognize your name. So I must not know you since these days many of us do not know each other closely anymore."

Nodding his head, Wah-yuuh-tyai said slowly, "That's true, that's true." And then he said, "Koo-nee-meh, I used to be. That was my name. Koo-nee-meh. That's who I was."

Koo-nee-meh! Upon hearing that name, I instantly recognized and realized at last who the man was. Why, of course, he was Koo-nee-meh! A name I knew him by when I was a boy! And then he explained that he gave his name, Koo-nee-meh, to his grandson, and he had taken the name of Wah-yuu-tyai for himself. At the end of this explanation, he added, "And then my grandson took my name to Arizona where he lives today!"

Wah-yuu-tyai went on to tell me he had walked from Deechunah, the village area about six miles east of where we were at my sister's house. He was going to chop wood and feed his turkeys at his daughter's mobile home trailer which was to the southwest on a hill which he pointed to out the living room window. I remarked on how he looked so hale and healthy for his advanced age and that he could walk around so well. And he smiled when I mentioned Shahrrlowkah, old man Tomato, who was legendary for his jaunts around the Acoma community even when he was at least one-hundred and twelve years old.

And then, because I remembered when Koo-nee-meh was Dzaahtyawa Hoochanih (Land Chief) many years ago, I said, "When my sisters and brothers and I were still young children, we used to look to the west." I pointed to the road three-quarters of a mile away. "And when we would see you walking on the road to Acoma, we would say, 'There's Koo-nee-meh walking to Aacqu.' You and Heerrludyai, who had very long legs, had very distinctive and recognizable walking strides."

When I said that, Wah-yuh-tyai laughed softly aloud. I was very happy to remember other Acoma elders who are long gone now, who he knew in his younger days. And because I did remember, I realized I was a link between the past and the present and that this role of being a writer-storyteller who is telling about the Acoma elder's visit adds to the significance of this story even more.

A sense of participatory listening and telling is absolutely critical with this story because of the responsibility required by me to convey its meaningful translation from the Acoma Pueblo language it occurred in, to another language and cultural context, namely the English language and contemporary non-Indian U.S. cultural society. For this "story" to be understood as an instance of "appropriate translation," I think there has to be a willingness on the part of readers-listeners to participate in the interstices of the Indian and American cultures where this narrative episode takes place.

Writing and oral narrative go hand in hand for me as a Native American writer, raised within the Acoma Pueblo cultural tradition of oral stories. The tradition is the source of my written stories and poetry. Without the stories I grew up with in Acoma, I would have written no stories, poems, or anything else. And, in the deepest sense, the consciousness brought about by oral tradition is the foundation of my sense of awareness as a human person.

It is not far-fetched for me to say that I, a Native American of Acoma Pueblo, would not know my identity nor my existence without the tradition. *Literally, I would not know myself as who I am individually-personally and socially unless there was a Native American culture which informed me of my existence, confirmed for me its validity and reality, and affirmed me of it.* This further means that my native Acoma culture is the proof and locus of my existence as a Native American and human being. I believe that for Native Americans who are living lives similarly founded upon such a cultural philosophy, this is the case.

I understand and appreciate the gravity with which Native elders say, "Know your indigenous heritage and traditions for without these you do not exist as a person, a human being. Know who you are, and love who you are." Without that knowledge and love, there is no Existence literally. That is why Native people will fight to the death to maintain their belief in their Native culture and its traditions, including the use of their Native languages as much as possible, maintenance of a Native community and its integrity, and the continuing use and possession of a Native land base.

These are all inextricably tied together. They cannot be separated and regarded piecemeal. And this knowledge and love, powerfully and profoundly, is made a part of Native American consciousness by the oral tradition and participation in it. Today, this tradition of participation is not only the source and dynamic of Native American writing, it is the important way by which Native identity and social-cultural assertion is struggled for, maintained, and conveyed.

Because oral tradition is the link with the past, most Native Americans will insist it is at the core of who they truly are. And when the Native American past is the crucible of Native American Existence, it is the truth, no matter how much Americanism through U.S. education and culture has tried to indoctrinate and acculturate Native Americans. "We are Indians" is a cry of affirmation and assertion, and it is a war cry of resistance.

Storytelling and writing today are a vibrant part of that resistance cry because Native American cultural consciousness is at stake. Because literature is at once an appreciation of experience, an expression of it, and a personal and social aesthetic perception that addresses and provides insight into many topics, issues, and ideas, Native American prose and poetry contain this truth.

I believe that proponents of Americanism deny this truth in order to silence resistance. They like to believe that the "past is past" and declare it is dead and gone, simply to deny that Native American people and their land, culture, and community continue to exist. Yet, the heritage and tradition of Native American oral narrative is the strongest feature and element of continuing Native American Existence, and this tradition, which insists upon participation by indigenous people especially, thrives in contemporary writing and storytelling.

Simon J. Ortiz

The Writing the Southwest *Interview*

David Dunaway
July 14, 1988

Ortiz: My family comes from the Acoma Pueblo reservation west of Albuquerque, and specifically, at McCartys on the New Mexico state maps, right off the Interstate 40.

Dunaway: Did you grow up in Acoma?

Ortiz: I grew up in the Acoma Pueblo community, at McCartys. McCartys is one of the villages, the other village is Acomita, and other additional small settlements at Anzac and some newer ones. I grew up there for the first twenty years of my life.

Dunaway: So what was McCartys and the Acoma community like in the '40s and '50s?

Ortiz: It was the war, World War II, of course, and the life there was sort of on the edge of something new happening. The war was going on, I remember that there were young men who were in uniform, going off somewhere, to California, wherever that was, and there were trains passing on the railroad, which runs about a mile north of my mother's house, and there were always these war things going up and down, west and east.

Acoma and McCartys, the little village, was very small at that time, and there didn't seem to be any more world out there except what was passing through. It was a very small community and I grew up within the community which was family, clan, grandparents, mother and father. Although, obviously, changes that had been

A shorter version of this interview was previously published as "An Interview with Simon Ortiz: July 14, 1988" in *Studies in American Literature* 16:4 (Winter 2004): 12–19.

taking place for many, many decades and in the past two hundred or so years—three hundred or so—years, were very much impressioned upon me as a child of the 1940s. There was something going on, mysterious, and, of course, somewhat fearful.

I found that when I started school that this world that was outside of Acoma and McCartys was so different, because most of that world and the exposure that I had to it was through reading—what I read, anyway, in the pages in the schoolbooks—was not really the Acoma and the Indian world in general. It was always some white-picket-fence in the West, or perhaps in California. When I was very young, things were changing so fast. The atomic bomb was exploded right at the beginning of my life. I was born in 1941, right at the beginning of that war. And, in 1945 and the changes that were wrought by the war, and especially the bomb, you know, are a part of the history that I was living. I didn't really know it, of course, as a child, just that it was happening. I think that the changes were exemplified by school, by the railroad, and the men, leaving. My father was a railroad worker. I didn't learn any English until I went to school at McCartys' day school, which was then a BIA federal school, when I was six, seven years old.

Dunaway: Was it a rural environment?

Ortiz: Very much so. Pueblo Indian people traditionally are agricultural people, cultivating the land with the traditional crops of corn, chile, pumpkin, beans, squash, those kinds of things. Bottom lands along the Rio de San Jose, which originates in the Zuni Mountains, were used for the growing of these crops, and then dry-farming in the Acoma valley, which is twelve more miles to the south, which is the traditional home—mother home site—of the Acoma people.

I was born actually at the old Albuquerque Indian Hospital, here in Albuquerque, and from there on I lived at home until I was about nineteen, when I went away to school—college—for the first time. In a couple of those years, because my father was a railroad worker for the Santa Fe Railroad, we lived in California, I think, when I was very young, when I was a baby. And then later on, when I was in the fifth grade, I remember, we went to Skull Valley, to go to school for one year. And then there were, I think, several occasions, briefly, when we went to California again, to be with my father. A lot of the employment for wage income was from the railroad in the 1940s.

So, after nineteen years of age, I've been away from the Acoma homeland. In essence I've never really left home, though, in actuality, physically, I've been living away for quite a number of years until last year, in 1987, when I returned to live at McCartys. Much of my work as a writer, as a teacher, takes me away from home, obviously, but there is always, and has always been, I think, with all the Acoma people, and, perhaps, with all the Indian people in the country, a real connection and a real sense of home. It's always with the community, as a society and the community as a people, and land, the environment, cultural, spiritual, political, social, economic, and so forth.

Dunaway: Going back for a moment to your childhood: What sounds do you associate with growing up?

Ortiz: A silence of the Southwest and music that I think is a mixture of my father singing and my mother speaking. Voices that were there all the time. Songs and stories, those sounds of an elder generation. And then the railroad which rattles, rumbles east and west, constantly, north of my mother's house, rattling, shaking the windows. And then later on, I remember the airplanes. But always the silence that connotes distance and something inner as a constant motion that was taking place.

Dunaway: Very nice. Did you have a radio?

Ortiz: We had radios that were battery-powered.... I remember the radio was very much a part of the late 1940s and early 1950s, and it was a voice from another world. It was like the connection that indicated the changes that were taking place.

Dunaway: Do you recall any groups or artists that you particularly enjoyed listening to when you were young?

Ortiz: My father was a singer, in the Acoma tradition. He made songs and he sang songs that were from the ageless tradition. My mother also was a singer; she sang, also Acoma songs that are part of stories, hunting songs with my father—hunting prayer songs when my father would go hunting in the fall time. And she also sang church music. The Catholic church, of course, is very prominent in the Pueblo communities, and I learned church songs, the Catholic ritual, the Gregorian chants back when. And, over the radio, I remember songs—early Elvis, you know, of course that was later on in the mid-fifties or so. But songs, popular music. Jimmy Dorsey, you know. Tommy Dorsey, those kinds. And, of course, since my sisters were teenagers, you know, they sang songs that they learned from the radio. He would sing railroad songs, folk songs from Jimmy Rogers or older folk songs, set into the context of the Acoma cultural life.

Dunaway: Could you tell us a little bit about Acoma storytelling?

Ortiz: The tradition of storytelling is part of the whole general oral tradition. The oral tradition is not necessarily only stories, but stories of say, the olden times, or another time before us, or the generation before our present ones. The oral tradition obviously embodies the ceremonial, social life that has been kept within the continuum of the Acoma people. The oral tradition also includes advice and counsel, that is, those items told to you by your elders to ensure that you are living responsibly, that the relationships among family members are correct and according to Acoma ways of life. There's also, of course, stories told to children to make sure that they're attentive to the principles or philosophies of the Acoma, and historical stories that include a look at the Spanish civilization or settlement or colonization that occurred. . . . There are stories of how America is seen, stories that provoke thought, speculation, and obviously provide insight into another way of life by which the Acoma people are faced. Stories which tell very clearly what the role of an individual is in Acoma and what the role of a person is in the whole scheme of life in the universe. I've always liked stories that give a good sense of who I am as an Acoma person within the whole way of life. Sometimes these are historical stories, sometimes these are personal anecdotes. In this sense, stories tie me into my heritage more than any other kind of story.

Essentially I think everything is story—in the sense that the tradition out of which poetry comes, and song comes, is like the story of the life of a people. That is, the culture survives because of the story of its birth, and goes on into its development and goes on to the end of a cycle. One's personal life, for example, begins with birth, although his personal story is only a continuation of a larger story; joined in with that, it becomes a part of and helps to continue it. The sense of a story for me is important at least in two respects. One is that it's a kind of a lifeline that connects the individual, me, back to that larger story. Two, it also expresses for American Indian people something very distinct, in terms of culture, language, kind of social structure, traditions, and so forth.

Stories in terms of what is written down—printed literature—is usually seen as very authoritative and defined and scripted according to certain rules. The oral tradition, which is the source of myth, of mythology, is a sense of the spiritual reality that all life is quite different. The oral tradition, in a sense, insists upon that affirmation of life. The Western culture's written literature is a kind of definition of life, rather than the essence of life, which the oral tradition is. So that the mythology is more than just, say, legends or tales or stories that have limited definition. Rather, it's literature—I'll go ahead and use literature to refer to these oral traditional texts—rather, this kind of literature has a spiritual dimension that doesn't necessarily, say, only evoke a creative source, but rather includes that creative source with what one's endeavors are as a human being.

Poetry is a part of that story as a form of the oral tradition. I think that the oral tradition lends itself very well to the narrative form of story, or the narratives that stories are. And poetry is certainly included within prayer and song: a sense of spirituality, a sense of being connected so inexplicably and forever to that whole general story of life as we live and know it and practice it. I think poetry is essentially story or language, language being an energy that forms us and also at the same time is the essence of how we come into being. Poetry being a part of language, then, is a part of this story of how we come into being.

In other words, the stories of this literature, of the mythic proportion, verify my existence right now. If I know the story and accept the story of the creation as told, as spoken, in that creative act of many millions and millions, trillions of years ago when life began as atomic activity. . . . They're true. And, if I accept them as true—when I accept them as true, then **my** existence is true. The literature, even the great masterworks of Western literature, has an entirely different purpose. It's more to define and even to limit it. Yet I think the oral tradition out of which the present-day texts, ceremonial texts, come from, really lets us realize ourselves, absolutely and completely.

Language has a kind of a neutrality at its very essence. There are different Indian languages in New Mexico: Navajo, and several Pueblo languages spoken. These are the languages that were here when the Spanish conquest settlement introduced European language and then later English and then others. Obviously people's language changes as they learn it, but I think that values and perspectives continue as long as there's not, say, political force and domination that begins to limit it.

The use of English as a political colonizing tool—weapon—was very useful to the settlement after the 1800s, in this part of the Southwest. This of course has changed the native, indigenous cultures of the United States of Indian America. There's many Indian people out there who are multi-lingual. People that are at Acoma, at Santo Domingo, at Taos, at Jemez, who are, say, ceremonial, spiritual elders, leaders, who speak English very well—maybe better than me—who speak Spanish also, certainly better than me; who may speak other Indian languages and yet they're still within the traditional selves that they've always been. So it's a contradiction perhaps, but I think that you have to recognize that the political nature of language can be, is, really what limits us.

Southwestern writers have a kind of consciousness that leads us to share identifiable images, metaphors that could only be Southwestern geographically. This, in terms of an identifiable place, makes us Southwestern writers. If there is a kind of interface [among Southwestern writers], it is struggle. I mean, the Southwest is essentially still a territory, colonized territory, colonial territory, so to speak. And I know that John Nichols with his own work tries to bring this out: the idea that the land here and the lifestyle culturally that has been lived by for centuries and thousands of years must resist the more destructive changes brought by western expansionism, including even by the railroads, by land developers, by uranium exploitation, by Los Alamos and Sandia National Laboratories and the lack of planning and purely for economic profit, affecting people's long-term lives and cultures.

For me, the landscape is just one vast, engulfing, enclosing place. The far mountains, blue, in the distance, the canyon lands, red, brown, orange, yellow. The plateau or semi-arid vistas, something so much forever and yet outlined in stark relief, giving it a sense of immediacy—so that that sense of vista is not only one of distance, out there, but also inside. And then, the landscape has given obvious inspiration to the art forms that have evolved, the architecture of the Pueblo people in an earlier, earlier tradition and epochs, you know, the cliff dwellings, the working with stone so that it's part of the landscape. The music, obviously, and the songs, using the drum and the songs which are muted, evoking a sense of that same cooperation, or adjustment and inspiration by the landscape to have a certain style and form and content.

I think that literature that refers to definite place names in the landscape, certain colors, the browns, and the dryness of the land— which I use, the images of blue skies that wait like me for rain to come from the west, and seeing the desert or our homeland transformed when the rain does fall—those kinds of environmental influences bring about inspiration. And more than that, the sense of how we have to live in a relationship with the land. The land is severe in some respects. It's hot, and it's pretty cold in the winter, and people faced with these forces can only be wise to respond appropriately, and to utilize those forces of nature. I think this lends a certain kind of linguistic outlook that also has that sense of economy—breathing in only a certain way, a sense of rhythm that evokes not grandiosity as a response, but certainly taking very great care with what you do with what you have in this sparse, arid land.

Dunaway: Who is your audience?

Ortiz: My audience in my early work was the land, a giving-back to the land that voice that it had given me. . . . You give back what is given you, your ability to think, your ability to feel, to have emotions, and then to have a voice, and a gift and skill for putting them into words. The audience in general is those people who are willing to listen, to hear. To some extent my politically engaged poetry is directed towards institutions that have wreaked destructive change, those minds and planners that often disregard the human cultural community. And then, of course, my voice is intended to be heard by those who would struggle against those institutions, somewhat inspirational. I believe that I might be following some of the traditions of poets that I admire, like Pablo Neruda, Ernesto Cardinal, who voice an appreciation and respect and love for life and land and people to inspire them as well as say something as criticism. To point out certain elements that need to be pointed out, especially those which are harmful and dangerous and potentially destructive. My audience is that great mass of people who I think need to be reaffirmed of their humanity. Kind of a tall order, but what's a poet for?

When I first began to see myself as a writer, there were really no

Native American writers. I've been writing for a long time. When I first became conscious of this specific use of words in writing, I was a writer; and maybe even before that I was a writer because I simply stepped into that energy that language is . . . A writer is a writer before he uses language on paper or by his voice, simply by his love for language. By the time I was, say, twelve or thirteen, I had started to make up songs, folk, country and western songs, singing along with the radio, you know, improvising, singing little things. I think by the time I was that age, I also had published my first Mother's Day poem. . . .

I would romanticize myself as a beginning writer; I had an ambition. That's when I fashioned myself that I would have a kind of grandiose stature, I don't know, an Acoma Hemingway or something. [laughs] You know how impressionable young people are. But there was really no models at all that were Native American. The models that were there were the popular American ones, at least that we were taught in school: Hemingway, Faulkner, the poets, Whitman, Carl Sandburg, Robert Frost. But Sandburg, obviously, and Whitman, who I felt spoke of a real America. I think that social conscious and socially committed writers: Theodore Dreiser, realists like Hamlin Garland, Steinbeck, Sinclair Lewis—these people were my models. Later on, in the 1960s, when I became aware of Native American writers, and I looked for them, we were all more or less contemporaries. N. Scott Momaday, the Kiowa novelist and poet was a student here at the University of New Mexico back in the late 1950s, early 1960s. He was a model eventually, but then we're at the same time contemporaries. Jim Welch, Leslie Silko, actually we all came along about the same time. We were interdependent models for each other. Inspirations, anyway.

Dunaway: Why weren't we hearing those voices in the 1950s?

Ortiz: Repression, mainly. Subtle repression and maybe not so subtle repression through the schools, the public school policy being that indeed there are no Native Americans: "they're all a vanishing race, right?" "There are no Native Americans east of the Mississippi." In fact, the Native Americans in the United States are not real "Indians," they're Indians who aren't "Indians" anymore because, well, they don't ride the painted ponies and live in teepees.

That was a method of repression: a non-acceptance, non-recognition, much less respect, non-sensitivity to Native American people and culture and ways of life. Obviously, within the communities, there were Indian people who kept telling the stories, who kept the ceremonies, who kept advising and counsel to the young, who kept the prayers. Even under the most severe repressive activities by state law, by church law or dictum, by federal law. And so this resulted in a real dark age for Native American literature. There was no encouragement of Indian expressiveness, in writing; there was some in painting and sculpture.

Culture and self-government are necessarily one thing. I think people would prefer to see culture as something separate, and self-government as another thing that's a political entity. But, the fact is that Indian people as self-sufficient peoples can only be so when their interests and concerns with sovereignty are regarded as a concern with culture as well. The fact of an integral culture means an integral sovereignty. That's one of my concerns.

Dunaway: When you begin a project, when you begin a poem or a story, what do you do for inspiration, and how do you actually begin writing?

Ortiz: I talk to myself. I stare at my typewriter, and sometimes I take my notebook out and look at it. I don't stop what I'm doing if I'm working at my desk on something else that's totally unrelated to poetry. I find that something insists on some investigation, some thought, an expansion. I find that I don't have large amounts of time, and I've lost some discipline to just demand time for myself to start on a project and block everything out.

In fact, I have chosen not to work so obsessively and compulsively as I used to; I'm trying to finish my latest poetry collection and I remember working on it five months, mornings I would get up, write. I would stay up—teach, then come home, fix supper, and I would write from 10:00 to 12:00 to 1:00. Every day, day after day. That kind of obsessive practice or method of writing is not productive. It's counter-productive because you're not enjoying yourself; you're not involved with what's around you. When I do start a project, it's a matter of writing something down, and then writing it again. And then I may even get bored with it, and I will just leave it alone for awhile. Then I go back to it. I revise and rewrite quite a lot. Earlier, I didn't; now, I do. Of course, it depends on what I'm writing. If it's an essay, that takes usually a lot of writing. Sometimes I dictate into a tape recorder, talk it out loud. But it takes sitting down, usually, and reading, studying.

When I feel that I've come to a point where I can agree with its own rhythms, with its own force, with its own energy, then I can say, "Thank you for coming about," "Thank you for coming from whatever source that you have come from." Then I can say, "This is the end of this work here." Essentially, it's at that point I'm able to respond to it gratefully, objectively. Usually up to that point, I'm very subjective with it, very critical of myself.

Poetry should be experience, and the writing should be experience, not just the product, but part of the process. You should participate in that inspiration. Inspiration is sometimes in sudden enlightenment, sudden power, and you accept it. You say, "Wowee, what a great idea!" But writing is ninety-five percent work, writing and rewriting, as most writers know. I'm one of the writers who depends on experience a lot, who has to have that experience of not only writing, but perhaps an experience that precipitates an idea.

Dunaway: When you think of yourself as a writer, how do you define yourself first? As an Acoma, as an Indian, as a father?

Ortiz: First? I don't know if there should be any priority list at all. I think a person who comes from an ethnic minority background can get into trouble with himself, maybe with other people, if he accepts a priority list. All these things are very important to me. I have some recognition and status out in the larger public as a writer of poetry. Yet I write short fiction. So am I a poet first, and then a fiction writer, or what? My thought on identity is that the writing expresses itself from me, a person who is Acoma. I'm an Acoma person who writes poetry and fiction, who is also a father, a family person, a tribal member of the Acoma people, who enjoys some travel and who enjoys literature and music.

Identity, I think, is more than that, though. Identity is a certain perspective. I can be all those things that every normal person can write about on an autobiographical form, on a resume. But identity has to do with a certain commitment to be that being that he is. And my commitment to literature is obviously Native American in perspective. My scope is universal, but my perspective is as a person who comes from a Native American heritage, as an Acoma in specific. If I have anything to offer to literature, it's as a Native American writer who specifically is an Acoma, from Acoma. Heritage is very important to insuring that we have a dynamic of variety in American literature, in world literature. Variety is what will ensure our human integrity, our human spirit. That's what gives us a common bond; variety makes us all-purposeful in our various, individual, cultural ways. It convinces us of the values of ourselves.

Dunaway: Well said. Thank you, Simon.

The Burden of Images and the Importance of Land, Culture, and Community

An Interview with Simon J. Ortiz

Susan Berry Brill de Ramírez

SBBdR: I'd like to begin this interview with a few questions about the development of Native Studies. Could you speak about what you've been doing over the past five years at the University of Toronto and how about how that university's commitment to Native Studies has evolved while you've been there?

SJO: I've been at the University of Toronto since August 2001 when I traveled from Tucson, Arizona, where I was living since 1993. I was asked to be a visiting professor. Two years before I went to Toronto, Ted Chamberlin, a professor at UT, asked me if I was interested in coming to Toronto to do a poetry reading, so I went up there. I met people there, and it was really nice. I liked the faculty of English, and then I met people from the faculty of Aboriginal Studies at University of Toronto. We just really talked about what I was doing and the teaching positions I had in the past. I had taught over the years on and off here and there. About two weeks after I got back to Tucson, I received correspondence from the University of Toronto, and the correspondence was a contract [laughter]. They weren't very subtle; they just said this is what we can do, we like you a lot, and we would like for you to consider what we have to offer. The offer was pretty good, very decent. I had never been really in Canada much except one time before when I was there for the Toronto Storytelling Festival in 1987, and I liked it then.

This interview was conducted in Peoria, Illinois, on November 4, 2005, when Ortiz had come to Bradley University to give a reading and to meet with faculty and students.

When the Canadian possibility at UT opened up, I felt it was a way of really making more of an international difference, not only because I would be living in Canada, but also because the University of Toronto is a very international and cosmopolitan university. I had become aware of its socially conscious curriculum offerings especially in aboriginal studies. The historical relationship of Aboriginal people and non-Aboriginal Canadians seems more positive due to the larger presence of Aboriginal people in Canada than in the United States. Not that there aren't problems; there certainly are as far as economic poverty and other stressful conditions are concerned with reference to Indigenous/Aboriginal Canadians.

Well, I did go in 2001 to Canada after I signed the contract. I am currently a faculty member in the Department of English as well as in Aboriginal Studies. I teach Creative Writing and Contemporary Native North American Literature. I am also an Aboriginal Studies faculty member teaching a full year course, Indigenous Thoughts and Expressions.[1]

Aboriginal Studies at the University is much more stable now than it was before, having started in the early 1980s when there were no Aboriginal Studies faculty working full time in Aboriginal Studies. Now, though, it has full-time instructors. When I arrived in 2001, they also hired another person. I also was the first Native person in the Department of English as a faculty appointment. I felt this signaled a really positive change for the University of Toronto. Even though University of Toronto is the biggest and the most prestigious one in Canada, sort of the Harvard of Canadian higher education, it hadn't demonstrated its commitment to Aboriginal Studies the way that it does now. Now the Department of English has two positions in Native literatures; there is one in the School of Law, another one in Aboriginal Studies itself, and they are looking for one in History. So the development of aboriginal studies has been moving rapidly over the last several years, and I am really glad to be a part of that change. We've also started two speaking series: one is called the "Distinguished Lecture Series," which I co-direct, and then the "Indigenous Literary Reading Series," that brings in poets and other people in the literary arts, which I started as well. So that is what I have been doing in Toronto at the university.

SBBdR: Can you speak about the ways that work is especially important because its being at University of Toronto and the distinctive stature that university has in Canada? Do you see the development of aboriginal studies there resonating outward from the university and being influential to academia more broadly in Canada and possibly even to the United States?

SJO: The University of Toronto and the university system in Canada as a whole makes it apparent and obvious that the Native population, the Aboriginal First Nations population, is fundamental to the educational goals of Canada. Canada's provincial university systems are verbally, rhetorically, and actually committed to this, and it is governmental federal policy to meet the people's needs. The Aboriginal First Nations population is really noticed; the wording of government decrees and policy statements always refer to the Aboriginal First Nations community in Canada. When the university announces plans and goals in the academy, such as curriculum initiatives, Aboriginal Studies is notified almost every time.

Regarding influence in the States, there is also a United States Studies Program that has invited or is inviting Native people from the U.S. to go up there. In its effort to provide education not only for Canada, the University of Toronto is also very aware of its role hemispherically throughout the Americas. One of the things that interested me about going to University of Toronto is that the university and country seemed to be very focused outwardly, not just nationally inward. There are welcoming immigration policies. The country is much more open than the U.S. You see people coming from Europe, coming from Asia, such as China or the South Pacific or India. Toronto is a very cosmopolitan city, and all kinds of languages are spoken there.

SBBdR: To date, the majority of Native studies programs have developed in universities and regions of the United States and Canada where there are significant numbers of Native students and/or nearby tribal nations, communities, and reservation lands such as University of Arizona, University of New Mexico, University of Montana, and the University of Oklahoma. Can you speak about the importance of Native studies, First Nations studies, aboriginal studies, Indigenous studies for Indigenous peoples?

SJO: Sure. This relates to the question that we just talked about a moment ago—making it very obvious that Indigenous studies (I'll just use that term to include all the Aboriginal First Nations studies [programs] in Canada or Native and American Indian studies in the United States) is important because Indigenous communities and populations are fundamental to any national and/or international development throughout the Americas. First of all, Canada consciously realized that its Indigenous population east to west and north to south is very much a part of the Canadian population and that they have to recognize them as the aboriginal citizens, original habitants of North America which is fundamental to any development concerns.

This is contrasted to other nations such as the United States where, often times, the Indigenous population known as Indians, American Indians or Native Americans, are almost incidental. To be included, we have to bring ourselves to the attention of the government to include us into its plans. It is almost as if we get attention only as an afterthought, which is sad because that means that we, the Indigenous populations of the U.S., find ourselves to be a last-minute issue with a federal government that resents us reminding it we are part of the population. Since the United States' political process, capitalism, and corporate money are in the dynamic and all are dependent on the market, the more of the market you demand attention to, the more power you have. The Native people in the United States don't have much money. Canadian Native people, the Aboriginal population, don't have much money either, but the federal government and the provincial governments in Canada include the Indigenous people anyway because of their socialistic orientation.

Native studies really can help to bring attention to Native peoples. When I arrived in Canada, I found my works were fairly prominent there and people knew about me and that's why, for example, in the speaker series I can contact people and have access to them simply by name recognition, and that is helpful. And if it does some good, then that is all right; if I can be helpful to the Native communities because of that, then that is fine with me. And if I am able to bring attention to community needs, then that's a good use made of my name and time. In general, both the U.S. and Canada need to be much more aware of Indigenous scholarship and artistic works of Indigenous people.

I see change. I think younger Indigenous peoples are much more assertive than ever before. I know some good scholars who are

working either as younger professional academics or else are in graduate school who are looking at professions in the academy, and they
will be very helpful in the future.

One of the things that is grabbing some attention are the links
being made internationally among Indigenous peoples. When I think
about Indigenous peoples, I am immediately concerned for independence here and throughout North, Central and South America, i.e.,
the Western Hemisphere. But there are Indigenous peoples beyond
the Western Hemisphere such as Indigenous peoples of Africa, Asia
and Arctic regions who we can link up with. Indigenous people presently in school or starting out in their careers are aware of this. For
example, Ned Blackhawk is coming out with a book [published as
*Violence Over the Land: Indians and Empires in the Early American
West* (New Haven: Harvard University Press, 2006)], that includes
a look at the slavery of Indigenous peoples who worked in the silver
mines in Mexico. It also looks at Nevada where Indigenous people
were dispossessed of their lands and dislocated. Today Nevada has
more federally designated land than anywhere else in the United
States—designations largely designed to dispossess Indigenous pop
ulations, making Nevada a real contested area.

SBBdR: This is research that would be valuable globally—for the diverse
Indigenous (and diasporized) peoples of the world.

SJO: The international nature of these studies, the global addressing of
Indigenous peoples, is not just local but stretches beyond into the
Arctic regions and into Siberia. And south into the South Pacific,
New Zealand, and Australia, because the peoples there are just as
Indigenous as we are with related concerns. One of the things I
found being in Canada and Toronto is that I've been in touch with
people from around the world. Recently I went to China and spoke at
a couple of universities, and I'm continuing to have contacts there. I
haven't gone to ethnic minorities meetings in China yet, but there are
Indigenous movements there. The universities I visited in Shanghai
and Beijing are very interested in Native American communities
here in the United States.

For whatever it means, China is really changing. I hope it changes
in a beneficial way, not just simply take over Western traits and char-
acteristics, which are not always the best to emulate and copy. I
don't necessarily see myself as one of the younger people anymore

but hopefully my spirit and my push toward some positive direction has some impact on younger scholars and artists so that they can be more aware of what is happening and what can be done.

SBBdR: At this point, I'd like to make a segue to talk about your writing.

SJO: All right.

SBBdR: You have been working on a number of prose projects recently.

SJO: I seem to have been doing that, more prose than poetry actually.

SBBdR: Well, that is my question. Would you describe your recent writing and also comment on why you have been working more in these directions?

SJO: I've asked myself that question, maybe not in a way to answer it completely or in detail, but it has been on my mind. Prose demands more study and extended detailed attention. This is not to say that poetry doesn't require and demand that kind of detailed attention, but it seems like prose requires it fully. It's more work to write prose. At least for me, it is. It is a much more involved dynamic that takes more time. Prose composition demands more intellectual thought. I don't simply write intuitively like I think poetry happens. Poetry is intuitive; you are very spontaneous with poetry. I don't really "think" when poetry comes about until afterward when I make revisions and think more analytically about it. I don't tend to write or compose intellectually in the English language, but if I do, then I look at it to make sure it is what I mean and not necessarily what I want simply to create an effect or impact. So that the poetry is sincere and passionate and has the emotional impact I want. I suppose it has to do with how I came to learn English. I respect English simply as language, and I love language. I write prose because it takes more work. Maybe I like work better than anything else. I love the work of language.

SBBdR: Your most recently published book responds to the past graphic photography of Native peoples. Can you talk about the origins of this book *Beyond the Reach of Time and Change: Native American Reflections on the Frank A. Rhinehart Photograph Collection*?

SJO: This may sound kind of funny or odd for me to say. I always used to feel intimidated or put out of sorts by pictures of old time Indians. That is, the Indians that were portrayed by Edward Curtis, who were dressed in elaborate tribal regalia, fur leggings and necklaces, and beautiful moccasins. They were always very fine-looking human people and specimens. They always were gorgeous, poised statues, like something to be admired and not touched. Well, I always felt that those pictures or images were more like burdens to me, pictures or images that I could never look like. Yet the pictures or images were identified to be Indians.

As far as I knew, I was an Aacqumeh Indian, an Indigenous person. To me that is what Indigenous people, Indians, looked like. Like people who were Aacqumeh hanuh. I never resembled those kinds of figures. Figures like the Apache warrior leader Geronimo. Or Cochise. Or Sitting Bull. But those were my models. So when I was younger, although I admired the figures as portraits of ideal Indians, that is, the images of them, I was intimidated, and I was put off by them because I wasn't like that. So if I wasn't the beautiful brave warrior, what did that make me? Either I wasn't an Indian or else I was a poor imitation of one. That's the way I saw those photographs. I mean they were photographs, of course, of homes and places long ago. Long ago when Edward Curtis took photographs of Acoma. They were photographs of a long ago time and place. They all seemed to be of a mythical place that really never was.

This was the other thing: it was a long time ago. The pictures were so old the Indians they showed were long gone. Well, of course, they were not really long gone. I mean there was Acoma; it was still there. And I was still there when I was there, but I was a boy. I still go there to Acoma, the old pueblo, when I go home to visit, and I go for fiestas or ceremonies or when the Kachinas come. I've seen old pictures of Acoma more than 100 years old. They're all static; they're all way back when.

In 1994 when I was speaking at Haskell Indian Nations University in Lawrence, Kansas, I was shown the Rhinehart photos by the Haskell Foundation Director. There were over 700 glass-plate negatives of this man's archive. He had made those photographs during the World's Fair, the American and International Exposition held at Omaha, Nebraska, in 1898. Haskell had the whole archive. Rhinehart was the official photographer for the Exposition in 1898. During this time, the American Bureau of American Ethnology (which became the Smithsonian Institute) had planned an exhibit, which was called Indian Congress of Native People. They invited or brought Native people from various reservations and photographed them. The photographs were really gorgeous, and they were just kind of stored haphazardly in cardboard boxes. Now they're more secured in a museum.

Eventually, I was asked to be the editor of this publication, and the first thing I did, of course, was to ask, "Do these people have relatives, descendants alive today?" I was told that there are descendants who are known. So I checked around, and I happened to know some of these descendants, like Greg Cajete (of Santa Clara Pueblo).[2] His great-grandfather is in there. Bob Haozous (Chiricahua Apache) is a painter and sculptor in Santa Fe, New Mexico; his great-grandfather was in the photographs there because he was with Geronimo when Geronimo was forced to surrender to the United States in 1886. There were a few Apaches with him in their continuing struggle against the United States and Mexico in Arizona, and when they surrendered they were made prisoners of war and were sent to Fort Marion in Florida, then later to Fort Sill in Oklahoma, where they were still prisoners of war in 1898. Geronimo and a few of his people were allowed to come up to the International and American Exposition at Omaha. And so they were photographed. Geronimo's picture is in there and others from the Dakotas, South Dakota and North Dakota and Iowa and Montana and New Mexico and Arizona. The book has about 100 photographs in all, out of 700 or so, mostly from that exhibition of the Indian Congress in Omaha.

At the beginning, I didn't like working with the photographs. I found I resented them. I resented the kind of image we, contemporary or present-day Indians, were expected to live up to. That if we weren't like those images and did not have those looks and were not as fierce and nor costumed like they are in the tribal outfits and tribal wear in the old time way, we weren't real Indians presently. I mean the Indians I knew at home were usually poor, unemployed, and living in substandard housing on reservations or were on rare occasions living in urban areas in Dallas or the San Francisco Bay Area or Oakland or Denver, doing the best they could. They weren't in any way anything like the old-time people in the photographs who looked like romantic, beautiful warriors. And so I found I was writing an essay that, at first, was mainly a diatribe.

Well, I changed my mind about how to do it. I decided not to do it by myself because I felt if I did it by myself, it would be just a one-dimensional, one-person diatribe about Native people depicted as static, old time, one-dimensional Native people. I decided instead to invite others to really change the course of how I would look at it. Instead of me being the only writer, I decided I would invite people I knew and others at large to look at the photographs and what the photography meant to them. I located the descendants of some of those who were photographed, and they provided their own views. The book has a variety of perspectives. There were at least seventy tribes at the American Indian Congress. That was the extent of my work. It turned out really well and it came out last year. I think it's a good look at what photographs have been to Native American people. Photographs can be a burden. I think Native people have never trusted photographs entirely. I don't know how they see these photos in *Beyond the Reach of Time and Change*. I haven't heard any reaction from them yet, but the book has gotten pretty good notice so far.

[At this point, there was a break in the interview. When Simon and I continued, he wanted to correct some misinformation that he had seen about himself on the Internet. He placed that correction within the larger frame of the topics of the interview.]

SJO: Indians are burdened by the images of the Native American and also how people see "Indians." I choose how people see me at times. Remember I said yesterday that some of the information out on the Internet is wrong about me. I think it is funny, but it is also irritating and aggravating. For example, I see time and time again that I have an M.A. or M.F.A. from the University of Iowa, which I don't. I don't have any college degree, but people like journalists and others want to see an image of a successful Native American or a successful person on their own terms. That happened in the photographs by Rhinehart or Edward Curtis to some degree, when they dressed up those Indians. They had them put on studio clothes. They put them in costumes like their images of the old Indians so that they presented what they wanted to see. So almost in the same way I end up in biographies with these degrees, with this M.A or M.F.A. from the University of Iowa Creative Writing Workshop program. I was at Iowa, but it was with a writing fellowship in the International Writing Program simply as a writer. I was honored to have that, but I didn't get any degrees. I haven't ever gotten a college degree. I went to school and got enough of a college education to be able to say that I went to college.

SBBdR: Was that at UNM [University of New Mexico]?

SJO: I went to Fort Lewis College at first. My gosh, in 1961. I didn't go to school right away after high school. I went to work up in the uranium mining area for Kerr-McGee. I was working up at the mill site for one year, actually less than a year because there was a big strike. The workers went out against the mining companies because of issues of pay and health, so I was saved by that. Then I went to Fort Lewis College, and I stayed three semesters. Then I quit and joined the Army.

I went back to school at UNM later on for several more semesters. I didn't get a degree, but I got invited as a fellow to the International Writing Program at the University of Iowa, which I took because, oh my gosh, we were broke. We—my wife and our two boys—didn't have any money, and U. of Iowa offered a stipend. It was a two-year program, but I only stayed one year because we had a growing family. So I only went one year and came back to Albuquerque. Then I started working at Rough Rock on the Diné [Navajo] Reservation. When I hear or see that I went to the University of Iowa, I know that people simply assume I have a degree from there, perhaps because the Masters' Writing Workshop at Iowa is very well known and because the director of the International Writing Program also used to be the director of the Writing Workshop in Iowa. I wanted to talk about this because it has to do with perceptions of Native people and the ways we are affected by such instances.

It is important Native literature be recognized for what it is. I think Native American literature is so important and the writers and the intellectuals in it have to be recognized for what they really are. They are the voices of Native people. They are the voices of their community. When Native writers speak, what they write is not necessarily themselves personally, but they are really reflecting and speaking from much more of a communal collective sense of themselves. I think that is correct because my story as an individual person is not a real story unless there is also the community and family and friends and culture which are also included. It is a real strength, and that's why I always refer to my children or my mother and father. I think it is an important difference from non-Indian people. This kind of voice is necessary to recognize for what it is. Then, we can get beyond the image of the Indian, quote unquote "Indian" which has been a burden.

SBBdR: In the ethnography based on Hopi/Tewa Albert Yava's stories, Yava says that it is important to understand that his people are not supposed to focus their stories on themselves. He said, "The stories that I tell even though I am in these stories, the stories are not about me." He says that "the stories have me in them just because I was there and that's how I know the story and I tell the story." Essentially he is saying that the stories are much larger than the storyteller, much larger than just him.[3]

SJO: That is, I think, a real good way to put it; what I was saying or trying to say. Because there is so much, sometimes so much emphasis on the individual personal story, it ends up kind of a misuse of what a traditional or original story was. Because it was a story always of the people, not just the people as people, human people, but as people that are a part of everything. Because the reason we are people is because we are part of the land and the belief system or culture that is a part of us. So when you look at people, you are not just describing flesh and blood or personal images, you are actually looking at the whole holistically.

SBBdR: Would you say that a writer is like a lens to help others see stories more clearly and in more focused ways?

SJO: Yes, I think so. I don't know if you recall a poem I did some time ago. It's in the first book, I think, *Going for the Rain*. It's about looking at a man, an Indigenous man who has fallen down on the street because he was inebriated. I was at that time in Albuquerque working for the National Youth Council, and I saw him, an elder man. It was winter. I saw him from my desk which was right by the window. So I got up, and I went across the street to help him get up, and I brought him over to our office across the street on Central. I wrote about that experience. I was actually telling a friend of mine, David, a Jewish guy, who always liked to hang around with us back then. After telling him about it, it was a story. I wrote it with a real concern for this elderly nameless Pueblo man, and then, of course, it became about me and all the Native people who have been too often in that condition. At the end, I wrote, "I let you see into me in order that you may see yourself." That idea: "I let you see into me in order that you may see yourself or into yourself." And yes, you are a window. You open up. You let yourself be seen so that other people can and, maybe, will see themselves.

SBBdR: Providing a focal point.

SJO: Yes, and it's not just really limited only to Indigenous people, but really everybody. I learned that from reading other poets. I told you I like Carl Sandburg, Sherwood Anderson, Hamlin Garland. Edgar Lee Masters—the *Spoon River Anthology*.[4] They reveal very human situations, human conditions. Sometimes the looking was very hard, very hard, very difficult because of the functions of society, the social systems, especially American social systems. I used to want to be able to look at that in order to understand myself. There had to be some kind of reasoning or something that could help me to cope with the pain of growing up Native American. Sometimes it was really painful. I didn't want to say it just because I am an Indian or just because of discrimination or whatever. It was the feeling of being an outsider when I was a boy. There had to be some kind of explanation or a kind of understanding that I could achieve.

By reading the work of these writers, I seemed to be coming to some insight into myself and the realities of the world. I was always a realist, I guess, in my preference for literatures. Some people may call these writings depressing: Thomas Wolfe's *Look Homeward, Angel*. Or *The Beautiful and the Damned* by Scott Fitzgerald which is a real depressing book actually. But the writers were realists; they were really looking at the turmoil of life. And it seemed I could understand why I felt, lots of times as a kid and even as an adult, tortured. So, yes, writing and/or reading was a window.

SBBdR: Both you and Leslie Marmon Silko have written and talked about the co-creative interactions in storytelling. Does this process inform your crafting of poetry? And in what way? And also, how do you see this involved in the prose writing as well?

SJO: I think that has so much to do with how writing/speaking is an expression of whatever is inside. At the same time, it is also a way we perceive. You express, but you also perceive at the same time. It's not a by-product but comes from the same dynamic when you express yourself. It seems to be like sonar; you throw a sound out, and something bounces back. It's a way in which what you say is creative. You say something as expression, but you say it in order to understand something. Like the sonar bats have, there is feedback. From that feedback, we have insight, understanding, comprehension, and creativity. That's where the creative act is. The creative spirit is the wondering function of the brain; the imaginary is the experience. That is the creative source we then make use of. This is where we come to discover whatever is.

Recently I wrote about my uncle and my dad in an essay that is part of a project I am working on. When my father passed away in 1978, it was the first time I had ever heard my uncle cry. It was such a deep, deep, deep grieving. It scared me at first because it seemed like he couldn't stop. He was kneeling by my dad, holding his hand, and it still emotionally reverberates in me. He cried, "Don't leave me, please. I love you very much." There is a history behind all of that. That expression was necessary for him, and for me to be able to see that. It was enriching, much more than I could ever really describe. It was true and deep emotional expression, and from that, understanding and comprehension take place.

SBBdR: As life has become more fast-paced and so many have very little if any quiet reflective time to listen and perceive with this sort of depth, most college students today prefer to read prose, tending to shy away from poetry and not knowing how to engage co-creatively.

SJO: I don't know if that is the reason, if limited time and a fast-paced life just leave so little time. I know we get torn personally; I should look at it personally. We get fragmented. We get fractured. We are pulled this way and that way. So many things are taking place. I just want to focus on one thing at a time and look at it. I know that, for me, prose writing takes work, much more than poetry. Poetry—I let it come about by intuition. I would say, spontaneously. Prose can do that too, intuitively or spontaneously, but prose takes work and focus and concentration and structure. I want something that demands my attention, so perhaps prose is a way of creating a context or creating a time or circumstance I have to be bound by. Maybe some young people prefer prose because prose requires or demands their attention.

SBBdR: The work is done for them by the writer.

SJO: [laughter] Well, perhaps you could see it that way. I get pulled into prose by the demands of it. It takes work, more work to read prose, I think.

SBBdR: Than poetry?

SJO: Yes. At least for me. It may be a personal preference. I can read poetry and just kind of assume it is going to be understood. It is probably the wrong thing to do, that I am going to come to understand just by reading it. It is not that simple. You have to study it as well. But, I mean, I guess I immediately relate to it and expect an understanding to come about, maybe by osmosis or something.

SBBdR: You have written a great deal about stone, stone building, stone-walls, and wind-sculpted rock faces, woven stone.

SJO: They're just sandstone.

SBBdR: What can stone teach about poetry and literature?

SJO: Stone is very solid, like this stone we see in this wall. It is something you can feel comparably. Stone has weight, you put it down, and it stays there and slowly disintegrates. But it stays there usually for a long time. Stone has a certain texture and feel that is hard and solid and concrete. At the same time, it can be used constructively, like in building walls or putting stones together in such a way they form a structure.

My father was a stoneworker, a stone builder. He built a lot of the homes around Acoma. He was the one who, back in the seventies before he passed away, rebuilt Buu-dzah-tyah, the Antelope people's main house. The Antelope people have the religious responsibility for the ceremonies. They are the ones who plan and set the religious ritual calendar for each year. And they work. The handiwork and the way you can work with stone is really, really meaningful.

Stonework is something very foundational that is carried from one generation to the next, from one era to the next. I would say in the Southwest, where I come from, stone is probably the main and the most significant and noticeable thing visually. It is the metaphor for what the Southwest is culturally. Going back and restoring culture and history of the people, stone is such an element, a cultural element in how people relate to stone. Stone comes from the original creation.

Sandstone is sediment. But there is also basalt stone, volcanic stone, very prominent around home because of Mt. Taylor, Kaweshtima, as we call it. That's a northern sacred mountain. It's a big volcano, an inactive one, and all around you, north and west and southwest lies volcanic lava, the lava beds. The inactive volcano provides real rich soil because of the volcanic ash. The San Jose River valley is good farmland; sadly, it is not farmed as much as it used to be. The soil of the Acoma valley is essentially a mixture of volcanic ash because the uplift to the west is old volcanoes and volcano bluffs. Some of it is sandstone, so it is a mixture of volcanic ash and sandstone. Before Spanish times and past Spanish times, it was good for farming. When I was a boy, there were good farmlands in the Acoma valley, dry farms making use of rainwater and snowfalls. There were some springs around there, but not a lot of springs. I don't think the land ever had a lot of water, but there were some springs. There is not as much farming now. There seems to be less water.

When I was a boy, I helped my dad when he was working building houses. It was a trade he learned I suppose from his father and grandfather and other people, building houses from stone. Looking back at stone in terms of cultural history, stones were the cliff houses or cliff dwellings my ancient ancestral people had. Stone is just so much a part of my own personal and cultural history. I mean stone is good poetic metaphor. And reality.

SBBdR: In what other ways does your Acoma Pueblo heritage inform your writing?

SJO: Discipline is a structure. It's not just dos and don'ts, but it's like a philosophical structure, a guide, and an outlook. It is part of the worldview my identity is really dependent upon. Acoma culture informs who I am as a person—a person who is not a person unless there is a whole context of family, clan, community, land, and a system of knowledge that is all tied together. In the past fifteen years or so, I've been using the three terms, "land," "culture," and "community," to signify all of that as a single entity. An entity made up of land, culture and community [which constitutes] a system of knowledge. Without that entity, I am not a person. My identity as a person is non-existent unless there is an Acoma Pueblo as land, culture, and community.

This goes back to how Indigenous peoples see themselves. That is why colonization has so effectively undermined our sense of Indigenous identity, identity and indigeneity are so often lost because Indigenous people do not relate consciously, intentionally, or purposely to their land and culture anymore.

What is really taking place is that when the land was lost from our control, a break severed us from the land, and the break created a barrier between the land and us. We no longer had access in terms of our identity to the land. Because our systems of knowledge were connected to the land; especially how we saw ourselves, that function of knowledge of ourselves was lost. Because of that loss, because of that barrier. The loss of language, the decrease of fluent language use is a part of that loss. So we found ourselves suddenly doubtful. We had less sense of being tribally identified if we couldn't speak the language or did not know ceremonial knowledge or lost language terms for relatives—mothers, fathers, aunts, uncles, cousins, and all that—you know, how we addressed each other. Then the community systems, the community in terms of sovereignty and self-government, that were lost. And now we sometimes don't know who we are. Am I a real Indian if I don't know these things and can't use those things? Colonialism really has devastated us a lot because of those things.

I find that discipline or structure really is what I look to. Sometimes I feel . . . of course, I have lived away quite a lot, like many other Native people who have drifted away from their home communities. But I've also tried to . . . even though I may have lived in Portland and San Francisco and now in Toronto, I consciously, probably every day, say, "This land is still me, this land is still who I am." Even if I am someplace else, I feel connected to the Earth, to the land, to the culture, to the community. Even though it may seem like a pointless exercise or simply a ritual, it is reassuring myself: this land is still me, this land is still who I am. It is necessary to do; it is a choice, an important choice. If I do this, it is like a prayer; it is a reconnection because prayers are really ways in which you reconnect or you connect and maintain the bonds, whether it is to God or to Yahweh or to Mohammad or to Bahá'u'lláh.[5] It is connection to your provider and sustainer, it is deliberate intentional reconnection. Being an Acoma person is really important to how I see myself and how I see the world and how I live as part of a community, a culture, and a land.

SBBdR: In *from Sand Creek,* you stated that your primary purpose of writing the collection was to revive the forgotten history of Native peoples. Was there a second and deeper purpose of helping contemporary Native peoples to be more widely known and respected through writing a corrective history of that one place and event?

SJO: A true history of the U.S. has never really been presented—especially the history of violence in the United States and especially the fact that the U.S. is founded upon violence. The trauma that violence causes and the reverberations of the trauma have never been really exposed. If you don't talk about the history of violence, of destruction, then it's almost as if it never happened. Of course, we know it happened. But if we know it happened, why don't we talk about it, why isn't it out there? It's always very difficult to talk about trauma and to talk about violence. I'm somewhat two ways about it. I mean I can either go along and say, "Well, it wasn't that bad or else it never happened" (avoidance and ignorance are easy choices), or I could just go ahead and say, "Well, you know we have to admit that there is a history." I think when I began to write *from Sand Creek* it was really with that in mind.

I came upon Sand Creek almost incidentally or came to admit it because I was an inpatient at the alcohol and drug rehab unit at Fort Lyons Veterans Administration Hospital, which is west of Sand Creek in southeastern Colorado. Fort Lyons was a former Army fort, and it had been built in order to win the West. These were lands that were formerly owned or used by the Cheyenne and Arapaho people in southeastern Colorado—buffalo country. So for settlers going west from the East Coast to the California and Nevada gold fields and so forth, Fort Lyons was on one of the routes they would take, either the Oregon Trail or the Santa Fe Trail and all of that. Much later on, it became a V.A. hospital.

There are crosses around outside the Veteran's Hospital: some unmarked graves. One time they, hospital personnel, took us on a field trip—to entertain the inmates, patients, clients at the hospital. One of the places we went was Sand Creek. It's just open grasslands, open prairie by a ranch, a small marked place. Then it [the connection between the past Sand Creek Massacre, the then-current Vietnam War, and all of us at the Veteran's Hospital] occurred to me.

This was 1974, and the Vietnam War was still taking place, although winding down. The Vietnam War had been taking place since the early sixties even though officially, the U.S. war did not officially start until about 1965. It had been taking place even before in the early 1960s when my younger brother was serving in Thailand and the U.S. military forces were building the Ton Son Nhut Air Base from where many of the later B-52 air strikes were eventually launched against North Vietnam in the later sixties and perhaps the early seventies.

So when I looked at the American invasion and occupation of Vietnam, there were striking parallels with what had happened at Sand Creek in the 1860s when the massacre of the Cheyenne and Arapaho took place in 1864. And that was just one hundred years before. In one hundred years since the Sand Creek Massacre, had the history of the United States changed? No, it hadn't. All the history of violence including World War I, World War II, the Korean War, and all the other times and places when and where U.S. military and government actions had been occurring was just a history of invasion and occupation.[6]

Let's see, you know, when I first came to know about the Sand Creek Massacre, it was in 1974. And then in 1975, when I was sent back to Fort Lyons Hospital for rehab again. I didn't immediately write *from Sand Creek*, but it stuck in my mind for the next couple of years. Later on, when I was teaching at College of Marin a year or two later, that is when I began to write about Sand Creek and the poems in it. It was a gradual realization and writing. It didn't take long to write it, but I felt it was necessary to write.

To recognize the history of U.S. violence was to recognize the history of blindness and national amnesia and denial, which are, of course, included as themes in *from Sand Creek*. One of the things I should say about it is that I almost saw it oddly as a piece of music like a symphony. I was living in Marin County at the time not far from the Marin College. I would go back to my apartment and lie down on the floor and turn music on, and then I would just write . . . write on loose-leaf paper. It seemed to me like a piece of classical symphonic music. I don't know a thing about a classical symphony, but that's the way it felt like to me, a piece of symphonic music. I think *from Sand Creek* had what is really necessary for me to write. And I still think it is very relevant, especially today.

Somebody said to me the other night it could be I just wrote it on purpose for the war in Iraq. But I didn't, of course. I didn't know the war in Iraq was going to happen, but I think that if people do not look at their history of violence, then it's going to repeat itself. That book was first published in 1981, and it was later republished by the University of Arizona Press. All these years, and it's 2005 now.

SBBdR: And it is still as relevant, if not even more relevant, globally today.

SJO: People teach *from Sand Creek* in history classes, I've heard. They teach it as history, not just as literature. I'm glad it works.

SBBdR: Thank you very much for your time and your words.

SJO: You're welcome.

NOTES

1. At the time of the interview, Ortiz was a faculty member at the University of Toronto. Currently, he is a professor at Arizona State University.

2. Greg Cajete is also the author of the preface to this volume.

3. The Yava volume was brought out by Harold Courlander, editor of *Big Falling Snow: A Tewa-Hopi Indian's Life and the History and Traditions of His People*. Initially published in 1978, the volume was later reprinted by the University of New Mexico Press in 1992.

4. Additional significance to this reference is that the interview took place not far from the Spoon River in central Illinois.

5. Here, Ortiz refers to the Prophet-Founder of the Bahá'í Faith because his interviewer is a Bahá'í.

6. Later during an informal conversation with Ortiz, we spoke about different U.S. interventions over the course of the century since the Sand Creek Massacre, including the Philippines (war and continued military bases), Cuba (the island's division and the missile crisis), Hawaii (which was taken for eventual statehood), Venezuela (Bolivar), Argentina (Pinochet), Panama (the appropriation of Canal lands and waterway), the Congo (the CIA's assassination of Patrice Lumumba), etc.

Simon J. Ortiz

In His Own Words

Evelina Zuni Lucero

I interviewed Simon J. Ortiz in three sessions in the summer and fall of 2005. The first interview took place in July at the Ortiz family home at McCartys, the second at the Native American Studies conference room at the University of New Mexico [UNM] in August, and the final one in Santa Fe in October. In this edited transcript of the interviews, Simon recounts his educational experiences and development as a writer. At the end of the interview sessions, we conversed about Native American literature, writing, and Indian gaming, a topic almost impossible to ignore in New Mexico with Indian casinos all around us.

Fairly early in the first interview, Simon spoke of the necessity to put his life, his writing, into a broader context. He said, "Gloria Bird and Elizabeth Cook-Lynn had a conversation I once read, and one of them said this: 'When you talk with one person, and the person tells you his or her story, you're not just hearing one person's story, you're hearing the whole story of their community, the people, the Hanoh. The Pueblo sense of identity is [that] the identity is not yours personally, or singularly, or privately, or individually. But your identity is part of the whole, so any person's story is really part of a whole.'" He began his story by situating himself within family, community, and history.

In 1903, my mother said it was around that time that people began to move down from Acoma [atop the mesa]. This area [where the family home is situated][1] is called Deetseyamah. These are mostly farming areas, but people began to move down because the schools were built in the villages, the day schools, by the federal government, probably in the 1890s or so, around the early part of the twentieth century.

The restaurant we ate at [Sky City Casino] used to be a little store, kind of a drive-in restaurant. It used to be a trading post. It was Phillip Bibo's store, owned by a family who became ranchers, who came into the Acoma-Laguna area about the 1860s, during and after the Civil War. There were two Bibo brothers, Jews. They were traders during the Civil War, who eventually emigrated to the West. I think they moved to Albuquerque. They had a trading company in Bernalillo, a mercantile, and then eventually they came up here and somehow got some land, probably in the Cubero land grant. They established a mercantile business in Cubero [where the younger brother, Solomon, joined them], and they eventually put the Acoma Indian people and people of Laguna sort of under their control. In fact, Acoma used to have a Jewish governor [laughs]. It's a colonial story.

Of course, the tribal government was organized and set up under the Spanish colonial era. Even the present-day governor [is called the] *govenador* or dah-buuph, translated as "governor" in the Acoma language. It's loosely based upon the traditional government, but it really was a Spanish-colonial invention, an adaptation of governing. The Spanish managed some control even after the Pueblo Revolt through this system of governorship (the governor, his staff, and a tribal council).

Solomon Bibo

Of the Bibo brothers, Solomon was the one who married into the Acoma tribe and became governor. By this time it was probably 1870s or '80s. He was married to a woman from Acomita. They had children, but there are no descendants living here on the reservation now. They moved to California. I met one of them years ago when I used to live in San Francisco. I think his name was Carl Bibo. He told me he was half-Acoma. I kind of didn't believe him. He just looked like some ordinary white guy, business-type, baldheaded, in his late seventies, I would say. I had done a poetry reading at Union Square. He came up to me afterwards and introduced himself and said that he was a descendant of Solomon Bibo—that was his father. I lived in the Bay Area in San Francisco in 1975 through 1979, so it must have been about 1977.[2]

The trading post clientele were people from Acoma and Laguna and Cubero, Indians and Mexicans. I didn't know the Bibos personally except when I was younger, I knew Phillip Bibo, who was the merchant. He was probably a son of the original Bibos. They owned quite a lot of land, some of the land right there [where the casino is], and maybe up on Mount Taylor, and land that is west of Acoma and southwest. There's this range called the Bibo Range, which Acoma now owns, and some of that eventually passed into Acoma hands by purchase. I don't think it was by deed, that is, heirship; I think it was all purchased. It was all Acoma land in the first place.

New Mexico didn't become a state until 1912, so this was still a territory. But of course the reservation itself was designated patent Pueblo land and was established in the 1860s. The Pueblo land-grant system had been set up, which was an adaptation of the Spanish land grant. But the U.S. federal government after 1851, after the Treaty of Guadalupe Hidalgo, recognized the Pueblo occupation of land, ownership, and supposedly, sovereignty. The Bibos had something to do with the land holdings because they were advisers and consultants to the federal government on behalf of the Acomas, and maybe even the Lagunas, too, which means they established boundaries according to their advice, their consultation. Of course, people still believe that we have less land because of the Bibos. This all came up during the Pueblo land-grant hearings and the commissions that took place in the late 1940s and into the 1950s. The Bibos had had a lot to do with what's taken place. So anyway that is where the casino is located—on that land, their land, supposedly, which is really Acoma land originally.

McCartys Day School

I was born in 1941 in Albuquerque at the Albuquerque Indian Hospital, which is where the people had been told that they had to have their children. Remember where you used to work at the *Pueblo News*?[3] Remember the red brick? That's where the hospital served Acoma. We went down there for medical services or any kind of illness. I was born there, May 27, 1941. I was schooled at McCartys Day School, which is about a mile and a half west from here. That's where I first went to school when I was six years old.

Before I was born, my mom was working with the school. When other people would talk about her, they would always designate her as a teacher. I don't know if officially she was a teacher in a formal BIA-employee-sense, but she did work there as a teacher's aide. She spoke English fluently as well as the Acoma language, and wrote fairly well. She was a graduate of Saint Catherine's Indian School [in Santa Fe]. Saint Catherine's was the model of the old missionary schools. The BIA contracted schools to religious orders, such as the Catholics. I think you find them across the country whether here in New Mexico, in Arizona, or South Dakota or Montana. A lot of those schools, maybe most of them, were missionary schools contracted by the federal government to provide educational services to Indian people.

She was born in 1903. So by the time she finished school, which was 1921, that would make her eighteen years old. She got a certificate of completion of school there, and then she came home. She was the oldest of seven girls in her family: Frances, Connie, Lolita, Juanita, and then Katie and Esther. Her name was Mamie.

Everybody went to school at McCartys Day School, which went up to the sixth grade. I liked school because I was a real curious child. That is, I was interested in things. I liked reading, and I liked writing for whatever it was. At that time, it was just general learning about things outside of Acoma. I always thought that school was a way in which one satisfied their curiosity. I was eager to learn. I think that eagerness came from wanting to know how things worked, how things operated, or how things in life were. I think that really came from an Indigenous sense of wonder. And that seemed to me a very normal way in which one learned how to satisfy that curiosity. So I found myself liking school. I didn't have any real problems with school, although sometimes I have questioned what the reasoning for that learning was. It may, in some instances, have been a way to form me into something that was not Acoma, something that resulted in me being less of an Acoma person because the idea behind the BIA education and the American schooling was to change Indian people, to make them different from who they were originally, especially the boarding schools.

I went to McCartys Day School except for one year when I was in the fifth grade in '52. That was when my father, who worked for the Santa Fe railroad, was stationed, working at a section crew in Skull Valley, Arizona. He worked for the railroad for over a twenty-year period, and then later on, he worked on a railroad track gang, both as a laborer and welder in different places.

He was away from home a lot when I was growing up. He used to work up here at the local railroad section, just a mile north where the railroad goes through. One of the earliest memories I have of him is of him coming home from work with his lunch bucket, walking down from the railroad section crew. There's a little river north of here, the Rio San José [with] a little bridge made out of railroad ties. All us kids would go rushing to see what my dad had left over in his lunch bucket. He worked [locally] for some years. But most of the time after that he worked away on welding gangs, track crews, out in Arizona and California. He was gone from home for weeks, maybe a month or more, which created a lot of hardship for us as a family, and for my mother. A lot of people worked away from home. Some people worked whatever kind of jobs they had in unskilled labor. Essentially, working for the railroad was unskilled labor for my father and for other men.

The year I was in the fifth grade at Skull Valley, Arizona, was actually the first time I ever wrote anything called a poem. It was published in a school newspaper we had called the *Skull Valley News*. It was a Mother's Day poem. I may even have copied it from some place. But it was written in my hand anyway, and my mother used to remember it. But I don't. It was something that was composed out of one's imagination because of how one learns, partly from meditation or rote; part of one's self is creative self-expression, whether it's humming or singing a song. It's your song whether it's a repetition of something you heard. So in that respect, that was in the form I wrote. I have no idea what it was about, something about the love of mother. My mother was quite a wonderful person. She was a very small woman. She was a beautiful woman.

Indian Boarding School

My seventh grade year was at Saint Kate's, and then, because I wanted to be closer to home, I came to Albuquerque Indian School because Albuquerque is closer to Acoma, to McCartys where I grew up. I had become aware that people were preparing for employment after they finished school. A way to get jobs, especially for Indian peoples, was to be trained for the job, and so AIS taught technical skills—auto mechanics, sheet metal, carpentry, and modern-day farming, dairy, taking care of animals, and domestic service for women, maybe pre-nursing.

I remember telling my mother and father in a letter—back home my dad worked in California and Arizona—that I wanted to go to Albuquerque Indian School to learn a trade. I was going to be in the eighth grade [and] that kind of brainwashing was already taking place. So the next year I went to Albuquerque Indian School along with a number of others from home. I suppose that was part of it, too. There were not many Acoma students at Saint Catherine's. Only one of my cousins, Clyde, went there. The others all went to AIS.

That was a big school around these parts. Santa Fe Indian School was also operating. It was intended for the northern Pueblos from Santa Fe and above, like Taos, Picuris, Tesuque, and San Juan, maybe a few students from Cochiti and Santo Domingo. But the southern Pueblos were mostly the student enrollment at AIS: Acoma, Laguna, Isleta, Santa Ana, Jemez, San Felipe, Cochiti, Santo Domingo. And then there were Navajo students as well. They did not have any English-speaking or writing knowledge, so they were put in a special program, intermediate, or even remedial.

By that time I was becoming aware of how the federal government or the American education was impacting Native people. I don't think I really thought as much about that critically, in terms of me and the general Native American population, although I was becoming aware. You know how adolescents are, very curious. You become concerned as an adolescent about your identity.

I was aware of the tensions of race, and cultural differences, especially on the Indian School level and in the Indian School community. There was a mixture of tribes. Mescalero and Jicarilla Apaches were also at the school. I remember the differences in terms of language and cultural behavior, like Pueblos stuck together, Apaches stuck together, and Navajos stuck together. And there were, of course, some conflicts.

I was also curious and interested in things, it seemed to me. I would ask and I would listen. I would watch and I would wonder. Even though I was sociable here, I tended not to be [either] a real extroverted outsider, or an apparent outsider, or a loner. But I liked to read a lot, and I liked to go off and wander around, more at Saint Catherine's probably. You could go off to the hills where Saint Kate's is located. I could go up into the hills, into the juniper and sand hills up there. I would go out away from the school and daydream. I would go over things that I knew from home, from the Acoma traditional oral literature. I would probably enact or re-enact those things, just like how you have conversations by yourself, just to be away in that world by yourself, up there in the sand gullies and hills.

I kept a journal at Saint Catherine's, a diary that was mostly my adolescent thoughts and longings, that was more emotional and probably sentimental, kind of flowery, and overly sensitive—notes that young people keep, and tell Dear Diary because the diaries are sort of your alter ego. I did write imitation poetry, not original or my own, in the most part. Although I think the first poem I wrote that other people called a poem was the Mother's Day poem [written at Skull Valley in fifth grade].

At that age, seventh, eighth grade, I was becoming very aware of what I guess you could term cultural dynamics, especially inter-culture dynamics. The tribal-cultural dynamics are very interesting to me because while we know the differences between each other in terms of language, there's also, I think, social-cultural dynamics taking place. There was, in some instances, open warfare. There were fistfights. It took place intertribal-culturally, as well as inter-Pueblos on that kind of tribal identity basis. There were some Pueblos that were more aggressive. We always thought that the Isletas were more aggressive than the other Pueblos, and the Lagunas. The Lagunas had another trait, and that was that they were better educated. What does better educated mean? They were more Americanized. We saw it as a synonym. Better educated meant that they were more aware of American ways, and practiced more American ways. At Acoma, we envied the Kawaikah-meh-titra because they spoke English more and better. Even though we admired them, at the same time, we also faulted them for how they said certain things, or thought certain things, or dressed certain ways. If someone is dressed better, you can look at them admiringly or else you think, compared to you, because they are wearing better shoes, they're chaa-rrhaanah, meaning that they are fancifully dressed.

As I said part of the [AIS] curriculum was trades-oriented with training, sheet metal, welding, and things like that. In the classroom itself, I was a fairly good student at McCartys Day School, at Saint Catherine's Indian School and here in Albuquerque. I liked school. I was very interested. I liked to read a lot. I was studious, probably a nerd of sorts. I used to like to socialize.

I did like Indian school for certain reasons. One was that I became aware at AIS of being an outsider. That is I felt different, the mental-intellectual phenomenon of being marginalized. Ethnic minority people are affected by the dynamic of marginalization even within their own cultural community—they become "otherized" even within their world—a colonial effect. Part of my sense of being an outsider had to do with personal self-esteem. I came from a family that was dysfunctional because of alcoholism in a community that if a family member was an alcohol abuser, he had a certain reputation, and his family, therefore, including his children, were burdened by this. So I felt inferior. Even though nobody knew that openly, I felt that. I knew that my dad, even though he was a railroad worker, had a certain identity in our home, and I felt badly about that as a family member. I think I felt I had to do well, and that's one of the reasons I studied a lot. I made fairly good grades I would say, maybe not the best, but fairly good grades, and they were consistent, like As and Bs. I remained an honor roll student. Education, to me, was needed. One of the ways in which one got ahead, I got into my head at that time, was to become educated. My feelings changed somewhat as I grew older. What did education really mean? Later on, you became much more of a conformist, you became much more part of the status quo and the establishment. And some of that status quo and establishment values just were not that good because often times they meant anti-Native ways and resulted in a loss of certain tribal values and the Native American views we had of ourselves.

Return Home

I finished my eighth grade at Albuquerque Indian School, and then the ninth year came along. I came back reluctantly [to AIS] because I didn't want to go to Indian school. I was the oldest of my immediate family, although I have three older sisters. One of them is deceased; two older sisters remain, but their father passed away. I was the result of my mother remarrying. She met and married my father, and they became another family. I was in the middle, but I was the oldest male of the immediate family.

So this came into play when I was away from home because since my family was dysfunctional—a lot of it had to do with my father's alcohol abuse—that left me to be the caretaker as the oldest male. The way that it worked out in our family was that my mother depended on me a lot. Of course, I was still a child; I was beginning to be a teenager. My father, when he worked for the railroad, was often away in Arizona, California, Texas, and Colorado. He was a laborer and semi-skilled worker, so he would be away for periods at a time, weeks, maybe even months. Most of the time it had to do with work; other times it had to do with being away because he was just away. He may have been involved in alcohol abuse. I learned to be available as an older sibling to help care for my brothers and sister, two younger brothers and two younger sisters. My youngest sister is actually my niece who was adopted by my parents because my older sister was unable to take care of her when she was an infant. She grew up as my younger sister.

I wanted to be back home for the sake of my family. I felt this a lot at Saint Catherine's and at Albuquerque Indian School. In that sense, I had a longing to be helpful and responsible to my family. When I think about people who were sent away to school back in the early years of Indian school, whether it was to Carlisle, or Haskell, I am sure [it was difficult] to be away from your home and community because Native people are so close knit that you were part of a community, part of your tribe, part of your family and your clan. To be away meant that you are away from that close knit group. And the way that we are raised within a cultural philosophy is that you are necessary to the integrity, to the wholeness of your family, to your clan, and to your people. So that as a result, if you were in Carlisle, Pennsylvania, or in Lawrence, Kansas, at Haskell, then you were not being part of that group anymore. You felt, what? Obviously at a loss, and confused, rootless. I'm sure this had been part of the whole decimation and loss of Native American and Indigenous integrity.

Public School

All that went into what I was feeling at the time. My ninth grade year came around, and it was time to board the bus at home at McCartys Day School, which is how they brought us to [boarding] school with our suitcases and trunks. We would get on the bus and they would bring us to AIS to check in and be assigned to a dorm, boys and girls. A lot of Indian school students were Acoma. I felt okay because I was part of the Acoma group. Nonetheless, I wanted to go back home, so that by the time December of 1956 came around, I decided that I was going to go back home. Indian students at home were going to Grants High School, the nearest public high school. The Indian students from Acoma and Laguna were the tribal groups closest to the high school. Grants is about ten miles west of the reservation. The nearest communities were McCartys and Acomita on the Acoma reservation, so they could go by bus. You could go up to the highway, U.S. 66, to catch a bus that went just on the highway all the way down to Laguna.

It used to be that the bus only stopped at certain places on the U.S. 66 highway to pick up Acoma students who enrolled in Grants schools before I-40, and before JOM [Johnson O'Malley], which was federal legislation which provided congressional money to public school systems that enrolled Native American students beginning, say, 1953 or 1954. It didn't occur to me [until now] that this may be related to the termination era of the early 1950s when the federal status of some reservations was terminated. It may have been a way in which eventually [Indian] people would all be educated within a public school system, not in Indian school. Of course, I didn't think about it then. It just seemed to be part of what may have been taking place.

Some Laguna and Acoma students were already going to Grants High School. But generally, the tribes and the parents from Acoma and Laguna did not feel comfortable with their kids going to school at Grants High School because it's a public school where non-Indians went. In the 1950s, there was a lot of discrimination, a lot of racism. The cultural and social contact was antagonistic, was conflictive, and was a barrier to good relations between peoples. In Grants at that time, the largest group of students were the Hispanics from San Rafael, San Mateo, Grants itself, Cubero, and San Fidel. The Hispanics probably were in the majority until the 1950s, when the uranium mining and processing era began in 1951 and '52 when the uranium boom brought in a lot of white people, Mericano hanoh, white American people. They became the majority.

By the time I enrolled at Grants High School in my second semester as a freshman in high school, the majority of the students were white. I graduated in 1960. By that time [1957], the JOM legislation had kicked in, and we knew Grants High School had been built using some of that money. Buses were provided to go onto the reservation, both Acoma and Laguna reservations directly. They used to only go on Route 66 and that was it. The kids had to walk up to the highway to get on a bus, but this time they brought buses into the reservations.

As for my writing and awareness, my interest in literature, it wasn't necessarily there in any overt or definable sense. But I was, as I said earlier, in my seventh and eighth grade years, very curious about certain things. I became aware of the intertribal and inter-cultural dynamics. I began to wonder about the relationships between white people, Hispanic people, and African American people.

Parental Influence

I loved to read. I would say my love of learning and evolving knowledge had to do with reading and literature. Also, my parents were fairly schooled or learned, but within an Indigenous or Native American sense of being. They weren't college-trained, that's for sure. My mother went to Saint Catherine's. She graduated in 1921. She finished the eighth grade, which was the highest Native people could go at that time. She was a good student from what I hear, but she didn't go beyond that. She learned to read, and she learned whatever they had to offer at Saint Catherine's. My dad had a different kind of education. He did go to Saint Catherine's several times. In fact, he was in the third grade three times. He used to run away from school. And then later on, I wasn't ever clear whether he really went to Albuquerque Indian School, or if that was part of his story about himself. And then he said [he attended] Grants High School.

My father was a very lively person, and he liked to tell stories. Sometimes his stories were stretched. He was fluent in Spanish and English, and of course, as an Acoma person, Keres was his native language, but he also spoke some Zuni. I would even say that my spark, or my interest in wanting to know things, came though his influence. He was curious about things. He knew about things and he would tell you what they were if you asked. Perhaps he'd add to the information so that it sounded plausible and sounded like he did know what they were.

He was also a traditional elder because of his clan membership. He was a Kuutsi hanoh, the Antelope People, who are by tradition the people who are in charge of the religious teachings and religious occasions. They were the leaders of the traditions of the katsinas. When he became older, he became much more active, much more central to the religious function of the tribe as a whole. They are also the clan that appoint and authorize the leadership of the Pueblo, the governor, the lieutenant governor, and so forth. Their clan elders along with those from the kiva fathers, the

kiva leadership, the medicine people, and that learning, intellectual echelon, select the tribal leadership. Acoma doesn't vote. It's not run by the
democratic system or elected offices. It's by traditional appointment.

My father was an interesting person. He was very vigorous. If I have
any kind of competitive spirit—I'm not competitive, but he insisted that
we had to be certain of who we are. It was important that you value yourself, that you have knowledge of who you are, and what you did, and how
you came to be so that when my awareness of differences between me and
others came, that kicked in. And it was important to say that I was Acoma
and that I am Native American. And he also demonstrated that if you have
a certain skill, that you make use of that skill in a good way. And that you
show it, not to show off, but to show that you could do something. I think
that my knowledge-gaining faculties follow that sort of guidance that he
and others like him provided, not simply to gain status or prestige or recognition, but that it was how you conducted yourself as a person.

And along with this, something that both my father and mother, and
other elders of the Acoma people counseled and advised about, was that
you were to help. You were always to help. Ah-yaamaatse is a principle,
to be helpful. When someone needed help, whoever they were, you didn't
make any cultural or race distinctions at all. You helped. You offered
to help. And it was your people as a whole—that was also a given—that
you were most directly involved with, your own family, your clan, your
community, your culture because your wholeness depended upon it.
Your sense of self, and your identity and how you felt about yourself, that
depended on you. You are a part of this wholeness and it's not going to
be whole unless you do your part. And it probably related to what I was
saying earlier, being away from home you felt "marginalized," and the way
to counter or resist the marginalization was to live your life in a "helpful" or "helping" way; by helping your family and community you were
not marginalized but part of the people, part of land, culture, and community vitally, even if the fact was your community was dysfunctional,
even if things were not so good at home and you knew this to be. It was
the idea of that wholeness.

I went to Grants High School because I wanted to be home. I wanted
to be part of this community, and wholeness. The Grants Municipal
School District was able to provide buses so we could go daily and come
back home at the end of the school day. That was much better than being
away at Indian school or being away long periods of time.

Racial Tensions and Realities

My writing came into play much more at that time, as far as a literary consciousness. I didn't really have a literary consciousness, so far as reading was concerned. I knew that stories were done. It seems kind of funny now. I seemed to be aware, but not entirely so, that there were writers, that there were occupations or careers as writers. Actually I didn't relate to it. Maybe I could not relate directly to it because Native Americans did not do those sorts of things because they were different. It was only the Shah-muutsi-hanoh Merican, the white American people, that had certain professions. And those professions were writers, thinkers, and leaders, governors and presidents, but Native Americans were not [any of these]. And this was part of the class and cultural consciousness that was taking place in me over the years.

I did not articulate it or know how to articulate it, not becoming even overtly or more expressively conscious of this until I went to Grants High School. This was in the mid-1950s, and there was much more of a mix, whites, Hispanics, and Indians, along with the differences and the conflicts and the dynamics that I was already aware of, having gone to school in the years previous at Saint Catherine's and Albuquerque Indian School, so that the intercultural dynamics became much more definitive: I was an "Indian," and the white kids and Hispanic kids made sure I knew that, made sure *we* knew that. The terms "Native American" and "Indigenous" were not in existence at the time. "Native American" did not come about until the 1970s. "Indigenous" is still not a common term. I knew that later on in college when I began to think about world populations and that there were populations who were original or who were native in the Indigenous sense. They were from there, and they were of that terrain or geography.

I became aware generally, and maybe even, specifically, because the 1950s was also the beginning of the Third World liberation struggle in the United States. That had a lot to do with the African American civil rights struggle, the Black Liberation movement in the U.S., beginning in the mid-50s when students were being integrated into schools in the South, especially when the Freedom Rides began to take place in the late 1950s. I was peripherally aware of that because it was in the news, and even though we didn't have television, we had newspapers.

My parents, because they were multi-lingual, especially in English, read to us even to some degree before I went to school. I remember several books from early childhood. I don't know why I remember them. One was [by] Pearl Buck, an American writer who lived in China, and wrote novels about that. And then I remember *Shangri-La*, that James Hilton book. They read to us out of that. And I remember *Robinson Crusoe*, not reading it, but hearing it. Then there was a book on Africa that I associate mostly with my dad. I remember Stanley Livingston. Maybe it was a biography, some kind of historical explorer book, Stanley Livingston in the deepest darkest part of Africa. So I was aware of the power of literature in some ways—written ways—although I didn't really read them. I looked them over later on when I was in college to see what they were.

The early inspiration for literature came from my parents. Also, of course, I grew up at the same time, especially in my earlier years, with the traditional oral literature that is in the Acoma language. A lot of it is religious knowledge: a lot of it is ritual meditations. The religious stories are the heart of Native traditions, knowledge, and cultural beliefs. I would not say that I was literate in the sense of reading these things, but I knew about them, how they were given to us as members of Acu, that we have this knowledge because we are people who must have and hold this knowledge, in order to be who we are, that it was necessary to have this knowledge in order to have a sense of ourselves as persons who are members of this community. The only way you are truly a member is if you took on the responsibilities that were part of being linked very critically and crucially. If you were not linked tightly to it, then you were out here on the edge somewhere, somehow. The way to belong was double-edged, a reciprocal tie that you had. Only in very, very absolute ways would it ever be broken. There was just no way that you could just break away from it. You were responsible, and it was responsible to you.

Being Indian

I became aware of my identity in high school. And it seemed to evolve, if I can recall, in that continuing sense of how I saw myself and began to see myself as Native American. The common term was "Indian," the only term that I knew, that we knew, to say that you're Indian, and that was your identity. And oddly, I began to be aware of a potential, negative association to the term "Indian" in this time because I began to feel, or become aware of, the discrimination and conflict between whites and blacks.

By the time I was in the tenth grade, I was aware that there were white students who didn't like black people. There were very few, maybe just a handful of African American students in Grants. And sometimes it seemed that they didn't stay, that they left to go someplace. Maybe their parents were miners. Later on when I went to work in the uranium mining, I didn't see any African Americans. There were some Hispanics, a few Indians, mostly whites. A lot of the white workers came from Southern backgrounds, and many of those miners were, I would say, heavily racist.

By the time I was fifteen or sixteen, I became aware of the racial prejudices, biases, and conflicts that were very open. I became aware of my identity as an Indian almost defensively. I think my father's influence also kicked in because, as I said, I am not really competitive. But it became important to me to be competitive because if you were good at something, then you became capable at showing what you were good at. And even if you were Indian, or if you were black, Hispanic, or even if you were a minority, then that goodness became an asset. I mean that kind of, not goodness in behavior, but if you were a good athlete, if you were a good student, that became the agent that you could demonstrate and show your qualities. My father could speak Spanish, and so he would show he was just as smart as Euroamericans. Or if he demonstrated his English fluency, then he was just as good as the person who spoke English. Or because he was multi-lingual in Acoma, English, and Spanish, that's even better. He showed his facility with language. I had become aware that making good grades was part of this, that if I felt belittled because of racist treatment by the so-called upper echelon society, whether or not they were smarter then me, I could show that I could make As, that I could be a student as good as they, simply because of how I carried myself.

I remember the tribe used to send the tribal officials up to Grants to the public school to have the officials, the governor, the lieutenant-governor, and his staff, gather the Acoma students in assembly, maybe in the dining room for an hour or so, and the leaders of the people would speak to the students in the native language to encourage us. In retrospect, I thought that was wonderful. They would repeat over and over again, "in order to help your people, their life, their quality, their home, their land, their culture. Ehmh-eh-hehyaa srai-stumeshstah. And that's why you are here."

That was a real affirmation act that they were doing. They don't do that these days as far as I know. I was conscious, defensively so, maybe even embarrassed because that definitely showed to the white students, to the Spanish-American students, that you were Indian, that you were different from them. Their parents, their community leaders, being white or Spanish, did not come and gather them into an assembly, but our people did. It also showed in a good way, in retrospect, I'd say, a real sense of pride in themselves, which is what they were showing to us.

Proving Ground

Anyway, in one of those meetings, I remember standing up to speak, one of the few occasions when I expressed myself. I was starting to be more extroverted, to show, perhaps, my ability as a student. And I was beginning to be a student leader—which I eventually did more and more as an athlete and scholar at Grants High School—saying that Indian students should not always stand back and be silent, that we had things to say, that we were smart, that we could be just as smart as anybody in the school, that we should be proud to be who we are.

At that time, I was sixteen, probably a sophomore. Some of the students probably thought that I was trying to brownnose, that sort of thing, which wasn't the case at all. I used to get tired of the Indian students being left out of things. One of the ways not to be left out is to insist on participating. I would always see the Indian students being the last to be chosen for anything, being the last to be called upon or being left out altogether. And I began to feel these things, and that's what I was addressing. Grants High School became a kind of proving ground at a young age for me. Then I began to make a connection between writing and literature, and that there were people who wrote. I became interested in literature as acts of human expressions, as expressions that spoke about what was important to you, and how you formed yourself in your home, and how that formation became significant to how you asserted yourself as Indian. Maybe this did not become more common as expression until later after I left high school. But in retrospect, at the time, it seems I was becoming aware of expression: How I said things became part of the way I would make my way in the world, and especially because of racism, you had to make your own path or journey through this maze. In this way, I became very aware of the largeness of society. It wasn't just the Acoma world, nor was it just Grants and Acoma. But there was a big world out there, and somehow you were part of this.

I didn't know, of course, the details of this big world, but I knew there was a world out there, and you are taking part of the formation or the engineering of this road, this journey. I began to articulate what later on I called "journey," or related to it more as theme. But that would be several years before that came about. I knew the concept of hih-yaa-nih, the road from here to the center, the road of life that you were born to, and when you were given a name, then you went forth on that road as a child. And you led yourself or other people followed, but it was a journey. You were on this path, always moving forward. That became a part of how I began to see what was in store for dealing with, or not dealing with, the world, whether it had to do with the local relationships between you and the non-Indian world, or you and other people personally, you and your family members.

And writing formed part of the way that road was being laid out for me. I would say that poetry was informed a lot by the American literature I came in contact with in school, not so much at Saint Catherine's or Albuquerque Indian School, but at Grants. For some reason, I know this literature more, poets like Robert Frost, Carl Sandburg, and then American fiction, like Ernest Hemingway, Sherwood Anderson, and John Steinbeck. I began to relate to plot, to characters, especially people who struggled, who came from the land, people who overcame big odds, poverty, racism. Later on, I read James Wright, Langston Hughes, and James Baldwin when I was in college. I was pretty much set in college on being a writer. I liked to think, I liked to talk, and I liked to debate. I liked to discuss.

Knowledge Versus Education

I graduated in 1960 out of Grants High School. I didn't have any real plans for college except that I felt that it was important for some kind of knowledge process or education. Education was a term that was used a lot by society in general, but also by Indigenous peoples, the Pueblos. Education also seemed to me a catchword to bring up the topic to young people and youth in general. For example, the elders would say, you must get educated in order to help your people to cope economically and healthwise, [with] resources, and so forth.

I never understood education as an Indigenous concept because I also thought education came more from the Bureau of Indian Affairs and the government. Education was what you got when you went to Indian school. Education was what you got if you were fortunate enough to get a grant to go on to college. Education was so you could get some kind of training so you could get a job. Education was also used to have Native people understand what you had to have in your life in order to become a real American, that is an awareness of, or [being] sophisticated as, an American.

I rejected and resented that. I felt instinctively that "education" was the wrong term. Yes, we needed to progress in terms of the knowledge that was natural to human social life, knowledge from when you passed from childhood to adolescence to adulthood, knowledge that insured that you were being responsible. That was the way in the Acoma culture, the Native culture, that one became knowledgeable because he was aware of his role in life. This was something very culturally traditional. It didn't mean necessarily that you got educated to go to college or that you graduated from high school. You know, it didn't mean that you would learn English well, or learn to be a mathematician, and so forth, and be an expert in American society. Knowledge, I felt, was the goal for human culture, life.

I had a contention internally about education. Also, remember this was the era of relocation in the '60s. Relocation was the federal policy to remove Native people from their homelands into urban areas so that "urban Indians" became a term used a lot. It became almost a pop-culture term.

Anyway, it seems "education" became synonymous with a job, on-the-job training. They would send people to Los Angeles or Dallas or Denver or the San Francisco Bay area. They would get some training, and that was education. Education seemed to be a move towards assimilation and acculturation more than anything else. But knowledge was something else. I didn't like simply becoming an American by gaining employable skills.

There was a man at home, Clyde Pasquale, Christine Pasquale's dad. He was kind of an advisor informally to the younger people at home, and he was also interested in helping young people with whatever they wanted to do. I know that he was anti-relocation. He said, "They just want Indian people to get off the reservations and go into the cities. Here at home, we have power if we learn to use that right. But in the cities, you just are part of the crowd."

He was a big influence in several of our lives. He wanted us to go to college, which eventually I did. I didn't have any ambitions to go to college although I wanted to be a chemist. Chemistry in high school interested me. If there was any kind of goal I had, it was to be a chemist, which was what my major was when I did go to Fort Lewis College in 1961.

Fort Lewis College

But I did want to get more knowledge in some ways. I did go to college in 1961 after working for about a year in the uranium mines, not in the mines itself, but in the industry. I worked at Ambrosia Lake at the Kerr-McGee processing plant. I was also kind of following other kids at Grants High School (mainly white kids, a few who were Hispanic), who were going to college. I knew I had made good grades in high school. I was fairly active. I was co-captain of the football team. I think I was student council vice-president. I wasn't one of the shy ones necessarily. However, I wasn't really vocal.

At college, I always felt sort of constricted in some ways even though there was a large number of Indian students at Fort Lewis in Durango, and we hung out together. It was sort of a constriction in that if you were Indian, you were supposed to belong to a certain group, which I did more or less, almost by default. But it was also important to expand beyond that in order to gain knowledge, to become part of a general community, which was my tendency. Not that I moved away from the Native group, but it was more an extension or expansion beyond that. And I didn't feel that I wanted to be restricted or constricted just because I was a Native American. I began to write seriously in college partly for that reason, to go beyond what it was that I had grown up with as a Native person, as an Acoma person.

I remember writing stories that—I think it's kind of funny [laughs]— had almost no ethnicity to them. It's true that as Native people we have a cultural identity that is unique as Native American—that term wasn't used a lot. It was "Indian"—and we did have that cultural identity, but it was also important to us that we were like other people in whatever we did. I wanted to be a chemist, and if other Native people wanted to be lawyers or doctors or whatever, they certainly should be. So my stories, if not anonymous, didn't have their identity on their sleeves.

That was a stage that I think lasted a year. I saw myself as a prose writer at that point. I was nineteen going towards twenty. I thought it was important to express myself simply as a growing human being. I didn't necessarily write about Indian issues at that point, although I was very, very aware. Of course, that was my identity, and I wasn't going to back away or deny that.

Eventually, I quit college. I had the beginnings of a problem with alcohol at that time, and I got thrown out, more or less. I was not thrown out completely, but I was allowed to be enrolled with conditions: I was not allowed to go off campus because if I went off campus, I might get in trouble or something. So I quit college.

I had a grant scholarship from the BIA. I remember going down to the Albuquerque agency. At that time, they sent you a check. I was received with somewhat of a gasp because there's this Indian kid, obviously bright, who was turning in his check because he didn't want to go to school anymore. I remember Mr. Tiger, and a woman, a real BIA type. I thought I would never forget her name. She was the classic white woman, always encouraging, very paternalistic, Miss Bradley, Miss Smith, or something like that. Anyway, she didn't want me to quit, but I was insistent, no, I wasn't going to go to college, and I told them my reasons.

Then she had me write an essay. I always wished that I had that essay. We had an hour, and she said, "Write it down on paper the reasons why. Write it out and we'll consider it." So I did. Mr. Tiger read it through, and he said, "Yeah, I understand." And so they took the check back, and then I said goodbye to college. I had three semesters at Fort Lewis College.

The Movements of the Sixties

So I went into the Army, which was a stupid thing to do. This was in 1963. The rest of the 1960s gave me a perspective that included what I had learned and what I was writing about and ruminating and musing about as a teenager. It became a way for me to be introduced into Third World liberation because that power had come into being. The Civil Rights struggle led by Dr. Martin Luther King, Jr., Ralph Abernathy and others, the Freedom Rides, and the Black Power movement, the Black Panthers in Oakland, Chicago, and L.A. caught the imagination of people like myself. I admit I was impressionable. I thought the civil rights issues of poverty, and the oppression of poverty, the lack of jobs, and discrimination were very much like we were undergoing at home as Native people.

And then the anti-war movement began because of what the United States was doing in southeast Asia which related to the colonization of Native people although it wasn't really apparent at the beginning. What the United States was doing in Vietnam was an invasion, and so that related to the invasion of Indian lands. Of course, there's a whole history of that going way back to 1541 and Coronado, not the Americans but the Spanish, and then later, Mexico's eventual independence from Spain and our being then colonized by Mexico. The Americans easily stepped in by 1851 with the Guadalupe Hidalgo treaty and became the caretakers, so-called, but it was simply colonialism.

Although the idea of colonialism didn't really become apparent to me at that time in the 1960s that this was taking place, there was the seed of it already from what I had seen and what I had heard from my elders, even my dad, Mr. Pasquale, and other people, and how we dealt with the Bureau of Indian Affairs and the federal government. We had endured the racism and the discrimination at home and in the nearby towns, Albuquerque, Grants, Gallup, and so forth, and the Indians had suffered dysfunctions due to the social restrictions we endured as Native people. That became a part of my writing at that point in the mid-60s.

The Freedom Rides were participated in by the younger Native people, the National Indian Youth Council. I first became aware of them in 1961 in Gallup. I was not in college yet. I had gone to Gallup Indian Ceremonial, and there was a small meeting in one of the rooms in a hall at the Gallup Ceremonial grounds. I was just a curious kid. There were college-aged Indian youth there, as well as Herb Blatchford, who was Navajo, Clyde Warrior was Ponca, and Shirley Witt was Mohawk, and Mel Tom was Paiute, I think, and maybe Jerry Brown, who later on became an acquaintance and friend. I think Clyde had participated in the Freedom Rides, which were down into the South. It wasn't Black Power yet. The Black Power became a part of what I call the liberation movement. It was based on the oppression that people of color, that black people, brown people, red people [had experienced].

The Red Power movement probably began in that time of Indian activism, radical philosophy, radical goals. Part of it, for me, was a romantization of Native American culture: it was easy enough to look at long hair and braids and beads and so forth, and also easy enough because Hollywood and the literature always talked about the brave, courageous Indian warrior, and all you had to do was show the traits of that. The other side of that was the real way in which Native Americans were just pushed aside, and the Americans and the white people were superior in power.

Writing Out of Life Experience

My writing began to drift towards a portrayal of Native people that was, I would say, genuine and authentic. A lot of it had to do with the kind of life that I experienced at home. We were a dysfunctional family. My father was an alcoholic, and there was a lot of alcoholism and alcohol abuse in McCartys and Acomita, the two main villages of Acoma. And people were in trouble with their families, general family/community/social dysfunction linked to alcohol abuse. I began in the late '60s to include such things in my writing. I have to admit that it was a form of therapy. I was writing these down, writing about the harsh realities, because they actually happened within my own life experience. I tend to be a realist. I try not to gloss over or deny that these things take place, but that there's real struggle. I think you have to look at the reality and the facts in order to understand the whole of your life.

By the late 1960s I began to write. I was out of the Army. I served 1963 to 1966, so I got discharged. I did have plans to go back to college by that point. I had written while I was in the Army. I even worked for an Army newspaper at one point. I was mostly a clerk, a personnel clerk, stationed in Puerto Rico. I was fortunate not to be a part of what was taking place in Vietnam. My younger brothers, Petuuche and Earl, also were in the military. That was the way the Native youth were regarded. They were expendable. So you found a lot of guys and women in the military whether it was the Marines, or Army, or Air Force, or Navy because the United States was open to recruiting Indians. And the draft came in, so a lot of people were drafted during that time. And the military was an option. But it was an option because of the social-economic conditions. Sometimes there were no other jobs, no other things you could get into because of discrimination, and so the military welcomes you, where you got to be treated equally sort of, but not genuinely or authentically.

University of New Mexico

I had gone back to school at the University of New Mexico, this time not as a chemist, but as an English major. My goal was to be a teacher. I was in the College of Education. But I still had problems with education mainly [being] geared toward assimilation and acculturation. By that time, it had become a strong enough idea in my mind, so I rejected it more or less. I wasn't enthusiastic about college as such. I had begun to see the University of New Mexico [was] bound by its colonial legacy, which, unfortunately, still persists, that image and that result. It's changed some, but not a whole lot.

I went to the University of New Mexico from 1966 to 1968, but I was there as a writer this time. There was no Indian studies program at that time. Probably if there was Indian studies, which didn't start until 1971, I would have become an Indian studies major. I had begun to publish in stu dent magazines. I was looking then for Indian or Native American creative expression. I became aware of Scott Momaday, Charles Eastman, D'Arcy McNickle, and others. But I was looking also for contemporary writers, and that's why Scott Momaday was one of the first names I had. And then there was James Welch. Leslie Silko was just a kid at that time, seventeen or eighteen. She was just out of high school, so she only had ambitions, aspirations at that time. She was introduced to me through my niece with whom she was friends. They worked together at the trading post store at the pueblo and that's how Christina, my niece—that's my oldest sister's daughter—introduced Leslie and me. I don't know whether I was actually a mentor [to Leslie.] It was more like an influence. Because she knew I was a writer, whatever image that she had of me in her mind impressed Leslie so she came to me. We influenced each other, I think. It was important to me to find other Native writers at that point. James Welch, Scott Momaday, and Leslie Silko. Those were the contemporaries for me, the Indian writing world. And I think those were good models to have.

I did not get a degree. I have never gotten a degree. It's embarrassing because some people claim that I have a degree from the University of Iowa. I don't, and I would never say that. But people, some writers, journalists, authors, take the liberty and assume that you aren't anybody unless you have a degree. I don't have any degrees, but people say that I have an MFA from the University of Iowa. I see this in very reputable anthologies and very reputable bibliographies. I publicly disclaim it. I don't.[4]

Iowa International Writing Program

I went to the University of New Mexico, and I was offered a fellowship to the University of Iowa International Writing Program, which is where that MFA fiction comes from. I was becoming known as a writer at least locally, regionally in New Mexico, so I was recommended by the [UNM creative] writing people, Gene Frumkin, Gus Blaisdell, and others, to be given a fellowship to the University of Iowa. It was an international writing program representing writers from other countries, like Europe, Africa, South America, and the Middle East. When I got there, I found that the participants were very accomplished writers and filmmakers and poets. Some of them were professional for years, and they were highly published. And here I am as an Indian nobody, comparatively. There were two Americans, me and a young black writer poet from L.A. who came out of the Budd Schulberrg Watts Writing Workshop in Los Angeles. I always remember Emery Evans, Jr. He was a tall, black kid—beautiful, beautiful young man with his magnificent laugh. He was very talented, but I don't know whatever happened to him.

I spent one year there. I was broke during those times. I would have gone back to school at UNM, except my wife was pregnant. That's Raho's mother, Agnes Good Luck. She's Navajo. She hung with me during those years. We had once upon a time gone to be hippies in San Francisco. We hitchhiked to Golden Gate Park because this is where the happenings and love-ins [occurred] in 1966 or 1967, or something like that. But by 1968, we were really, really broke. The only money I had was the G.I. Bill, which had been reinstituted during the Vietnam War. So I was receiving like maybe $75 a month to go to school, and then I worked work-study in the history department at UNM. That was about all the money I had. The [Iowa] fellowship offered real money. It was a monthly stipend, maybe $350 a month. I mean $350 a month was three times, four times, what I was getting from the G.I. Bill, $75 a month, plus my work-study time. And so I said, "We're going." Agnes was pregnant, and Raho was about to be born, so I went ahead by myself for two months to Iowa and enrolled in that international writing program. They stayed [behind] until Raho was born.

We had this little car. We called it "the Green Turtle." It was a green 1960 International that we had bought for $150. I was so broke that I remember going down to the BIA and asking Mr. McGurl [for assistance]. He worked with the Southern Pueblos Agency. Maybe he was in education with Ms. Bradley or whatever her name was. He had something to do with the relocation program because I remember making the argument. I said, "You have this BIA relocation program, and you provide travel, transportation to people who take part in the program, who move away from the reservations and go to California or Denver or Texas or wherever. Here I get a scholarship or fellowship, and it seems like I would be able to qualify for transportation assistance to get to where I am going to work [Iowa for the writing fellowship]. Look, on my own initiative, I'm going out. This is not relocation. On my own initiative as a young writer and wanting to develop my writing, I have this opportunity. Is there any way I can get a bus ticket to go to Iowa City? You know, it would be about, I don't know what, sixty dollars, maybe."

But I didn't qualify because I was not taking part in the BIA program to get relocated. They couldn't do it officially. They just didn't do it officially. There just was no way. This was an outstanding example of a young person, an Indian person, on his own who was getting a chance, an opportunity. It was not on-the-job training in the same way that the BIA's relocation program was, or employment assistance, or whatever it was called officially. He was sympathetic, but he said, "No. There just doesn't seem to be any way."

I didn't know what to do. I was ready to hitchhike out to Iowa. This was early September or mid-August or something, and school was going to start. I was going to borrow money, and then I would get a bus ticket. It was almost $60 to go one way. One day—and this is almost something from the katsina—in the morning, there was an envelope hanging from the door of our apartment in Albuquerque with $60 in cash with a little note that said, "Good luck, Robert McGurl." It was enough for a bus ticket to go to Iowa City. He understood. He couldn't do anything bureaucratically according to the rules of the BIA and its relocation program, so on his own, he put that $60 there. While I criticize the Bureau of Indian Affairs officially as an agent of colonialism, in this case he acted on his own, personally and very humanly. I always appreciated that.

Evolution of a Writer

So I went there for a year. It was a two-year program. Eventually $350 per month wasn't enough because Brian, my stepson, Agnes's older son, was starting school. As a young person with a limited income, it was just hard, so I came back to New Mexico. Agnes hated being in Iowa as a young mother. It was cold in the winter time. It wasn't like New Mexico. It was freezing. So we all came back. They came back first. Then I came back to New Mexico.

I started teaching at the University of New Mexico as a counselor/part-time instructor. I was out of the University of Iowa with some education but no degree. I could have gone back to Iowa to finish off the two years, but I didn't. Instead, I took a job. I actually had a fellowship on top of that to Columbia. I sometimes regret that I didn't take it. But I don't know how we as a family, Agnes and the two boys, could have functioned in New York City at Columbia University if we had gone. It would have been a struggle and a strain. So I went to work, instead. I could have either gone back to Iowa 'cause I still had that fellowship, or else, I could have gone to Columbia. But I didn't do that. I went to work for Rough Rock [Demonstration School] [RRDS] and became the public relations director out there, publishing a newspaper, *Rough Rock News*. I thought the work they were doing at Rough Rock, running a demonstration school with local control of Native education on the Navajo Nation, was important. The point of RRDS was local control by the local Navajo community, the Indigenous community; it was their community and they were in control of it, why not their learning system as well? We at RRDS were trying to make it a national program.

This all was part of my own evolution as a writer, as someone who was finding his own voice personally. But I always thought it was just not my voice alone, individually, or only exclusively me, because I always felt the community, the whole of the community, was what was important. Community education meant the whole of community: Learning by the community and for the community, and the community teaching the world. Then I began to expand beyond just the Acoma world or the Pueblo world, although that was always the base, and it still is the base as I regard myself as a voice. Anyway, I began to seriously write more poetry. By this time I wasn't writing a whole lot of prose except in my journals. Eventually other stories became published.

I only worked at Rough Rock for one year, and then I received a grant from the National Endowment for the Arts. By that time, the National Endowment for the Arts had started. I think Leslie got the same kind of grant. It was a Discovery Award. There were more people beginning to write, but it was still [primarily] myself, James Welch, Scott Momaday, and Leslie. And then other people began to come into the picture.

The 1970s Activism

The 1970s was a reassertion of the Native American voice. Some people have dubbed the '60s and '70s as a renaissance. It may have been to some degree. But it was almost like a first-time awareness that we were expressing of ourselves. It wasn't militant or radical or red power, but it had those features. It had those adjectives that could be ascribed to it because it was an insistence on who we were. N. Scott Momaday's *House Made of Dawn* had gained a lot of publicity when Scott was awarded the Pulitzer Prize in 1969. And Vine Deloria had come onto the scene, not as a literary person, but as an essayist and important commentator with his book, *Custer Died for Your Sins.* Native American voices began to coalesce into, I would say, an organized, or at least a persistent, identifiable challenge to the United States, and it was real—it was an expression of cultural sovereignty. Actually, it was political sovereignty if you associated a political message to it.

Canada became part of the picture. Harold Cardinal's *The Unjust Society* had come out in Canada in 1970. And Buffy Saint Marie, who had been adopted away from her Cree family and ended up living in the United States, became a strong voice. I first met her in 1970 at the first Convocation of Indian Scholars at Princeton University, which was organized by Alfonso Ortiz from San Juan Pueblo, who was a young professor at Princeton University, and Jeannette Henry, who put out that newspaper [*Wassaja*] with her husband Rupert Costo, who was Cahuilla from southern California. That was a good convocation, where Scott Momaday delivered the "Man Made of Words."

I was there that day. I was still in my self-destructive mode. I had come from Minneapolis. There was a poets-in-the-schools program there. I remember coming to this conference in Princeton, New Jersey, where people were dressed in suits, and I was there in my dirty Levi jacket, my scuffed boots, and my long hair down to my waist. I tell you, it was a full-blown image. The 1970s were very important. We Indigenous Native American people had been talking about oppression. The way in which to express this fact of loss of land and culture and community was to talk about it, was to say it in realistic terms, not in that romantic, lo-the-poor-Indian way. A lot of that, of course, was taking place. It's easy enough to get sympathy for that lo-the-poor-Indian sentiment, but it's used simply as pitying. You're encouraging that self-pitying mode that people can use to get what they can. Or "You don't understand us." Though it's true, people don't understand Native American communities, culture, or issues that are brought up.

Of course, the history is that the people have been in resistance for a long, long time, [against] 500-plus years of European, American colonization, European and American imperialism. We were becoming a part of that. We were, of course, victims. The demographer, Henry F. Dobyns, says that before Columbus, there was an estimated population from 90 to 112 million people in North, Central and South America. It wasn't an empty continent. Some historians and cultural anthropologists say it was relatively empty; therefore, it was easy enough to acquire, for Europe to get its hands on it, with first the Spanish, and later on with others, the French and the British.

It wasn't empty. You look at the land and the evidence, the pre-Pueblo people who are so-called cliff dwellers. It's an extensive area. It was a very extensive society, and [there was also] the Mississippi, the Ohio River Valley, and then also in Mexico with the Mayans and the Aztecs and others, and through Central America with people who were known as the Incas, although there's many other people as well. It was an extensive civilization, extensive population.

Native American Literary Renaissance

This became a part of our consciousness in the 1970s. It became a part of our assertion and affirmation that it wasn't just simply an Indian Pride thing, at least for me, when you talk about the realities of that loss, culture, community, and land. We as a whole began to be joined in this by people who were concerned about the ecology, the environmentalists. They began to look towards Native people. And then, of course, there were books that came out like *The Teachings of Don Juan* by Carlos Castaneda, who became exploitative of Indian culture. That was just one of them, and then the movies continued in their own way.

The 1970s was a genuine time of self-assertion and affirmation. I began to teach again in 1974 after Rough Rock (which was in the late 1960s). By 1970, I joined the National Indian Youth Council (NIYC). At that time, I moved to Albuquerque. NIYC was a militant organization. They were concerned about water rights, land rights, civil rights, legal rights. During the time I was there, I was the editor of the *ABC, Americans Before Columbus*, which was an organizing tool, [providing] information as well. It was a way in which to get people interested in Native Americans and Native concerns and issues. We were involved with the closing of Indian schools, Intermountain Indian School, Chilocco Indian School, and others, because of the way that they treated Native American students and the same accul-turation, assimilation goals that the teachers, the administration, the Department of Interior, the Bureau of Indian Affairs had used.

Emerging Writers

I think the 1970s was a writing period for many of us. I published my first book in 1971, a chapbook called *The Naked in the Wind*, which was about thirty pages long, published by this friend who was at Pembroke State University as a teacher. I became seen as part of the national poetry crowd. I became friends with Gary Snyder, [Allen] Ginsberg, and others. I was called a rare bird, even though there were others. Those of us who became identified as writers of Native American heritage and identity, such as Scott Momaday, and James Welch—Leslie wasn't well known until she published her first book, *Ceremony*, in 1978—you could even say we were victimized as the "rare birds," known as the modern-day voices of Native Americans in the United States. I think it's really important to have writers today, poets and writers and filmmakers and others, to see that there has been a progression, and this is part of the progression.

In the 1970s, I published *Going for the Rain* and also *A Good Journey*. James Welch published *Winter in the Blood* at the time, which was good for him. Scott continued to write, and then other people came about: Paula Gunn Allen, Ray Young Bear, Duane Niatum, and the first antholo-gies of Native American literature.[5]

Land, Culture, Community

By the late 1980s or early '90s, for certain, I began to use "land, culture and community" as a refrain so that in the past fifteen years or so, it is a refrain that runs through the theme of my writings. By that time, I had begun to expand into essays that focus on land, culture, and community concerns of the Indigenous peoples. Our struggles as Native people, as Indigenous peoples of the Americas, always goes beyond us. It always goes beyond to other Native peoples, other Indigenous peoples. It's a worldwide matter because other people have been colonized. Other people have been affected by invasion and occupation, by imperialism in general.

Our concerns are not just ours. They go beyond our local or regional attention so that we have a sense of what the old people would say, that we are not the only people who are oppressed. And they [the elders] even include, I think, white people, the Mericano hanoh, the American people in general. There's a system at work. Call it witchery—Leslie Marmon Silko's term in *Ceremony*—call it evil, call it confusion, call it capitalism, call it exploitation or dehumanization, or technological oppression. Oppression is oppression. Just because we are Indians and we have been colonized to a large degree doesn't mean that we're the only victims of colonization because there's a phenomenon of reverse colonization, where the people who are powerful and rich and wealthy and supposedly in power, are just as dependent upon this dynamic of exploitation, are just as dependent upon the mechanics and machinations of imperialism—in fact, maybe even more so than the people who are so-called victims.

To bring these out, to refrain it and repeat it time and time again brings about results. The old people would say to always care for the land where you live, the people that you come from, to always work for them, to help them because that's the only way that true health comes to you, and to overcome these conditions. So resistance is a part of that. Resistance is a phenomenon where you are in opposition to what is oppressing you, but it's the kind of opposition where you also have alternatives, what's beyond that oppression and beyond even the struggle itself so that there's always something that comes about as result of that creative resistance, like water rights in New Mexico.

I used to hear about water in the 1950s, where the Winters doctrine was applied or brought up about the Rio Grande, that waters that arise in Indigenous lands that Native people have primary and full rights to it. It was a matter that was very significant and important in the 1950s, and to some degree in the 1960s. In the 1970s, '80s, '90s, I've wondered whatever happened to it because Isleta was able to accomplish some results using that doctrine and using the water rights issues.[6]

But we still don't have any real power. Albuquerque does what it wants. New Mexico does what it wants. And the matter with the water is so important. If we have sovereignty and are recognized as a self-determining people, the tribes should have something to say about it, but nobody talks to us about it or things like that. In New Mexico, people still want to build statues and monuments to Oñate. How can anybody resolve anything if you continue to honor and idolize the oppressive?

Indigeneity

Presently in this twenty-first century, it's important that you go beyond self-assertion and identify with other Indigenous people, whether it's in Africa, or the circumpolar areas because we have a worldwide struggle. There is worldwide resistance that needs to be waged. And literature or philosophy—I always consider that literature is more a discourse in philosophy than anything—I think that we can no longer look at ourselves—when I say "we," I mean Indigenous peoples, Indian people—we can no longer see ourselves as isolated or exclusive communities. We are part of a larger *Hanoh*. We are the Hanoh, the people of this earth, responsible for the earth. I don't think this necessarily puts us above anybody, but we have to constantly remind ourselves that people have to speak for themselves in this age of globalism, where in a way the boundaries between nations due to the economic power and economic power dynamics sometimes almost don't make any difference whether it's Canada or the United States, or United States and Britain. It's all the same. Capitalism and business, in general, make those boundaries irrelevant.

Recently, I was in China. I was appalled. I was shocked. Sure, [people] have kind of a romanticized notion of ancient China. I didn't see ancient China much when I was there in August [2005]. It's become so Western. I don't know whether you could call it "Westernized." But Chinese economic-minded people and industrial society see capitalism as an opportunity that the people, the society, can make use of. I don't know. Maybe it is. I almost automatically disagree. This is why I'm not a supporter of gaming for Indian people because economic development can be simply acculturation and assimilation, like we used to hear "education" being used. Yes, we need economic development, but economic development can lead us down into the same path of capitalistic self-destruction because whatever the financial gain, the tradeoff is more harmful than good.

Discussion

Lucero: It has been so interesting listening to you and being able to make connections as you're talking. I can see, based on everything you said in the last interview and today, that there's this natural movement in your life toward becoming a writer. And even though that wasn't something that Native people did as a profession back then, yet you eventually made the move toward doing that. I have a couple of questions out of that. Everything in your life is so interconnected, your family, culture, education, politics, and community, all these things you mentioned. And that's coming out of the larger context of Pueblo people and what has happened to Pueblo people through colonization. Could you talk a little bit about that—your life experience, what has happened to Pueblo people throughout history, how your writing fits into that larger context.

Ortiz: Okay. I don't know—was it inevitable that I became a writer? It was part of my orientation pretty early on. How I understood the Indigenous philosophy to work, that fate, what's a part of this inexorability of fate is that I was born a child and became part of the human family with the name that I received, Hindruutsi. And that henceforth I was now bound by the power of my name and the power of that philosophy. It was like a cultural dictum that was part of this philosophy that you were now bound to your family, and you were bound to the people, the community as a whole. That you were part of the Acoma people henceforth, forever. You could not step away from it. But you had to do certain things that had to do with responsibility, not only acknowledging, but practicing, and performing as a Native person in order to maintain this connection.

But this inexorability was not going to stop. You were going to keep going forward. And the only way you could continue your life was to take part, was to be involved voluntarily. And also, I think we have to remember that, at least in the Native American philosophy that I know, that, in a sense, you are limited by—you cannot step away—you are limited by this inexorability. You are determined by this inexorable force, or fate, you might say, although "inexorable" and "fate" are not quite the same, but the fact that you choose to, and that you are part of this process, is a plus because it will be what will keep you alive. It will keep you living and it will keep you going towards something. It will maintain your life, your lifeway, forever, and you will always be on this road. You will always be a part of this process.

Waiting is a part of this. It's not so much as to define what it is a person is, but actually making note of your process and that you are part of this experience that is not only teaching you, but that you are also at the same time contributing to this knowledge. In other words, it's a road of self-discovery. You are seeing how you develop and how others with you are developing, but you must make notations along this journey as you go. I know that it relates to, say, guwah sraa hanoh taimeeshi dzeh eh meeshe (how our people lived in the past). It relates to way back when to how the Pueblos lived before we were colonized, but it also relates to what they experienced by colonialism, the fact that another people, another culture, came upon them in the 1500s, and that challenged the life and the life mechanisms of the Pueblo people. And I think this really comes into play in the modern age, in our modern times.

I have sometimes thought about this: that if there had not been that cultural confrontation that occurred when the Spanish came, would I have been a writer? I don't know, though my tendency is to say, I don't think so. Yet this cultural encounter, as some people call it, or cultural trauma, came about. And because it did come about, this radical experience came about for us, which became a part of this inexorable force that was going forward on which we are living and continue to live. So I may have become a writer but perhaps in a different form. There were such things as cultural artisans whose responses, whose profession, was to maintain and to live and demonstrate and articulate what they were living. Perhaps in that form, I would have been. But since I don't know that, I would have to say that there were certain decisions that were made, not necessarily by me, but forces at work that resulted in me becoming a writer, intellectual, articulator of what I have experienced and what might be in store into the future.

I don't question this too much about why I am a writer. I think I used to, but I don't do so anymore. It's still not absolutely defined for me what a writer is in the modern Indigenous world. Because while we have become so fluent and glib in the colonial language of English, we don't really know the harm caused by our fluency. I think that we've learned to articulate what these changes have meant to us and what the potential of these changes are, and that we're not certain what they truly and finally, or ultimately mean. I am real guarded about it myself. In fact, I've said some critical things about how some of us are fluent, not only as speakers, but as writers, as articulators of the Western cultural system without being aware of the potential dangers of our fluency in expressing ourselves. I think that there are real potential dangers in how fluent we are in another cultural way of life, the Western culture way of life. I think that writing or using a language that is not originally of us can be more an arrogant act than we know of. I think we are in danger of losing the original core of ourselves if we become too skilled.

Lucero: Again, listening to what you said, it seems that maybe Indian people, particularly Pueblo people, have always been doing this, processing history. We just didn't take it to that other step of writing it down and printing and publishing, and disseminating it in that way. But do you think where the danger of fluency might lie now is that there's not always a connection to or a sense of responsibility to community? I mean, is there some of that there, or how do you see it?

Ortiz: I think you're right in looking at how a writer or an artist, or anybody who expresses thoughts and emotions very well has a right and responsibility to do this only if they are responsible back to their resource, the source. The source and the resource is the core of culture. And the only reason they are able to do it, to be articulate, artistically, or intellectually express it and articulate it, is because of this cultural core. If they're not responsible back to it, and are instead way out there being articulate, then there's a danger of arrogance. The fluency may be counterproductive: rather than an expression of the core culture, then it's expressed individually or personally, or simply an arrogant act. If we lose footing or foundation of this core, if we are not responsible for this core, then we are doing our own thing as artists, as intellectuals. Western culture even encourages that. Western culture has lost its footing, its foundations because of this skill, this fluency in speaking proper English, good English. Do we want to lose our cultures, our abilities to speak our own languages? Ultimately, I think that we have to be responsible to be human, not superhuman, but human. Not grandiose, not being super-Acomas, super-whoever, super-Navajos, super-Apaches, super-Cherokees. Who we are—that is the base, that is the core, and that is what we must be responsible to. I think there are real dangers in that. I have to watch myself and see how I say things.

Lucero: I was thinking when you say it's important that we remain human—it's like even being honest. I think that is what will keep your humility as opposed to being arrogant, when you can confront and even talk about hard issues in your life, like how you mentioned the dysfunction in your life, the alcoholism, which is true of Native life, of all of us. Probably far too many of us come from that kind of background. And then to be able to talk about it publicly—to me, that's important, and that is part of keeping that humility, part of humanness.

Ortiz: I'm glad you used the term and the idea of humility. I have found myself sometimes less than humble. I used to repeat to myself years ago that we must always be humble. This is a kind of self criticism; humility was always one of the principles that we had. Even though you might be good at something, have athletic ability or intellectual ability, with that, you have to be humble. You have to be willing to be second. I don't think it was just a way to rationalize, but it was a way, I think, to keep a check on yourself, so that you would not be arrogant, you would not be vain. And you would be honest.

Lucero: I think so. When we're honest with ourselves, we're really human. We make mistakes. We're just not perfect. But a lot of times there can be an attempt to not let that part of us be known. Who do you write for? What prompts your writing?

Ortiz: I think that writing as a distinct ability to express yourself in script—that is written form and then to refine it and define it more to what literature is—I think that there are two ways to look at it. What is the purpose of writing, of literature? I think one is to inform people. That is, inform them objectively. You provide them information, you provide them knowledge, you provide them news. And that's to help them be aware of what life is about and of course, to help people through your articulation. Then another way is to persuade people. This is more than just providing objective knowledge. You want to convince them, to persuade them to a certain perspective to either agree with you, or want to agree with you generally about something. So I would say that considering these two things, who do I write for? I think I write for those who are closest to me. That is, if I were to help people, it would be those people who are closest to me. I think there's a certain kind of bias built in. I would say they were the people I immediately have close association with.

Lucero: And could this be people of any race, any culture? Are you talking about specific families?

Ortiz: I think if there were people out there who did not agree with me, and who would not side with me, or that I identify with, I think that through the persuasive nature of my writing, if I draw them into my circle, into my interest group, I think that includes them. Even people I oppose or that I defend myself against. I think there's also a portion of my argument that is not only opposition. Yes, they could be people from other countries. Ultimately, you have to look at people who are not part of your personal experience because we know that there are more worlds beyond the Indigenous. Ultimately, as you go on this road, then you want to find new experiences, new peoples that you have to address as well. So I would say that I write for everybody, first of all those that are close to me, and then those ones that I want to include. Who do you write for?

Lucero: I write primarily for Native people with the idea to tell them a story that they can see themselves part of, because that's not necessarily part of the Native experience to pick up books and find your life, or people who are like you, in them. But at the same time, like you, I realize that that's not necessarily who our audience is or that it's an exclusive audience. I mean other people read it and are just as interested, and need to learn about us in order to understand us. So I guess I write with those people in the background, knowing that they are part of the audience as well, so that makes me more conscious of how I am presenting Native people, and also at the same time wanting to be true to the Native people that I also am writing to.

Ortiz: When I say I am writing for everyone and anybody, I find that real broad, and I tend to lose some concrete sense. So the ones that are closest to me are those in my immediate neighborhood who identify with me and I identify with them. So that's the one that I think I can immediately see. Now I know a while ago I said that as we go on this journey, I project this to other people as well. As we go out of this Native world, we are going to encounter people that we don't know. The ones I have found myself most responsive to, that I can relate to most, are the people most immediately around me. That seems to me the most immediate responsibility.

Lucero: It's interesting that when you're writing for those closest to you, that at the same time it can speak so powerfully to people who are far away from that experience. When I read literary criticism of your work, that's what scholars, particularly non-Indian scholars, say. They focus on the universals, or the humanity, or the humanness of the experience, which is maybe a very Acoma or very Indigenous experience. I'm amazed at that.

Ortiz: Universality is like looking from the larger perspective and focusing upon the very smallest. And I think that has to do with how the smallest has to do with the largest way out there somewhere. Again, like you say, it has to do with the Indigenous philosophy, like that which took place a long, long time ago that we are not even aware of, that we have some connection with where we are right now in this room at Native American Studies at the University of New Mexico. Consciously, that is, we have to look at it that way. Our role as present-day human beings has something of what the great-great grandmothers, grandfathers were, and also looking toward the future to the great-great-great grandchildren. We have to choose to be responsible to the future.

Lucero: I want to ask you a question about the development of Native American literature and how you are very much a part of how that literature has developed, though perhaps you don't see yourself as such, but you begin writing just as the Native American Literary Renaissance, began to pick up steam. And you have this consistent presence up to now, and are identified as one of the major Native American writers. What are your thoughts on how this literature developed, where it was when you started out and where it is now?

Ortiz: I've never quite agreed with the term "renaissance." I've never known what that "renaissance" refers to. But I will say the [decade of the] 1960s was very important, not because it was a renaissance, but because we began to see ourselves openly as members of the whole human race. Not that we didn't always know this, but we began to be very open about it, in a sense, in a radical way, even militant. The dynamics of it then made us very visible because we were asserting and even being aggressive about it, challenging the accepted view that Native people were a dying, disappearing, vanished race, and we would no longer be distinct as a living entity, not socially and certainly not politically. We made an appearance new in source, but not new because the native Indigenous resistance had been ongoing all along from the very start of European and Western colonization, and had never stopped. There were the cultures and traditions that were maintained and practiced, even underground, like the Pueblo religion; it was outlawed because it was already obvious to the non-Indians that as long as there was Pueblo integrity [and] wholeness demonstrated as remaining with the land, and religious practices that maintained this identity and integrity, it was going to be political fastness and insistence on being. And so this had been ongoing since the very beginning. Of course, there were occasions when they became very openly resistant, like the Pueblo Indian Revolt, but there were other occasions of personal and individual resistance.

But the Pueblos were not the only people. You see across the country, across South America, and Central America, that this was the case, although colonialism has worked on various levels. One of those levels has been the recognition of a certain kind of Indian—an Indian who was perhaps docile, less resistant, and malleable. I think that kind of Indian has been accepted to a certain degree and given some recognition, but not political recognition, although in such nations as Bolivia, Ecuador and Venezuela, there are Indigenous people who can determine the course of a nation and perhaps entire continents. I would say that this is happening, that Indigeneity has taken form and force in more ways than we realize. For example, President Evo Morales was elected president of Bolivia; he's an Indigenous man representing his Native community as well as the nation of Bolivia. I think the Americas have become more Indigenized than people appreciate and people realize. Not that it's making us, at least currently, pivotal, although I think it can become pivotal. I think that a great deal of the environmental movement comes from Native American energies; attention that has been gained through an insistence on an ecological connection to people and lands and cultures.

I think that the future, as far as consciousness, is becoming more obvious, we see Western culture on a decline. I don't know how many people would agree with this. I mean, given [the present year] 2005, going back to whatever numbers of centuries that the United States has become such an imperial country, it seems like it is on the rise. But I think it's clear that capitalism and imperialism are falling apart. It's just the quality of life. We may think we're doing good and that life for everybody is secure. I think more and more, people in society in general feel a sense that we are insecure. Those are signs of degradation of life and Western culture.

For the past five years, I have been using the word "Indigenous" more because while we are Native or Indigenous to the Americas, in terms of the world, there are Indigenous peoples all over the world, the people of Africa, the people in the Mid-East, the people in the Pacific, Indigenous cultures that are in the forefront of changing the world. Indigenous American peoples in what is now called America, who are for the most part tribal peoples, are a part of this change. If Western culture is dissipating and eventually falling apart, Indigeneity is very much a going back to the roots in a sense— not going back to the original roots, but going back toward a way in which the earth is in relationship to us and we with it in a very reciprocal way. We're not just using the earth to be our technological Garden of Eden. The earth is not necessarily under our control, but the relationship is one of responsibility, so that the relationship is [a] reciprocal and creative one.

Lucero: And do you see Native writers as articulating that message in whatever form it may be to others in the world?

Ortiz: Artistic and intellectual expressions of this articulation is a major responsibility of writers, intellectuals, artists. I don't think we're necessarily doing it now, but I think that's the potential. And I think if the grandmothers and grandfathers are approving of us, or can be approving of us, it is that we speak about responsibility in the way that we think—we believe—they did, so that we are actually their good future. I'm sure that there were thinkers, intellectuals, artists, expressers, articulators way back when who wanted us to live in the future so that we are conscious of their own efforts. We are their future in how we are living responsibly by what their practice and ideals were way back when. And I think, today, it is up to us to live in such a way to be reciprocal with them in expressing that we are responsible. How well we are doing that, I don't know. Sometimes I have some doubts. We are fluent about it, but we don't know yet whether it is the correct way.

Lucero: Back to the dangers that you mentioned earlier.

Ortiz: Yes, in a way it may even have to do with how culture is changing and how the culture of Indigenous peoples may be changing in inappropriate ways. I have concerns about the gaming phenomenon and how that has become such a powerful dynamic of change on culture. But we don't know the end result yet [of] our people, our tribal and political leaders' venture. But at least as my own argument goes, it is participating in the capitalist energy of destruction.

Lucero: That's an excellent example of an impact on culture we need to think through carefully.

Ortiz: I know that gaming does employ the people in the local area. I'm real leery of the gaming matter. I don't know how many [casinos] there are across the country. Some of them are more public, more successful than others.

Lucero: I think that just like what you were saying about Westernization in China, that it has some benefits but ultimately, it's corrupting. I don't necessarily mean corrupting of character but of the values of ancient societies.

Ortiz: The gaming on Indian reservations or Indian communities—you can't even say reservation because some are off-reservation in the urban areas—is really the biggest cultural change, changer, in the past thirty years. That's fairly recent. It's amazing that it's caused enormous changes. Several years ago, I wanted to do a whole book, a project, a kind of a research. I was going to go to each reservation, each community, that had a gaming casino and just talk to the people and write out what they say. Someone has to do it.

Lucero: It seems like in a lot of communities, when it's put to the vote of the people, often they don't want it. It's something that's not well thought out. What is this going to mean for us? Or how can we use it ultimately for our own benefit? Right now, it's just to meet the immediate needs, and it's not been thought out beyond that. And I think that's the problem.

Ortiz: [Indian gaming] has really broken up solidarity, the integrity of Native communities in big ways. And we don't even see it. I mean I go to the casinos to use the restroom or to get a bowl of soup at Acoma, or to meet somebody there. I have put money into the slots 'cause it's easy, that extra ten bucks or something, and do it almost mindlessly. But that's how capitalism works. I mean, I carry credit cards. They're useful. They're handy. I use the telephone. I use the computer. I mean, I drive a car and I use the gas, and yet I have concerns about this. I have arguments against, I have opposition to, I have resistance to exploitation, and yet we are part of the system that does these things.

Lucero: It would be very interesting to research the stories about the Gambler, about gambling in old Indian stories to see what they have to say. I bet the answers are there, and we conveniently look past them because gambling is something that, in the stories I've heard, isn't a positive thing. It can turn out badly. In the attempt to gain something, ultimately, you lose something of greater value. I guess we're playing that game.

Ortiz: I don't think people have really looked into the cultural concepts to see when you gain something easily or by chance, it's not a reliable thing. Of course, in the present time in which we know the experience of oppression, we are so tired of being poor. It's easy enough to say, "Gosh, this ten dollars could turn into a million dollars." You hear this story of how it actually happened. And yeah, I'll do that. And ten dollars is gone just because you are sort of backed up into a desperate space. If [gaming] should fall, and it's on a downslide right now even though people are denying there is no recession or signs. But if we give ourselves over to this capitalist energy, if it falls, we fall. It's as simple as that. Maybe I'm looking at it too simplistically. We become expert casino workers, but what if the casino culture and culture-economy collapses? What have we invested our time and energy in?

Lucero: Yes, and what has happened to us in the meantime as well?

Ortiz: It's a cross-country dilemma. The casinos are all over. And there's just millions and billions of dollars, and we don't know what's taking place. And I don't know if we really want to know. There are probably deliberate ways in which we are shielded from, or there's denial of knowledge or denial of information if they are corrupt. On the way down here this morning from McCartys, I was listening to a commercial for the show at the Sandia Casino. It was a big act. I mean they're multi-million dollar acts at the casinos now. I mention that because the Sandia Casino, the Isleta Casino, and the Santa Ana Star Casino are all in a radius of forty miles. And Albuquerque is the big cultural, social center for New Mexico. So Native American people are affecting not only Native people in their own pueblos, but they are affecting the culture as a whole. Albuquerque is the biggest city and in a sense, the cultural spokesperson for New Mexico and the Southwest. Native casino culture is a big factor in that in Albuquerque and New Mexico. Are we then defined by what takes place in the casino and by what they are on the surface representing? As you know, sometimes Indians are now seen as casino bucks.

Lucero: Yes, there's a misconception that we're all casino rich.

NOTES

1. The family home where the interview took place is now owned by Simon's sister, Angie. The home was passed down to her by their mother. His brother, Petuuche, who was transitioning from head tribal council man at the time to *fiscale* (sheriff), lives in the home. Almost all the homes nearby belong to his other sisters.

2. Interestingly, a children's book, *Katzimo, Mysterious Mesa*, about the Bibo family was published in 1974, written by Bobette Bibo Gugliotta, and illustrated by Lorence F. Bjorklund. The novel is based on the family of Solomon Bibo, a German-Jewish trader, and his Acoma Pueblo wife, Juanita. In the first chapter the Bibos return to Acoma Pueblo, New Mexico, for a summer visit from San Francisco, California; seeing Enchanted Mesa for the first time, thirteen-year-old Carl Bibo determines to climb it by summer's end. Thanks to Debbie Reese, who maintains the *American Indians in Children's Literature* blog, for providing this information in April 20, 2008, e-mail correspondence.

3. I had interviewed Simon in 1978 as a staff writer for the *Pueblo News*, which was published by the All Indian Pueblo Council (AIPC). The offices of the AIPC were located in the building Simon indicates, which was located on the campus of the Albuquerque Indian School on Indian School Road NW. The building and the school are no longer in existence. AIPC has built office buildings on the property, which now house offices of the Bureau of Indian Affairs. Acoma people now receive medical services at the Indian Health Service Acoma-Canoncito-Laguna health center located at San Fidel on the Acoma reservation.

4. Ortiz was awarded an Honorary Doctorate of Letters by the University of New Mexico in May 2002. In awarding the honorary degree, UNM noted the array of Ortiz's accomplishments: recipient of two fellowships from the National Endowment for the Arts, the Pushcart Prize for Poetry, a grant from the Lila Wallace-Reader's Digest Fund, and the Western States Arts Association Lifetime Achievement Award; inclusion of selected works in the *Norton Anthology of American Literature*, a volume of American literature used worldwide; his teaching experience at UNM, 1979–81, the University of Arizona, the University of California at Irvine, and the University of Toronto; and serving as lieutenant governor of Acoma Pueblo.

5. Ortiz is referring to *Carriers of the Dream Wheel: Contemporary Native American Poetry,* Duane Niatum, ed. (New York: Harper and Row, 1975), and *The Man to Send Rainclouds: Contemporary Stories by American Indians,* Kenneth Rosen, ed. (New York: Random House, 1975).

6. In 1996, the water quality standards for the Rio Grande set by the Pueblo of Isleta in 1992 under the Clean Water Act were upheld by the 10th Circuit Court of Appeals. The city of Albuquerque, an upstream user, had filed suit in 1993 against the Environmental Protection Agency for its approval of the tribe's standards, claiming that the standards were too stringent, had no scientific basis, and that EPA failed to follow proper administrative procedures in approving them. Isleta's water quality standards were set to protect ceremonial use, which includes some immersion and ingestion of river water. The river is also used by the tribe for irrigation and fishing. This marked the first time a tribe in the U.S. established water-quality standards that were challenged and then upheld. See "Isleta Water Standards Upheld," Evelina Zuni Lucero, *Indian Country Today,* October 28–November 4, 1996, C-1.

PART II

Short Creative Nonfiction Essays by Native Women Writers and Scholars

Morning Star Song

Kimberly Roppolo

There is a revolution going on;
it is very spiritual and its manifestation
is economic, political, and social.
Look to the horizon and listen.
                    —Simon Ortiz, *from Sand Creek*

Simon, I want to thank you in this way.
I want to honor you for what you have done for us.

I don't want to use the language of academia
or its forms
because I want to thank you from the place where you
        touch me . . .
somewhere in my spirit.

You spoke to Tsis-tsis-tas sorrow
and I saw your word-magic
ease the hardness in the eyes of tomorrow.
You have taken our wounds and showed us
their counterparts
in each other,
from place to specific place,
from tribe to tribe,
from man to woman to child,
from generations past into the future.
You took our Aunties and Uncles,
writers from many tribes,
and showed them a road,
back in Al . . .bur-quer-que,

This poem was originally published in the special *SAIL* issue devoted to Ortiz's
work (*SAIL* 16.4 [Winter 2004]: 89–92).

back in the '70s.
You put their feet on a path
and held their hands,
pulled them along into song
and re-story-ing the Peoples.

Yes, I know you all had your tears,
Your moments of cloudy anger,
but Love was at the center of it all,
and fire spread from your belly to theirs.
We still warm our hands at it now.
It still creeps through our palms,
en nos brazos,
en nos corazones,
and flames out in our tongues,
filling the air with smoke, cinder, and new growth.

You have gifted us—Wa-do.
You have fathered us—Ma-do.
You have mothered us—Ya-ko-ke.
You have guided us—Ni-a'-she-men.

Tonight, when I look up,
You are there.

I will follow you until morning,
where, transformed,
our children will map trails by you
for seven generations more.[1]

---

1. The Cheyenne look to the Morning Star to find their way, and that is how
   they regrouped after the massacre at Sand Creek. Because of the impact of
   his book, *from Sand Creek*, on my Cheyenne students, I thought this was an
   appropriate metaphor for Simon. Also, Simon has guided us all—he really is
   the one who broke ground and guided the whole American Indian literary
   renaissance back in Albuquerque in the seventies. Where would any of us be
   without him? Moreover, he taught us all to look beyond a narrow tribalism
   and see what we have in common with each other, with the world. The
   moccasin in the graphic is a Cheyenne Morning Star pattern. Beadwork by
   Bobbi Ann Blackbear Osage. Photo courtesy of the author.

The Same Family of Stories

Leslie Marmon Silko

I was in high school when I heard about Simon Ortiz and his poetry from his cousin, Chris, who worked with my parents, sisters, and me at our small family store. She told me Simon was at UNM and some of his poems had been published. Poetry was very mysterious to me then, so I was impressed. When I got to UNM in the summer of 1965, the poet Gene Frumkin, who taught creative writing and poetry, spoke highly of Simon's writing, both the poetry and the short fiction. Gene showed me some of Simon's poetry, which had been published in a small magazine. Finally, Simon and I met at an English Department party in the fall.

I began to feel more comfortable with poetry after I took Gene Frumkin's class on the Beat Poets because they'd reclaimed poetry for ordinary people from the academics. But I wonder if I would have tried to write poetry if it hadn't been for Simon's poems. The Beat Poets wrote about cities, usually large cities that were far away, and I had the impression the cityscape was necessary to the poems. But as soon as I read Simon's poems about the sandstone, the mesas and hills around the Laguna-Acoma villages, I realized what he had done. Simon made world-class poems with yellow sandstone and old piñon trees; he made poems as good as any of Pound's, but with coyote, raven, buzzard, and all the others. If T. S. Eliot or Ezra Pound could use chunks of Greek in their poems, he could use tasty morsels of the Acoma language as often as he needed for spice and for music as he does in his short story, "Howbah Indians," in which the people tease Eagle by saying, "Gaimuu shtuunu kudra gas station." Simon's work helped make way for poets like Rex Lee Jim, who writes strictly in Diné, and for Ofelia Zepeda, who writes like an angel in both O'odham and English.

Simon's poems became models for me—I loved the humor, and the way he straddled great expanses of space and time in a single line. My poem *"Toe'osh'*: A Laguna Coyote Story" (first published in my chapbook *Laguna Woman* in 1974 by Greenfield Review Press) is dedicated to Simon and is an acknowledgment of the huge influence he has had on me and on my work. Even now, when I write something, Simon is one of the few whose opinion matters to me.

Back then, in the '60s and '70s we all were busy with our small children and with classes and jobs, so I didn't meet up very often with Simon except at UNM poetry readings or the parties afterwards. Wherever we were, whatever we were doing, we wrote letters about the writing we were working on at the time. I carefully saved all his letters because they were so beautifully written—clear, concise, and laced with excerpts from poems in progress. Later, the boxes with the letters were lost.

And there were the occasional late night phone calls. I remember the phone calls, especially when Simon traveled out of town and the demons of the road hounded him. If the phone rang at 3 a.m., I knew it was probably Simon in some airport somewhere or in some hotel on the road. My husband at the time didn't like it, but I didn't care because Simon always had the best stories to tell me at 3 a.m. The short story titled "Uncle Tony's Goat" is my rendering of a story Simon told me over the phone in the middle of the night in 1971. Simon said it was a true story, and since I kept goats, I knew it was true. I couldn't resist re-telling the story to needle people who don't want to admit goats are as smart as some humans; also, I loved the route the goat took home through the high mesas and piñon forests southwest of Acoma. Simon is a generous teacher.

In a phone call one time, Simon told me about the old man who died twice. Another time, Simon told me about these Acoma women quarreling over which household fed the most slop to their old uncle's pig. Years had passed since he'd told me the stories when suddenly I got the urge to see how many stories within a story I could manage to fit. I knew the old man who died twice and the women fighting over the pig must be part of it. Somewhere, I heard a story about the Hopi woman who went away to live off reservation for many years. Then at retirement, she moved back to the family house at Oraibi. She did not like the way village people just walked through her front yard to get someplace. She was used to property boundaries from the years of living away; so she put up a fence with signs that read "Private Property." Then everyone made fun of her. I was hooked on the inclusiveness of the novel at the time, and I wanted to see if it was possible to widen or complicate the structure of the good old "American short story" as practiced by Hawthorne and Hemingway.

A great many of my ideas about the oral tradition and storytelling were expanded and corrected as a result of lengthy conversations and letters from Simon. No one evokes the spoken word with the written word better than Simon does in his story "Home Country." Whenever I reread the story, I can actually hear the voice of that woman who narrates "Home Country." She speaks correct English like one who lived in the outside world among white people. Simon gets her just right. I recognize her in the choice of words Simon gives her. I can see her face. Her hair is cut and permed; you can tell she wore it that way to fit in better with the white people. In the old days, Pueblo people who'd been sent away to Carlisle Indian School returned with distinctive traits—a subtle inflection to their English (from Scotland perhaps) as well as colorful phrases such as "precipitous cliffs" or "faggots of wood" that Aunt Susie talked about.

I recognize the old man in "Men on the Moon." I grew up with old folks just like him—people who bravely tried to interpret the new technologies but who just as often misinterpreted things like the old man did when he watched TV. The humor that enriches Simon's stories is integral to the heart of the Pueblo universe. Life can't continue without laughter. Our families, and neighbors, all the people we knew when we were growing up—these people helped us become who we are. These old-time people who helped rear us were tough, funny, generous, and fair-minded—more so than later generations; maybe the world wars are to blame for this. Anyway, the people who helped us form into ourselves continue to live on in us, in the words they spoke to us, in the stories they told us, in their gestures and actions. So when we are writing (I'm thinking of Simon now, myself, and others when I write "we") and we are imagining a character in a difficult situation, without hesitation we know what that character will do. What comes to us is the clever invention, the way out of the seemingly impossible situation which we know because we heard something similar one time, something brilliant some old woman invented long ago, and we use it for the story. That's how writers bail themselves out in the middle of a story they're writing. That's the way the people keep themselves going, on and on.

When I wrote my short stories, I wanted them to belong to the same family of stories Simon wrote. Now, years later, what great pride and happiness I feel as I reread the stories in *Howbah Indians* and *Fightin'*. Beautiful and strong as ever, the stories brilliantly stand the test of time. "Kaiser and the War" is as powerful today as it was more than thirty years ago when Simon, a Vietnam-era veteran, wrote the story.

Which brings me to the five hundred–year resistance of Pueblo people against outside colonization and Simon's courageous stand for human rights and justice for all human beings and all beings, really. More than ever, in the publishing world and in the world of academia, those critical of the empire are scarcely tolerated and rarely rewarded. But across international boundaries, among the masses, in the remote communities of Indigenous people across the Earth, among the artists and thinkers, Simon is our poet champion.

Generosity in Continuance

The Gifts of Simon J. Ortiz

Gwen Westerman Griffin

The most cherished gifts in our lives come in the simplest ways. One of the first conferences I attended as a new faculty person in 1994 was the Third International Conference on the Short Story in English in, of all places, Iowa Falls, Iowa. Every other year, this conference brings together writers and readers from all over the world to discuss the short story and its interconnections with other forms of literature and art, as well as its embodiment in history and geography. Sponsored by the Society for the Study of the Short Story, the event provides a forum for practitioners and critical readers from a broad range of diverse fields and interests. The lineup of speakers was impressive: Amy Tan, Ernest Gaines, Isabelle Allende, Amiri Baraka, Sonia Sanchez, Bharati Mukherjee, Simon Ortiz, and others. Not knowing quite what to expect, I sat through the sessions and panels, and was in awe of the internationally known writers there who were willing to share their stories and their time.

During a luncheon, several of us sat at a table with Simon Ortiz. He very purposefully made room next to himself and asked my eleven-year-old daughter, who had been enduring the conference events rather patiently, to sit by him. This invitation was gracious and unpretentious, and what followed were gestures of generosity and inclusion that made lifelong impressions upon my daughter and me. Throughout the meal, this acclaimed Native poet talked with my daughter, made her feel grown up, and included her in the conversations. He was unassuming and gentle. And he was generous to a young girl who did not know him to be anyone other than a nice man who looked like one of her grandfathers. Then from his bag, he pulled a copy of his first children's book, *The*

People Shall Continue, and signed it for her: "Erin, Always in continuance, Simon J. Ortiz." That book is still one of her treasured possessions.

So, what does Simon Ortiz's interaction with a young girl many years ago have to do with his importance as a storyteller for the people? His attitude and treatment of my daughter, his storytelling embrace of all of us at that table, such a seemingly insignificant event in the grand scheme of things, made a lasting impression upon me not only as a professor of literature, but also as a mother. In person, Simon reached out to each of us with his words and actions, bringing together a diverse group of people at that luncheon who shared, if only for a short time, a sense of community. His graciousness that day, especially toward Erin, affected my response to his work and the way in which I would teach it from that point forward.

Coming to a regional comprehensive university in the northern Great Plains, my students are predominantly white and from rural areas. Eager to complete their general education requirements, they view my Introduction to Multicultural Literature course as a "triple hitter" that fulfills writing intensive, human diversity, and cultural diversity categories, rather than as a door to a wider world beyond southern Minnesota. They are hesitant to "get into" literature, especially poetry that couldn't possibly relate to their farming or small-town experiences. That is, until they read "My Father's Song," in which Simon writes about missing his father's voice and presence in the stories that he told. The beginning of the conversation appears simple, but runs deep with memories of corn planting, new life, and love:

> Wanting to say things,
> I miss my father tonight.
> His voice, the slight catch,
> the depth from his thin chest,
> the tremble of emotion
> in something he has just said
> to his son, his song:
> We planted corn one Spring at Acu—
> we planted several times
> But this one particular time
> I remember the soft damp sand
> in my hand.

> My father had stopped at one point
> to show me an overturned furrow;
> the plowshare had unearthed
> the burrow nest of a mouse
> in the soft moist sand
>   (*Woven Stone* 57–58).

As the students *listen* to the words of Simon's poem, they begin to make connections as they recognize that they are included in the conversation. Then, they talk about the size of today's tractors and combines and how difficult it is to see anything in a furrow, let alone "the burrow nest of a mouse / in the soft moist sand" (58). They talk about how closely their lives are connected to the land and the weather, yet how disconnected they are when, inside a climate-controlled cab complete with stereo sound system and GPS, they drive a tractor pulling a ninety-foot-wide planter.

Often, their first comments on the poem are about the generosity and kindness of the father and what he taught his son when he took the tiny mice "to the edge / of the field and put them in the shade / of a sand moist clod" (21–23). And then we connect that small act to the "important knowledge" in *The People Shall Continue*:

> The Earth is the source of all life.
> She gives birth.
> Her children continue the life of the Earth.
> The People must be responsible to her.
> This is the way that all life continues (3).

From starting out as a classroom full of students who professed not to like poetry, they respond to Simon's generosity of sharing his story by writing about their own memories of a time when they felt close to the earth, were taught to respect life, or were drawn close to their parents. Months, even years later, they will see me on campus or e-mail me and say, "Do you remember that poem we did in class by Simon Ortiz, the one about the mice? It is still one of my favorites." I realize then that in addition to the basics of literary analysis they had learned (or not), they are carrying with them the "important knowledge" of continuance.

It was almost ten years before I saw Simon again, when he was a keynote speaker at the 2003 Native American Literature Symposium. After mis-communication about his pickup at the airport in Minneapolis, he man-aged to arrive smiling and generous, as I had remembered him. A mark of a truly great human being is his treating those around him as no less important than he is, and during the conference he made time for every-one. Simon attended sessions, signed books, listened to others' stories, and encouraged each person he spoke with to continue his or her important efforts, whether it was through teaching or writing or learning. During his keynote address, he shared his stories from *Out There Somewhere* in his gentle and unassuming way. He sang and then read "In the Moment Before," reminding us of the work we carry on: "And today, we must think as we pray: / always one with our struggle, hope, and continuance, / always for the sake of the land, culture, and community" (9–11).

As a storyteller, Simon has been teaching us how to live for the sake of our communities and guiding us as we struggle against the appropria-tion and misinterpretation of our work for many years now. In "Towards a National Indian Literature: Cultural Authenticity in Nationalism," he helped us understand what makes American Indian literature "authentic":

> It is also because of the acknowledgement by Indian writers of
> a responsibility to advocate for their people's self-government,
> sovereignty, and control of land and natural resources; and to
> look also at racism, political and economic oppression, sexism,
> supremacism, and the needless and wasteful exploitation of land
> and people, especially in the U.S. (12).

For it is when we talk, write, and teach about these issues that those col-leagues who are uncomfortable with our words and our concerns label us "angry Indians" or "essentialists." They hear what they want to hear, not what we say, and then repeat it as often as it takes until they convince themselves that they are right and we are wrong about our own cultures, languages, and literatures. Interestingly, rural Midwestern students, who come to learn how to listen with open hearts and minds, understand the importance of that authenticity and begin to engage literally and literarily in a conversation with inclusive voices like Simon's and other American Indian writers.

For far too long, Native voices have gone unheard or been co-opted outside of our communities by federal, state, and local governments, by the news media, by the academy, and rank-and-file non-Indians. Yet, it is Simon who has modeled the way forward for us to address our imposed invisibility, our silenced voices, and our dreams that do not end. In *from Sand Creek*, he leaves us with a vision of the power of our stories:

> That dream
> shall have a name
> after all,
> and it will not be vengeful
> but wealthy with love
> and compassion
> and knowledge.
> And it will rise
> in this heart
> which is our America (95).

That promise is what keeps us writing and sharing our stories in the face of continued war, invasion, occupation, domination, and dysfunction. His words bring us together to protect our community connections (both Indigenous and non-Indigenous) and to help us endure.

Simon's love of storytelling and his compassion for others is evidenced by his mentorship of emerging Native writers. In 1983 with *Earth Power Coming*, one of the earliest collections of Native American fiction published, he gathered some of our most recognized voices: Linda Hogan, Gerald Vizenor, Louise Erdrich, Elizabeth Cook-Lynn, Gordon Henry, Maurice Kenny, Mary Tall Mountain, Carter Revard, Paula Gunn Allen, Luci Tapahonso, Geary Hobson. In the introduction, Simon tells us that "it has been through the words of the songs, the prayers, the stories that the people have found a way to continue, for life to go on" (vii). Then in 1998, he provided a space for Native voices to be heard in his edited volume of essays, *Speaking for the Generations: Native Writers on Writing*. Pointing out that people and land are interdependent and cannot be separated, Simon brought together representative voices who are "simply carrying on a traditional way of life that the oral narrative has expressed since the dawn of indigenous Native American humankind and its culture" ("Introduction," *Speaking for the Generations*, xiv). Simon remains consistent in this collection with his call back in 1981 for "an authentic voice of liberation" ("Towards a National Indian Literature," 12) that addresses the reciprocal and delicate relationship we have with our world, a traditional belief that we are a part of all creation: "I feel it is necessary to do so; there is no way to avoid that responsibility as a member of today's Native community" (*Speaking*, xv).

Responsibility and community—"important knowledge" that is passed to us through stories by a writer who reminds us that we are not by ourselves. Simon brings his gifts to us singing, "remembering, always remembering" that "despite traumatic change, Native American people have endured" (telephone interview with author). In a world where corn can be planted thirty-six rows at a time and tiny pink mice never seen, where the dreams and voices of a people can be ignored, Simon's voice rings clear from Acoma or Minneapolis or Gambier, Ohio: "Don't anybody ever tell you that it is all in vain" (*Out There Somewhere*, 156).

Simon Ortiz probably doesn't recall his gift of recognition to a little girl at a big conference in 1994, but it opened up the world of his storytelling not only to her, but also to me and to hundreds of students in my classes through the years. His generosity is, as are the gifts he gives us through his words, "always in continuance."

WORKS CITED

Ortiz, Simon J., ed. *Earth Power Coming*. Tsaile, AZ: Navajo Community College Press, 1983.

———. *Out There Somewhere*. Sun Tracks: An American Indian Literary Series 49. Tucson: University of Arizona Press, 2002.

———. *The People Shall Continue*. Rev. ed. San Francisco: Children's Book Press, 1988.

———, ed. *Speaking for the Generations: Native Writers on Writing*. Tucson: University of Arizona Press, 1998.

———. Telephone interview with author. 22 February 2006.

———. "Towards a National Indian Literature: Cultural Authenticity in Nationalism." *MELUS* 8, no. 2 (Summer 1981): 7–12.

———. *Woven Stone*. Tucson: University of Arizona Press, 1992.

Poetry Can Be All This

All of You, All of Me, All of Us

Joy Harjo

*The smoke of student riots still lingered in the air the
fall I arrived at the University of New Mexico with
my three-year-old son to begin my studies in pre-
med and dance. The Kiva Club, (the Indian student
club), was my community, my center of gravity. We
were dedicated to defining, securing, defending,
and protecting Native rights. We didn't just talk;
we acted. After classes and meetings, we'd often
gather to continue discussions, or to party. We were
a pivotal generation and urgently understood the
need for cultural regeneration, political and social
renovation; we did everything passionately, hard.*

One night that first fall at UNM, I met Simon Ortiz. It
was at a gathering of Native students and activists. Simon started the
conversation. He was working for National Indian Youth Council with
Gerald Wilkinson up on Central Avenue, and had been sleeping on the
floor of the offices. I don't know what I said or if I said much of anything at all beyond my tribal affiliation and school major. I was shy, self-
contained. He was a poet, he said. What do you say to a poet? Sure, I
knew about Emily Dickinson, Henry Wadsworth Longfellow, and the
Beats, but there was no such thing in our circle, though we did respect
the power of words. I'd admired eloquent native speeching at press conferences and in circles of meaning and consequence, from my own quiet

This essay was previously published in the special issue of *SAIL* devoted to Ortiz's
work (*SAIL* 16.4 [Winter 2004]: 47–50).

distance. And many students at Indian school wrote poetry. Mostly, I'd always imagined poets as pale men (and the rare spinster) declaiming in long aristocratic coats, hailing from wet, cold lands. I had never met an Indian person before who introduced himself as "a poet."

Simon Ortiz invited me to a reading he was going to do the next morning over live radio. I don't think I went the next morning to the radio show, but he persisted and we became a couple. He obsessively wrote poems and journals, labored hours at his typewriter at the kitchen table or on some other improvised desk. He had meetings, associations, even at times, an entourage of followers. I painted. He was the one with words. I was wordlessness. I had always preferred the silence and space of painting and drawing, after taking care of a child, then children. As I watched Simon work, I had to admit that I was amazed at the creation of a poem, how a kernel of meaning and sound condensed to one page could stagger the world with meaning. There was Garcia Lorca, Pablo Neruda, Gabriela Mistral, and I held their poems in my hands. And not just their words, but in these words lived souls, lands, and peoples. What blew me open next was the realization that poetry lived within our Native lands, our communities. And that poetry could be about the everyday of washing dishes, sunrise, crows carrying on, and crickets in the corner of the room making a huge racket as well honoring songs for those we loved, for those who were working with us for justice. Poetry became a refuge in those times of gathering together, standing up and reconfiguring. Poetry was Simon's gift to me, and it was here that my poetry began.

© Joy Harjo May 17, 2004

3 AM
in the Albuquerque airport
trying to find a flight
to Old Oraibi, Third Mesa
TWA
is the only desk open
bright lights outline New York
Chicago
and the attendant doesn't know
that Third Mesa

is a part of the center
of the world
and who are we
just two indians
at three in the morning
trying to find a way back

and then I remembered
that time Simon
took a Yellow Cab
out to Acoma from Albuquerque
a twenty five dollar ride
to the center of himself

3 AM is not too late
to find the way back

Are You Still There?

there are sixty-five miles
of telephone wire
between acoma
and albuquerque
i dial the number
and listen for the sound
of his low voice
on the other side
hello
is a gentle motion of a western wind
cradling tiny purple flowers
that grow near the road
towards laguna
i smell them
as i near the rio puerco bridge
my voice stumbles
returning over sandstone
as it passes the canoncito exit
i have missed you he says

the rhythm circles the curve
of mesita cliffs
to meet me
but my voice is caught
shredded on a barbed wire fence
at the side of the road
and flutters soundless
in the wind[1]

NOTE

1. Joy Harjo, *How We Became Human* (New York: W. W. Norton, 2002).

The Stories He Lives By

Evelina Zuni Lucero

Summer 1978. I was a young journalist, in love with words, thriving on deadlines and adrenaline rushes, disbelieving that I actually got paid to meet and interview Indian leaders and newsmakers, the ordinary and extraordinary, the movers and shakers, like poet Simon Ortiz. Simon and I sat on the grass, in the thick shade of cottonwood trees that dominated the then-existing campus of the Albuquerque Indian School. The All Indian Pueblo Council (AIPC) was in the process of taking over the school from BIA control. The aging buildings were being condemned one by one, and AIPC was looking into how they could provide a better education for Pueblo youth. It was a fitting place for an interview with this poet, what with the political implications in a boarding school setting, and Simon's confrontation of issues facing America and Native America in his writing.

I was only vaguely aware of his writing, though by this point he already had four books to his name. His book, *Howbah Indians*, had just been published, his reputation growing. It was amazing to me that Indians could be authors. There had been none as I grew up, no characters I recognized in all the books I had read. I listened hard as Simon spoke, not only because that comes with journalistic training, but also because his words resonated within me: "As Indian persons, each of us has different roles and tasks, and I decided I would write to carry out the responsibility of teaching Indian and non-Indian people" (Zuni, "Writer Ortiz Tells Indian Joys, Struggles, Victories and Sorrows," not paginated).

Even if it had only started as an adolescent dream, I still harbored the thought that someday I could write a book. And here before me was an *Indian* author, a Pueblo, no less, who wrote of people and places with which I was familiar, who showed in his poems and stories that our lives were as important and worthy as any. Like Coyote, he had been all over the country, working all kinds of jobs, meeting all kinds of people, and then writing about those experiences. His hands gestured as he spoke passionately about writing, about themes in his work, about responsibilities, about the value of language.

The sixties were a defining moment for Simon: "I think a lot of us went through quite a change. We came to a point in time where we had to make a decision either to keep on being treated as a stereotype image of the quiet Indian or to speak out and to demand respect. Not just quietly ask, but to act, to confront the non-Indian power structure. I think this happened within the communities, Indian and non-Indian, and within ourselves. We gained a more firm idea of ourselves, what our human capabilities were, and could become.

"Most of my writing is part of a story of Indian people, life, land, America. Most Indian people grow up with the thought of being useful for the sake of the land, the people. This kind of philosophy is really what I want to make my writing be," he told me (Zuni, "Writer Ortiz Tells Indian Joys, Struggles, Victories and Sorrows," not paginated). It amazed me that an author was down-to-earth, a "regular" guy not caught up in arrogance, but someone interested in community and in speaking to community. Looking back, I see so clearly that he, who had also been without Indian models, was making the way for all the Native writers who followed, including me.

Eight years later, I was in the graduate program at the University of New Mexico in the creative writing program, studying Native American literature, not knowing then the Native American Literary Renaissance was beginning to roll, with Simon as one of the major writers at its forefront. Since then, I have become well familiar with Simon's work and have heard him read and speak many times, and have had many conversations with him. Returning to this interview twenty-six years ago, I am struck with how Simon's message has remained constant over the years, as only a message that comes with conviction can. What he said then is what he always has said and is what literary scholars have written about as a common theme of resistance in his work and in Native literature in general: "Indian people are really energetic and enthused about how we can work, not only with organizations just on specific levels, but throughout all things. There's a lot of inspiration by looking at the long history of resistance. If our ancestors hadn't fought, we wouldn't be here" (Zuni, "Writer Ortiz Tells Indian Joys, Struggles, Victories and Sorrows," not paginated).

He told me in 1978 that in his writing, he strives for an in-depth insight into people, not just their personalities, but also into the events which surround people and in which they grow, sometimes even destructively: "People's lives aren't always successful. I have always tried to find, even in defeat, inspiration for others" (Zuni, "Writer Ortiz Tells Indian Joys, Struggles, Victories and Sorrows," not paginated). I think it is this quality in his writing of providing hope and inspiration that resounds with readers.

He's an important writer, well regarded, revered, even, by some. He has contributed much to Native literature with his essays, poetry, and short stories, always with that seeming simplicity that overlays complexity. His Native language, the stories of his people, his traditional upbringing permeate his thought, his writing, his voice, his presence. He speaks forth the Indian experience in a way people, white and Indian, urban and reservation, recognize and embrace. Always he opens with a greeting in the Acoma language. His voice is resonant. He speaks slowly. His words are deceptively simple but in their brutal honesty, they hit with a twang to the heart like an arrow to the bull's eye. He writes out of a tender compassion for the harsh political and social realities of Native life. He writes and speaks from his heart.

In addition to his writing, his significant contribution to Native literatures is his constant support of emerging writers and support of the Native American studies program at the University of New Mexico and the creative writing program at the Institute of American Indian Arts. I admire this community consciousness. No matter where he is, he always comes home to reconnect, to contribute, to participate. His writing, his life, truly is for the land, the community, the next generation.

WORK CITED

Zuni, Evelina. "Writer Ortiz Tells Indian Joys, Struggles, Victories and Sorrows." *Pueblo News*, August 1978, not paginated.

"It Was That Indian"

Simon Ortiz, Activist Poet

Laura Tohe

"It was that Indian. . . ." (3). The first time I heard Simon
Ortiz read this line from his poem with the same title was in the 1970s
at the University of New Mexico. He was reading from his recent work,
Fight Back: For the Sake of the People, For the Sake of the Land. These
poems spoke powerfully of the uranium mining that was taking place on
Laguna land in New Mexico. Simon's poetry was a reflection of not only
his experience as a former mine worker, but also of the Southwestern
Indigenous people's experience in the mining industry.

"It was that Indian. . . ." A little revolution exploded in my mind. It's
been twenty-four years since he wrote this line, but it continues to stick
with me. Few Native writers were getting their work published in those
days. At this poetry reading, Simon named places I knew and people who
worked for the mines near Laguna and Grants, New Mexico. With each
poem he read, I became more immersed in his words. As we used to say
in the '70s, "he blew me away" with his words.

I grew up on the Diné reservation in New Mexico and Arizona, in
a remote place and mostly disconnected from the outside world. At the
elementary Day School, I learned to read from the Dick and Jane reading series. When we got to see television once a week, it reflected a white
America: *Our Miss Brooks, The Real McCoys, The Three Stooges, The Man
from U.N.C.L.E.* Here was one of the first Indigenous writers speaking
of border towns, capitalism, exploitation, environmental pollution, and
racism. Though they were his words, he spoke powerfully for those of us

This essay was originally published in the special issue of *SAIL* devoted to Ortiz's
work (*SAIL* 16, no. 4 [Winter 2004]: 54–56).

who were silent. Simon's reading made us feel the power of language, the power of speaking for The People and for the land.

Further on, he read, ". . . and never mind also / that the city had a jail full of Indians" (3). Simon voiced a silent truth that we Indigenous peoples had been living under for nearly 500 years of colonialism. In those days, no one was writing of border towns, those little havens of racism and exploitation that simmer near the reservations, except for Simon. My childhood memories are still clouded by the times when my family parked in the J. C. Penney's parking lot and saw Diné men and women shout greetings to their family below from behind the shadowy windows of the upper floor of the Gallup city jail. His words continue to explode in my mind as they do today when I'm at his readings or read his work. My earliest writing, stirred with Simon's activism, influenced me as I tentatively put words on paper. His work as an activist poet has helped raise our social and political consciousness and, I believe, influenced the present generation of Indigenous poets and writers. Simon, as informal mentor, has generously given his time and editorial skills to beginning Indigenous writers. I am especially grateful for his editorial help on my manuscript, *No Parole Today*. With Simon's early encouragement and support, I published some of my earliest work as a fledgling poet. During this time, I sorely needed a mentor to give me the kind of encouragement that he volunteered.

"We have been told many things, / but we know this to be true: / the land and the people" (36), Simon wrote in the same work. In each new book, Simon has taken us on his journeys, sometimes as trickster Coyote, sometimes as father, as husband, as lover, as son, as urban derelict, as teacher in his comments on the Indigenous peoples in America, and on America. He once said, "My education comes from experiencing all of America." While some of his revelations are hard to take, he avoids descending into cynicism and bitterness. Instead he reaches for hope, for the continued struggle to survive. His activist poetry converges with the spiritual values of his Aacqu/Acoma upbringing and his compassion. Simon, like Ella Deloria, Vine Deloria, Elizabeth Cook Lynn, and Leslie Marmon Silko, speaks from The People's consciousness for the sake of the land and The People. These word warriors past and present have helped defend the sovereign status of Indigenous nations and the struggles of Indigenous peoples on their terms. Simon is also one of the few Indigenous writers who use the Aacqu language in his work.

Simon defined colonialism in his work when no one else spoke of it. Before there was such a thing as the Native American Literary Renaissance, Simon affirmed the spirit and values of The People while many of us were struggling with the residual effects of boarding schools. Simon's body of work consistently responds with the deeply rooted values and beliefs of Indigenous peoples toward the earth, toward each other, and for continuance as Indigenous peoples. Perhaps for this reason his work has been often glossed over by critics.

While it would be easy to simply describe Simon as a "Native American poet" or "Acoma poet," his work speaks of issues that confront our national consciousness, issues such as the U.S. military presence in the Middle East and Iraq. Closer to home, he has written of American genocide in *from Sand Creek* and U.S. policies that affect Indigenous lands and Indigenous peoples that bear parallels to the U.S. presence in the Middle East. At his readings, he exhorts us to challenge national issues that face us as American citizens and, most particularly, as Indigenous nations.

Simon Ortiz's body of work spans four decades. He gives us a rich and enduring legacy of poetry, stories, including children's stories, essays, and film work. He is a nationally and internationally recognized poet. Locally, he has been acclaimed many times over and was awarded the Life Time Achievement by the Word Craft Circle of Native Writers and Storytellers. His recognition as one of America's foremost poets and writers is long overdue. He once said, "[T]o demystify language is to use language as clearly and succinctly as possible." For that I say, *ahé'hee', thank you,* for bringing forth our history and our stories for survival, for continuance.

WORKS CITED

Ortiz, Simon J. *Fight Back: For the Sake of the People, For the Sake of the Land.* Albuquerque: The Institute for Native American Development—Native American Studies, University of New Mexico, 1980.

———. *from Sand Creek.* Tucson: University of Arizona Press, 2000. New York: Thunder's Mouth Press, 1981.

Simon Ortiz, "Cored Tightly" in Prayer, Song, and Protest

Kathryn W. Shanley

When I first met Simon Ortiz, back in the early 1980s, a friend and I had gone to visit him at his home outside of Albuquerque, New Mexico. We brought with us a tree, a sapling, as a gift to honor Simon's newborn daughter. Now that daughter and that tree are grown, but memories of our first visit remain vivid.

Simon asked me if I knew him, and I said no, except for knowing his work. He balked, as if offended, and said something about how knowing his work *is* knowing him, or at least that's how I read his response. Later Simon asked my friend to tell the stories back to him that Simon had told him the last time my friend had visited—stories about slaying monsters and how such events account for how the world is today. My friend was chastised for not being able, or not having the courage, to tell the stories himself, and Simon began again telling us many of the stories that identify him as human, as Aacqumeh. Like an ancient mariner of the desert, just such a contradiction, he was compelled by the stories to give them voice.

That evening, Simon would go off from time to time to the bedroom to lie down for a while, and we would visit with his wife. But just as we were about to leave, he would be up again, ready to talk, to tell stories. I love him for that night. I can't exactly say why, except to say that people seem tallest when they walk with a deep belief. At those moments, they are "carriers of the dream wheel," as N. Scott Momaday says: "They shape their songs upon the wheel / And spin the names of the earth and sky. . . ." ("Carriers of the Dream Wheel," 26). They help others among us

An earlier version of this essay was previously published as "Prairie Songs and Poor Prayers" in the special issue of *SAIL* devoted to Ortiz's work (*SAIL* 16.4 [Winter 2004]: 101–2).

transcend our timidity and speak the reality of experience, ground it in place, and make the most of it in that compelling way that stories bring coherence to our agonies, our struggles, and our hopes.

Although Simon does not drink now, he was drinking at the time, drinking the way my mother used to drink and the way I have drunk myself, to obliterate sorrow while at the same time remaining aware, even intimately in touch with people, places, ideas, and feelings. At times like that, you want to keep the buzz going no matter what.

Believe me, I don't romanticize drinking or alcohol addiction or glamorize the longing and loss it entails, and neither does Simon. No, I speak of those three things together—being known through one's words, knowing the importance of remembering stories, and having the courage to climb on the beast called Grief—Sorrow or Shame—determined to ride, to let 'er buck! They are the truth and fierce beauty I associate with knowing Simon J. Ortiz: a child, a tree, a story, a lesson, a life, a sorrow, a joy, and a raging grief. The joy comes with recognizing another one of the people, too, someone who knows how the land was lost, the people pushed down, and the hollow silence created. Sometimes we can't do a damn thing about it, but recognize another who knows.

Simon knows the howling winds of my own prairie homeland, too, both as geographical and as spiritual space, and knows them as if he were born there. In "The Prairie Song," Simon writes,

> This is our poor prayer; it is despair
> . . . .
> More than anything else
> what we want to feel and finally know is the prairie's song.
> With this cored tightly always and forever enduring in
>   ourselves,
> we can know
> all manners and dimensions of grief and we will not fail
>   ourselves (*Out There Somewhere*, 83).

We pray our "poor prayer," as he calls it, when eloquent words fail us and when our pitiful selves know keenly how pitiful we are.

Simon insists on enduring, "cored tightly always and forever." Those who love Simon's words understand how that can be because his "before" and "after the lightning" become more than brackets around a season.

> For now, the turn of one time into another is nothing.
> It is only the prairie of blue light that is the dawn prayer.
> Only that, the animals and the core in the margin
>> ("Prairie Changing Prayer," *After and Before*
>> *the Lightning*, 119).

He invokes a ceremonial space of grace and forgiveness, healing and remembering and being beyond all those abstractions into sky-gazing and wonder—a gratitude for being alive. Speaking out brings the forces of prayer and song together in favor of purposeful political change—the personal and the political merged. As he writes in the introduction of *Speaking for the Generations*, "As an influence—in fact, as an essential element—in the development of my writing, my Native voice has come from the concept of the necessary and essential relationship of the land and people, and it is my hope and wish that this voice will have Continuance as the land and people continue to have Existence" (xviii).

I admire the risks Simon takes in allowing himself to be known, both his telling of the things that make him cringe in shame and the things that make him want to strike out in anger. "Sometimes I feel like killing somebody" ("Headlands Journal" in *Out There Somewhere*, 11), he writes; and he adds,

> After poetry readings though, most times, usually,
>> people are polite. And
> they say thank you, sometimes referring to something
>> I brought up in
> poetry.
> This time I overheard a tall, blonde, freckled woman
>> with broad shoulders
> and an intense manner say, "Indians are hard to save" (11).

What is a person supposed to do when he opens himself, as one does in giving a poetry reading, and finds that another person sees him as pitiful, "hard to save," as if that is her task. Such occasions call for wisdom and spiritual strength of an extraordinary order. It is no small thing to ride through that complex of emotions (shame, anger, grief) to humility.

In the Nakoda language, we have a word that gets translated as "pitiful." The word is *unshiga*, with the "n" nasalized. "Pitiful" in the language means something broader than the English word. It means something related to Trickster philosophy, a paradoxical state of power and failure and the recognition of an innate insignificance. We are all reduced to pitiful states as humans. Sometimes people combine *Iktomi* (the Spider Trickster) with *unshiga* to produce a new word (one the community owns), telling of a pitiful state that has come about because a person has been tricked by his or her greed or lust or appetite to do something, and now is paying the price—like a hangover. In tribal communities, people participate in telling the stories of others' pitiful states. Pitiful states constitute a shared fate, imperfection and insignificance, and the stories about them provide social instruction. Within honor- and shame-coded Indigenous cultures, states of pitifulness draw us back to ourselves and humble us before our kin. The recognition of ourselves as pitiful ultimately gives us the strength to stand up for what is right.

That powerful idea is outside the hegemonic paradigm of Christian thought, with its "original sin," on the one hand, and Freudian "id," on the other. So many scholars have written about trickster figures and philosophy, it's hardly news. Yet, the American popular mind flips too easily into images of clowns or memories of humorous, bawdy tales, missing the profundity of the philosophy. Speaking personally, I abhor simple-minded labeling of Things Trickster, and I would never attach such a descriptor to Simon Ortiz or his work. Rather, I point to the philosophy that runs deeply through Indigenous peoples of grasping the paradoxical human ways of being innately powerful, yet insignificant and capable of, if not prone to, foolishness and failure. In *Out There Somewhere*, Simon leaves the poem having planted the idea in the listeners' heads of Indian salvation, and begins the next poem, "Before and Behind Me," with the simple statement, "I look in the mirror." He does and does not need saving; he can and cannot be saved. The dynamic making of a self comes through the making of a day, offering pollen and prayer for the sun to rise, a ritual obligation. Simple things become equivalent to offering and opening oneself, like a tear that falls easily down the cheek of a seemingly placid face.

Other contraries embraced in the scope of his writings include a high value placed on Indian workers, while also descrying the exploitation of those people's labor. "Woman Singing," an early Ortiz story, hits at the commodification of human labor and the sexual extortion that goes with it. Not unlike the master's sexual abuse of black slave women, use and abuse of American Indian women by non-Indian men has occurred and continues to occur with such severity and regularity that Amnesty International is going to study the problem. (Andrea Smith's *Conquest* tells the same sad tale in nonfictional prose.) The despair experienced by place-centered, Indigenous peoples who have to leave home for work, because of systematic capitalist exploitation, is compounded by the treatment they receive while working. More than any other Native person writing now, Simon shows how all kinds of work that people do holds value. Although the subject of exploitation of labor, appropriation of Indigenous lands, and other oppressions of capitalist patriarchy most often enter the academy through neo-Marxist theorists, there is no substitute for the voices of people who know that suffering intimately. Being immersed in the financial need to provide for others, families sacrifice dearly; their experiences lend an acute gut-level perspective that theories of economics hardly capture. Mike Rose, a specialist in language and literacy studies, captures that idea well in the opening to his book, *The Mind at Work*: "I grew up a witness to the intelligence of the waitress in motion, the reflective welder, the strategy of the guy on the assembly line. This, then, is something I know: the thought it takes to do physical work. Such work put food on our table, gave shape to stories of affliction and ability, framed how I saw the world" (xiii). It's not just "the values such work exhibits [the work ethic]," it's the thought it takes, "a mind at work in dignity" (Rose, *The Mind at Work*, xv). In writing about one of his bosses in the poem "The First Hard Core," Ortiz describes the layers of racism and the subordination of workers who seem expendable to the boss, and the thought it takes to survive bad work situations:

> Herb used to have an observation
> which was the same as a rule
> for him too I think.
> We white people got our niggers
> to look down on.
> Mexicans here got you Indians
> to look down on.
> and you all got Navajos
> to look down on.
> But who the hell Navajos
> got to look down on
>   (*Woven Stone*, 307)?

As if addicted to the poetic structure of his own pecking order joke, not the least bit funny to Indians (especially Navajos) or Mexicans, and blacks, as if enamored with the very idea of his own philosophical musing, "Herb" poses a rhetorical question. The narrator follows with an explanation that he could not articulate at the time to his boss:

> I couldn't figure out how to answer
> that one either if it was a question at all.
> I guess I wanted to tell him
> we were working on land stolen from Acoma
> and that Martinez was a Navajo man
> on whose land was discovered uranium
> which gave us our jobs.
> But I just said, I don't know
> (*Woven Stone*, 307–8).

Being "just a kid then," Ortiz cannot explain what he really thinks to this ignorant man, but he does reply later, when he can, in a poem that will outlast "Herb" and give something valuable to every person who understands and sympathizes with the narrator for enduring the demeaning atmosphere described. The narrator says he learned from Herb nonetheless, "the first hard core / I ever met personally" ("The First Hard Core" in *Woven Stone*, 308). Ortiz's poem reminds me of my first job at age fourteen in a café/bakery, and how "Bill" would chase me around after closing, trying to get hold of me, all the while saying ugly things about my mother and her drinking. I outran him each time, because he was old and always drunk; I stayed at the job, because I needed the money.

Ortiz also portrays the dignity of work, and the parent's teachings to the child through example and explanation. In his poem tribute to his father's work, "A Story of How a Wall Stands," Ortiz writes,

> My father, who works with stone,
> says "That's just the part you see,
> the stones which seem to be
> just packed in on the outside,"
> and with his hands puts the stone and mud
> in place. "Underneath what looks like loose stone,

there is stone woven together"
(*Woven Stone*, 145).

The poem builds around a metaphor of strength and the fruition of human effort and intention—the walls of a home—and that wall will endure "a long, long time." Although no earth dwelling lasts forever, his father's good, honest work will long signify to readers the foundational truth Ortiz extols. Dignity abides in such stories and storytelling, a father's legacy to a son.

The visions of dignity in the face of difficulty is Simon Ortiz's legacy to me, the beauty in his belief in being rooted to our places and our ancestors' ways of enduring, even singing, and most certainly praying. He autographed my copy of *Woven Stone*, "May you always know the courage and strength of our people, land, and culture. Always, Simon Ortiz." I pray for those things for him as well.

WORKS CITED

N. Scott Momaday. "Carriers of the Dream Wheel." *In the Presence of the Sun: Stories and Poems.* New York: St. Martin's Press, 1992.

Ortiz, Simon J. *After and Before the Lightning.* Tucson: University of Arizona Press, 1994.

———. *Out There Somewhere.* Tucson: University of Arizona Press, 2002.

———. "Introduction." In *Speaking for the Generations: Native Writers on Writing.* Tucson: University of Arizona Press, 1998.

———. *Woven Stone.* Tucson: University of Arizona Press, 1992.

Rose, Mike. *The Mind at Work: Valuing the Intelligence of the American Worker.* New York: Viking, 2004.

Smith, Andrea. *Conquest: Sexual Violence and American Indian Genocide.* Cambridge, MA: South End Press, 2005.

PART III

Critical Essays

No Mistaking the Boundaries

Esther Belin

no mistaking the fall weather
no mistaking the river
yet Simon still makes note of it
he defines it: we are on the Mormon
side of the river
camping
our northern boundary is
a monumental sandstone wall
and a barbed wire fence protects it
with a feeble sign:
STAY OUT. DO NOT CLIMB.
about ten feet high is a row of hearts
carved into the wall

DENNIS
+
MARILYN

autumn
+
river

red
+
deep red

what is
boundary
+
what is
beauty

red + skin
+
heart
+
home + land

Simon Ortiz and the Lyricism of Continuance

"For the Sake of the People, For the Sake of the Land"

Roger Dunsmore

I started out to write this piece honoring Simon's work by taking a close look at his widely anthologized, much loved, early poem, "My Father's Song." I wanted to show how such a deeply personal, short poem expressed that pre-eminent value, continuance, which he invokes to focus Native tradition and resistance beyond mere survival. But along the way I got ambushed. I got ambushed by his father, by poems and statements about his father and his father's influence on his work. I was easy to ambush because in an eighteen month time-period a year and a half ago I lost four fathers: First, my wife's father, then thirty-seven days later, my father, eight months later my mentor, the philosopher Henry Bugbee who brought me to Montana, and six months later, Buster Yellow Kidney, the Blackfeet elder and friend. So Simon's statements about his father would not leave me alone. And, the continuance (a word I initially resisted due to its abstract quality) that he invokes so eloquently probably has no more direct and forceful path than through the parents and grandparents, in this case, through the father.

I want to look at his father as a stone-worker, as a carver, as a singer, and at the influence of these on Simon as a writer. There is an early poem, "A Story of How a Wall Stands," in which his father explains the care, the mystery, and the mastery of weaving stone into a wall for a graveyard at Aacqu. The picture we are offered of this stone-working craft is created by his father's hands as he shows Simon the motions these hands must make in the making of stone walls.

This essay was first published in the special issue of *SAIL* devoted to Ortiz's work (*SAIL* 16, no. 4 [Winter 2004]: 20–28).

At Aacqu there is a wall
almost 400 years old
which supports hundreds
of tons of dirt and bones—
it's a graveyard built on a
steep incline—and it looks
like it's about to fall down
the incline but will not for
a long time.

My father, who works with stone,
says, "That's just the part you see,
the stones which seem to be
just packed in on the outside,"
and with his hands puts the stone and mud
in place. "Underneath what looks like loose stone,
there is stone woven together."
He ties one hand over the other,
fitting like the bones of his hands
and fingers. "That's what is
holding it together."

"It is built that carefully,"
he says, "The mud mixed
to a certain texture," patiently
"with the fingers," worked
in the palm of his hand. So that
placed between the stones, they hold
together for a long, long time.

He tells me these things,
the story of them worked
with his fingers, in the palm
of his hands, working the stone
and the mud until they become
the wall that stands a long, long time
        (*Woven Stone*, 145).

What's crucial about this particular wall is its support of "hundreds of tons of dirt and bones" on a steep incline—for 400 years—its being the wall for containing the bones of the ancestors at Aacqu. The craft skills, the understanding, the qualities of patience and carefulness, reside in his father's hand-bones as their movements tell the story of the wall—stones *woven* together with mud. The story of how a wall stands might also be the story of how a people stand, on the steep incline of history. For any wall, especially one on an incline, is a balancing act, stones standing amidst the forces of time and gravity and shifts in the ground that might bring them down. The bones inside his father's hands know this story and these forces; and they know the supreme value of a certain texture of mud that must be mixed if the stones are to hold together, in time and space, and with the people, the ancestors, the unborn. The title of Simon's volume collecting his first four books of poetry, *Woven Stone*, is taken directly from this poem, and from the sense that his own written work must contain the craft of weaving stones and mud, hand bones and emotion, only with words, weaving tradition into the present, as others have done in stone, cloth, mud, song for countless generations. Simon makes this point clearly in his biographical essay, "The Language We Know," in *I Tell You Now*:

> Our family lived in a two room home (built by my grandfather shortly after he and my grandmother moved with their daughters from Old Acoma), which my father added rooms to later. I remember my father's work at enlarging our home for our growing family. He was a skilled stoneworker, like many other men of an older Pueblo generation who worked with sandstone and mud motar to build their homes and pueblos. It takes time, persistence, patience, and the belief that the walls that come to stand will do so for a long, long time, perhaps even forever. I like to think that by helping to mix mud and carry stone for my father and other elders I managed to bring that influence into my consciousness as a writer (188–89).

The awareness that his consciousness as a writer has been influenced by helping to mix mud and carry stone as a child who takes part in something enduring in the life of the people, is at the heart of Simon's strength as a writer, is itself an act of continuance. The act of writing must contain the act of stone-working, just as the wall standing at Aacqu contains the bones of the ancestors. One thinks of the well-known story of the Navajo students who were given video cameras and asked to make their own documentary on the craft of weaving, how they filmed the grasses, the plants, the sheep, the mesas and the clouds, all that the weaving contained.

A further look at the influence of his father's craft skills on his writing comes from Simon's essay "Song, Poetry and Language—Expression and Perception" in *Symposium of the Whole:*

> My father carves, dancers usually. What he does is find the motion of Deer, Buffalo, Eagle dancing in the form and substance of the wood. . . . and his sinewed hands touch the wood very carefully, searching and knowing. . . .
>
> His movements are very deliberate. He holds the Buffalo Dancer in the piece of cottonwood poised on the edge of his knee, and he traces—almost caresses—the motion of the Dancer's crook of the right elbow, the way it is held just below midchest, and flicks a cut with the razor-edged carving knife. And he does it again. He knows exactly where it is at that point in a Buffalo Dance Song, the motion of elbow, arm, body and mind.
>
> He clears his throat a bit and he sings, and the song comes from that motion of his carving, his sitting, the sinews in his hands and face and the song itself. His voice is full-toned and wealthy, all the variety and nuance of motion in the sounds and phrases of the words are active in it; there is just a bit of tremble from his thin chest (400).

In this memory of his father carving, Simon shows us the wholeness of the act—that wholeness involves knowledge of the exact motion of the dancer's body and *mind*, of the motion in the body of the piece of wood being held in his hands, the motion of the Buffalo itself being sung/danced, in and by his hands, mind, knife, even by his sitting. It is no surprise, then, that later on in the essay when Simon asks his father about a particular word he has used in speech or song,

> "What does it break down to? I mean, breaking it down to the syllables of sound or phrases of sound, what do each of these parts

mean?" And he has looked at me with an exasperated—slightly pained—expression on his face, wondering what I mean. And he tells me, "It doesn't break down into anything."

For him, the word does not break down into any of the separate elements that I expect. The word he has said is complete (400).

The father's act of language is complete, just as is the act of carving. It is this older sense of completeness in word, in song, or in carving that Simon strives to bring on over into his writing, and this is not something learned at school.

Later in this same essay he elaborates on this sense of completeness in reference to song, to his father's singing, which we saw as a part of his carving. But first he tells a funny story about an older man named Page who went along with a hunting party as the camp cook because his eyesight wasn't so good, and, thinking he was tracking a big deer at one point, was actually tracking a pig—which he knowingly goes ahead and shoots. For the rest of his life his nephews ask him, "Uncle, tell us about that time the pig was your deer." This story is to remind us, I suspect, that humor, too, is as much a part of a hunt, or of a poetics, as anything else. He goes on to say about song—

> The song as expression is an opening from inside of yourself to outside and outside of yourself to inside, but not in the sense that there are separate states of yourself. Instead, it is a joining and an opening together. Song is the experience of that opening . . .
>
> When my father sings a song, he tries to instill a sense of awareness about us. Although he may remark upon the progressive steps in a song, he does not separate the steps or components of the song. The completeness of the song is the important thing. . . .
>
> He makes me aware of these things because it is important, not only for the song itself but because it is coming from the core of who my father is, and he is talking about how it is for him in relationship with all things. . . .
>
> A song, a poem, becomes real in that manner. You learn its completeness. . . . You learn a song in the way that you are supposed to learn a language, as expression and as experience . . . (404–5).

And finally,

> My father tells me, "This song is a hunting song: listen." He
> sings and I listen. He may sing it again, and I hear it again. The
> feeling that I perceive is not only contained in the words; there
> is something surrounding the song, and it includes us. It is the
> relationship that we share with each other and with everything
> else. And that's the feeling that makes the song real and
> meaningful and which makes his singing and my listening more
> than just a teaching and learning situation (406–7).

When Simon was in Montana last April for a lecture/reading I asked
him, naively, why he used the word song in the title of the poem, "My
Father's Song," since it was a story. As answer, he directed me to another
short poem, "My Father Singing," from late in his second book, *A Good
Journey*. The poem goes like this:

> My father says,
> "This song, I like it
> for this one old man."
> And my father moves
> his shoulders, arms
> and hands when he sings
> the song.
> My father says,
> "When the old man
> danced this song,
> I liked it for him"
>   (*Woven Stone*, 264).

Simon then said, "It isn't so much his song as the way he moved his body
when he talked, his body gestures," and he got up from where we were sitting outside, and moved *his* shoulders, arms and hands, moved his whole
body in gestures like his father's, and said, "It was like this that he moved
when he spoke, that's why I call it his song." His father's body danced its
affection in him, the son, re-membering his father's life as motion and
sound and emotion together, the father's life continuing in these gestures
of affection "for this one old man who used to like to sing—and he danced

like this" (*Song, Poetry*, 407). This connection between sound and motion, and emotion, between singing and dancing and telling an affectionate story, is inherent in Ortiz's way of receiving and giving experience. It lends to his poems an active silence that we feel in and with the words.

> My existence has been determined by language, [he says], not only the spoken, but the unspoken, the language of speech and the language of motion. . . . Memory, immediate and far away in the past, something in the sinew, blood, ageless cell. Although I don't recall the exact moment I spoke or tried to speak, I know the feeling of something tugging at the core of the mind, something unutterable uttered into existence (*I Tell You Now*, 187).

In these descriptions of his father carving, singing, talking about language or explaining how a stone wall stands, Simon Ortiz has suggested a Pueblo Poetics—and reveals his father as a primary inspiration for his work as a writer. We see the completeness of voice and self that is at the core of what Simon's work continues, how such voice embodies the language of movement—the muscles and sinews, the way the skin is wrinkled, even how one sits being a part of it, the way a person is moved by the whole of the heritage he or she carries, as well as by their own individual nature and experience. This language of motion that he says has shaped him reminds us of a comment by Gary Witherspoon, in *Language and Art in the Navajo Universe*, that the Navajos have over 350,000 conjugations of the verb "to go," so important a part of their world is the experience of motion.

In closing, I want to quote a note to my students that I scribbled on the inside cover of my almost decade old copy of *Woven Stone* and dated December 11th, 1995:

> When I say Simon Ortiz is the most important poet writing in America today, I mean (to borrow a phrase from Jason, a Wilderness student who went on to receive Rabbinical training)—I mean that Simon's poetry is thoroughly prayerful—full of prayers and praising. And prayerful in a way that works today because that isn't the result of any doctrine or creed or religion. It is an extension of thousands of years of dry land farming *culture* in what is now called the Southwest, and the pain

of five centuries of colonialism. He knows the loss because he
has lived it—he also knows the life, the renewal, the fertile power
in everything, including us. And he just tells it, sings it, moves it
in language so that all the time it is praying, praising, respecting,
alive, living. Always, even in anger, Simon Ortiz has "gone for
the rain."

I want to add a couple of points to this statement. (1) What makes this
prayerful or sacramental quality so powerful in his work is that it does
not call attention to itself as such, is left unstated and takes place almost
casually in the course of writing about seemingly ordinary events, like
the standing of a stone wall or moving mice out of a cornfield or bringing
home a skinny dog. (2) These poems also are an extension of the "ferociousness" with which the Acoma Pueblo people have "held to their history, culture, language and land despite . . . the forces surrounding them
since . . . the advent of Euro-American colonization." (3) We must learn
to listen for that "something that surrounds the song"; to listen for that
"something more than memory or remembering that is at stake," we must
catch the language of motion/emotion, and, if we are to have a regard for
"the sacredness of language," we must, like old man Page, know when to
let a pig become our deer.

WORKS CITED

Ortiz, Simon. *Woven Stone*. Tucson: University of Arizona Press, 1992.

———. "Song, Poetry and Language—Expression and Perception." In
Symposium of the Whole: A Range of Discourse Toward an Ethnopoetics,
edited by Jerome Rothenberg and Dianne Rothenberg, 399–407. Berkeley:
University of California Press, 1983.

———. "The Language We Know." In *I Tell You Now: Autobiographical Essays
by Native American Writers*, edited by Brian Swan and Arnold Krupat, 185–
94. Lincoln: University of Nebraska Press, 1987.

Witherspoon, Gary. *Language and Art in the Navajo Universe*. Ann Arbor:
University of Michigan Press, 1977.

Sacred Journey, Poetic Journey

*Ortiz Re-turning and Re-telling from
the Colonized Spaces of America*

Kimberly M. Blaeser

*I have learned that to be spiritually conscious means
to undertake a journey that is often a political one.*
—Linda Hogan, "The Two Lives"

*I am most conscious of my life as a
journey, and what I write is a map*
—Simon Ortiz, *After and Before the Lightning*

Returning. Remembering. Retelling. These steps inform much of the literature of sacred journey in American Indian traditions. The journeys themselves vary greatly in length and circumstance, but the hearkening toward the sacred nearly always involves ritualized repetition of motion, memory, or voice. Somehow through the enactment of connection, the immersion in the cyclical reality of experience and being, we outstrip our individual essence, are infused with a knowing power, or arrive back on sacred ground.

The literal and linguistic enactment of this kind of ritualized motion forms an important foundation for the poetry of Acoma writer Simon Ortiz. Movement in individual poems, the buttressed structures of entire collections, and the philosophical framework for the large body of his poetic works reflects a particular kind of preoccupation with cultural and spiritual continuance. His books *Going for the Rain* and *A Good Journey*, for example, involve the entrance into and re-speaking of sacred journey cycles on many levels. This literary and cultural continuance in Ortiz's work is inevitably linked with political awareness and activism.

Collections like *Fight Back: For the Sake of the People, For the Sake of the Land* and *from Sand Creek* embody particularly strong strains of political critique. Clearly, the journeys Ortiz has undertaken in his life—spiritual, cultural, literary, political—overlap and nurture one another.

Comments in Ortiz's introduction to *Woven Stone* articulate his own awareness of the overlapping of these realities. There, for example, he describes *Fight Back* as "a literary work intended to be a political statement" (30). In the same introduction, his comments point to the characteristic literary migrations of his poetry, noting the relationships they articulate. First, he names the several elements important to the 1984 collection, *A Good Journey*: "the oral voice of stories, song, history, and contemporary experience" ("Introduction," *Woven Stone*, 17). Then, several lines later he describes the dual trajectory of the movements in that volume: "The poetry in the book is styled as storytelling narrative ranging from a contemporary rendering of older traditional stories to current experience: from Grandmother Spider to my children, from Coyote to being in the Veterans Hospital for alcoholism treatment" (18). Ortiz makes a literary journey of return and remembrance as he poetically recollects and retells the traditional stories. He also carries them forward, upholding their continued significance by rendering contemporary experience through the lens of traditional story.

Often, given the circumstances of Indigenous realities in the Americas, Ortiz also draws parallels between historical and contemporary experiences. In *Fight Back*, he explains:

> I had looked back three hundred years at the Pueblo Revolt of 1680 when the dispossessed, oppressed poor led by the Pueblo Indian people rose up against the civil, religious, and military rule of the Spanish. The rebellion was against theft of land and resources, slave labor, religious persecution, and unjust tribute demands. The people and the land had been colonized and dominated for almost a hundred years by Spanish power, and there seemed to be no other recourse but to overthrow oppressive Spanish rule. . . . Three hundred years later, some of those same conditions existed (30–31).

Thus, the 1980 volume became a political offspring of the historical story—Ortiz hoped to incite the contemporary public, particularly the

Native segment of his readers/listeners, to a new political awareness and to action. Historical story informs his contemporary interpretation of circumstances and, by extension, historical action will, he hopes, incite contemporary revolt. "Fighting back," he claims, "is fighting on, and this is the continuance. . . . It must be a part of every aspect of Native American life and outlook" (*Woven Stone*, 31).

Despite living in a future-oriented American culture, Ortiz recognizes the significance of the Native mythical reality and historical past as guideposts and tools for continued survival. Metaphors of map and journey, literal pilgrimage and physical placement, consistent literary orienteering inform the poetic territory of his more than thirty years of publications. "When the poems came about and I wrote them," he says in the preface to *After and Before the Lightning*, "I felt like I was putting together a map of where I was in the cosmos" (xiv). Most if not all of Ortiz's publications across the genres also clearly have supra-literary intentions, working as they do toward challenging the philosophical underpinning of colonialism, raising awareness of contemporary justice issues, and hearkening after the healing associated with ancient ritualized practices. "As an Acoma Indian in the Americas," Ortiz like many other Native people has experienced "the dreaded reality of despair, death, and loss because of oppressive colonialism" (xv). So in his life and his writing, he has turned to older cultural practices, traced them as maps in his journey toward survival.

The altered spaces of Native lives resulting from colonial displacement, cultural subservience, and ecological destruction, have, however, as Susan Brill de Ramírez notes, wrought changes as well in the "idea and practice of sacred journey." The "horrors of conquest, flight, and dispersion" have resulted in a tradition she characterizes as "more necessary now than before, more complicated now than before."[1] Throughout his poetic performances, Ortiz recognizes the need to adapt the ancestral sacred journey patterns and practices to contemporary and to literary ends.

I. Taking Bearings

Journey has always informed Native life. From the too-frequently stereotyped vision quest to the seasonal subsistence migrations, travel, repetitive patterned movement, forms the basis for physical survival and spiritual

well-being in many tribal societies. The history of previous journeys frequently serves as map for the contemporary undertaking, and the oral
retelling of those journeys fixes in memory a physical landscape as well as a
kind of spiritual terrain. The written journey literatures of Native American
people frequently retain a connection in form and function to those earlier
verbal mappings. The contemporary journey is often made in tandem with
the historical, or its telling is linked to the early spoken accounts.

Karl Kroeber's 1983 comments in "Poem, Dream, and the Consuming
of Culture" about the "recreation" involved in the performance of Native
poetry help us to understand the emphasis in contemporary travel literature that is placed on maintaining these continuities with older ritualized patterns of sacred journey. "The poem," he writes in *Smoothing the
Ground*, "is means by which psychic energy flows into sociological structure, thence into practical activity . . . which makes the participants effective in the natural world, provides them with power" (331). He speaks of
the "focusing on reenactment" as a source of "continuity of power-flow"
and describes the link between the verbal and physical re-upping: "Hence
the repetitiveness *in* the poem is reflective of the performative repetitiveness which constitutes its persistence as a practical social force" (331). In
cultures in which oral tradition involves the social and sacred kinship
relationships among human and all other beings, the "spoken" inevitably
extends beyond mere language, and entwines with the activities of being.
"Oral tradition," Ortiz claims, "is inclusive; it is the actions, behavior,
relationships, practices"; it "evokes and expresses a belief system, and it is
specific activity that confirms and conveys that belief" (*Woven Stone*, 7).
Thus the *acts* of pilgrimage are always likewise manifested through the
whole cycle of ritual: preparation, verbal performance, physical enactment, spiritual transformation, followed again by re-turning and re-
telling. The gesture in Native pilgrimage encompasses all time and being:
the past spoken and enacted, the present re-creational performance, the
anticipated continuance in future verbal and physical reenactments. We
see this inclusive healing vision manifested in Ortiz's poetry as it works
to reintegrate mythic stories and personages with contemporary global
communities, to verbally transform the lives and realities of a world still
entangled within the destructive machinery of colonialism.

Because the authors of contemporary written accounts of travel somehow attempt to place their writing within or seek to understand the place
of their work within a long tradition of tribal movement in the Americas,

the texts often exhibit or enact a kind of duality or multiplicity. The stories of pilgrimage in Native American literature then are seldom the account of individual movement or of a search for a single isolate destiny. More often they are braided accounts that entwine with the destinies of communities, generations, tribal nations, the ecosystem of a region, the spiritual inheritance of a people, the colonial legacy, and struggle for decolonization.

In twentieth and twenty-first century journey literature, the creation of a storied context becomes an ever more complex process as the layers of re-speaking and re-enacting themselves multiply. Journeys originally tied to the seasonal cycles, for example, often have a link to ritual or to ceremonial oratory. These verbal performances exist somewhere within the complicated terrain of language relationships: they may waver in the space of alteration between spoken and written, between Native language and English. Travel might in its enactment invoke the long historical tradition of an older journey, of migrations, of particular subsistence activities, or of harvest celebrations. Contemporary undertakings of ritual journeys that were halted because of military interventions, removals, or other colonial repressions and were later subsequently revived may be placed in the context of historical survival.

Many tribal and sacred geographies, though formerly entwined through various kinds of ritualized practice, have experienced a breach. Whether brought about by physical distance courtesy of colonial removals or by current government "ownership" and control of crucial religious sites, this "broken" connection itself becomes a storied element in repair-ations of older practices. Current enactments might involve a somewhat tentative, evolving revival or a physical reorientation. Essentially the new process may become, for a time, an ongoing search for appropriate adaptation that engages in different ways with older movements, texts, and ritual acts.

The verbal performances of journey literature then reveal an intricate network of relationships, simultaneously traversing wide ranges of time, experience, and belief. The author's sometimes self-conscious act of reconnecting supplies another layer of story in the telling, and itself becomes one of the ritualistic motions invoking spirit. The verbal pilgrimage speaks the actual which repeats the former as it was both spoken and acted, and in this process, it respeaks identity.

Because the contested histories of Native nations in the Americas inform the structure of the acts and literary reenactments of pilgrimage, the sacred sought and realized within the accounts may not necessarily involve a traditional, much less a biblical, salvation, but instead may involve an embracing of the inheritance of loss. Abenaki writer and scholar Joseph Bruchac has characterized "the tradition of 'tribal travel poetry,'" as ranging from "sacred journeys and pilgrimages on the one hand to tragic tales of displacement on the other—Trails of Tears and Long Walks that ancestors survived and their descendants will never forget" ("Introduction," *On the Good Red Interstate*, not paginated). Indeed, the process of remembering that plays a crucial role in any of the many ritualized travel accounts that have come to form the genre of sacred journey cycles in the Native American literary canon might more accurately be described as the motion or attempt at re-membering—putting back together—as Laguna writer Paula Gunn Allen has refashioned the term. Such is also the case with Ortiz who, by story or allusive gesture, often engages in a recollection acknowledging the legacy of loss, and then works to transform that history through the literary journey of renewal. Likewise, arrival for the pilgrim in many American Indian accounts signifies an-other outcome from classic western pilgrimage narratives. It involves no golden chalice or other object of desire, no secret to the lost cities of gold, but simple survival. The Holy Grail in these accounts is the blessing of continuance for a tribe or nation; it is the privilege to proceed in the journey, the search, the sacred motion of existence. Ortiz's "Survival This Way," for example, offers an effective poetic rendering of continuance as the outcome of literal, metaphoric, and verbal journey:

> Survival, I know how this way
> This way, I know.
> It rains.
> Mountains and canyons and plants
> grow.
> We traveled this way,
> gauged our distance by stories
> and loved our children.
> We taught them
> to love their births.
> We told them over and over
> again.
> "We shall survive this way"
>   (*A Good Journey*, 28).

The cycle of journey in Indigenous representations, gift though it is, also often includes hardship, danger, and loss. From the early accounts of actual pilgrimages (such as the sacred salt journey of the Tohono O'odham as described in *Singing for Power* by ethnographer Ruth Underhill) to more recent Native-authored creative works recounting journey (including novels of pilgrimage like Linda Hogan's *Mean Spirit,* N. Scott Momaday's *House Made of Dawn,* and Leslie Silko's *Ceremony*), endurance and ceremonial repetition remain at the center of motion and verbalization. The pilgrim-seeker often travels the difficult path, following those who have made the journey before, following ancestors who knew suffering, deprivation, and loss as teachers whose presence heralds spiritual transformation. In this construction of pilgrimage, the sacred duty to re-turn and re-tell holds as much significance as does the actual repetition of the physical journey, since future continuance of the ritual depends upon embedding the pattern in tribal memory. Hence the role of poetic pilgrimages like Simon Ortiz's looms large; contemporary written literature in Native America takes on the stature of sacred vessel.

II. Poetic Leavetakings

The outcome of the journey in tribal accounts, especially in contemporary retellings, might be understood as preordained, as somehow merely another variation of an older mythic "arrival." Myth in many tribal societies provides the storied context for understanding present-day experiences or for investing them with sacred meaning. For example, Peggy Beck, Anna Lee Walters, and Nia Francisco, in their book *The Sacred: Ways of Knowledge, Sources of Life,* explain how the "journeys outside the bounds of the everyday world" are "similar to traveling back to points and places of origin and reenacting events which occurred in the stories" (75–76). According to one of their sources, Blackhorse Mitchell, in the initiation rites for young women among the Navaho (Diné), "the girl reenacts what Changing Woman did in observation of her first menstrual period." For that short time the girl "becomes" Changing Woman (76). The mythic Changing Woman is said to live with the Sun in the west and every day, sunrise to sunset, is retracing her journey to her home in the west. Her journey from birth to old age is commemorated in the daily and yearly cycles, and the story of her life is well known to the initiates.

So the puberty "journey" of the young women is premapped in story; the reenactment is used to "bind the everyday world with other worlds" (Beck et al., *The Sacred*, 76).

This common grounding in the mythic often supplies one layer of resonance in contemporary journey accounts as well. In his writing, Ortiz frequently invokes traditional stories, demonstrating their relevance not only for Native Americans, but also for Indigenous and all "other" peoples. Through his poetic reflections of ritualized motion, he demarcates a path we can follow even in the maze of postmodern America.

Ortiz's 1976 poetry collection *Going for the Rain*, for example, traces a literal journey he made in the southern and eastern United States and entwines the telling of that pilgrimage to "look for Indians" with a ritual going "for the shiwana" or rain spirits (37).[2] He structures the collection in a cyclic pattern which includes a prologue and four sections titled in turn "The Preparation," "Leaving," "Returning," and "The Rain Falls." Isleta/Ohkay Owingeh Pueblo novelist Evelina Zuni Lucero has noted how the poetic movement aligns neatly with Pueblo emergence stories, even to the extent of evoking axis points.[3] The text thus creates a layered metaphorical journey through time and space.

The poems in the volume range in subject, but many concern themselves with the small motions of existence, with a woman at a loom, with planting corn, giving birth, travel by Greyhound bus, with everyday conversations. And yet, we come to understand them, as Ortiz does, as the very center of the spiritual. When, in his prologue, he characterizes the physical, spiritual, and literary journey represented in the pages, he claims an exalted purpose in the sometimes commonplace encounters: "His traveling is a prayer as well, and he must keep on" (37).

Ortiz begins to create this spiritual context in his prologue, linking his own journey to that of the ritual "going for the rain," by invoking a traditional song:

> Let us go again, brother; let us go for the shiwana.
> Let us make our prayer songs.
> We will go now. Now we are going.
> We will bring back the shiwana.
> They are coming now. Now, they are coming.
> It is flowing. The plants are growing.
> Let us go again, brother; let us go for the shiwana (37).

In the prose passages of his prologue, Ortiz writes in a manner we can understand as referring to the ceremonial journey to bring rain, to the specific travels his narrator recounts in the collection, and to the universal journey of "humankind." He offers this reflective summary:

> A man leaves, he encounters all manner of things. He has adventures, meets people, acquires knowledge, goes different places, he is always looking. Sometimes the traveling is hazardous; sometimes he finds meaning and sometimes he is destitute. But he continues; he must. His traveling is prayer as well, and he must keep on (37).

Hence the poet aligns his journey with the older one, as emerging from and merging with the ritualized, ceremonial going for the rain. And, in a world threatened by environmental degradation and subject to increasingly complex political contexts, Ortiz offers a metaphor for the vital human journey we must undertake together to restore balance on many levels.

In the opening poem of the volume, in the "Preparation" section of the book, Ortiz adds the mythic context to the ceremonial.[4] "The Creation, According to Coyote" offers a short telling of the Keresan Pueblo creation myth and the story of the War Twins who lead the people "upwards through successive worlds until they emerge through a single *sipapu* (hole in the ground) onto the earth's surface" (Scarberry-Garcia, "Simon J. Ortiz," 210). Ortiz gives us these important accounts as if in the voice of Coyote, a trickster/storyteller who is also among tribal mythic figures. But with this mythic telling, Ortiz intermingles the colloquial voice of the narrator who thinks Coyote was probably "b.s.-ing" (*Going for the Rain*, 41), and he recalls the same story being told by his uncle. He thus prepares his own role as poet/storyteller as it overlaps in places with that of the trickster and alludes to the multiple ways of story and journey. The journey of the twins he characterizes as containing "many exciting and colorful and tragic things of adventure," and says of them, "and this is the life, all these, all these." He thus invites us into his own poetic tellings of the varied terrain of America in the era of 1970 and suggests the relevance of mythic stories across time and cultures (42).

Also a part of the "preparation" for the journey are several poems in this first section which might be understood as the kind of "prayer songs" alluded to in the "departure" of the traditional song. Recalled with a prayerfulness are the birth of Ortiz's daughter, Rainy Dawn, in "To Insure Survival," and a remembered conversation and encounter Ortiz shared with his father (48–49). This latter, appropriately titled "My Father's Song," describes with precision and delicacy a pause in the planting of corn when father and son discover "the burrow nest of a mouse / in the soft moist sand" and his father scoops "the tiny pink animals / into the palm of his hand" and together they carry them to safety beyond the planting field (57–58). The "song" of Ortiz's father is never spoken within the range of the poem, and the "song" of the poem itself we understand as the power of longing for and remembrance of a prayer of being in a certain way.

III. Traveling Songs

The journey of *Going for the Rain* figuratively and literally covers much ground. In the "Leaving" and "Returning" sections of the book, the poems find Ortiz or his persona "Passing Through Little Rock," "Crossing the Colorado River into Yuma," "West of Ocotillo Wells," "Crossing the Georgia Border Into Florida," and going "All the Way to New York City" (98, 103, 69, 74, 87). Filled with the poetry of place, some poems offer lyrical descriptions of landscape, some a litany of names: Casa Grande, Dateland, El Centro, Tuba City, Gallup, Amarillo, Tucumcari.[5] Filled as well with casual meetings, small incidents, the poet's everyday, the poems ground the reader in the sense of common reality. In "Small Things Today," we find "a tortilla with some honey," the "smell of apples, wet fields"; we also find the kind of transformation that comes with a haiku moment: "Wind blows, shakes the tarp, / water falls to the ground. / The sound of water splashing" (71–72). As the prologue suggests, the poet is "always looking" and "finds meaning" (37). In these sections, much pleasure comes with simply following the poetic glance.

But together with these common scenes, Ortiz interweaves the unsettling: racist incidents, political unrest, and personal struggle. Repeatedly asked if he is Indian and encountering various manifestations of racism, he writes sometimes with righteous anger, sometimes with humor, of his encounters with injustice. In "Travels in the South" he confesses, "I worried about my hair, kept my car locked. / They'd look at me, lean, white, nervous, / their lips moving, making wordless gestures" (74). In "I Told

You I Like Indians," he writes playfully of an encounter with Native ste-
reotypes in Flagler Beach, Florida. The narrator, asked once again if he is
Indian, replies, "'Yes, ma'am.' I'm Indian alright. / Wild, ignorant, savage!
/ And she wants me to dance" (107).

Many of the poems are slight, informal pieces, presented as if they
were simply lifted from the author's travel journal. Others present crafted
political commentary, like that in "The Significance of a Veteran's Day"
(108). Here the narrator identifies himself as a veteran "calling for significance" when "no one answered." But, although Ortiz did actually serve
in the military, in the poem the author reaches for a context beyond an
individual experience. He writes, "I am a veteran of at least 30,000 years"
and talks of wars against "foreign disease, missionaries, / canned food,
Dick and Jane textbooks, IBM cards, / Western philosophies, General
Electric." In the poem, as the poet searches for an understanding of our
longer, larger journey as "the people," he explores some of the central
questions of this literary pilgrimage toward meaning:

> And then later on in the ancient and deep story
> of all our nights, we contemplated,
> contemplated not the completion of our age,
> but the continuance of the universe,
> the traveling, not the progress,
> but the humility of our being here (108).

Thus in the literal, and in the literary journey which recounts it, the passage finds meaning in continuance, simple going on, the process of the
journey, the process of being. The final line in "Veteran's Day" declares,
"I am talking about how we have been able / to survive insignificance"
(108). This line reverberates, drawing and subtracting meaning on several levels. Alluding to the 30,000 years of Indigenous history and its
erasure in the "Dick and Jane textbooks," it might ask, as Norma Wilson
suggests, "How Native people can feel significant in American society"
and how anyone can survive without a sense of worth (53)? Alluding to
"the humility of our being here," the relative unimportance of a singular
person in "the ancient and deep story of all our nights," with verbal gesture the passage may point beyond the ego of I toward the mythic, the
historical, and the ceremonial, as does the larger text of the book.

Ortiz offers his ironic observations of America in many poems in these middle sections and in some traces his own failings and despair. "Blues Song for the Phoenix Bus Depot Derelict"—who could be the narrator himself "Waiting to leave. / Waiting to come."—pleads for protection or peace from "Phoenix streets / cold gray and hard," and concludes "I'm waiting for everything / to arrive / just this one time for me" (64–65). Bus depots, bars, harsh city scenes in Gallup, Denver, New York City, or the generic "Somewhere Else City, USA," become the settings for encounters with lost Indian people, symbols of personal or national disintegration. This pervading sense of disintegration Ortiz embodies in specific incidents and in political references throughout the collection. In "Travels in the South," for example, he incorporates allusions to Alabama governor George Wallace and to the protest and killings at Kent State (74). In "East of San Diego" he offers a warning—"Keep to the hills / and avoid America / if you can"—which gives voice to the schism he sees between the homelands of Native peoples and the larger "other country" of America (111). Writing in the first person in "Relocation," a title which alludes to the U.S. government policy of the 1950s that placed reservation peoples from across the nation in alien city settings, Ortiz laments its affects:

> So I agreed to move.
> I see me walking in sleep
> down streets, down streets with gray cement
> and glaring glass and oily wind,
> armed with a pint of wine,
> I cheated my children to buy.
> I am ashamed.
> I am tired.
> I am hungry.
> I speak words.
> I am lonely for hills.
> I am lonely for myself (76–77).

The desperate city images he often pairs with longing for or images of the land or of home, and frequently with chant-like prayers for recovery. In "For Those Sisters & Brothers in Gallup," the litany of prayer recalls the object of the poets' quest, the cleansing rains of tradition and the traditional reenactment that will bring order and peace:

Be kind, sister, be kind;
it shall come cleansing again.
It shall rain and your eyes
will shine and look so deeply
into me into me into me into me (89).

The sense of this pilgrimage is strong as well in the lines of "Passing through Little Rock," in which Ortiz voices his search, his longing for the symbolic rebirth inherent in the ceremonial reenactment:

I just want to cross the next hill,
go through that clump of trees
and come out the other side

and see a clean river,
the whole earth new
and hear the noise it makes
at birth (98).

Finally, in "East of Tucumcari," the narrator arrives home to see "the brown water / falling from a rock" where "it felt so good / to touch the green moss" and "smell / the northern mountains / in the water" (116). He encounters again the life force of water, the green growth of moss, and his "placement" in the northern mountains. This "homing in" of the narrator in the poem involves the cyclical return to place and the symbolic return to remembered ceremony.[6]

The last section of the collection, "The Rain Falls," is filled with the thirst-quenching waters of Ortiz's poetic vision, with several of the richest poems of the book. "The Story of How a Wall Stands" and "Dry Root in a Wash" from this section have been reprinted in many anthologies. Among the other strong poems in this section is "Curly Mustache, 101-Year-Old Navaho Man" (140–42). A minimalistic poem, more tightly constructed than many of the narrative, more colloquial poems of the book, "Curly Mustache" depicts, as the title suggests, an elderly Diné man. Ortiz characterizes the ancient quality of the human species and of the individual in the poem by aligning his description of the man with elements of the ageless natural world:

Motions
with long hand,
brown fingers
shape the mountain
ridge
of his knuckles.
Meadow wind
flows in channels
of his skin (141).

As the references of the lines move back and forth between the man's hand
and the mountain, the wind and his skin, the two become linked in a timelessness heightened by the Zen-like questions of the next stanza: "How
many times / the mountain tops? / How many times / the roots?" The last
stanza of the poem suggests that, just as the old man has learned "the life
flow / of earth places / of his mind," so too can the traveler who continues
in his journey, continues past the notion of that kind of "progress" deni-
grated in the "Veteran's Day" poem toward a kind of ceremonial wholeness. And in the very last poem of the volume, entitled "It Doesn't End,
Of Course," Ortiz's text gestures back to the words of the prologue: "The
cycle has been traveled; life has beauty and meaning, and it will continue
because life has no end" (38). In words and gesture, the text thus respeaks
itself, as does life.

IV. Poetic Activism

The various layers of myth and meaning, the multiple movements enacted
in *Going for the Rain*, continue to appear in Ortiz's later works. His poetry
develops in different directions during his career, but never leaves behind
the basic sense of mythic reality, the strong engagement with place, the
influence of orality, the mapping based upon traditional practices, and
especially, the intercessions for historical truth, resistance, and justice. He
sees the United States, for example, as a country that "doesn't face or deal
with" its atrocious history, that instead "insulates itself within an amnesia
that doesn't acknowledge that kind of history" (*from Sand Creek*, 6). In his
work, then, Ortiz grapples with how to expose the truths of historical realities; and for him, the historical reverberates in contemporary conditions.

The volume *from Sand Creek,* for instance, recalls the massacre of 133 peaceful Arapaho and Southern Cheyenne by the troops of Colonel John Chivington at Sand Creek, Colorado in 1864, and it links this atrocity to the more generalized domination of Native peoples in America and to specific narratives of loss. Ortiz wrote the poem while he was in the Veterans Administration Hospital in Colorado in 1974 and 1975, undergoing treatment for alcoholism. He reads in the faces and histories of his fellow patients the legacy of personal and cultural loss, and he opens the collection with an indictment:

This America
has been a burden
of steel and mad
death (9),

As the book unfolds with short one- or two-line prose passages on the left-hand side of the pages and free-verse poems on the right, Ortiz intermingles an account of the western movement and "conquest" with thought-provoking and challenging commentary and contemporary scenes. He recalls the historical destruction of the buffalo herds and the murder of tribal leaders; he speaks of the contemporary conditions at the VAH (Veterans Administration Hospital); and he comments on the negative effects of the cultural trends of "scholasticism and intellectualism" (20–21, 28, 10, 44, 58). Ultimately, the volume seems to suggest that only by confronting our complicated dualistic relationship with the idea of nationalism, only by the revolutionary act of truth-telling, will colonized peoples construct a viable place of survival in twentieth century America. Near the end of *from Sand Creek,* Ortiz writes, "There is an honest and healthy anger which will raze these walls, and it is the rising of our blood and breath which will free our muscles, minds, spirits" (84). Two pages later, employing a partial echo of the opening "mad death," Ortiz voices the possibility of change when he writes, "The future will not be mad with loss and waste though the memory will be there; eyes will become kind and deep, and the bones of this nation will mend after the revolution" (86). Although he clearly insists upon the need for some kind of revolutionary realignment, he still expresses a hope for survival, even picturing symbolically the alteration in the remembered place of massacre:

but, look now,
there are flowers
and new grass
and a spring wind
rising
from Sand Creek (9).

Indeed, in the final passage of the book, Ortiz even goes so far as to invoke
a sense of ultimate belonging, writing of a "dream" and claiming:

And it will rise
in this heart
which is our America (95).

The claiming of America as "our America," clearly marks a change from
the accusatory representation with which the book opened. The volume
is, as Thomas McGrath has claimed, "A vision of damnation and resistance which is nevertheless understanding and even hopeful" (comment
on the book cover).

The same might be said about other Ortiz volumes: They refuse to
whitewash America's historical culpability, and yet the conversation they
undertake with the reader includes gestures towards a path of healing or
renewal. The most overtly political of Ortiz's books, the 1980 *Fight Back:
For the Sake of the People, For the Sake of the Land* was published in com-
memoration of the Pueblo Revolt 300 years earlier in which, Ortiz baldly
explains, the people rebelled against "theft of land and resources, slave
labor, religious persecution, and unjust tribute demands" (*Woven Stone*,
31). One of several of his collections that combine poetry and narrative prose, the book offers a strongly critical view of the various colonial
interventions in the Southwest. The pieces cover the time from before
first contact with the Spanish through the passing of "ownership" with
the 1848 Treaty of Guadalupe Hidalgo on through events up to the 1980
publication of the book. Ortiz provides clear indictments of many of the
historical actions as well as indictments of the colonial and later capitalist philosophies behind the exploitations of land and people. Among the
specific targets of the collection are the uranium mining in the Laguna-
Acoma-Grants region, the fallout from atomic bomb detonation at
White Sands, the Navy takeover of the Coso Hot Springs, and the callous

display of Native remains as tourist attractions. Although the circumstances of exploitation differ from instance to instance, Ortiz succinctly summarizes the greed in "Returning it Back, You Will Go On":

> Power companies and corporations
> railroads, agribusiness, electronics,
> states, cities, towns,
> the men and women who work in them,
> all of them—all of America—
> take and take from the land and People
>   (*Woven Stone*, 330–31).

He exposes the self-interest of the U.S. government in its dealing with the Native peoples of the region, the government's collusion first with railroad interests and later with the mining industry, and exposes the false justifications of their actions: "It would be in the national interest, of course, with the U.S. economy at stake that Indian lands and people, whose affairs were ruled by the BIA, would be exploited" (354).

Early on and throughout the collection, Ortiz links the various generations who experience injustice and ultimately he calls on the People to "fight back" just as the earlier Pueblo Indians did in the 1680 Revolt. His poems also call for this new revolution in voices from several generations. He recalls, for example, "Mama's and Daddy's Words"—"You have to fight / by working for the land and the People"—as well as the words of an "elder Paiute man"—"It will come, / the moving power of the voice, / the moving power of the earth, / the moving power of the People" (329, 324). Ortiz himself states plainly the need for the struggle to continue and clearly his poetry becomes a part of that ongoing struggle as it works to educate and to incite action. What he calls the "national sacrifice area" in the Southwest can exist as long as Americans remain indifferent to the dynamics of exploitation. He claims, "The American poor and the workers and the white middleclass, who are probably the most ignorant of all U.S. citizens, must understand how they, like Indian people, are forced to serve a national interest, controlled by capitalist vested interests in collusion with U.S. policy makers, which does not serve them" (361).

This unvarnished understanding is what Ortiz tries to bring about through his work, and therein lies the hope for change. Throughout his poetic career, he has re-turned to both the ceremonial and the historical pathways of Native peoples, and in his poetry, re-tells these journeys. His stance is ever that of one who resides in occupied territories, in the colonized spaces of America. The poetic gesture he makes points us beyond.

NOTES

1. I am grateful for the insight of these comments, which come from e-mail correspondence with Brill de Ramírez.

2. Ortiz spoke about his journey to "find Indians" in an oral performance of his work given on November 19, 1975. An audiotape of the reading is available from American Poetry Archive at San Francisco State University. References given are for the reprint of *Going for the Rain* in *Woven Stone*.

3. Herself a part of the Pueblo tradition, Lucero sees in the volume "the connection/movement from below, to emergence to the middle (sipapu), to the four directions, and then back to the middle (homing/returning/ rebirth) and up." I offer my thanks for these comments, which came through e-mail exchanges.

4. For a discussion of the many mythic connections inherent in the poems, see for example Scarberry-Garcia.

5. Like many Native writers, Ortiz links place and identity. Indeed, his collection *A Good Journey* contains a poem comprised primarily of place names. After the listing of names, "Some Indians at a Party" concludes, "That's my name, too. / Don't you forget it" (88).

6. I allude here to William Bevis's use of the phrase in "Native American Novels: Homing In."

WORKS CITED

Beck, Peggy V., Anna Lee Walters, and Nia Francisco, eds. *The Sacred: Ways of Knowledge, Sources of Life.* Rev. ed. Tsaile, AZ: Navajo Community College Press; Flagstaff, AZ: Northland, 1990.

Bevis, William. "Native American Novels: Homing In." In *Recovering the Word: Essays on Native American Literature,* 580–620. Berkeley: University of California Press, 1987.

Bruchac, Joseph. Preface to *On the Good Red Interstate: Truck Stop Tellings and Other Poems,* by Lee Francis, not paginated. San Francisco: Taurean Horn, 2002.

Hogan, Linda. *Mean Spirit.* New York: Atheneum, 1990.

———. "The Two Lives." In *I Tell You Now: Autobiographical Essays by Native American Writers,* 231–49. Lincoln: University of Nebraska Press, 1987.

Kroeber, Karl. "Poem, Dream, and the Consuming of Culture." In *Smoothing the Ground: Essays on Native American Oral Literature*, edited by Brian Swann, 323–33. Berkeley: University of California Press, 1983.

Momaday, N. Scott. *House Made of Dawn*. New York: Signet, 1966.

Ortiz, Simon J. *A Good Journey*. Tucson: University of Arizona Press, 1977.

———. *After and Before the Lightning*. Tucson: University of Arizona Press, 1994.

———. *Going for the Rain*. New York: Harper, 1976.

———. *from Sand Creek*. Tucson: University of Arizona Press, 1981.

———. *Woven Stone*. Tucson: University of Arizona Press, 1992.

Owens, Louis. *Other Destinies: Understanding the American Indian Novel*. Norman, OK: University of Oklahoma Press, 1992.

Scarberry-Garcia, Susan. "Simon J. Ortiz." In *Dictionary of Literary Biography: Native American Writers of the United States*, 208–21. Detroit, MI: Gale Research, 1997.

Silko, Leslie Marmon. *Ceremony*. New York: Signet, 1977.

Underhill, Ruth Murray. *Singing for Power: The Song Magic of the Papago Indians of Southern Arizona*. 1993. Tucson: University of Arizona Press, 1938.

Wilson, Norma C. *The Nature of Native American Poetry*. Albuquerque: University of New Mexico Press, 2001.

"The story goes its own way"

Ortiz, Nationalism, and the Oral Poetics of Power

David L. Moore

In the four "Lightning" poems that frame Simon Ortiz's 1994 collection *After and Before the Lightning*, he charts the internal agonies of the winter of history. Spending an academic year in the Standing Rock Sioux nation while teaching at Sinte Gleska College, Ortiz experienced the bitter winter of the northern Plains. The extreme temperatures, wind, and snow that threatened survival provided the impetus for his poetic reflections. By the last of the four poems and the finale of the volume as a whole, an emergence arrives with all the labor pains of spring. There is not only survival, but an affirmation of power. And power, for Ortiz, pulses in the land.

> We do finally know why we don't turn
> from danger or beauty or sadness or joy.
> How completely we feel the tremoring
> and shuddering pulse of the land now
> as we welcome the rain-heart-lightning
> into our trembling yearning selves
>   (*After and Before the Lightning*, not paginated, 134).

Those feelings, that yearning, the give and take of power in the "shuddering pulse of the land," remain a constant affirmation throughout his work. Perhaps more than any other writer, certainly than most, Ortiz demonstrates an acute sensitivity to the life of the land, its forms, its history, its peoples. In an earlier 1980 collection, *Fight Back*, he writes,

---

This essay was originally published in an earlier version in *SAIL* 16, no. 4 (Winter 2004): 34–46.

This land yearns
for us.
The people yearn
for the land.
Loss and separation
are hard to bear (62).

Ortiz's work is dedicated not only to bearing that loss and separation, but somehow to reversing it, reuniting the people, and as he says,
"not just Indian people" (*Fight Back*, 73), with the land. He maps that process in the historical and political spheres, and increasingly in the inner
territories of the mind and heart as well. Ortiz is generous in showing
his readers how to overcome fear of "danger or beauty or sadness or joy,"
as he articulates the relationality that strengthens and connects one as
part of a much larger creation. He even shows how we "finally know why
we don't turn" from that danger. Understanding profoundly the role that
language, story, and poetry play in this process, he writes,

Choosing words is a waste of time. Let the words choose you, let
them choose their own place, time, identity, meaning. . . . They
have their own power, their own magic, wonder, brilliance. Where
and how they fit, that has nothing to do with us. The only thing we
can do is recognize, admit, and accept that. Let words choose us.
Let language empower us, give us beauty and awe. We cannot do
anything about it. When we think we can, when we choose words,
it is a waste of time (*After and Before the Lightning*, 51).

His assertion of the "power . . . magic, wonder, and brilliance" in words
celebrates the multiplicities of language and human discourse as the
creator of our expressions of experience and ourselves. This view is in
direct contrast with romantic literary nostalgia over the so-called "death
of the author." Echoing Roland Barthes' famous 1967 essay by that title,
Ortiz privileges the communal power of language over the individual-
ity of the writer. Here, the life or death of the author is not the core issue
as long as the stories continue. Ortiz demonstrates that the transformative power of language requires a focus on the larger unfolding stories that connect persons as part of a much larger creation. He thereby
connects his voice with the oral tradition, with what Louis Owens calls

"the authorless signature" of traditional storytelling. This dynamic gives Ortiz's discourse a quality categorically different from the more self-referential writing that is oriented to selves. Offering his words to his readers as a gift from a larger cultural field, Ortiz presents himself as a vehicle for the creative and connective power of language. Beyond some "prison-house of language" (see Fredric Jameson's book by that title), he sees a celebratory source of life in language, with the author and readers dancing along.

If what makes a poet is openness to that larger power in language, one of the particularly magnetic qualities in his writing is the fearless way that Ortiz maintains such openness in the midst of a devastating history. This warrior courage is based on love of land and community and on faith in life itself. Faith is always elusive and can be misread as optimism. In a remarkable, reciprocal logic of encouragement, we can read this faith in simply "life and its continuance" through this passage from *Fight Back*:

> We must have passionate concern for what is at stake. We must understand the experience of the oppressed, especially the racial and ethnic minorities, of this nation, by this nation and the economic interests, because only when we truly understand and accept the responsibilities of that understanding will we be able to make the necessary decisions for change. Only then will we truly understand what it is to love the land and people and to have compassion. Only when we are not afraid to fight against the destroyers, thieves, liars, exploiters who profit handsomely off the land and people will we know what love and compassion are. Only when the people of this nation, not just Indian people, fight for what is just and good for all life, will we know life and its continuance. And when we fight, and fight back those who are bent on destruction of land and people, we will win. We will win (73).

Those fighting words are filled with the courage of passionate certitude. In the heart of the storm of colonialism, which he names—"This America / has been a burden / of steel and mad / death . . ." (*from Sand Creek*, 9)— his aesthetic of openness merges with the ethics of power in Native nationalism and authenticity: ". . . the indigenous peoples of the Americas have taken the languages of the colonialists and used them for their own purposes" ("National Indian Literature," 10). This ability to transform oppressive discourses and use them "for their own purposes" derives from a returning affirmation of dynamic cultural authenticity. "It is by the affirmation of knowledge of source and place and spiritual return that resistance is realized" ("National Indian Literature," 11). In Ortiz's definition, this is a dynamic, not static, authenticity that moves through that very act of resistance by which the people use colonial languages "for their own purposes." Inside that historical burden of America, he thus can go on to write, "but, look now, / there are flowers / and new grass / and a spring wind / rising / from Sand Creek" (9).

But how does this work? On the one hand, Ortiz writes, "Let the words choose you"; and on the other, he states that those words must be used by Native artists "for their own purposes." How can the words "choose" you when you "use" them for particular purposes? His negotiations of this complex dynamic run parallel to ancient Western questions of free will and predestination, to ancient Eastern mystical tensions between visualization and acceptance, to postmodern tensions between individual agency and social construction, to critical linguistic tensions between personal expression and social language. Ortiz has addressed many of these binary questions in his work. His essays such as, "Song, Poetry and Language— Expression and Perception" and "Towards a National Indian Literature: Cultural Authenticity in Nationalism," written more than twenty years ago, contribute to these ancient discussions. He provides not only the conceptual spark but also the practical example of how to make the leap that transcends or deconstructs these binaries basically of spirit and matter. Ortiz shows us the way out of or through a paradox—out of choosing between two opposing possibilities, such as openness to language versus reinvention of language—in the courage of dynamic focused energy, a leap of faith across or around the abyss of that divide. We are witness to that leap of faith as we discuss how these two tendencies work for a Native nationalist, to "let the words choose you" and to take "the language[s] of the colonialists and [use] them for their own purposes."

Are these two tendencies, with their various aesthetic and ethical dimensions, a contradiction or a mystification? Is he being co-opted by the romance of language? For many Native writers, this challenge is added to the other tough questions about how Indian voices reinvent their stories in the enemy's language. Through Ortiz's oral aesthetic of resistive and regenerative cultural authenticity, we find a single root in that certainty which knows that "The story goes its own way" (*After and Before the Lightning*, 20). In his description of the power of the oral tradition, there is little room for powerlessness. For instance, this affirmation of an oral aesthetics of power is from his "Introduction" to his edited volume, *Earth Power Coming*:

> There have always been the songs, the prayers, the stories. There have always been the voices. There have always been the people. There have always been those words which evoked meaning and the meaning's magical wonder. There has always been the spirit which inspired the desire for life to go on. And it has been through the words of the songs, the prayers, the stories that the people have found a way to continue, for life to go on.
>
> It is the very experience of life that engenders life. It is the act of perception that insures knowledge. For Indian people, it has been the evolvement of a system of life which insists on one's full awareness of his relationship to all life. Through words derived from one's thoughts, beliefs, acts, experiences, it is possible to share this awareness with all mankind (vii).

Because of this root of certitude in his aesthetic, and its ethics, he can give himself, his writing and even history over to such an affirmation. Yet for Ortiz, the affirmation of the power of "the voices" and "the people" is far more than platitudes. It is experiential, accepting a participatory role in the unfolding of language and "the meaning's magical wonder." Thus he holds to the power of language and story to effect change in people's lives. For example, in a remarkable moment in *After and Before the Lightning*, Ortiz inserts an internal, contemplative voice into a communal story:

> "In those days, people would go on top of Horace Mesa to gather pinon nuts. Once in October, they went for two days. On the second day it started to snow. It snowed all afternoon and into the night. . . ." No, it's not that way. The story goes its own way. In my mind the words go their way, following the basic story plus the imagination and memory, plus the way I have experienced things. It is how the story goes, my mother's and father's words, their experiences in my mind, and my mind's own knowledge.

Imagination is a harking back to the source but it is also more than source.

[. . .]

Snow that October, the language of experience, sensation, history, imagination are all in the story and how it carries forth. Story has its own life, its very own, and we are the voice carried with it (*After and Before the Lightning*, 20).

By his explanation, such letting go so that the story may go "its own way" is only a loss of illusion. Control gives way to that reciprocal certitude. We become empowered, as we let ourselves be "the voice carried with" the story, "as we welcome the rain-heart-lightning / into our trembling yearning selves." This empowerment becomes a writer's balanced embrace of the power of craft and the power of language, and that embrace functions on fundamental faith in those powers.

Throughout his work, Ortiz marks many expressions of this reciprocal certitude in references to "Existence," or "continuance," or to "the creative forces of life" (*Fight Back*, 1). The affirmation often remains submerged as the *a priori*, the foundational dynamic of his language and perception. He rarely lands directly on faith in these forces as its own focus, perhaps because of a difference between optimism and faith: where optimism is vague and passive and faith is specific and active, like the focused energy of reciprocal certitude which turns in Ortiz's words. His prose can be explicit about that cycle, "[. . .] my own writing comes from a similar dynamic of reciprocity shared by the land, water, and human culture" (*Speaking for the Generations*, xv). Often this dynamic affirmation of faith focuses the process that drives his politics. For instance, he writes, "*There is a revolution going on; it is very spiritual and its manifestation is economic, political, and social. Look to the horizon and listen*" (*from Sand Creek*, 54). By mapping those manifestations of spirit, his works direct the active reader to the full spectrum of grim history both as it is written and as he would rewrite it to revise a future.

As Robin Riley Fast suggests, "Having given his testimony, Ortiz can finally rely only on hope, but the terms in which he imagines hope, in the context of this history, must be limited unless his witness compels his listeners to faith and action" (59). In that momentum of action, Ortiz gives many phrases to this ineffable "Existence." Again in dynamic relation, he invokes "the creative ability of Indian people to gather in many forms of the socio-political-colonizing force which beset them and to make those forms meaningful in their own terms" ("National Indian Literature," 8). That "creative ability of Indian people" is linked in turn to the creative force at the center of "Existence," a term which he frequently capitalizes. In his introduction to *Speaking for the Generations: Native Writers on Writing*, Ortiz writes,

> Acoma Pueblo people believe they came into Existence as a human culture and community at Shipapu, which they know is a sacred mythic place of origin. Shipapu and a belief in Shipapu, therefore and thereafter, is the mythic source of their Existence. Coming into Existence from a source like Shipapu is indisputably an assertion of their direct relationship with the creative spirit-force-dynamic of the earth (xiii–xiv).

His connections to this "spirit-force-dynamic of the earth" take many forms of expression, which we might approach through Ortiz's own general categories of manifestation—economic, political, and social—and he maps those categories onto a ground which we might call ecological. Thus there emerge in his writing four foci of his "spirit-energy-dynamic of the earth": first the ecological "for the sake of the land"; second the social "for the sake of the people"; third the political, how "Warriors will keep alive in the blood" (*from Sand Creek*, 33); and fourth the economic, how he addresses "this heart which is our America." Of course, any one of these bears the weight of each of the other categories, as the economic is ecological, the political is social, etc. What is key here is his originary faith in the "spirit-energy-dynamic" which can envision active human choice in each of these realms.

For the remainder of this essay, I would like to discuss briefly only the last two of these areas in conclusion, and leave "for the sake of the land" and "for the sake of the people" to the other essays in this collection. I am intrigued by the warrior anger which Ortiz wields with such skill, a warrior ethos not "frightened by emotion, / the sheer joy of being men, / of being children" (*from Sand Creek*, 59). There is a fascinating link from that warrior ethic in his work to the particular ways that his redefinitions of "America" offer the enemies of that warrior a vision of compassion. The warrior who is open to anger is also open to compassion. Thus, speaking of the settlers, he writes, "They should have eaten

/ whole buffalo. / They should have, / like the People wanted for them" (*from Sand Creek*, 51). If they had taken more than just the tongues and hides, if the hunters had had compassion for the buffalo, the invaders might even have discovered how "Warriors could have passed / into their young blood" (*from Sand Creek*, 35). By openness to feelings, they would be open to the warrior spirit which survives. Ortiz is generous in battle.

I think this generosity rises up because his work is courageous enough to imagine balance in a crazy world, in a crazy psyche. Indeed, Ortiz faces the most brutal history in the most personal ways, only to transform it into "a spring wind / rising," as we saw as in his seminal book-length poem, *from Sand Creek*, cited earlier. Contemplating the 1864 massacre by the Colorado Militia of a peace-seeking Arapaho and Cheyenne camp, as he works out his own internal legacy from that history in an alcohol treatment ward of a nearby VA hospital, Ortiz achieves a remarkable complexity of historical and personal voicings in this text. In a passage on shell-shocked warriors in the Ft. Lyons veterans hospital, he writes, "*There is an honest and healthy anger which will raze these walls, and it is the rising of our blood and breath which will free our muscles, minds, spirits*" (*from Sand Creek*, 84). Having also written, "I am so mad / with love for these derelicts" (*from Sand Creek*, 63), he personalizes that proclamation about anger in the lines that conclude the accompanying poem:

> I could only cry,
>   mangled
> like his anger,
> amazed
> and dismayed (85).

As Ortiz conveys throughout the volume, when that anger cannot find an outlet, it injures the self. "*Repression*," he writes, "*works like a shadow, clouding memory and sometimes even to blind, and when it is on a national scale, it is just not good*" (*from Sand Creek*, 14). But as we saw in *Fighting Back*, the courage to resist is linked to the passion for life, and that passion is linked to compassion even for disappointed colonizers and "settlers," for "Even the farmer has become a loser" (*from Sand Creek*, 30), he writes. That compassion is aimed even toward deluded soldiers at Sand Creek,

> ... and breathing
> self-righteously they deemed
> themselves blessed and pure
> so that not even breath
> became life—
> life strangled
> in their throats
> (*from Sand Creek*, 75).

Yet that warrior spirit survives even the assault of self-righteous massacres, enough to convey a tone of tenderness which is the only way to catch the attention of despair. Traditional warriors know their honor comes not merely from self-advancement, but from serving their people. They are willing to sacrifice themselves for their culture. Thus Ortiz keeps the warrior focus on the life of the people, as here in the corn:

> Don't fret now.
>
> Songs are useless
> to exculpate sorrow.
> That's not their intent anyway.
>
> Strive
> for significance.
> Cull seeds from grass.
> Develop another strain of corn.
> Whisper for rain.
>
> Don't fret.
> Warriors will keep alive in the blood
> (*from Sand Creek*, 33).

A faith in the warrior spirit is a faith in life, in corn, as the prose statement accompanying this poem declares: "*In this hemisphere, corn is ancient and young; it is the seed, food, and symbol of a constantly developing and revolutionary people*" (32). The energy of revolution is the biological cycle of sunlight in corn as food for human bodies. Despite droughts, diseases, conquests, wars, and the theft of land and body, continuance requires effort, that one must indeed "strive for significance" in the most direct ways, through corn, grass, rain, blood.

In the next category where his pragmatic faith in "the spirit-force-dynamic of the earth" addresses "this heart which is our America," his alternate vision of history evokes a cross-cultural nation where whites unlearn Puritanism and relearn from Indians that death is not sin, that suffering is not evil, that they did not have to mask their fear and guilt in a myth of Manifest Destiny, that "We do finally know why we don't turn / from danger or beauty or sadness or joy" (*After and Before the Lightning*, 134). As Ortiz has shown in his writing and in his life, we make choices each day, and here he affirms the power, the responsibility and culpability, of our choices. Rather than destiny, conquest is a choice. The appropriation of land and its resources is a set of choices. Objectification and genocide are, too, the results of choices made and ignorance reified. In *from Sand Creek* he writes both about the massacre of innocent Arapaho and Cheyenne people and about the men in the Colorado Militia who had their own choices, to live as fellow humans with the Indigenous peoples of that region or to brutally objectify them to the point of massacre. *"Pain and death did not have to be propagated as darkness and wrong and coldness; they could have listened and listened and learned to sing in Arapaho"* (*from Sand Creek*, 34). Such a fantasy does not ring hollow, because Ortiz hooks that alternate history onto internal, psychological losses that are real. He even offers counsel to the white warriors:

> They should have seen
> the thieves stealing
> their most precious treasure:
> their compassion, their anger (*from Sand Creek*, 59).

Again, his faith in that spirit-force-dynamic categorizes compassion and anger together as a warrior energy requisite for the humanity of any person, especially warriors. Here Ortiz suggests how a white military was out of touch with its compassion because it was out of touch with the roots of its anger, horrifically displaced upon the objectified people of that camp. Speaking to the white culture in a voice like a matter-of-fact mother earth, Ortiz suggests what could have been history:

> There was no paradise,
> but it would have gently and willingly
> and longingly given them food and air
> and substance for every comfort.
> If they had only acknowledged
> Even their smallest conceit
>   (*from Sand Creek*, 79).

Presumably there is still a future in that yearning and longing of the land for the people. Ortiz even articulates for them their arrogance and their acquisitive assumptions: "*There is probably no way to verify if people become self-righteous and arrogant because they are dissatisfied or failures, but they certainly do*" (*from Sand Creek*, 76). Through his own clarity about that spirit-energy-dynamic, Ortiz is able to diagnose the problem:

> And onward,
>   westward
> they marched,
> sweeping aside the potential
> of dreams which could have been
> generous and magnificent
> and genius for them.
>
>   It is
> no wonder
> they deny regret
> for the slaughter
> of their future.
> Denying eternity, it is no wonder
> they became so selflessly
> righteous (77).

In a collection which takes the Sand Creek Massacre as its central metaphor, it is a remarkable twist for Ortiz to point to the "slaughter / of their future," referring to the destruction of America's own compassionate heart in the violent extremes of that self-righteous mentality— played out in the volume's passages that focus on the largely forgotten casualties of those men's lives in a Colorado Veterans' Affairs hospital not far from Sand Creek. In that same context, we can see further his point that "Denying eternity" is the consequence of denying humanity in America's "others" by that tragic militarism which slaughtered and mutilated Black Kettle's peaceful camp. Even so, *from Sand Creek* begins not only with America as "a burden / of steel and mad / death," but astonishingly frames the intimate, angry, celebratory poems with this affirmation at the end:

> That dream
> shall have a name
> after all,
> and it will not be vengeful
> but wealthy with love
> and compassion
> and knowledge.
> And it will rise
> in this heart
> which is our America (95).

"Mad / death" has become "compassion / and knowledge" through this very process of retelling the story so that all the voices may be heard. The reader, and "this heart / which is our America," may thus know and thus feel compassion for those hearts and those voices that both died and killed. Then we are "wealthy with love." It is a stunning transformation by a Native American poet. Indeed, we are primed for this "dream" that "shall have a name" in the first poem of *from Sand Creek*, which begins "Grief / memorizes this grass" of Ft. Lyons, Colorado, the staging ground for the 1864 massacre. Ortiz provokes his readers to the act of believing in that primary energy which survives such grief. In this instance, he calls that spirit-force-dynamic "raw courage":

> Raw
> courage,
>   believe it,
> red-eyed and urgent,
> stalking Denver.
> Like stone,
> like steel,

the hone and sheer gone,
just the brute
and perceptive angle left.

Like courage,
              believe it,

left still;
the words from then
talk like that.

Believe it (11).

He can deliver this imperative to believe in the timelessness of words
spoken with raw courage because that is what he does. Here again Ortiz
gives us not only the urgency but the example of how to see and what to
do with the history of our America, which he loves as *"something precious
in the memory in blood and cells which insists on story, poetry, song, life,
life" (from Sand Creek*, 92). By faith in that *life*, he writes, *"Women and
men may be broken and scattered, but they remember and think about
the reasons why. They answer their own questions and always the truth
and love will make them decide" (from Sand Creek*, 56). His readers and
his nation, Acoma and America, can now decide on these questions.

WORKS CITED

Barthes, Roland. 1977. "Death of the Author." In *Image-Music-Text*, translated
    by Stephen Heath, 142–48. New York: Farrar, Straus, and Giroux, 1988.

Fast, Robin Riley. "'It is ours to know': Simon J. Ortiz's *from Sand Creek*." *SAIL
    (Studies in American Indian Literatures)* 12, no. 3 (Fall 2000): 52–63.

Ortiz, Simon J. *After and Before the Lightning*. Tucson: Arizona University
    Press, 1994.

——. *Fight Back: For the Sake of the People, For the Sake of the Land. Institute
    for Native American Development Literary Journal* 1, no. 1 (1980).

——. *from Sand Creek: Rising in This Heart Which Is Our America*. New York:
    Thunder's Mouth, 1981.

——. "Introduction." In *Earth Power Coming: Short Fiction in Native
    American Literature*, edited by Simon J. Ortiz, vii–ix. Tsaile, Arizona:
    Navajo Community College Press, 1983.

————. "Song, Poetry and Language–Expression and Perception." In *Symposium of the Whole: A Range of Discourse Toward an Ethnopoetics,* edited by Jerome Rothenberg and Diane Rothenberg, 399–407. Berkeley: California University Press, 1983.

————. "Introduction: Wah nuhtyuh-yuu dyu neetah tyahstih (Now It Is My Turn To Stand)." In *Speaking for the Generations: Native Writers on Writing,* edited by Simon J. Ortiz, xi–xix. Tucson: Arizona University Press, 1997.

————. "Towards a National Indian Literature: Cultural Authenticity in Nationalism." *MELUS (Multicultural and Ethnic Literatures of the United States)* 8, no. 2 (Summer 1981): 7–12.

Reading Simon Ortiz and Black Diasporic Literature of the Americas

Sophia Cantave

In the fall of 2006, I heard Simon Ortiz speak at Tufts University's annual Native American Speakers Series. When he read his prose poem, "More than Just a River" from his *Out There Somewhere* collection, I found myself thinking about the relationships that first generations of Africans in the Americas tried to maintain with their respective homelands in Africa and how they and their descendants in the Americas went about making the unknown rivers, trees, plants—and the lands they were forced to work—"more than just [these] rivers," trees and plants. As long as the landscapes around them were alien, the unknown geographies reinforced their captivity and subalterity. In Julie Dash's 1992 classic film, *Daughters of the Dust*, the Unborn Child and sometime-narrator, in the shape of a five-year-old black girl, races across space and time to spiritually assist the Peazant family on the eve of their migration north, from the Gullah Sea Islands to the South Carolina mainland. In one scene, the Unborn Child follows her father to the family graveyard and says, "In this quiet place, years ago, my family knelt down and caught a glimpse of the eternal. We left our markers in the soil, . . . in memory of the families who once lived here. We were the children of those who chose to survive" (Dash, 133).

As a descendant "of those [first Africans] who chose to survive," I wondered what it must have been like for the early African slaves brought to the United States, Haiti, and Jamaica to try to find *Ginen*[1] or Africa in these foreign lands; to credibly identify in the new environment the sacred and the meaningful that existed alongside the brutality of a white plantation system founded upon genocide. How was it that people who had been violently taken from one world to another were able to redefine an alien landscape into a geography of belonging? As Ortiz read about his memories of his place and of a home forever connected to the *chunah* (the Keres name for the Rio de San Jose which runs through Acoma Pueblo land), I was moved by thoughts of those early enslaved ancestors, how they believed they could and would adapt the elements of this new environment to fit with their memories of another place and, in the process, create a sense of home and, thereby, a place for me. I also thought about black people like my parents, leaving one country, Haiti, to start over in another, the United States, and what that did to their certainty of place and to their sense of belonging. To address the rupture of leaving Ibo landing for the U.S. mainland and the prospect of some family members never returning, the matriarch of the Peazant family, Nana Peazant, makes a protective "hand" or charm for the ceremonial gathering using the "scraps of memories" contained in her tin can. She says to her family,

> When I was a child, my mother cut this from her hair before she was sold away from us. Now, I'm adding my hair. There must be a bond . . . a connection, between those that go up North, and those who cross the sea. A connection! We are as two people in one body. The last of the old, the first of the new. We will always live this double life, you know, because we're from the sea. We came here in chains and we must survive. There's salt water in our blood . . . (Dash, *Daughters of the Dust*, 151).

Creating a space for me meant coming to terms with the unspeakable horror and grief recollected in Julie Dash's groundbreaking film and in early Haitian spirituals that to me lamented the loss of home while simultaneously putting the new place within the powers of ancient *lwas*, gods. "Solèy, o, Moin pa moun isit o, solèy / Moin sé nég gin[e]n, solèy / M'pa kab traversé / Min batiman~m chaviré, solèy" (Montero, *In the Palm of Darkness*, 13).[2] My translation of these Haitian Kreyol words reads, "Sun, I am not of a people from here. Sun, I come from Ginen and I cannot crossover. Sun, my boat has sunk." In this lament to the sun and the *lwa* (god) Damballah, who makes the sun's rising possible, my ancestors cried out their displacement from their African lands and their disorientation on another continent, another hemisphere, another place. The importance of belonging and identity is affirmed in the song's prayerful address to the constancy of the sun traveling across a sky which looks down upon all humans. With this blues lament and the many others sung throughout the Americas, the process of becoming "black" and of the Americas began. The blues lament and all that it encompassed—loss, anger, resistance, resignation, adaptation, hope—continues to be the hallmark of black music-making. Grounded in the beliefs that Africans brought with them, these initial prayer songs became the soul-saving and spirit-saving measures that made a counter-narrative of black American humanity possible.[3]

That spirit of Indigenous agency (as Africans became part of the American landscape) and personal resistance to cultural and physical erasure is also what I heard in the voice of the Native American writer Simon Ortiz and what caused me to recall and want to reach out to a similar spirit that I knew was possessed by those first Africans, who had to submit to multiple levels of life-altering changes while finding ways to remain constant as people of African descent. The poems and stories that Ortiz read from *Out There Somewhere, After and Before the Lightning,* and *Men on the Moon* demonstrate his quiet but firm insistence that his Acoma Pueblo claims to an identity with the land and that the similar claims of other Indigenous people will not go away. My people, too, are Indigenous peoples with ancient homelands, even though we have been dispersed to new lands we had to make into new homelands. Ortiz's reading prompted this subtle, yet profound, difference in my understanding of the ways people of African descent lay claim to their new environments, the conflicting nature of those claims, and the struggle for black American continuity within the fact of white hegemony. In time, they would find the corresponding trees, waterways, and wooded enclosures that would become the New World home of this *lwa* or that *orisha*.[4] They would also identify, for example, the warrior god *Ogou*'s favorite food and drink, recreate with cornmeal and flour the *vèvè*'s, or the signatures, that would help call *Ogou*, and a pantheon of other gods, to their "New World" homes.

I thought about these and other transformations that came out of that violent transplanting of so many Africans into the unknown, who I am and what, as a modern black person, I am not always "allowed" to simultaneously honor, grieve, and take strength from: what it took for African peoples to transport and transform their entire worldview and reimagine what constituted hallowed ground. In *Voodoo: Search for the Spirit,* Laënnec Hurbon says, "The displacement of millions of black slaves to the New World led to the rebirth of African beliefs and practices in the Americas under various forms and names: *candomblé* in Brazil, *santería* in Cuba, *obeayisne* in Jamaica, *shango cult* in Trinidad, and *vodou* in Haiti" (13). In the Georgia and South Carolina sea islands, Nana Peazant says, "[W]e've taken old Gods and given them new names" (Dash, 159). Everything sacred had to be reconfigured, often out of and in spite of what the enslaving culture profaned. Though forced to work the land, and in becoming synonymous with laboring on the land, Africans and their descendants created spaces of resistance through spirit and through a reverence for the freedom to be found in both wild, green spaces and also in built spaces that enabled the expression of unchecked African-based spirituality hidden from white institutional interpellation.

These were the early spirit-saving acts that granted the enslaved a space of humanity and also began, for those who "chose to survive," a way to resist their dehumanization and inscribe blackness onto the new and often unforgiving environment. Often the acts that ensure survival and shape future resistance can be as unassuming as stressing, via repetition and story, the connections to place—for my people, the knowledge and intimacy gained clearing and seeding the plantations while secretly renewing "[e]ach *lwa* ['s] tie[s] to a specific realm of nature (air, earth, water, or fire), tree or plant, human behavior, color, and ritual" (Hurbon, *Voodoo*, 140); for Ortiz, a life-giving and living river that winds through the arid landscape of the desert Southwest and his series of personal memories. But those personal memories also shed light on a colonial legacy of conquest currently manifested in the Acoma people's struggle "with the State Game and Fisheries people," as well as on the people's reliance on this river "as a water source [and] a life-giving force," or even as a place to perform the clan's regenerating ceremonies. Where do African Americans in the United States and people of African descent throughout the Americas go to regroup as communities and descendants of first Africans? Where are their fonts of sustainable "life-giving" energy and can they get to them? I considered these questions as I listened to Ortiz speak in a university lecture hall.

Ortiz offers invaluable guidance towards the establishment of deep connections here in the Americas, despite the imperial legacy of the past 500 years. In part, Ortiz's resistance to systematic domination, erasure, and relegation to the margins of hegemonically created societies comes from his determination to reaffirm his people's connections to their lands and what existed before. That reaffirmation begins with investing every-day activities with meaning, like learning to swim in the *chunah* or committing his earliest act of sabotage. Out of this meaning and purpose, he speaks as an Acoma poet, storyteller, and activist. The memories that are more than memories, the stories that are more than stories, along with attendant rituals and prayers helped those leaving ancestral lands or fighting dominant cultural encroachments on their land to resist psychic annihilation. The alternative to not investing a space and its harsh elements with personal meaning is to drift unconnected, aimlessly, in anger and resignation, and powerless in the dominant group's meaning. Many of the characters in the novels I study as a scholar of Black Diasporic literature of the Americas, *General Sun, My Brother* by Jacques Stephen Alexis, *No Telephone to Heaven* by Michelle Cliff, and *In the Palm of Darkness* by Mayra Montero, struggle to do what Ortiz does in his poems and short stories: find adequate ways to resist psychic annihilation and cultural erasure in majority white environments and the debilitating marginalization of the places they come from by the dominant culture. In either case, home, the history attached to that space before and after the fact of whiteness, has to be dealt with, especially in the case of people who are forced to migrate—again and again in moves and removes that relocate and dislocate persons, families, and communities.

In the preface to *Out There Somewhere*, Ortiz says that the title is an Acoma response usually said by someone inside a home about someone "outdoors and beyond the house walls" (ix). But that person who is "out there, somewhere" remains a vital part of the interior home space. As Ortiz relates, ". . . I've imagined the outdoors to be out there somewhere in everyday experience somewhere in America. I've spent a large part of my lifetime away from Acoma Pueblo—out there somewhere in America . . . away from the Acoma village area of Deetseyaamah where I grew up" (ix). Many Native peoples in the twentieth and twentieth-first centuries share this experience (ix). Even so, for many, the Indigenous connective ties to one's ancestral lands and communities endure. As Ortiz explains, "Yet at the same time that we are away, we also continue to be absolutely connected socially and culturally to our Native identity. We insist that we as human cultural beings must always have this connection because it is the way we maintain a Native sense of existence" (ix). So too, black people who have become *native* to the Caribbean, North America and South America have to keep reenacting the rituals that will confer native, environmental recognition. They have to keep affirming their humanity in environments, home spaces that continue to deny their access to clean drinking water, adequate schooling, and proper waste removal. Three Caribbean works of fiction, *General Sun, My Brother, No Telephone to Heaven*, and *In the Palm of Darkness*, demonstrate the extent to which people's relationships to their environments (Indigenous or diasporic) are compromised by the appropriative interests of big business and central and local government agencies.

Ortiz's words help me, a black woman in the Americas, consider anew the racism that does not allow black people in the Caribbean to make a living or raise a family in the places where they were born. How do these often displaced, dispossessed people see themselves in relation to the land that centuries after enslavement leaves them with either an unaffirmed spiritual connection or only the old rituals as their only form of redress? How exactly does this struggle affect people of African descent in their overall sense of belonging or alienation? Drawing upon Ortiz's emphasis on the importance of a person's grounded orientation to her or his environment, I have found that the protagonists in black Caribbean literatures struggle with this challenge, with being "out there, somewhere" without the enduring connection implied by the Acoma phrase. Black protagonists struggle with their conflicting emotions both within and outside of their birthplaces. In the Jacques Stephen Alexis and Michelle Cliff novels, the protagonists wrestle with claiming a certainty of place and a certainty of self within an era of outright colonization, post-enslavement. The powers-that-be either deny or keep unofficial the facts of African enslavement, African resistance, and the empowerment that descendants can derive from their ancestors' choosing to identify as African and American. For Cliff's Clare Savage, a young woman visibly bred out of Africanness, reconnecting with the stories of Jamaica, the Coromantee language of the warrior woman Nanny, enables her to end her rootless travels in a "white chocolate" body and to come back to a homeland and a black identity rooted in the struggle for freedom (Cliff, *No Telephone to Heaven*, 4, 99, 199). On the other hand, Alexis's Hilarion Hilarius has the traditional stories and ancestral rituals, but no real way to turn them into an impetus for political action or even to improve his material condition in the slums of Haiti (Alexis, *General Sun, My Brother*, 5). Mayra Montero uses what the book jacket calls the "ever-volatile" yet exotic backdrop of Haiti to pit the black Haitian Indigenous knowledge and Thierry Adrien's storytelling against the Western science

and specificity of Victor Grigg, a white U.S. American herpetologist, looking for the last remaining *grenouille du sang*, a blood-red frog (Montero, *In
the Palm of Darkness*, 19).

All three of these Caribbean novels demand that readers enter into
the sights, sounds, and smells of their storytelling environment. Through
sensory detail the Caribbean world explodes. There is no way around
the harshness and the extremes of black Native life in these texts: the
extremes of poverty and wealth, the use and misuse of spirit, the failed
political apparatuses or the Western drive for research or exploitable
commodities in these subject island nations. The novels also force readers to come to terms not just with the struggles of the living, but also to
reckon with the complex legacy of dead, angry spirits they've trauma-
tized, and also with the specter of the walking dead—those still physically alive whose spirits have been taken away from them. To understand
the importance of burial ceremonies for the dead and the fear of the spiritually unsettled dead in these novels requires the story of those earlier
Africans who, when they had the opportunity, chose death as a way to
return to Africa. In *Haiti, History, and the Gods*, Joan Dayan says those
deaths were undercut by policies that decreed that the dead, mutilated
bodies remain unburied or else be buried without any rites in unconse-
crated ground to deter others from attempting the same opportunistic
choice (Dayan 259–60). "Slaves were ordained to be suspended between
the promise of sanctified earth and the curse of defilement which meant
an unquiet wandering, a state of unrelenting restlessness" (Dayan 260).
The mutilation of the dead by the enslaver would ensure that he or she
would be unrecognizable to Africans waiting on the other side of the
water in both body and spirit. Left unburied and unclaimed, or else violently killed, the spirit of these dead roamed on this side of the water:
angry, restless, unable to leave or to stay. "The landscape of Haiti [and the
Jamaica described by Michelle Cliff] is filled not with the spirits of the
dead seeking rest and recognition but with other corporeal spirits who
recall the terrors of slavery and the monstrous, institutionalized magic
of turning humans into pieces of prized and sexualized matter" (Dayan,
Haiti, History, and the Gods, 264). Thus, to survive the institution of
slavery, people of African descent had to find ways to access their own
meaning-making powers against this "monstrous" dehumanization.

Those choosing to survive, despite cultural, ethnic, and linguistic
differences, brought their collective knowledge together, as Nago, Arada,

Ibo, Congo, to form not just new alliances but also new identities as Africans and as blacks. But to get to these identity-forging spaces in the forest, to learn the arts of healing, curing, or poisoning, they risked life and limb and the possibility of being rendered not only unrecognizable in the afterlife but of being trapped in a space of pure captivity (physically by the slave owners and slave traders, or spiritually through a compromised death and burial). The most famous Black Diasporic literary example of this phenomenon may be Toni Morrison's *Beloved* in a novel of the same name. The fear of becoming angry, wandering spirits without the possibility of ever finding peace or justice also runs through these works of black Caribbean literatures—the angry, wandering spirits of slaves and that of their descendants down to this day.

The folklore and oral history of the African Diaspora also contain powerful countering stories to the angry restless dead so that not all the dead walk this side of the water do so with misdirected rage or venom. For example, one of Haiti's earliest folk heroes, Makandal, would escape being burned alive at the stake by turning into a mosquito and helping to sow the seeds of what would become the only successful slave revolt in modern times. Before his capture and supposed death, the one-armed Makandal spent most of his time studying the environment surrounding the plantations. While tending the livestock, he experimented with different plants and left a legacy of plant-based poisons and cures. He identified the places that would support communities of escaped slaves, maroons, in their preparations to overthrow slavery. Because of his spiritual and mystical connection to the land, a connection made on his terms, Makandal was able to fight for the land and for his place it. He did not die to wander as a captive, angry alien. "After his death, his followers believed he would be reincarnated in the body of a new leader who would undertake the final struggle for liberation" (Desmangles, *Faces of the Gods: Vodou and Roman Catholicism in Haiti*, 34). Jamaica's Nanny and Cudjoe have a similar mythic status. For those in the Black Diaspora seeking home on this side of the Atlantic—reading and listening to Simon Ortiz's work is invaluable in placing this oral narrative within a framework that emphasizes the spiritual aspects of the Black Diasporic relationship to the natural world.

Often the spirits that helped to make foreign land Native cannot be celebrated in the open and seem to exist outside of the dominant environmental discourse. In *No Telephone to Heaven*, Clare's healing begins with reclaiming maroon warriors Nanny and Cudjoe from their relegation to the margins of her story as a Jamaican descendant of Africans who chose to undergo the painful process to make that identity possible. In the novel, Clare's journey culminates in her return not only to the place where she was born but also to the history and the stories she was never taught in the colonial classroom. With this reclaimed history of her mother's people, she also claims a people to fight for and a better understanding of what nations like Jamaica are up against in the global economy. By moving the societally marginal into the center of the story, Cliff shows readers post-slavery Jamaica using a more nuanced, more focused lens. In his preface to *Men on the Moon*, Ortiz says,

> Story has its own power, and the language of story is that power. We are within it, and we are empowered by it. We exist because of it. We don't exist without that power. As human beings, we, as personal and cultural entities, are conscious beings because of story, no other reason.
>
> I've known "story"—or stories—all my life, just like everyone else. For me, there's never been a conscious moment without story. That's simply the case, that's simply fact. Cultural consciousness, whether personal and individual or social and collective, is determined by our awareness of the self within circumstance, experience, and event. Place and time and motion: something happening (viii).

Whether experiences are defined in the specificities of enslavement or their enduring legacies, Ortiz's words provide a useful interpretive frame to focus upon both Cliff's and Alexis's stories about similar yet different black urban experiences and the attempts of their characters to resist physical and psychic violation as well as cultural erasure in a world dominated by Western globalization and an overwhelming sense of powerlessness.

In *General Sun, My Brother*, Alexis captures the tension of being both of African descent and of American birth. In the angry lines of a starving "real man of Haiti," the protagonist Hilarion says,

> On the mountain, that mon over there, a little drum is sounding an insistent complaint. A little drum begging forgiveness of a life

that is at once so harsh and so sweet and that brings so much pain
to so many people. The mountain lies collapsed like a sleeping beat!
That stupid little drum with its piercing beat, like a migraine! That's
Africa glued to the flesh of every black man like an extra penis.
Africa will not let a man alone, regardless of where he was born—no
matter what place he comes from or heads towards (3–4).

The drum signifies absence, distance, and violent diasporization, and yet
in the very next lines, Alexis captures the other side of what that drumbeat has meant: African survival, retention, and adaptation. "Every night,
misery and its companion, despair, make the heart beat in a complaint—
the naked, heartrending drum of Vodou and its spirits. But with each
new, triumphant day, the living drum carves out its own place, that gay
and joyous yanvalou drum, or the laughing kongo drum, the high ring-
ing conical drums that sing out life" (Alexis, *General Sun, My Brother*, 4).
Those who survive did so and continue to do so by turning the despair
and complaint into songs of hope, freedom, and resistance—songs that
have traveled the world. Through song and music, people of African
descent psychically and physically survived unimaginable horrors.

The insistent drumbeat has followed Hilarion all his life, chronicling
his forced migration from the countryside to the posh suburb of Bois
Verna as a *restavek*, a child servant, his escape into the woods for solace
and to avoid being punished by the people he worked for, his time as a
street boy along with other runaway *restaveks*, and his life in the outskirts
of Port-au-Prince at the start of the novel as a young man coming of age
during the 1915–1937 U.S. occupation of Haiti. He hears the drumbeat as
he returns to his one-room shack "in the old suburb of Nan-Palmiste, [a]
neighborhood rotting like an open wound on the flank of Port-au-Prince"
(Alexis, *General Sun, My Brother*, 3). The urban squalor and decay Alexis
describes point to the disparities between those who have access to a life
beyond the slums in the city proper and those who do not. To get to his
home, Hilarion jumps from rock to rock to avoid stepping into the open
sewage that runs freely in the ditches along the roads and often covers the
roads when the rains come. Hilarion describes the sewage as a "kalalou
and djondjon [okra and black mushroom] soup" (Alexis, *General Sun, My
Brother*, 3). Once home, his delirium from hunger will force him to leave
his room "made out of rotten old crates because the poor residents in the
suburbs of Port-au-Prince have no place to park their bodies, and the rich

folk, or rather the rich mulattoes—same thing—have this kind of ajoupa, shack, built. With a few old crates of kippered herring, soap, or corned beef, you can have a serviceable house, a shack good enough for workers, those dirty black folk. The shack looked like the wire-covered cage of a chicken house" (Alexis, *General Sun, My Brother*, 5). Hilarion and the others in his makeshift community live away from the manicured homes of the well-to-do but close enough for them to work in those homes or sell their wares in the city. How does one maintain his or her connection to one's fellow humans or find a sense of self in connection with an environment made up entirely of waste? What meaning can be derived from such a place? Hilarion vacillates between anger and pride, disgust and sympathy for himself and his fellow slum-dwellers.

In *No Telephone to Heaven*, Cliff also writes of the same makeshift homes built with crates that contained goods manufactured elsewhere and sold to those in the Caribbean and elsewhere who can afford them. The Jamaican poor, like the Haitian poor, are left with the empty crates, poignantly emblematic of the nothingness that the powers-that-be grants the world's destitute. In the Jamaican shantytown "outside of Kingston" described by Cliff, only "women and children jammed together with other women and children, and a few old men discarded elders, scattered about" lived in "the Dungle" (Cliff, *No Telephone to Heaven*, 32). Though Christopher's "rotting wound of a neighborhood" has women, children and the elderly, Cliff focuses the reader's eye on the women foraging for food behind the tourist hotels, fighting mangy dogs for scraps and sometimes keeping an anxious eye on other mothers (Cliff, *No Telephone to Heaven*, 33–34). Enduring the physical and psychological hazards of living near and around the stench of open sewage, without access to any government agencies, the women and all the community members, including the children and the elderly, are left to either survive or perish. As Cliff says, none of these children go to school, eat balanced meals, or have access to any form of health care. Thus when Christopher's grandmother dies and leaves him an orphan at the age of eight, the city simply removes her body and leaves him to fend for himself in the Dungle. The other women help him as much as they can, but they cannot take full responsibility for him, since they are already stretched to the limit trying to provide the bare necessities for their own children's survival.

Two years later, Christopher is delivered from his invisible life in the Dungle into a marginal existence as a child servant to an affluent, aging woman in the countryside. The patriarch of this affluent light-skinned family, only referred to as "Mas' Charles," comes looking for Christopher's grandmother to replace a recently deceased maid who turns out to be Christopher's great-aunt. Not finding the boy's grand-mother, "Mas' Charles" takes the boy instead. Cliff makes clear both the disruption of family ties and the disconnection to the place in Jamaica where Christopher's people are from when she says, ". . . [His grandmoth-er's] passing had not been noted in her homeland" (Cliff, *No Telephone to Heaven*, 42). To be saved from the Dungle, Christopher reenters and reestablishes his family's historic role as servants to Mas' Charles and his family. The cycle of dispossession and displacement continues, for when he enters manhood, the sister of Mas' Charles turns him out, giving him only a pair of long tweed pants and bus fare to the Jamaican capi-tal, Kingston (Cliff, *No Telephone to Heaven*, 42). He takes with him his only possessions, a little black statue of Jesus and his machete. Yet again Christopher's Native country has failed him, abandoning him to a pre-carious existence as a young teenager with no one and nothing to anchor him or help give his struggle and anger meaning.

Neither the yardboy Christopher nor Hilarion, the former *restavek*, child servant, gets to enjoy "the sleep of the righteous" or the well-fed. Hilarion's hunger-driven run from his shack leads him to the red-light district of Port-au-Prince, then past the medical school, through the city square, *Champ-de-Mars*, and finally to a random middle-class villa in Bois-Verna. Overcome by the memory of his physical and verbal abuse in a similar villa with creeping bougainvilleas, Hilarion enters the gated garden and, after a few moments hesitation, decides to break into the home. Upon entering he thinks, "There are people who have lights to watch over their sleep. . . . Hilarion found it difficult to comprehend this peaceful state of sleep, the neatness of the room, and the useless blue light. These things suggested wealth to him and the separate world of the rich to him, more than did a sort of luxury that was not so unex-pected" (Alexis, *General Sun, My Brother*, 13). In this moment of mount-ing outrage, he decides to steal the sleeping man's wallet as "evidence of his rights. The right to defend his existence, the right to ransom the ransomers. In an instant, he had conceived an entire social philosophy. He thought he understood their values perfectly. The two contradictory worlds, cohabiting face to face—the world of the deprived and the world of the wealthy" (Alexis, *General Sun, My Brother*, 13). In his self-righteous anger, Hilarion forgot why this man could sleep so peacefully. As soon as he steps out on the grounds, Alexis says, "The whistle of the forces of order swept over him in peremptory and arresting salvos. Then there was a shout. . . . 'Stop, thief!'" (Alexis, *General Sun, My Brother*, 14). Hilarion's act of retaliation ends in his immediate, brutal capture and subsequent imprisonment. After his release, Hilarion spends the rest of the novel struggling to make a living in his Native land.

Similarly, one night when Christopher is hungry, drunk, and driven by an impossible hope, he enters the bedroom of his occasional employers (the same Mas' Charles and his wife who found him in the Dungle) to ask them to help him find the remains of his grandmother and allow him to bury her on their land. Neither master nor mistress jump up in alarm, so sure are they of his complete subjection. Mas' Charles's laughter at his request, at his attempt to honor his grandmother and fix his place and home, causes him to snap. Cliff describes what happens to Christopher at that moment as a possession by a spirit that Christopher cannot control. Before the night ends, Christopher will use the sharpened machete, the sign of his casual laborer status, to kill and mutilate the entire family as well as Mavis, the maid, because "they were dead and she was still taking care of them" (Cliff, *No Telephone to Heaven*, 48). Because no one in the area knows him and none cared for him, he is able to slip away into the woods and the cemetery and eventually slips into madness. This particular type of erasure does not happen to light-complected Clare, Christopher's polar opposite in the Jamaican social hierarchy. Because of the "chance" for financial, educational, and social mobility that her surface whiteness promises, Clare's family, friends, and even her nation seem to encourage her to pass for white. Clare becomes materially secure and able to travel to the United States, Britain, and France and enter most white institutions uncontested, but her inheritance from the history of the trans-Atlantic slave trade and the Black Diaspora nevertheless yields an interior displacement and loneliness similar to Christopher's— yet it is Christopher whose madness and displacement is the sign of the unspeakable horror of their lives and histories in the Americas. Never apprehended and haunted by his grandmother's roaming, restless *duppy* (ghost), Christopher becomes the crazed Watchman of downtown Kingston, a mock folk hero.

Christopher's tragedy, of not belonging and not being connected to anyone or any place, remains largely unspoken and thus uninterrogated.

"He lived as he was used—hand to mouth" (Cliff, *No Telephone to Heaven*, 44). Cliff says he carries within him the spirit of *Ogún*, "the iron worker god who bathes in blood" who is sung about in an old Yoruban hymn, but Christopher is unaware of this knowledge and how this god might be working in him to give voice to his mute rage (177). Understanding *Ogún* and his power, Christopher could have channeled this powerful energy and save himself from his own restless roaming. *Ogún's* story and many others that could have "empowered" Christopher and given him a "cultural consciousness . . . [and] awareness of [him]self within [a particular] circumstance, experience, and event" (Ortiz, *Men on the Moon*, viii) could have prevented his psychic annihilation and his physical reduction into serviceable beast. Whether in the Jamaican countryside or shantytowns of Kingston, Christopher did not feel he was connected to a place and to a people. Though the ceremonies and stories conferring this identity exist all around him, it is the returned exile, Clare, who reclaims the stories of her Native land and says with certainty, "The history I have learned . . . rather, recognized . . . since my return is something else. I know only that the loss, the forgetting . . . of resistance . . . of tenderness . . . is a terrible thing" (Cliff, *No Telephone to Heaven*, 196). Ortiz speaks to the horror of "forgetting" and the importance of being grounded in a particular place and time that is just as important for people of African descent.

The way "Ortiz's voice interweaves a tribally indigenous and a colonialist dominant U.S. culture into a powerful postcolonial articulation that is hemispherically and globally powerful" (Brill de Ramírez, personal communication, September 2007) also shows up in Mayra Montero's novel *In the Palm of Darkness*, in which Indigenous Haitian knowledge is placed side by side with western knowledge. Herpetologist Victor Grigg comes to Haiti to look for the last specimen of the *grenouille du sang*, a blood-red frog. If any remain, they will be found in Haiti. With Thierry Adrien, his guide, who was guide to another celebrated herpetologist, he pursues the frog at the exclusion of everything else. Frogs and people disappear in Haiti, but the mounting number of dead frogs causes more alarm that the violent deaths of Haitians caught in the political crossfire. To blacks living by open sewers in makeshift shacks with little access to clean drinking water, the priority given to saving the trees or finding a particular frog or a plant can provoke violent anger, disgust, or cynicism. The concern for the frogs and silence regarding the deaths of black people are offensive and reenact white disregard of black humanity.

Thierry agrees that the frogs are disappearing but that the rising number of human bones should be of even greater concern. He also notes the other animals that are declining in numbers, asking Victor to tell him where all the fish have gone (Montero, *In the Palm of Darkness*, 11). Here we have a difference between a learned researcher and a Native observer regarding what is important.

Throughout their search for the frog, Thierry's comments and behavior within the Haitian environment repeatedly leaves the scientist, Victor, in awe. Victor did not just hire a guide, but someone with a strong sense of his identity and his groundedness in the country of his birth. For Thierry, frogs are only part of the story of his life and experiences. He connects the frogs to people and events that he readily shares with the single-minded Victor. Thierry's stories include valuable information about Haiti's flora and fauna, rivers and mountains, knowledge that his ancestors inherited from the Indigenous people who escaped into the mountains to resist the Spaniards. Thierry also tries to give Victor a deeper insight into the different levels of violence and fear that many Haitian people live with. Thierry speaks with the understanding that the "[b]lack experience in any modern city or town in the Americas is a haunting" (Brand, *A Map to the Door of No Return*, 25). The search for the blood-red frog becomes a series of stories about family, friends, and events that need reckoning with and remembering. Thierry, always thinking about the meaning of his own life choices, forces Victor to do the same. In one of Thierry's stories, he tells him how he buried the first herpetologist, Papa Crapaud, and protected his corpse from violation. His fears for the corpse were proved right when he found the grave dug up the next morning. Having done his duty to the dead, Thierry says, "... I was at peace inside.... At peace means with grief in its proper place" (Montero, *In the Palm of Darkness*, 88). While Thierry and Hilarion, and Clare to certain extent, get to put "grief in its proper place" by remembering the old ways and adapting some of those ways as the need arises, Christopher does not.

The violence and anger of captivity in all its forms always threaten to erupt and take over. Black ceremonies called on the *lwas* or *orishas* and the ancestors for the strength and courage of the warrior and for the rage of the violated, maligned mother to fight their captors. And even then, that rage, especially if not properly channeled, may not be enough to match the determination and the singular focus of researchers, missionaries, or colonizers. But not remembering stories of "resistance," of "tenderness" savagely reduce one's humanity and connection to a group, leaving only the reactionary violence, the blood oaths, and sacrifices that were also needed to make this space a space for black people. Even in Ortiz's earlier work, the tight anger, the desire to do violence, to commit acts of sabotage, to retaliate, and to defend can be heard, but in his later work, Ortiz focuses more on Native people's survival and his belief that "[m]emory is more than story; it is symbol and gift" (*After and Before the Lightning*, 45). Thierry's stories quickly become such "symbols and gifts" in the midst of a legacy of violence and violation. In his alternately troubling and lyrically beautiful stories, we get glimpses of "[h]uman beings learn[ing] from the pressures exerted on them. One strength buckling under sometimes [and that becoming] the main learning process" (Montero, *In the Palm of Darkness*, 53).

All that Africans and their descendants called upon and needed to survive, to resist, remain and still need attending to. Though he does it in his work and activism, Ortiz says, "Sometimes it's kind of hard to explain 'Indian things' to non-Indian people" (*Out There Somewhere*, 109). What would it look like to reenact the revolutionary ceremony of 1791, to take the oaths again that so many Africans and Creole blacks took in the Bois Caiman area in Haiti? This "ceremony was commemorated for the first time in two hundred years, on August 22, 1991" (Hurbon, *Voodoo*, 125) under great Protestant protest. In Jamaica, what would it mean to honor Nanny, woman warrior, or Cudjoe of the Accompong Maroons and the resistance they set in motion in the way that Cliff does in her novel? Can I openly wear my ceremonial white to honor the spirits of U.S. African Americans on the hallowed grounds of St. Helena Island and call for a healing circle for black women; for black men only? We continue to fight for these spaces and explain the need for these types of rituals and symbolic acts that recall both the brutal oppression and the resistance to such attempts of physical and psychic annihilation. We challenge the notion that remembering gets in the way of progress. I pose these questions because so much of the secrecy that enabled African beliefs systems to thrive remains while many more "Christophers," "Clares," and "Hilarions" struggle with their own meaning and place in the twenty-first century. The opposition to African-based celebrations as well as the stigma often associated with black ancestor worship makes public acknowledgment of Nana Peazant's African ways doubly difficult. As these diasporic works show, it is forgetting not remembering that gets in the way of progress. I take courage from Simon Ortiz's work and the cultural resilience and resistance in his poetry, storytelling, and in his certainty in these uncertain times.

In the Americas and elsewhere, black and Indigenous peoples' histories overlap. This struggle to decide what to hold on to and what to let go of, and how to use what we have, remain constants that Native American people and people of African descent must be vigilant about. In the prose poem "More than Just a River," Ortiz mixes poignant memory with righteous anger regarding the loss of lands and the loss of a sacred river. Ortiz shares his culture and his people's history with us all; what they signify resonates for me with the need for a multifaceted understanding of the cultural and spiritual practices of African-based beliefs of the New World. "Place and time" always need to be transformed by black people for it to become, possibly, our place and time. Only in doing so can we continue to create the resistance needed to carve out free, safe, and sustaining spaces that counter the dehumanizing European practices that began our story in the Americas and that continue to affect us in the present, as they do the people of whom Ortiz writes. For both our peoples, "The struggle for freedom / is too strong an urge still" (Ortiz, *After and Before the Lightning*, 45). Only with our stories can new generations make sense of their struggles *in* freedom and fully access their meaning-making powers in the twenty-first century.

NOTES

1. *Ginen*, or *Afrique Ginen*, has come to stand in for the place Haitians believe they originated from and will return to when they die. *Ginen* takes on mystical and religious qualities especially when identified as the undersea home of the *lwas* and the ancestors.

2. I use Mayra Montero's spelling from *In the Palm of Darkness* where she references the song. I provide my own slightly different translation.

3. The enslavers did not intend for enslaved Africans to become *native* to the Americas as human beings.

4. Haitians call their African gods in the New World *lwas*. Elsewhere in the Americas, in places like Brazil and Cuba, the gods go by the name of *orishas*.

WORKS CITED

Alexis, Jacques Stephen. *General Sun, My Brother.* Translated by Carrol F. Coates. Charlottesville: University Press of Virginia, 1999.

Brand, Dionne. *A Map to the Door of No Return: Notes to Belonging.* Toronto: Vintage Canada, 2002.

Brill de Ramírez, Susan. Personal communication, September 2007.

Cliff, Michelle. *No Telephone to Heaven.* New York: Plume, 1996.

Dash, Julie. *Daughters of the Dust: The Making of an American Woman's Film.* New York: New Press, 1998.

Desmangles, Leslie G. *Vodou and Roman Catholicism in Haiti.* Chapel Hill: University of North Carolina Press, 1992.

Gilroy, Paul. *The Black Atlantic: Modernity and Double Consciousness.* Cambridge: Harvard University Press, 1993.

Hurbon, Laënnec. *Voodoo: Search for the Spirit.* Translated by Lory Frankel. New York: Abrams, 1995.

Montero, Mayra. *In the Palm of Darkness.* Translated by Edith Grossman. New York: Harper Flamingo, 1998.

Morrison, Toni. *Beloved.* New York: Plume, 1988.

Ortiz, Simon J. *Out There Somewhere.* Tucson: University of Arizona Press, 2002.

———. *Men on the Moon: Collected Short Stories by Simon J. Ortiz.* Tucson: University of Arizona Press, 1999.

———. *After and Before the Lightning.* Tucson: University of Arizona Press, 1994.

———. "Towards a National Indian Literature: Cultural Authenticity in Nationalism." MELUS 8 (1981): 7–12.

"They should look in the space that is in here"

Developing an Ethics of Reading
American Indian Literature

Jeff Berglund

In Simon Ortiz's story "What Indians Do," an elder remarks that we should all look within the unexplored spaces of our own hearts and souls, the space inside, rather than expending so much effort to get to the moon. In numerous stories from *Men on the Moon*, Ortiz creates noticeable narrative spaces, what others might call silences, though I suggest these spaces resonate with meaning. Ortiz's work in this collection encourages readers to appreciate and honor limited access to privileged knowledge by cultural and tribal outsiders. This requires of literary scholars an unusual reading practice, an ethical poetics that honors the existence of internal spaces in texts, meant to be understood only by those who are prepared and have privileged access to spiritual and cultural knowledge systems and traditions. The upshot is that readers must accept that not all knowledge is available for consumption. Ortiz's stories in this collection also encourage careful attention to the ways tribal traditions are inculcated and transmitted—quite different than might occur in the academic scenario, in which reader-critics in the spirit of scholarly inquiry are encouraged to become knowledgeable about particular cultural knowledge systems. Ortiz's stories masterfully convey cultural knowledge without giving full access to all readers, thus creating coded spaces for cultural insiders in possession of this information.

My thinking on this topic emerges from classroom experiences, when I try to model a reading practice attuned to tribal specifics. I share criticism such as *Red on Red* and *American Indian Literary Nationalism* and have developed units where students read multiple works—in many different genres—by writers from specific tribal groups. I am compelled by literary models of sovereignty, of discussing tribal canons and intellectual traditions, and the legitimacy of designing tribally specific modes of inquiry. But this provocative and positive approach has also encouraged scholars and students—many of whom are not Indigenous—to commit cultural transgressions as they cite privileged knowledge or distorted knowledge circulated by academic outsiders.[1]

My experience using Rex Lee Jim's brilliant essay "A Moment in My Life" in classes with Diné and non-Diné students in a unit on Diné writing, though, has led me to more complex thinking about the position of different readers and appropriate reading methodologies. Several, although not all, Diné students have raised concerns about the appropriateness of Jim sharing his understanding of hózhóójí/the beautyway with the reading public.[2] The critique extends to my course design, as well; one student cited her grandfather's remark that the sort of information conveyed by Jim is so powerful that it must not be put into the wrong hands—cultural outsiders or those who are too young, or unready to be educated. Our education system has always encouraged the pursuit of knowledge as the highest goal, irrespective of the emotional, psychological, or spiritual readiness of the student. Paula Gunn Allen characterized this as an American discomfort with "secrets and mystery": "the white world has a different set of values, one which requires learning all and telling all in the interests of knowledge, objectivity, and freedom" (382).[3]

The forces of colonization and genocide over the last 500 years have forced tribal cultures to grow increasingly protective of spiritual and religious practices. Those who practiced tribal religions were all too often persecuted—this was especially true for many Pueblo peoples—and Native religious freedoms were not officially protected in the United States until the 1978 passage of the American Indian Religious Freedom Act (AIRFA). Because of these historical realities, many Native people view academic inquiries and even casual observation by unknowing, unprepared outsiders as part of a continuing effort to colonize them. For example, Nambé Pueblo scholar Debbie Reese, who studies children's literature about and by American Indians, discusses the efforts of Pueblo people to resist such colonizing strategies: whether it be the Hopi Tribal Council's development of research protocols, her own process of reviewing quality chidren's books, or a Kiva elder's requested removal of Pablita Velarde's *Old Father Storyteller* from the open shelves of the Santa Fe Indian School library because its circulation could not ensure that storytelling protocol will be followed.[4]

Simon Ortiz's stories clearly employ strategies that indicate to his readers that not all subjects are appropriate for all public readers. When I examine his writing and other works by Native writers, I work hard to recognize strategies of inclusion and exclusion. Literary works featuring such protective articulations force all readers to examine their own positions, their relationship to cultural knowledge and tribal traditions, as well as their right to probe further. As the title of my essay suggests, such texts encourage readers to practice an ethical reading practice; in this regard, I suggest that these sorts of literary texts offer readers an ethical-theoretical reading practice. I encourage readers—especially my students—to look within texts for embedded metacommentary about appropriate reading practices, if not theories of reading.[5] For most readers of this volume, it is not too much of a leap to suggest that in his essays Simon Ortiz is a theorist of the highest order; hopefully, then, it is not too great a leap to propose that his poems and stories advance theories as well. While there is no unified system of interpretation or reading, I want to highlight how a number of his stories in *Men on the Moon* draw attention to the interactions between individuals and their cultures, and between people from different cultural traditions, and the possibilities for and failures of cultural sharing. The characters' and narrators' dilemmas shape the way readers see themselves and create new paradigms for interpreting literature, paradigms that allow for the existence of the unknowable—for some readers, the unmasterable—and the possibility of finding value in recognizing why one might be excluded from full participation in the world of the poem or the story.[6]

One essay-like story, "What Indians Do," relays most of the issues surrounding cultural appropriation and the tensions and misunderstandings between insiders and outsiders. The narrator, either Ortiz himself or an individual quite similar to him, is at a poetry reading engaged in conversation with a Hopi friend: "'Do you ever get set upon by Indian people who question what you're teaching in Indian literature? By your writing, I mean. You see, I teach history, and sometimes I get the feeling my people think I'm giving away secrets. You know, Hopi secrets.' I understood. The Hopis don't want to lose anything more. So I said, 'Yes, I do. That's why I talk about Private Property Week instead'" (133). This humorous retort sheds light on one strategy: using humor to protect the culturally sensitive subjects and to expose social injustice. The inside joke here is dependent on making the link between the nontribal notion of "private property," the very principle that underpins the doctrine of Manifest Destiny, and the protection of valued and personal tribal experiences.

In another section of the same story, the narrator jokes with his co-presenter, Roxanne: "'I'll tell them you're a show-and-tell Indian: "This is an Acoma Indian. He will show and tell." I'll tell them alright. And then I'll take it out and show it to them.' Laughing—sometimes it's better to laugh" (Ortiz, "What Indians Do," 135). This satirical take on performance for tourists, academic or otherwise, is yet another rebuttal to the attempts to pry inside the narrator's culture. His presentation "Land, Water, Indians, and Power" will tell, and his indecent exposure, implied only, will "show" and in essence, tell the tourist to piss off: there's no cultural demonstration going on here today.

Readers of another story, "The San Francisco Indians," meet an elderly Indian man searching for his granddaughter in San Francisco. He's recognized as "Indian" and brought by hippie "wannabee" Indians to an apartment where Chief Black Bear resides. A young blonde woman says, "'I heard Chief Black Bear found an Indian. Are you the Indian he found?'" (120). She is going to join the Black Bear tribe, and wanted the chief to find "an Indian to guide us in the ceremony. So it can be real when I join the Tribe" (120). Unfamiliar with tribal traditions, she believes that any Indian person possesses essential spiritual information that she may acquire. But, "the Indian man did not know anything about peyote. He had heard some songs and prayers for the ceremony, but he did not know anything about the ceremony. And he did not know how a person could *join* a Tribe" (121). Troubled by the strange interest these white hippies possess, and unsuccessful in finding his granddaughter, the elderly man leaves. The last thing he hears is the white girl lamenting, "I want it to be real" (121). More than anything, this story explores the desire for a presumed authenticity that can be borrowed from and acquired through contact with Native people. I encourage student-readers to see this story as a reframing of the issue of cultural borrowing and exploitation; it is part of the continuum of interest in acquiring intimacy with elements of cultural and tribal experiences that may be inappropriate or entirely off-limits.

In the opening anecdote in "What Indians Do," the narrator's friend Alvin tells of a play he's writing about an old Eskimo uncle who hears of American space exploration and the efforts expended to explore the "unknown depths of space." And this old uncle says, "But they don't know that they should look into the space that is in here"—touching his chest (129). The narrator admits, "Sometimes it's difficult to explain about the space inside oneself. It's almost as if it is easier to talk about space that's outside, and away from oneself. Because of that, it's often hard to answer convincingly enough a question such as the one asked by a non-Indian college student: 'What do Indians do at a powwow, anyway?'" (129). The space inside is the part that matters, not the performative actions observable by outsiders, "scopophiliacs," those in love with looking. In some regards, other sections of this story attempt to further illustrate the space inside the narrator's self—as well as others' misunderstanding of the space inside. Ortiz relates how listeners to stories need to be actively engaged in the coming into being, in a happening, not like people watch TV where "the world of that box within the plastic box is so far away" ("What Indians Do," 130). To illustrate this self-involvement and interpolation, the narrator responds to his friend's Alvin proposed play with a story of his own about an elderly Grandpa/Nana watching the moonwalk on television, a story that recalls Ortiz's "Men on the Moon" and suggests, possibly, its genesis. In this version of the story, an elder brings a rock in from outside to show his grandsons who have been discussing the astronaut's lunar sampling. They believe the grandfather is playing tricks on them. No, he responds with a laugh and quick look at the TV, "That's knowledge." While the grandsons within the story think their grandfather confuses rocks from outside his house with extraterrestrial evidence, the grandfather is really affirming his Pueblo culture's perspective concerning the interconnection of all of creation, including earth and celestial bodies. For the grandfather, the reality of creation is much greater than the limited geologic identifications of contemporary science. The narrator watches his friend Alvin, the first storyteller, listen and believes he is "thinking about that Eskimo uncle looking into the space within himself" ("What Indians Do," 132). The rock from outside the grandfather's home, a place he has lived his entire life, represents to him truth and knowledge of self. The rocks remind him of his place in this world, part of his family's legacy, but also likely a place mentioned in creation stories and given to his people as their homeland.

This notion is explicitly explored in "Men on the Moon." Grandfather Faustin watches the lunar landing on his new television; he struggles to understand the astronauts' motives and his grandson Amarosho explains, "They're trying to find out what's on the moon, Nana. What kind of dirt and rocks there are and to see if there's any water. Scientist men don't believe there is any life on the moon. The men are looking for knowledge" ("What Indians Do," 5). As he tries to understand, Faustin "wondered if the men had run out of places to look for knowledge on the earth. Do they know if they'll find knowledge?" ("What Indians Do," 5). That night, Faustin dreams of Flintwing and Coyote's encounter with a ferocious metal mahkina; unable to fathom this loud, dangerous machine, Flintwing and Coyote pray with cornfood to the four directions, asking for power and guidance. Flintwing tells Coyote he must tell everyone what he has seen: "The people must talk among themselves and learn what this is about, and decide what they will do. You must hurry, but you must not alarm the people" ("What Indians Do," 9). The next day, when the astronauts' moonwalk is being televised, Faustin still "couldn't figure out the mahkina. He wasn't sure whether it moved and could cause harm" ("What Indians Do," 11). He and Amarosho talk about the astronauts gathering samples, and Amarosho tells Faustin, "They say they will use [the knowledge gained from the rocks] to better mankind . . . and to learn more about the universe in which we live . . . and in finding out where everything began a long time ago and how everything was made in the beginning" ("What Indians Do," 11–12). Faustin asks, "Hasn't anyone ever told them?" ("What Indians Do," 12). Faustin is astounded that the astronauts are missing this vital information about their origins, something as knowable to him as the truth of his own beginnings, linked to the very earth outside his own home.[7] When Amarosho questions whether his grandfather is teasing or telling him the truth about his dream, Faustin responds that it may be a dream, but it's the truth. There are such moments through many of Ortiz's stories in this collection. Characters learn something of cultural traditions from their elders, but intricacies of these truths are merely alluded to, and not always understood by the usually young characters. This is both a realistic depiction and the author's strategy to protect sacred information. I like to draw attention to these significant and brief moments because they remind students of the spiritual dimensions of the world Ortiz writes of, but they also illustrate the measured ways he gives access to outsiders while providing an open space, a window, to cultural insiders who may bring their own knowledge to bear.

Opening a space for familiar and/or initiated readers is in keeping with Pueblo storytelling tradition. As Leslie Marmon Silko notes, "So in the telling (and you will hear a few of the dimensions of this telling), first of all, as mentioned earlier, the storytelling always includes the audience, the listeners. In fact, a great deal of the story is believed to be inside the listener; the storyteller's role is to draw the story out of the listeners. The storytelling continues from generation to generation. Basically, the origin story constructs our identity—with this story, we know who we are" ("Language," 5). This sort of learning, the acquisition of cultural knowledge, comes over time and with experience. The story may exist within the listener but it is not fully understood by the young until they have processed the story with other retellings and other knowledge that has been gained. Without cultural or ancestral connections to such stories, though, listeners are ill-prepared, and in dangerous proximity with sacred and privileged knowledge. In Ortiz's narratives, then, he creates a space for familiar readers to access traditional and/or sacred knowledge, depending on their own readiness. For readers unfamiliar with sacred cultural traditions, Ortiz still invites them to discover knowledge of the human condition, although it may be a different sort of, or level of, knowledge.

In a number of stories Ortiz illustrates the way young people are repeatedly introduced to significant cultural knowledge. There's no assurance that such knowledge will be fully understood, but its ritual sharing helps ensure that values are introduced and will be inculcated over time. For example, in the story "Kaiser and the War," the titular character, Kaiser, is blessed by the grandfather before he enters the military after some initial resistance: "Grandfather blessed Kaiser then with prayer and counsel, just like Faustin had done, and he talked to him of how a man should behave and what he should expect—general and significant things that Grandpa always said. He turned sternly toward us kids—who were playing around, not paying much attention, as usual—since it was important we should know those things too. My father and mother spoke too, and when they finished, Grandpa put cornmeal into Kaiser's hand for him to pray with. My father and mother told us kids to tell Kaiser goodbye, good wishes, and good health" ("Kaiser and the War," 35). Here, Ortiz uses the perspective of a child, who doesn't clearly understand the import of the grandfather's prayers, to protect possibly sacred knowledge conveyed in the prayers. More significant, however, is the illustration of the children's lack of awareness of the significance of the grandfather's words, an understanding that will only come through a lifetime of experiences and familiarity with such prayers and knowledge.

Such moments reiterate for readers that quick access to spiritual or cultural knowledge is neither possible nor desirable.

In the story "Something's Going On," readers are given another example of when specific circumstances require that knowledge be shared. Such moments remind readers that this sort of knowledge is not for the taking, but is context-bound. In "Something's Going On," Willie is sought by the police for the murder of Mr. Glass. Filtered through the perspective of Jimmo, Willie's nine-year-old son, the narrative recalls the hunting stories that Jimmo's father told:

> He would say, "When it was deer season, men and boys would
> go hunting together. But before they went hunting, they made
> careful preparations. Hunting songs and prayers were part of their
> preparations. They made and painted sacred sticks so they would
> be successful in their hunt, so they would be able to beckon the
> deer to them, and so the deer would gladly come to the village
> with them. It was always very carefully done in the old days. Now,
> although it isn't exactly like it was in the old days, you must always
> do the best you can" (70).

The narrator's father in turn had sung hunting prayer songs to his sons, instructing them. "This is what you're to do because a long time back this is what was done. This is what the people of the old times did. Always remember this" ("Something's Going On," 70). This brief passage is one generation's reflection of his father's and preceding generations' experiences of prayer and ritual. Values are shared with unfamiliar readers in general ways. In each instance, there is a motive for the parent or elder to tell these stories, to pass down these traditions. Of course, cultural traditions and protocol are context dependent; children learn about traditions when they are deemed ready and when the time is appropriate. These action- and context-specific passages remind readers why those of us outside of this specific tribal tradition should perhaps refrain from further inquiry about spiritual practices; without proper guidance, we're unprepared to gain such access.

The situation of inappropriate access is depicted in a story in which a non-Native character, the first-person narrator, gains intimate proximity to Indigenous spiritual practice quite by accident. One afternoon while watching birds and enjoying nature on a cliff overlook, the unnamed narrator in "Hiding, West of Here" observes two older Indian men engaged in a ritual: "[T]hose Indians, they were up to something. They were dressed in blankets . . . and they had beads around their necks and a little pouch at their sides. I seen pictures of Indians about like that" (193). He positions himself to remain unnoticed and "I didn't know whether to keep watchin or what. I mean, it was private, see, and I could see they were looking around like they might be checking to see if someone might be watching. When the younger man turned his head towards me, I ducked my head below his line of sight. I thought about my watching, and later I looked again. I had never seen anything like it" (194). This episode is a stand-in for intercultural moments when outsiders gain access to prayers or ceremonies without the proper education or preparation. The narrator has no frame of reference for understanding these strangers' rites. A shift in the wind occurs and he hears "something":

> It was a kind of singsong. Words, Indian words, I suppose, but spoken in a rhythm. Praying, that's what I figured. The Indians were praying by the big rock split in half. I couldn't stop myself looking at them, and somehow I couldn't help but feel it was somehow fateful I happened to be there. . . . And then it seemed like I was part of what the Indians were doing. Like they wanted me to be even though they didn't know I was there. The wind would change and drift the sound away and then bring it back, and it felt like I was part of that prayer that was going on. Something like that. It was an odd feeling, and then not odd too ("Hiding, West of Here," 195).

Students have responded strongly to this story and the narrator's experiences. The reactions are ambivalent: the narrator is simply curious, or a voyeur, a cultural outsider not interested in knowing about such spiritual matters in an intimate, culturally sensitive way. His deliberate attempts to keep himself hidden tell readers that he knows he is doing something wrong and inappropriate. One student suggested that this story is an allegory for how outsiders to Native culture approach even subjects such as Indigenous literature. At the same time, students are struck by how moved the narrator is and how much he connects with the prayers offered by the two men.[8] Native students, in particular, point to the power of spirituality as it affects all of us, but they also underscore their elders' concerns that outsiders will misuse prayer-knowledge because of improper preparation. Most importantly, Ortiz discusses these spiritual matters in a generalized way; thus, in a story about cultural transgression, we avoid committing such transgressions ourselves because of the author's narrative strategies.

While the previous story explores *uninvited* cultural observation, a great companion piece for analysis is "To Change Life in a Good Way," which explores cultural interchange and *invited* cultural sharing, reciprocity, and friendship. First published as a long narrative poem in *A Good Journey*, "To Change Life in a Good Way" focuses on Bill and Ida, a non-Native couple from Oklahoma, who become the friends of Pete and Mary, who are Laguna. Both of the men work for Kerr-McGee. Over time they become close friends, learn from each other, and get to know each other's families. When Bill learns of his brother Slick's death in Vietnam, Mary and Pete respond in the Laguna fashion they have been taught: "This is just corn, Bill, Indian corn. The people call it Kasheshi. Just a dried ear of corn. You can take it with you to Oklahoma or you can keep it here. You can plant it. It's to know that life will keep on, your life will keep on. Just like Slick will be planted again. He'll be like that, like seed planted, like corn seed, the Indian corn. But you and Ida, your life will grow on . . . . " (113). Mary and Pete have grown close to Bill and Ida over time; their friendship means they share in both life and death. The loss of Bill's brother is a shared loss and means that they are interested in sharing their own ways of coming to terms with death. Like several of the previously mentioned characters who practice ritual with incomplete knowledge of its mysteries, Pete says,

I guess I don't remember some of what is done, Bill. Indian words, songs for it, what it all is, even how this is made just a certain way, but I know that it is important to do this. You take this [prayer offering] too, but you don't keep it. It's just for Slick. For his travel from this life among us to another place of being. You and Ida and Slick are not Indian, but it doesn't make any difference. It's for all of us, this kind of way, with corn and with this, Bill. You take these sticks and feathers and you put them somewhere you think you should, someplace important that you think might be good, maybe to change life in a good way, that you think Slick would be helping us with ("To Change Life in a Good Way," 112–13).

This exchange of prayer, between a Native man and non-Native friend, I note to students, has grown out of a deep bond of earned friendship and intimacy. Ortiz demonstrates here the openness and generosity of Pueblo culture, but an openness that is dictated by the familiarity and character of the individuals who have demonstrated they are worthy of trust.[9] Andrea Smith, in "Spiritual Appropriation as Sexual Violence," points out that this sort of intercultural exchange is likely, but only if one has earned the trust of a community by being one with the community:

> Within the community, I always hear elders say, if you want to learn, be quiet and pay attention. Only through being part of the community over a period of time and developing trust does knowledge come to you—very slowly. Meanwhile, in the classroom setting, teachers are encouraged to present the information very quickly and completely so that students can learn it for the final exam. Consequently, academics promote the misperception that Native traditions are easily learned, can be learned quickly, and can be learned outside of a community context (109).

In "To Change Life in a Good Way," Ortiz engages his non-Native characters over time, has them travel across space, and slowly come recognize the power and wisdom of tribal knowledges. His Pueblo characters have their own questions and concerns about their traditions, as well, and these spaces encourage readers to engage and thereby, on some level, understand. Despite their close connection, Bill initially thinks: "Just corn, just Indian corn, just your life to go on, Ida and you . . . And then he wondered about the husk bundle. He couldn't figure it out. He couldn't figure it out" (113). In this, Ortiz acknowledges this lack of understanding and creates a character who in despair refuses his dear friend's practice. He decides not to take the bundle to Oklahoma and leaves it in a cupboard in his locked mobile home. When they return to New Mexico from Oklahoma, not comforted by all the platitudes they have heard—Slick died for a democratic America, for example—Bill knows exactly what he is going to do with the bundle. He takes it with him to work, stops the lift, and sticks the bundle behind a slab of rock. He remembered what Pete had told him to say something about it. He prays:

> Slick, you was a good boy . . . I got this here Indian thing, feathers

and sticks, and at home we got the corn by your picture. Pete and Mary said to do this because it's important, even if we're Okies who do this and not Indians. It's for your travel, they said, from here to that place where you are now. And to help us from where you are at now with our life here, and they said to maybe change things in a good way for a good life. . . . Pete said he didn't know exactly all the right Indian things to do anymore, but somehow I believe Indians are more righter than we've ever been led to believe. And now I'm trying too. So you help us now, little brother Slick. We need it. All the help we can get. Even if it's just so much as holding up the roof of this mine the damn company don't put enough timbers and bolts in ("To Change Life in a Good Way," 115–16).

Bill may not fully understand the nature of the blessings and prayers that his friends have bestowed upon him, nor does he fully understand the "right way" to pray, but it is clear his friends' gift of the corn and prayer bundle has given him a means to cope with the various stresses facing him, including the Vietnam War, mine safety, degradation of the environment, in addition to the loss of his brother, Slick. The sacred objects and a model of prayer given to him by his friends gives him access to the power of intercessionary prayer and communication across worlds.

The sensitive nature of this scene in the story requires careful teaching, for I clearly do not want to leave my non-Native students with the idea that they can willy-nilly pick up some objects that they identify as "Indian" and then "play Indian." This is especially problematic when the appropriative "play" tends in presumably sacred and religious directions. A story such as this is accompanied by readings on this very subject, whether it be excerpts from Vine Deloria, Jr.'s *God Is Red*, which warns consumers about hustling shamans who have no sense of the way "tribal religions created the tribal community" (197), or Wendy Rose's "The Great Pretenders," which notes the ways "White shamanism functions as a subset . . . within the matrix of contemporary Eurocentric domination" (332).[10] To guide students to greater insights into such issues, I invite them to do word annotations relevant to this story or its themes. One recent semester's work yielded the following: respect, self-discovery, mourning, love, understanding, grief, the human condition, humanity, knowledge, beliefs, religion, prayer, transformation. When given the chance, students readily engage with the entirety of the story, reading

Bill's ceremonial healing prayer and conversation with his deceased brother within the larger frame that Ortiz provides. Most students look to the title, "To Change Life in a Good Way," and note how Ortiz emphasizes the transformative power of Indigenous practices for all people. Of course, for students in a class of mixed Indigenous and non-Indigenous students in the American Southwest, this perception is focused on indigeneity of North America. Were the class taught in the Middle East, Africa, or Asia, one would imagine that Indigenous students there would also note relevant parallels, for prayer and sacred rituals for acknowledging and honoring those who have passed have been part and parcel of human cultures around the world and across time. Ortiz's challenging story is an important counterweight to the other very real episodes in which cultural outsiders are the transgressors. Instead, Ortiz emphasizes a common humanity that reaches across cultures: Bill and Ida are close friends invited to partake of another community's wisdom in a time of great need. Pete and Mary are not the "show and tell" Indians Ortiz jokes about elsewhere,[11] but they do share.

Each of these stories and episodes require readers to self-consciously examine their own positions and their own aims in reading literature in the first place. We shouldn't automatically pry open a cultural window because a space is available in the text and because current theorization suggests that a culturally specific mode of analysis is preferred. Indigenous writers like Ortiz make very conscious decisions about which windows to keep closed and which to open, and readers are well advised to respect those parameters and work *with*, rather than insistently *against*, them. Just as we examine the intent of writers, we need to examine our own intentions as readers. Indigenous theorists such as Linda Tuhiwai Smith (Maori) and Daniel Heath Justice (Cherokee), to name but a few, have made persuasive arguments about the need for "cultural insiders" to take control of their own destinies, particularly in the realm of research. Smith even explores the challenges posed by academic researchers from the very same culture; one's status as researcher alters the tenor of insider-outsider dynamics and places the ethical burden of proof on the researchers. Justice, in his essay "Seeing (and Reading) Red: Indian Outlaws in the Ivory Tower," notes,

> *We must not forget to be both responsible and humble.* This inheritance, however, brings with it two vital and connected

understandings: responsibility and humility. Most of our traditions hold us accountable to one another and to the world for our behaviors. . . . Humility will remind us that we're just part of the community, not the entirety. To ignore this interconnection and our mutual dependence is to harm both ourselves and our communities—no one hurts a family more than one of its own members turned bad (102).

In *Decolonizing Methodologies*, Smith also stresses the need for this sort of humility: "It [the insider researcher's approach] needs to be humble because the researcher belongs to the community as a member with a different set of roles and relationships, status and position" (139). Elsewhere in this book, Smith explains that

through respect the place of everyone and everything in the universe is kept in balance and harmony. Respect is a reciprocal, shared, a constantly interchanging principle which is expressed through all aspects of social conduct. . . . The denial by the West of humanity to indigenous peoples, the denial of citizenship and human rights, the denial of the right to self-determination—all these demonstrate palpably the enormous lack of respect which has marked the relations of indigenous and non-indigenous peoples (120).

The insights provided by theorists such as Smith and Justice about insider research protocol clearly remind us that any ethical reading practice—especially by outsider researchers—must be respectful and must consider the relationship of individuals to one another and to the community. Moreover, our reading practices must consider the colonialist and historical context of our efforts as well as the impact on dynamic, living communities. Critics of a positioned and ethical reading practice might assume this tactic is essentialist and assumes a narrowly defined ideal reader. Rather than making assumptions about genetic identity of readers, this ethical approach—for insiders and outsiders to a culture—assumes that individual readers must be respectful and committed to the needs of the community, both in terms of historical accuracy and in terms of the effects our researcher judgments have on living communities.[12]

Mastery of a text doesn't require us to understand every cultural allusion or gain access to every cultural tradition, particularly where spiritual matters are involved: mastery need not be our primary end. There is great value in enlightenment that is firmly grounded in the literature, working with it, rather than struggling to make it what it is not nor should be. This paradigm shift will require us at different times to have an uneasy relationship with the material under discussion. Giving up "mastery" of a text, I would argue, is an important decolonizing tactic; recognizing different levels of access is a way to honor Indigenous cultures.[13] But this shouldn't be seen as a free pass for non-Native students to learn less about Native peoples and cultures: rather, this ethical reading practice should serve as a reminder to learn appropriately, to follow cultural protocols. This resistance to typical academic models of common mastery is intended to interrupt the cycle of academic objectification of Native peoples. Such a reorientation of the academic pursuit of mastery of content and an emphasis on contextually appropriate and ethical methodologies give greater emphasis to cultural ownership of material and remind outsiders of the privileges and responsibilities of the initiated and of the protocols that cultural outsiders should be aware of. This results in mutual respect: no longer are Native peoples—vis-à-vis literature—in the position of being curatorial objects put on display, available for consumption and analysis. This reading practice acknowledges not only the challenges of moving across cultural-spiritual traditions, but also across different languages. Even though Ortiz has generously characterized storytelling as a force uniting us all,[14] he also notes in the introduction to *Woven Stone* that our differences also create different possibilities:

> Since we're all human with the same human feelings and
> responses to feelings, we understand and share hurt, love, anger,
> joy, sadness, elation, a gamut of emotions. However, human
> cultures are different from each other, and unique, and we have
> different and unique languages; it is not easy to translate from
> one language to another though we egotistically believe and *think*
> we can. And that is when I found myself objectifying my Acoma
> language and at emotional odds with myself (6).

This admission about Ortiz's own experiences moving across languages within his own cultural tradition should make all readers cautious about efforts to move across cultural traditions. Moreover, Ortiz's experience of self-alienation should make all readers attentive to the ethical dimensions of interpretation and the impact on ourselves and others. A reading practice such as I have been outlining values the way writers and artists reach different audiences through different modes. This discourse should not run the risk of making Native culture or spiritual traditions unknowably exotic to non-Natives, but it should remind readers of the complexity of systems of knowledge that take a lifetime—not a few class meetings or a good journal article—to understand. Such a model of reading in which stories have different iterations depending on the connection between readers and authors/storytellers is also in keeping with models of Pueblo storytelling, as described by Leslie Marmon Silko in "Interior and Exterior Landscapes": "Even conflicting versions of an incident were welcomed for the entertainment they provided. . . . The ancient Pueblo people sought a communal truth, not an absolute truth. For them, this truth lived somewhere within the web of differing versions. . . ." (32). The open spaces within Ortiz's stories ensure that different narratives are conveyed depending on the knowledge possessed by different readers.

This model of reading and interpreting borrows obviously from literary separatist models of tribal interpretation, but it also borrows from social justice theories of being allies.[15] As readers, we don't often perceive ourselves as allies to the cultures represented by authors, but we can be. Being an ally across differences—tribal versus non-tribal, black versus Indigenous, and so forth—requires us to self-consciously examine our own value systems and unconscious attitudes. Propelled by a sense of ethics and an interest in seeing the full humanity of others, the ally exposes systems of oppression and structures of bias. In academia, one system of oppression that still exists is that Native cultures and people are all too often the objects of study rather than the agents of theory-making and knowledge brokering, although we know this is changing. The ally needs to be versed in taking multiple perspectives in withholding judgment, in possibly making mistakes. The ally takes care not to erase differences to create a false sense of harmony, and the ally has open, truth-seeking dialogues that require more emphatic listening than talking. As Simon Ortiz's work demonstrates, with its multiple examples of internal spaces, it's a relationship founded on mutual respect, on the need to examine ultimately not the truths or knowledge that lie "out there," but the truth that resides in the "space inside."

NOTES

1. Robin Riley Fast briefly explores this in her essay "Outside Looking in: Nonnatives and American Indian Literature."

2. Readers may remember the controversial reactions to the publication of Paul Zolbrod's *Diné Bahane': The Navajo Creation Story*. Charlotte Frisbie's review of it in *American Indian Quarterly* 10, no. 3 (Summer 1986) briefly acknowledged this controversy:

> Many Navajos were reportedly hostile to the idea of having "The Creation Story" written down, finding that print was inappropriate for oral narrative. Others supported the idea, some obviously equating the process with salvage work which might enhance ethnic identity for future generations. The production of such a work in today's world raises many questions, perhaps the most basic of which are should it be done at all, and if so, by whom? Are the countless versions of Navajo origins considered sacred or secular by contemporary Navajos? If outsiders are invited to record them, or opt to retranslate earlier recordings, will such actions be viewed by some as continuing examples of unwarranted appropriation of cultural resources? Do many Navajos want to share these materials? If so, then what, from their perspective, is the appropriate medium for sharing that which properly lives in the oral tradition—regular print, manipulated print, audiotape, videotape? And how does anyone convey the fact that numerous versions of "The Creation Story" exists, each of which is just as important and valid as the next? (261)

    Zolbrod himself acknowledges the fluid and changing nature of ceremonial narrative, but its textual forms tend to freeze this transformative ceremony. Others, including Susan Berry Brill de Ramírez, especially in her emphasis on the conversive nature of much of Leslie Marmon Silko's work, have suggested that written texts can also be seen as "co-creative." It could even be argued that Silko's *Ceremony*—the entire presentation of the novel—is one large ceremony emphasizing that healing is co-creative and extends beyond the bounds of any specific "sing."

3. This comment comes from Paula Gunn Allen's controversial essay, "Special Problems in Teaching Leslie Marmon Silko's *Ceremony*" in an issue of *American Indian Quarterly* from 1990, and republished in *Natives and Academics*. Allen discusses her discomfort with teaching the novel because culturally sacrosanct values are shared with outsiders; she is also troubled that clan stories are told to the public at large, not just those who are clan members. She finds herself torn as an educator while teaching a work such as *Ceremony*: as a professor she sees the need to help students understand the spiritual and ceremonial underpinnings of the novel; as an Indian person, she is categorically against this methodology. David Moore's essay "Rough Knowledge and Radical Understanding: Sacred Silence in American Indian Literatures" discusses Allen's essay in detail.

4. See Reese's blog at http://americanindiansinchildrensliterature.blogspot.com/.

5. Susan Berry Brill de Ramírez's *Contemporary American Indian Literature and the Oral Tradition* (1999) discusses different models of protective coding. This book examines how some works by Indigenous writers are incredibly "conversive," inviting readers to understand with writer-storytellers how our "individual meaningfulness comes from one's intersubjective interrelationships with other persons (human and otherwise) in the world" (182). But, even in these situations, the degree of success with conversivity depends on the relationship between the storyteller and storylistener: "Teller and listener both have responsibilities in relation to the telling. Part of the responsibility of the listener-reader involves sufficient familiarity to be able to approach and enter the worlds of the stories" (144). David Moore's incredibly insightful essay "Rough Knowledge and Radical Understanding: Sacred Silence in American Indian Literatures" examines the way writers protect the sacred through silences: "Their literary silences gesture to a rough mode of knowledge that allows for uncertainty, for relationality in understanding, for fallibility. The rough form fits the rough content, redefining the limits of understanding. Especially around sacred experience, Native American writers often invoke such indeterminate ways of representing and knowing, in order to traverse the difficult territory of cultural property issues. In so doing they are not merely maintaining secrecy, but in fact are redefining ways of knowing. This very particular use of silence that surrounds the issue of cultural property in American Indian writing can guide an ethics of criticism" (634). In my analysis of Simon Ortiz's writing, I choose to avoid using the term "silence" since these moments are loud, resonant with meaning for insider-readers, cued into cultural traditions which they are appropriately ready to understand and know.

6. Emphasizing the position of readers and their influence on textual interpretation is by no means original. Reader-response theorists, notably, have considered the roles that textual communities have on shaping readers and readings. Feminist theorists likewise have considered the influences of gender and sexuality on the reading process. The approach to interpretation I share in this essay borrows from the insights of theories of positioned readings, no doubt, particularly in terms of theories that examine how differences—be they racial, ethnic, class, or sexuality-based differences—affect our reading practices. Elizabeth Flynn's groundbreaking essay on the subject, "Gender and Reading" from *Gender and Reading*, discusses three different relationships between reader and text: "The reader can resist the alien thought or subject and so remain essentially unchanged by the reading experience. In this case the reader dominates the text. Or the reader can allow the alien thought to become such a powerful presence that the self is replaced by the other and is so effaced. In this case the text dominates the reader. Either the reader resists the text and so deprives it of its force, or the text overpowers the reader and so eliminates

the reader's powers of discernment. A third possibility, however, is that self
and other, reader and text, interact in such a way that the reader learns from
the experience without losing critical distance; reader and text interact with a
degree of mutuality. Foreignness is reduced, though not eliminated. Self and
other remain distinct and so create a kind of dialogue" (268).

My approach here comes closest to Flynn's third strategy, though I'm not
convinced "mutuality" is the end-goal; rather, I suggest that reader and text
interact with a degree of *respect* founded on an understanding of one culture's
desire to protect itself from colonization by outsiders. When my students read
works by Ortiz in class, some from other Puebloan tribes (Hopi and Tewa, in
particular) respond with a clear understanding of and identification with his
worldview, but with respect and acknowledgment that they will never fully
understand or possess an Acoma perspective. This sort of perspective influences
the entire multi-ethnic classroom, as it models intra-tribal respect and a
recognition of the limits of our understanding and our rights as scholar-students.

7. In a section of *After and Before Lightning*, Ortiz refers to this story after
mentioning the then-superpowers' expenditure on satellites to photograph the
tail of Halley's Comet: "In one of my short stories, an elder who's a grandfather
asks, 'And then will they know?'" (38). Right after this reference, an example of
the multiple access points through which Ortiz explores this topic, he includes
a poem about the same grandfather and the materials in the short story "Men
on the Moon." This poem, titled "Possibility," explores the real possibilities of
knowing the mystery and power of what lies within and before us, not only that
which lies out of reach, requiring the investigative mode of modern science:

> The old man could have told them.
> His grandson explained to him what was happening.
> "See those astronauts, Grandpa," he said,
> pointing to the tv screen. "They're on the moon
> to find out what's up there, to find the origin
> of life, and where and how all things began."
> The old man couldn't believe it,
> and he couldn't believe his grandson talking,
> talking like the scientists who didn't know.
> He thought about stone, water, fire, and air.
> And he had to believe it was possible—some men
> didn't know or had forgotten
> stone
> water
> fire
> air.
> He couldn't believe it, but it was possible (38).

8. Ortiz's works contain countless moments of intercultural generosity. I'm particularly struck by this resonant chord in *from Sand Creek* where he characterizes the missed opportunities by settlers to gain from the deep knowledge base of Indigenous peoples, a knowledge base that would benefit all: "but they could have / matched the land / like those / who had searched / the plains and tied themselves / to stars, / insects, / generations and generations, / instinct / for millennia" (47). In the last story in *Men on the Moon*, "Pennstuwehniyaahtse: Quuti's Story," Ortiz explores how intercultural generosity is a two-way process. Recounting his difficult escape from a school like Carlisle, Pennstuwehniyaahtse says, "Those people, got me to understand that they knew about long journeys and enormous difficulties. . . . We never spoke any of the Mericano language, but I learned to speak their language a little, and they learned to speak a little of ours. . . . I have never forgotten them and their name. . . . That journey was hard, but if it wasn't for those people, I would never have made it home" (203).

9. Ofelia Zepeda's poem "Deer Dance Exhibition" features an interlocutor, a cultural outsider, maybe a friend, asking questions about a sacred deer dance. The Tohono O'dham speaker, perhaps Zepeda herself, perhaps another, respectfully answers a number of questions: about the dancer's regalia, offering insights about its symbolism; about the drum and the speaker invites the questioner to participate: "Listen." Then, about the drum, "Go ahead. Touch it. Bless yourself with it. It is holy. You are safe now" (50). "When the drum beats, it brings the deer to life. / We believe the water the drum sits in is holy. It is life" (50). When the questioner asks a potentially more invasive question, "How does the boy become a dancer?" the speaker replies, "He just knows. His mother said he had dreams when he was a little boy. / You know how that happens. He just had it in him. / Then he started working with older men who taught him how to dance. / He has made many sacrifices for his dancing even for just a young boy" (51). After this brief explanation, the interlocutor doesn't probe for more details about the dancer's preparation. Instead, the questioner wonders what the dancers will do with the money earned from the dance: a mundane, realistic answer is delivered: "Oh, they just split it among the singers and dancer. / They will probably take the boy to McDonald's for a burger and fries. / The men will probably have a cold one. / It's hot today, you know" (51). This beautiful poem illustrates the speaker's generosity and willingness to share the sacred; it's a balancing act, though, between sharing privileged knowledge and maintaining some privacy, particularly when the outsider-recipient is observed to be unready or unable to fully understand—unable to fully appreciate the importance of the experience, asking as s/he does about mundane issues such as the dancer's profits rather than more significant subjects or fully participating in the shared beauty and wonder of the experience. The speaker's comments at the end remind her interlocutor of several things: 1) the dancers and observers

are contemporaries and share the same mundane needs like refreshment; and 2) no matter what intimacies have been shared, the outsider continues to analyze the dance and dancer from the perspective as an outsider, something the speaker recognizes, and exaggerates through colloquial ethnographic caricature.

10. In addition to Vine Deloria, Jr. and Wendy Rose, see Kate Shanley's essay "The Indians America Loves to Love and Read: American Indian Identity and Cultural Appropriation," *American Indian Quarterly* 21, no. 4 (Fall 1997): 675–702.

11. I'm referring here to the section of Ortiz's story "What Indians Do" from *Men on the Moon* that includes a joke made about the narrator: "I'll tell them you're a show-and-tell Indian: 'This is an Acoma Indian. He will show and tell'" (135).

12. Daniel Heath Justice writes about his privileging of Indigenous voices in his Native American literature classes, as both a decolonizing tactic and as recognition of those whose voices are most allied with Indigenous communities' needs. In my article "Facing the Fire: American Indian Literature and the Pedagogy of Anger," I similarly discuss the worth of privileging an Indigenous perspective (87). Critics might assume this is an essentializing move as well, although it's a measured, thoughtful response to the institutional history of Native studies. Perhaps in the future, once decolonizing research strategies have gained a meaningful foothold, this will change.

13. I feel compelled to mention Ortiz's *from Sand Creek* once again as it sets forward a model of compassionate reading and understanding for all readers, at the same time recognizing that we each bring different knowledge and worldviews to bear on a text, or in the case of this particular book, on a bloody and tragic chapter of history. Ortiz demonstrates a way for readers to have a deep understanding of a story even if we were not part of the originating story; as non-Arapaho and non-Cheyenne people, we can come to understand that tragedy of Sand Creek through our parallel stories as veterans, as Native peoples of other tribes, as the otherwise marginalized and oppressed, as the diasporized, as the struggling survivors of our own respective histories. In no wise is Ortiz saying that we can understand Sand Creek in the way of an Arapaho or Cheyenne can, but that we can attain meaningful access, after our own fashions and within the rubric of our respective worlds and worldviews. Acknowledging the specifics of our own identity and identifications is a means of showing respect and making transparent our ethical engagement.

14. In a forthcoming essay, "Writing the Intertwined Global Histories of Indigeneity and Diasporization: An Ecocritical Articulation of Place, Relationality, and Storytelling in the Poetry of Simon J. Ortiz," Susan Berry Brill de Ramírez argues that Ortiz "demonstrates how a deep sense of place, belonging

and community can be communicated and realized (becoming real) across times, worlds and geographies through the power of conversive storytelling. Distances are affirmed, yet traversed within storied moments" (not yet numbered). I share Ramírez's perspective on the power of storytelling, but still note the limits of outsider readers, in particular, to fully access the sacred. Even Ortiz, in his preface to *After* suggests that while he writes about his experience among the Dakota because that is part of his reality—"every moment, every act of my being was defined by the reality I had to acknowledge" (xv)—he also understands that he will never possess the knowledge the Dakota have of "the sacred beauty of the prairie homeland which they regard with wonder and awe" (xv).

15. Much of my thinking here is usefully summed up by an appendix, "Becoming an Ally," in Maurianne Adams, Lee Anne Bell, and Pat Griffin's *Teaching for Diversity and Social Justice: A Sourcebook* (New York: Routledge, 1997).

WORKS CITED

Adams, Maurianne, Lee Anne Bell, and Pat Griffin, eds. Appendix 6B "Becoming an Ally." *Teaching for Diversity and Social Justice: A Sourcebook.* New York: Routledge, 1997.

Allen, Paula Gunn. "Special Problems in Teaching Leslie Marmon Silko's *Ceremony*." *American Indian Quarterly* 14, no. 4 (Autumn 1990): 379–86.

Berglund, Jeff. "Facing the Fire: American Indian Literature and the Pedagogy of Anger." *American Indian Quarterly* 27, nos. 1 and 2 (Winter and Spring 2003): 80–90.

Brill de Ramírez, Susan Berry. *Contemporary American Indian Literatures and the Oral Tradition.* Tucson: University of Arizona Press, 1999.

———. "Writing the Intertwined Global Histories of Indigeneity and Diasporization: An Ecocritical Articulation of Place, Relationality, and Storytelling." In *Stories through Theory/Theory through Stories: Native American Indian Writing, Storytelling, and Critique*, edited by Gordon D. Henry, Jr., Nieves Pascual Coler, and Silvia Martinez Falquina. East Lansing: Michigan State University Press, forthcoming 2009.

Deloria, Jr., Vine. *God Is Red: A Native View of Religion.* Golden, Colorado: Fulcrum, 1973; rep. ed., 2003.

Fast, Robin Riley. "Outside Looking in: Nonnatives and American Indian Literature." *American Quarterly* 46, no. 1 (March 1994): 62–76.

Frisbie, Charlotte J. "Review of *Diné Bahane*: The Navajo Creation Story by Paul Zolbrod." *American Indian Quarterly* 10, no. 3 (Summer 1986): 259–62.

Jim, Rex Lee. "A Moment in My Life." In *Here First: Autobiographical Essays by Native American Writers*, edited by Arnold Krupat and Brian Swann, 229–46. New York: Modern Library, 2000.

Justice, Daniel Heath. "Seeing (and Reading) Red: Indian Outlaws in the Ivory Tower." In *Indigenizing the Academy*, edited by Devon Abbott Mihesuah and Angela Cavender Wilson, 100–123. Lincoln: University of Nebraska Press, 2004.

Moore, David L. "Rough Knowledge and Radical Understanding: Sacred Silence in American Indian Literatures." *American Indian Quarterly* 21, no. 4 (Fall 1997): 633–62.

Morris, Irvin. "Nahaghá (The Ceremony)." *From the Glittering World*, 103–12. Norman: University of Oklahoma Press, 1997.

Ortiz, Simon. *After and Before Lightning*. Tucson: University of Arizona Press, 1994.

———. *from Sand Creek*. Tucson: University of Arizona Press, 1991.

———. *Good Journey*. In *Woven Stone*, 149–283. Tucson: University of Arizona Press, 1992.

———. *Men on the Moon: Collected Short Stories*. Tucson: University of Arizona Press, 1999.

Shanley, Kathryn W. "The Indians America Loves to Love and Read: American Indian Identity and Cultural Appropriation." *American Indian Quarterly* 21, no. 4 (Fall 1997): 675–702.

Silko, Leslie Marmon. "Interior and Exterior Landscapes: the Pueblo Migration Stories." *Yellow Woman and a Beauty of the Spirit*, 25–47. New York: Touchstone, 1997.

———. "Language and Literature from a Pueblo Indian Perspective." *Yellow Woman and a Beauty of the Spirit*, 48–59. New York: Touchstone, 1997.

Smith, Linda Tuhiwai. *Decolonizing Methodologies: Research and Indigenous Methods*. London: Zed, 1999.

Smith, Andrea. "Spiritual Appropriation as Sexual Violence." *Wicazo Sa Review* 20, no. 1 (Spring 2005): 97–111.

Tapahonso, Luci. "Starlore." *Blue Horses Rush In: Poems & Stories*, 15–16. Tucson: University of Arizona Press, 1997.

Weaver, Jace and Craig Womack and Robert Warrior. *American Indian Literary Nationalism*. Albuquerque: University of New Mexico Press, 2006.

Womack, Craig. *Red on Red: Native American Literary Separatism*. Minneapolis: University of Minnesota Press, 1999.

Zepeda, Ofelia. "Deer Dance Exhibition." *Ocean Power: Poems from the Desert*, 50–51. Tucson: University of Arizona Press, 1995.

Zolbrod, Paul. *Diné Bahane: The Navajo Creation Story*. Albuquerque: University of New Mexico Press, 1984.

Men on the Moon and the
Fight for Environmental Justice

Elizabeth Ammons

*Native American and indigenous cultures worldwide
have understood and experienced life as a continuum
between human and nonhuman species and between
present, past, and future generations. . . . Corporate
globalization sees the world only as something to be
owned and the market as only driven by profits.*
—Vandana Shiva, *Earth Democracy:
Justice, Sustainability, and Peace*

The title story in Simon Ortiz's *Men on the Moon* (1999)
opens at Acoma Pueblo in 1969 with a grandfather, Faustin, receiving
a TV on Father's Day. His grandson tunes out the snow on the screen
to bring into focus a wrestling match. One fighter is Apache, the other
white. "The two men backed away from each other for a moment and then
they clenched again. They wheeled mightily and suddenly one threw the
other. The old man smiled. He wondered why they were fighting" (2).[1] The
Apache wrestler wins, and immediately a new image appears: the Apollo
spaceship on its launchpad about to head for the moon.

The two television images—a wrestling match between an Indian and
a white man followed by the live broadcast of the Apollo moonshot—set up
environmental justice themes in the book. Indian and white values lock in
combat, as the two wrestlers suggest. And the white world has finally gone
completely insane, as evidenced by the race to conquer space: the phallic
flight to the moon where, upon arrival, three bizarrely dressed white men
carrying "heavy-looking equipment on their back[s]" (10) skip like boys and
then float oddly as if underwater. "Are those men looking for something

on the moon, Nana?" the old man asks his grandson (5). Knowledge, Amarosho tells him. "Scientists say the knowledge will be useful in finding out where everything began a long time ago and how everything was made in the beginning" (12). Suspecting his grandson is joking—after all, he "had gone to Indian School for a number of years, and sometimes he would tell his grandfather some strange and funny things" (5)—Faustin realizes he is serious. "Well, then, do they say why they need to know where and how everything began? Hasn't anyone ever told them?" (12). People have tried, Amarosho answers, but the white people "want to find out for themselves, and also they claim they don't know" (12). Earlier Amarosho had explained that scientists believe no life exists on the moon. "Yet," Faustin thinks incredulously, "those men were trying to find knowledge on the moon. Faustin wondered if perhaps they had special tools with which they could find knowledge even if they believed there was no life on the moon" (11).

Placed first in the volume, "Men on the Moon" lays out basic Indigenous environmental justice themes that challenge all readers to work for social change. That is why I, as a white scholar, am writing this essay about Ortiz's book. "Men on the Moon" indicts the western military-industrial complex's insatiable drive for mastery of the universe; white people's refusal to listen to the wisdom of Indigenous people; the elevation of western science to godlike status; the strange idea that some parts of the creation are not alive; and the West's rapacious consumption of natural resources. In a vignette that will echo in several stories in the book about mining, we watch one of the men on the moon "in the bulky suit" with "a small pickax in his hand. He was striking at a boulder. The breathing of the man could be heard clearly. He seemed to be working very hard and was very tired" (12). Cracking boulders on the moon *is* hard work. It's not easy to conquer creation, whether on the surface of the moon or in the boardrooms of Kerr-McGee, the huge energy conglomerate that Ortiz mentions various times in the volume.

In this opening story, the magnitude of modern, western, environmental devastation comes to Faustin in a dream. The Pueblo culture hero Flintwing Boy watches a huge machine walk down a hill, crushing all the plants in its path and frightening even Coyote.

The Skquuyuh mahkina was undeterred. It walked over and through everything. It splashed through a stream of clear water.

The water boiled and streaks of oil flowed downstream. It split a
juniper tree in half with a terrible crash. It crushed a boulder into
dust with a sound of heavy metal. Nothing stopped the Skquuyuh
mahkina. It hummed (8).

Faustin's dream-vision reveals seemingly unstoppable domination and
rape of the earth. The mahkina spills oil into pristine waters, topples
ancient trees, crushes huge boulders. Flintwing Boy places an arrow in
his bowstring and says, "The people must talk among themselves and
learn what this is about, and decide what they will do" (9). The declaration sounds an alert and specifically serves as an instruction in right
thinking for Faustin. At the end of the story, he hopes more wrestling
will come on TV. He plans to root for the Apache.

In "A Society Based on Conquest Cannot Be Sustained: Native
Peoples and the Environmental Crisis," Anishinaabe scholar and activist
Winona LaDuke lists well-known facts about the disproportionate negative impacts of corporate and governmental environmental devastation
on Indigenous people:

- Over one million indigenous people will be relocated to
  allow for the development of hydroelectric dam projects
  in the next decade;

- The United States has detonated all its nuclear weapons in
  the lands of indigenous people, over six hundred of those
  tests within property belonging to the Shoshone nation;

- Two-thirds of all uranium resources within the borders
  of the United States lie under Native reservations—in
  1975, Indians produced 100 percent of all federally
  controlled uranium;

- One-third of all low-sulphur coal in the western United
  States is on Indian land, with four of the ten largest coal
  strip mines in these same areas;

- Fifteen of the current eighteen recipients of nuclear-
  waste research grants, so-called monitored retrievable
  nuclear storage sites, are Indian communities ("A Society
  based on Conquest," 99).

Environmental justice as a concept and as a political movement focuses on precisely such targeting of communities of color. As the important scholar and activist Robert D. Bullard explains in *Confronting Environmental Racism: Voices from the Grassroots*, environmental racism constitutes the foundational issue that movement activists and scholars must attack because dominant-culture institutions are "providing advantages and privileges to whites while perpetrating segregation, underdevelopment, disenfranchisement, and the poisoning (some people would use the term genocide)" (8) of people of color.[2] In the United States and globally, Indigenous communities face hugely disproportionate and often catastrophic environmental threats to members' health, lives, economic survival, and cultural and religious well-being because of governmental and corporate policies and practices that target them.[3]

Reform cannot address the size and depth of the problem. The achievement of environmental justice requires social transformation. Richard Hofrichter calls for "major restructuring of the entire social order" and argues that basic change begins with "a challenge to absolute property rights and the logic of industrial capitalism's emphasis on growth without limit" (*Toxic Struggles: The Theory and Practice of Environmental Justice*, 5). This radical social transformation cannot come, Ortiz shows in *Men on the Moon*, without a fundamental spiritual reorientation to an inclusively relational ethic that recognizes the place and value of all people, their communities, and the natural environment. Vine Deloria Jr. explains in *God Is Red* that the environmental and human crisis faced by the modern world results from centuries of western dominance shaped by organized Christianity's ethos of conquest and conversion, including the hyper-logical demythologizing of that ethos as promulgated by thinkers such as Nietzsche. Change requires a profound mind shift:

> The imminent and expected destruction of the life cycle of world ecology can be prevented by a radical shift in outlook from our present naive conception of this world as a testing ground to a more mature view of the universe as a comprehensive matrix of life forms. Making this shift in viewpoint is essentially religious, not economic or political (290).

The white colonial ethic of unlimited conquest and consumption pictured in Ortiz's opening story—white men with pickaxes cracking rocks on the moon—is not just odd. It is the root cause of the suffering and destruction experienced on earth by people of color, poor whites, animals, and the planet itself. It manifests the white world's basic spiritual disconnection from creation. Environmental justice will only become a reality, Ortiz's work insists, when white people and western culture undergo deep religious reorientation.

Theft, Death, and Lies

> It is
> no wonder
> they deny regret
> for the slaughter
> of their future.
> Denying eternity, it is no wonder
> they became so selflessly
> righteous.
>   *from Sand Creek*[4]

Two stories in *Men on the Moon* explicitly highlight the classic environmental justice issue of disproportionate negative health impacts on people of color caused by environmentally harmful late capitalist labor practices.[5] "Woman Singing" narrates the experiences of Native American migrant workers in the potato fields of Idaho: the wretched living conditions, the constant dislocation and loneliness, the sexual exploitation of a woman worker by her employer, and the killing escape of alcohol addiction, encouraged by a capitalist system that has already stolen Indigenous homelands and now attacks the workers' bodies and souls. When the white potato-farm owner, Wheeler, hands out biweekly wages, he warns the workers to stay sober. "'It's getting cold out, and we don't want no frozen Indians.' The potato boss laughed" (170–71). Then he gives them a lift to the bar in town.

This theme of deliberate entrapment of Indian workers in poverty, work hazardous to human health, and alcoholism likewise structures "Crossing," which tells of migrant Indians' labor for the railroad early in the twentieth century. With their best farmland stolen, Pueblo men in desperation take jobs constructing and repairing the rail beds. Forced to follow the work to California, they live in "little firetrap houses on company-owned land" in an area literally named "the Indian colony," where the workers no longer even try to protect themselves from the toxin of cheap alcohol that provides their only escape. Years later, one man recalls his father's life:

> "It's no wonder he and other men drank until they couldn't feel anything." . . . Drunkenness was common at the Indian colony. There were always fights; there was always screaming and yelling. Charley would hide every time his father got drunk. At the Indian colony he would see the men trudging off to work in the morning and returning in the evening looking like they had just lost a battle (184).

As many environmental justice texts argue, migrant labor does constitute a battle, one which Indians and other exploited workers are meant to lose: economically, physically, spiritually.[6] Ortiz's "Woman Singing" and "Crossing" expose the capitalist greed and disrespect for life at the system's core.

The same greed and disrespect—for Indigenous people, for the earth—drive the cultural imperialism that Ortiz indicts in "What Indians Do," a series of vignettes that reveal some of the many ways in which the environmental injustice of interconnected white exploitation of the earth and racist exploitation of Native people permeates Indians' lives all the time. The narrative opens with a conversation about space exploration that echoes "Men on the Moon"—an old uncle, pointing to his own breast, says of Western scientists: "'But they don't know that they should look into the space that is in here'" (129)—and goes on to quote a *San Francisco Examiner* headline that proudly blares: "PRIVATE PROPERTY WEEK BEGINS TODAY." Promised "the truth about Uncle Sam," the narrator imagines the newspaper article will be about environmental injustice: "I thought the *Examiner* would tell about U.S. corporations building suburbs outside Albuquerque and Phoenix on Indian lands, taking what little water Indians have left. I thought it would tell about the Indians pocketed into tiny leftover enclaves in San Diego County. But, of course, it didn't" (132). Another vignette shows U.S. Forest Service archaeologists refusing to talk about the real issues: "interstate highways, Kennecott

Copper, coal mines, power plants, land and water, and Indians" (132–33). And at a session on "The Anthropologist and the Indian" at an academic anthropology conference, we see the white experts hold forth so long about "preserving" Indians that the narrator never even gets to hear the invited, living, Indigenous speaker.

Cutting back and forth between white theft of land and resources and white theft of Indigenous identity and voice, "What Indians Do" presents the bitter reality of cultural imperialism for Native people, which, as Laurie Anne Whitt explains, "embraces a spectrum of expropriative strategies. At one end of this spectrum we find legal theories of acquisition that facilitate the dominant culture's ownership of indigenous land and of the material remains of indigenous peoples within the land. At the other end, we find theories of acquisition that rely on laws of intellectual property to legitimate the privatization of less tangible indigenous resources" (176–77). In "What Indians Do," white mastery of the earth through private property and resource confiscation and white mastery of Native peoples through silencing and erasure emerge as completely interdependent phenomena. Each requires the other for its successful accomplishment, and both come from exactly the same basic western ethic of insatiable conquest and dominance.

The deep pathology of that ethic appears many places in *Men on the Moon* but nowhere more horribly than in the story "Distance." On a nice white family farm, a spirited young billy goat, George, butts and knocks down the farmer's little girl. Her knee is scraped, so she cries. The farmer says kindly, "'We'll get that old goat tamed down'" (163). He then proceeds to torture the animal to death by withholding water. As the days pass, the goat strains against the rope holding him, his legs weaken, he falls to his knees, his bleats stop, his eyes glaze. The little girl asks when he can be loose again. "The father looked at his little girl, and he smiled and said, 'When George learns, sweetheart, when George learns not to be so mean'" (165). Slowly dehydrated by the calm, superior, white father protecting his darling in an exercise of brute force that he defines as "taming," the goat is murdered for being a goat, for having his own spirit and will. For readers, George is a living being sadistically subjugated until he dies. For the white farmer, George is property to be dealt with as he wishes.

"Distance" makes vivid the spiritual sickness at the heart of the dominant Euroamerican ethic of conquest, exploitation, and ownership that the environmental justice movement and countless Indigenous texts foreground. Winona LaDuke explains that "the system of capitalism and other forms of industrialism . . . lack respect for people and their environments in an insatiable quest for resources. This is particularly obvious in the United States, which consumes one-third of the world's resources and hosts only 5 percent of the world's population." LaDuke directly ties such wholesale and wanton abuse of the earth to the ethic of conquest motivating Columbus and responsible for genocide in the Americas:

> Columbus provided the entree for this system into the Western hemisphere. The holocaust that subsequently occurred in the Americas is unparalleled on a worldwide scale, and in its wake was the disruption necessary to destroy many indigenous economic and governmental systems. It is the most comprehensive system of imperialism ever witnessed by humanity. While no one knows exactly how many people were killed since Columbus's invasion, one conservative estimate suggests that the population of indigenous people in 1492 was 112,554,000 in the Western hemisphere and 28,264,000 in 1980 ("A Society Based on Conquest," 101).

It is often asked: How could Europeans and Euroamericans do what they have done to Indigenous people in the Americas? How could people systematically murder thousands—millions—of other people? I believe "Distance" answers with this question: How does the farmer murder George? The story speaks to the history of western imperialist violence against Native peoples. Massacring unarmed people and abusing children in the many boarding schools; controlling and withholding the earth's water and other resources; forcing all created beings such as George to submit to white authority and ideology or die: all are of one piece. The same value scheme dictates all three.[7]

"Distance" is not an allegory, I need to emphasize. Although it has powerful allegorical resonances, it is literally and importantly about a white man denying another living being the sacred right to his own life. As Vine Deloria Jr. states: "Any violation of another entity's right to existence in and of itself is a violation of the nature of the creation and a degradation of religious reality itself" (*God Is Red*, 299). The deadly dominant ethic that the farmer embraces cannot conceive of people as simply one part of creation. The farmer's philosophy insists on human beings as supreme, the rulers of the earth, the apex of creation, and then himself as the apex of the apex. If we read the story as an allegory, we occlude its representation of that literal, lethal arrogance. We ironically reproduce, in other words, precisely the western blindness that the text makes so horrifying.

As "Distance" articulates, the problem that *Men on the Moon* addresses as an environmental justice text is at bottom spiritual: the alienation of white culture from the earth, the learned ignorance with reference to the sacred nature of life in all its forms: lunar, goat, human, igneous, vegetable, oracular, interstellar. Huge relearning by whites must take place for justice and healing to occur. These stories in particular illustrate this point: "To Change Life in a Good Way," "Hiding, West of Here," and "Pennstuwehniyaahtse: Quuti's Story."

Mind Shifts

> It is by the affirmation of knowledge of
> source and place and spiritual return that
> resistance is realized.
>   —Simon Ortiz, "Towards a National Indian Literature"

Mines appear frequently in *Men on the Moon*. They are where the gargantuan lust of the energy conglomerate Kerr-McGee expresses itself most sickeningly, literally and metaphorically. Also, and less expected, they create a context for Ortiz where change can occur: where healing might begin if white people are willing to listen to Indigenous people. Anticipated by the earth-slashing mahkina that Flintwing Boy watches in "Men on the Moon," Kerr-McGee dominates "To Change Life in a Good Way" and "Hiding, West of Here." Now a subsidiary of Anadarko Petroleum, which bought it and Western Gas Resources for $23.3 billion in 2006 and was in the news in 2007 for failing to pay $7.6 million in petroleum royalties to the U.S. government,[8] Kerr-McGee in the 1960s and 1970s, the time-frame of Ortiz's stories, operated huge uranium mines in the U.S. Southwest, including the Ambrosia Lake mine in New Mexico that provides the setting for both "To Change Life" and "Hiding." Most people know Kerr-McGee as the focus of Karen Silkwood's successful environmental justice lawsuit in 1979, but the mining company also made the news in the 1970s for other environmental hazards affecting people, animals, and the earth. It conducted an experiment to test the idea of using treated liquid uranium waste as fertilizer for grassland grazed by beef cattle. It also served as an industry model for the practice of backfilling active mines with uranium tailings to shore up collapsing walls with toxic waste by-products.[9] The largest uranium tailing in the Western world can be found at the site of the Ambrosia Lake mine.[10]

"To Change Life in a Good Way" revolves around the friendship between two Kerr-McGee mining families, a Laguna Pueblo couple, Pete and Mary, and a white couple, Bill and Ida. The story moves back and forth between the dangerous mine where Pete and Bill work bringing up ore from the earth and a landmine that kills Bill's brother, Slick, a soldier in the Vietnam War. When Bill learns about his brother's death, he stumbles in a drunken fog to the door of his mobile home:

> Pete, Bill said, Slick's gone. No more Slick. Got killed. Stepping
> on a mine. A goddamned American mine. Isn't that the shits,
> Pete? Pete. . . .
>
>   Pete didn't say anything at first, and then he said, Aamoo o
> dyumuu. And he put his arm around Bill's shaking shoulders (112).

The American mine that kills Slick, of course, links directly to the American mine that is slowly siphoning off the lives of the two working men, Bill and Pete, who descend into the Kerr-McGee shafts every day. Each is explicitly designed to support warfare. Landmines kill people in Vietnam and uranium fuels the nation's atomic bombs.

These two mines—one just below the surface of the ground and openly designed to kill, the other deep underground and also deadly—get all confused in Bill's mind at Slick's funeral in Oklahoma. Bill tries to think of the Vietnam War as heroic; he tries to believe Slick's death was worthwhile. But he senses something is wrong with what he has always believed. He can't turn the Vietnam War into a just war. He can't suppress the thought that Slick's own country killed him. He can't turn either "mine" into an enemy weapon. Each is his own nation's weapon, and it is turned against its own people: working class and poor soldiers and American Indian, Latino, and rural white miners. Bill surfaces from his muddled thoughts to hear mourners ask him about his job at Kerr-McGee. They say: "[T]he company has built itself another building in

Tulsa. [Senator] Kerr's gonna screw the folks in New Mexico just like he has folks here" ("To Change Life in a Good Way," 114). These things merge in Ortiz's text: Kerr-McGee, the Vietnam War, the waste of American and Vietnamese lives in that American Cold War aggression, the racist history of killing Indians in the United States, the corruption of elected U.S. officials.

Bill struggles to figure out what Slick died for—"Well, because of the mine, stepping on the wrong place, being in a dangerous place, but something else" ("To Change Life in a Good Way," 115)—and his dawning awareness guides ours. The wrong place that the young white man stepped was Vietnam, Wounded Knee, Sand Creek.[11] The mine-made-in-America that blew him up is the imperialism poor people have been taught from the founding of the nation to fight for, until they are discarded, their blasted bodies, as in the current war in Iraq, making rich men richer.[12] Also the mine-made-in-America that blew Slick up is Kerr-McGee itself: the violent, dangerous, ticking bomb in the earth poisoning his brother and the many Native miners working its tunnels; polluting the soil, air, and water on which Indigenous people depend; and providing the raw materials to conduct the modern warfare that sends Slick halfway around the world to die.[13] "To Change Life in a Good Way" intimately links the U.S. imperialist war machine—Slick's death—to the foundational environmental justice issue of people of color and poor whites—Pete and Bill—being disproportionately affected by the toxic practices of hugely profitable corporations such as Kerr-McGee, which require poor people to choose between health and a paycheck.

Equally important, "To Change Life in a Good Way" addresses the underlying environmental justice imperative of the need for radical white religious reorientation. When they hear of Slick's death, Pete and Mary make a Laguna prayer bundle for Bill and Ida. "They sat at the kitchen table with the kids and tied feathers and scraped cedar sticks and closed them in a cornhusk with cotton, beads, pollen, and tobacco" (112). They also give their white friends an ear of Indian corn. Pete doesn't know all the old words or exactly what the Laguna rituals were. But he knows the sacred bundle can help Slick on his journey and aid the living. He tells Bill:

It's just for Slick. For his travel from this life among us to another place of being. You and Ida and Slick are not Indian, but it doesn't make any difference. It's for us, this kind of way, with corn and

with this, Bill. You take these sticks and feathers, and you put
them somewhere you think you should, someplace important that
you think might be good, maybe to change life in a good way, that
you think Slick would be helping us with (113).

Bill takes the bundle deep into the mine at Kerr-McGee. He travels the
tunnel alone and leaves it for Slick with these words: "Pete said he didn't
know exactly all the right Indian things to do anymore, but somehow I
believe Indians are more righter than we've ever been led to believe. And
now I'm trying too. So you help us now, little brother Slick. We need it. All
the help we can get. Even if it's just so much as holding up the roof of this
mine the damn company don't put enough timbers and bolts in" (115–16).
Ida plans to plant the ear of Indian corn: "If he's gonna hold up the roof of
Section 17, Slick better be able to help me break up that clay dirt too" (116).
The story says that Laguna wisdom—given in friendship, not something
that can be bought, taken, demanded—may ease Slick's journey and may
keep Kerr-McGee from killing more miners. It may be able to break up the
rock-hard clay of white people's gardens so a new crop can grow.

    "To Change Life in a Good Way" is not about non-Indigenous people
becoming wannabes: fake or imitation Indians. It is about non-Indians
listening to and following the religious wisdom that Indigenous peoples
have not forgotten and others may also know if friendship and humility
guide them. Nor does Ortiz's story present modern-day Noble Savages,
New Age stereotypes of essentialized primitives somehow innately pro-
grammed to cherish the earth and reject all things western. Pete and
Mary are Laguna people who have survived 500 years of colonial assault
with enough of the old knowledge intact to understand the basic spiritual
truth that all of creation is sacred and to be lived with in balance, not in
a hierarchy of dominance and subordination, conquest and rape, profit
and plunder. The contemporary Cherokee Appalachian writer Awiakta
explains in *Selu: Seeking the Corn Mother's Wisdom* that "Western
thought is based on dichotomies, which separate spirit from matter,
thought from feeling, and so on . . . and that detachment has increased
in a society now geared to technology and the domination of nature,"[14]
a society, Ortiz maintains, that is tearing the earth apart for profit and
can't wait to colonize the moon. But the sacred inheres in the material world. The two are not different realms, much less hierarchically
arranged ones.

That basic Indigenous environmental justice message repeats in "Hiding, West of Here," the penultimate placement of which in the book underscores the importance of hearing repeated what the earlier stories have already taught us. We all need to listen many times, as so much Native American literature emphasizes. The dominant-culture master narrative of conquest and consumption is very powerful. It is difficult to break the stranglehold of what Leslie Marmon Silko calls in *Almanac of the Dead* (1991), the Destroyers.

In "Hiding, West of Here," the white narrator (son and grandson of West Virginia coal miners and now a mechanic at Kerr-McGee's Ambrosia Lake mine) takes us with him into the mountains on his day off. He reflects on his job: "Sometimes you feel good and strong, but it's shitwork too, so you feel there's no profit in being a man. So I come sometimes on Sundays, come up here, and well, yeah, hide out. It's my time, the mountain at my back, over my shoulder" (192). Two Native men come into view, and the narrator, unseen, watches them take out a bundle, "sticks and feathers wrapped up in cornhusks, it looked like" (195), sing, and then place the bundle in a crack in a large rock. "I guess it's praying of a sort, yeh. And then it seemed like I was part of what the Indians were doing. Like they wanted me to be even though they didn't know I was there" (195). Into the narrator's mind come the West Virginia strip mines and how the earth must have looked before the mining, and still does in places. He senses that the thought means something, but what? The Native men leave; the story ends: "And I just felt, in fact I could see myself, like I was still hiding with the quiet and the mountain and the praying that had been going on" ("Hiding, West of Here," 196).

Echoing "To Change Life in a Good Way," "Hiding, West of Here" pushes the idea that white people must learn from Indians a step further. The "Hiding" narrator does not need anyone to tell him to get out of the mine, the town, the house, the shopping center, the bar, the church, and enter the mountains on a Sunday. He knows where he needs to be. What he does not know is how to pray there. Ortiz's nameless white (every?) man understands at some level that the earth is sacred, should not be strip mined, should be honored and thanked. Deep in him are those truths. To find them, however, he must listen to those Indigenous people who still remember the sacredness of creation, in this case Indians. And he must do so in a spirit of respect or "hiding"—not intruding, appropriating, presuming, leading, or otherwise reproducing the colonial arrogance that has brought the world to its present "shitwork" state. Then he may become part of a prayer that leads, as we see in the story's last line, to a small vision: a human being in the quiet, in the mountains, in prayer, not alone.

A basic difference between Judeo-Christian and Indigenous religions, according to Vine Deloria Jr., has to do with Native religions being place-based and experiential, precisely the truth that the narrator in "Hiding" comes to. Instead of creeds, doctrines, sermons, and theological arguments driving and dictating belief—"all products of the intellect and not necessarily based on experiences" (*God is Red*, 292)—Deloria stresses that Indigenous religions understand that knowledge of the sacred comes to humans experientially and that those experiences occur at certain places on the earth. Consequently, "unless the sacred places are discovered and protected and used as religious places, there is no possibility of a nation ever coming to grips with the land itself. Without that basic relationship, national psychic stability is impossible" (*God is Red*, 294). Of American Indian literatures, Ortiz says, "In terms of literary theme, land is a material reality as well as a philosophical, metaphysical idea or concept; land is who we are, land is our identity, land is home place, land is sacred." Indigenous literature represents "'resistance literature'"— "decolonization and liberation literature"—for Ortiz. He emphasizes that, "The spiritual aspect of literature is . . . responsibility and the insistence on that common shared responsibility."[15] Environmental justice from Indigenous points of view can never be simply about economics, politics, or social equity. As Ortiz's words, *God Is Red*, *Selu*, LaDuke's *Recovering the Sacred*, and stories such as "To Change Life" and "Hiding" argue, environmental justice must always be grounded, literally, in place-based and experientially arrived-at spiritual values.[16]

Ortiz takes tremendous risks in "To Change Life in a Good Way" and "Hiding, West of Here." The history of Euro-American theft of Indian land, lives, bones, children, health, resources, art, stories, and religion is so long and horrendous that the mere suggestion that white people might participate in Native spiritual ways, even at a distance, carries with it the danger of encouraging further colonial depredations. Indigenous scholars and activists and non-Natives allied in the struggle against anti-Indian racism uniformly condemn the racism and cultural imperialism of whites pretending to be Indian, finding the hidden Indian within, discovering their long-lost Cherokee princess great-grandmother, deciding to write fake Indian books, setting up shop as "shamans," descending on reservations to acquire wisdom, or hiring out as supposedly Indigenous healers.[17] Ortiz's fiction is not suggesting whites try to become Indians. "To Change Life in a Good Way" is saying that hope and healing have the possibility of coming from bonds between working-class whites exploited by the system of late capitalism and Indigenous people oppressed by the system of capitalism for centuries, *if* the white people are able to approach such affiliation in a spirit of respect and thus learn from Indigenous people how to see and live life differently. "Hiding, West of Here" suggests, further, that the potential for that changed awareness already lives in at least some white people. A memory exists that can be awakened, a desire that wishes to express itself, as the repeated trips of the white man into the mountains and therefore into the prayer of the Pueblo men reveal. Each story offers hope. Neither pretends that transformation will or can be anything but tentative, very fragile, and certainly only a beginning.

Pennstuwehniyaahtse

Our children will welcome the call and song into their breasts.

Their dreams will be engendered by Popee, Tecumseh, Crazy Horse,

Chief Joseph, Geronimo, and all our grandmothers and grandfathers.

And they will hear them say their lives are our lives, their hearts our

hearts.

And they will come to know it will not be the thieves, killers, liars

but our people who will have victory!

—Simon Ortiz, *Out There Somewhere*[18]

"Pennstuwehniyaahtse: Quuti's Story" moves back in time to call us to a different future. Echoing themes in "To Change Life in a Good Way" and "Hiding, West of Here," but also reiterating the white sadism of "Distance," the cultural imperialism of "What Indians Do," and the environmental racism of "Crossing" and "Woman Singing," the story acknowledges trauma and chooses hope. "Men on the Moon" begins Ortiz's volume with a story about a Pueblo grandfather and his grandson watching U.S. imperialism blast into the future, the "last frontier"—the conquest of outer space about which Flintwing Boy says to the grandfather, "The people must talk among themselves and learn what this is about, and decide what they will do" (9). "Pennstuwehniyaahtse: Quuti's Story" closes the circle with another story about a Pueblo grandfather and his grandson, but this narrative speaks not about the future of white imperialism, but about its past. The story has been handed down orally to the grandfather by Quuti who lived it, and it tells of two remarkable things: a Native boy's courageous resistance to genocide and the love for the creation practiced by a few white people. The story's placement last in the volume says that in such a past retold, rather than in the neocolonial attempt of late capitalism to conquer the universe with rockets and lunar pickaxes, lies the future, the wisdom, that the grandson—and all humankind—need.

"Pennstuwehniyaahtse" opens with Santiago and his grandson, Cholly, walking back to the pueblo from the sheep camp in the mountains. As they make the long walk, Santiago tells Cholly the story Quuti told many years ago about how white people stole him at the age of twelve from his Pueblo home to attend the Carlisle Indian Industrial School hundreds of miles away in Pennsylvania. The whites who tear Quuti and the other Pueblo children from their protesting, grief-stricken families, like the farmer in "Distance," proceed with supreme sadistic confidence in their own rectitude and superiority. They throw away the food Quuti's mother sent with him for the journey, force alien cultural practices on the trapped children, forbid them to speak their Native languages, impose harsh regimes of manual labor at the school, and use methods of torture such as starvation to enforce their cruel rules.[19] At fifteen, Quuti runs away.

The escapee walks for days until a snowstorm leads him to seek shelter in a barn, where cows warm him. Then, in a scene evoking all the many references to mining in the book, as well as the snow on the screen of that TV in the opening story, the boy, desperately hungry, tunnels through the deep snow toward the farmhouse. Digging, he hears something: "Suddenly the snow fell open and there was a man standing in front of me who was so startled he dropped his shovel" ("Pennstuwehniyaahtse:

Quuti's Story," 201). The two try to communicate but speak different languages. So they travel back through Quuti's tunnel to the cows the farmer
was trying to reach.

> When he came into the barn and saw his cows, he was so happy
> to see they were alright he started to kiss them and hug them and
> rub their hides to warm them up. And talk to them in this strange
> language. And I knew then he wasn't one of the Mericano, for I had
> never seen any of them act like this man ("Pennstuwehniyaahtse:
> Quuti's Story," 201–2).

Ortiz's last story imagines a bizarrely un-American white man, one who
loves animals, hugs and kisses them like fellow beings, talks to them
as he does any other relative, warms them with his hands, and relieves
their painful udders. They in return give milk and friendship. The animals reassured and cared for, the white man and Quuti go back through
the tunnel they had unwittingly made together and enter the farmhouse,
where Quuti is bathed, fed, and made safe.

This story unequivocally names white imperialism as the deadly
enemy of Indigenous people and shows that Carlisle Indian Industrial
Boarding School epitomizes environmental racism. Along with the 1887
Dawe's Land Allotment Act that forced Indigenous people to become private property owners and therefore abandon Native lifeways, the theft of
Indian children beginning with Carlisle in 1879 was part of a U.S. government land-based plot to reduce the size of reservations and steal yet more
land for whites. The schools, in some cases far from the children's home
communities, existed for the express purpose of fracturing continuity
between generations by teaching the young to hate all things Indigenous,
including the traditional place-based religions of their elders and ancestors, without which, as Deloria emphasizes, there cannot be true or lasting environmental justice in the Americas. The removal of the children
constituted a systematic, environmentally focused, life-threatening
attack on Native communities as lethal as the earlier slaughter of the
buffalo or the later poisoning of the people through uranium mining.
The white invaders, having stolen land, plants, animals, warriors, bones,
water, and minerals, now stole the minds and often the lives of the next
generation (many died at the boarding schools), and thereby inflicted life-
depleting blows on entire nations, the wounds of which endure.[20] Quuti

says of his decision to run away from Carlisle: "I was worried—I thought about this a lot—that I was becoming more like an Mericano than one of our own people" ("Pennstuwehniyaahtse: Quuti's Story," 200). Quuti has to return home or he will, as Pratt wished, die.

The crucial thing about the farmer in this story, of course, is that he does not speak English. He represents whiteness, or some possibility of whiteness, outside the Anglo paradigm. Incredibly, amazingly, this story about courageous Indigenous resistance to genocide says, there lives a non-English-speaking national space that can be imagined, returned to, accessed. There are, and always have been, non-Indian allies. There still is or might be in America a white man who doesn't know the language of the conqueror, who speaks some other language.

The first word of the story conveys that possibility. "Pennstuweh-niyaahtse" undoes the dominance of English. It forces readers of many backgrounds to try to comprehend a different language, one most of us don't know how to pronounce, much less what language it is. Keres? Diné? Apache? Perhaps the reader flips the pages to look for a glossary at the end of the book, or goes online to Google it. But if confused readers give up this need to be in charge, the need to plant an American flag on the moon, or never indulge that ethic of mastery to begin with and simply read, simply listen, the text reveals soon enough that we do know the word after all. Most of us just never heard Pennsylvania named by a Pueblo boy before.

So too, when it comes to the white farmer. The story confronts readers with a new and unfamiliar language—a white man who openly hugs, kisses, and talks to cows, a person so different from all the whites Quuti has ever known that the boy states categorically that he can't be one of the Mericano ("Pennstuwehniyaahtse: Quuti's Story," 202). This farmer's language (verbal, physical) constitutes a nondominant (not English) possibility in the nation's past that can be recovered if we listen to the stories of the ancestors. Much as the unnamed narrator of "Hiding" and Bill in "To Change Life" can begin to think new thoughts when they listen to and learn from Indigenous people who have not forgotten traditional truths, this story says new ways of thinking and being are possible, and they are actually the old ways. Immigrant as well as Indigenous. They can come to the reader if, like Cholly, one walks with and listens to Santiago.

Men on the Moon insists on the injustice and pain caused by the ongoing history of genocide in the Americas, represented in

"Pennstuwehniyaahtse" by the infamous Carlisle Industrial School which flew Pratt's deadly motto on a banner above the door: "Kill the Indian, Save the Man." White colonial dominance—the insanity of men on the moon—requires courageous resistance, which is the meaning of Quuti's story and the reason why Santiago tells that story to Cholly, his grandson, on their long walk home. Ortiz's concluding story is not some hug-in with white America. It is a warrior story about and for a Pueblo boy that diverse readers are privileged to hear, as the narrator in "Hiding" becomes part of the prayer, if we remain silent and listen. And the story does offer hope. There is a nondominant ancestral past—Indigenous and immigrant—from which strength and wisdom can be drawn. Apparently new but actually very old languages and ways of being exist. As various Ortiz critics note, one of the most astonishing of the many astonishing features of Ortiz's work is, as Matthew E. Duques puts it, "the manner in which Ortiz can in so few words convey both the horrific tragedy of conquest and colonization, while at the same time find a space for possibility, a means for recovery that is never about forgetting but always occurs as a kind of recuperative remembering."[21] Quuti names his first born son Yoonson, for the farmer who helped him on his long journey home.[22] The immigrant in this story gets absorbed into Pueblo life, not the other way around. It is possible.

"Pennstuwehniyaahtse" is for most people an unfamiliar word. Not English or Dutch or Swahili or Cantonese or Spanish. It signals some other possibility. A Pueblo way of naming a place in America that lives in oral history to be retrieved and brought to life now in the stories told to the children, all the children, on the long walk home. Ortiz states in "Towards a National Indian Literature":

> It is also because of the acknowledgment by Indian writers of a responsibility to advocate for their people's self-government, sovereignty, and control of land and natural resources; and to look also at racism, political and economic oppression, sexism, supremacism, and the needless and wasteful exploitation of land and people, especially in the U.S., that Indian literature is developing a character of nationalism which indeed it should have. It is this character which will prove to be the heart and fiber and story of an America which has heretofore too often feared its deepest and most honest emotions of love and compassion. It is

this story, wealthy in being without an illusion of dominant power and capitalistic abundance, that is the most authentic (12).

Ortiz's words eloquently define environmental justice. In a non-Mericano America tunnels can exist not to line the pockets of Kerr-McGee but to support life. The abuse of land, people, animals, sacred truths, and the very universe itself that *Men on the Moon* as an environmental justice text chronicles with painstaking honesty comes to rest in Ortiz's last story in a vision of hope. A boy and a man from opposite sides of the earth create together—to their mutual, enormous surprise—a tunnel that does not fuel wars, poison the planet, or kill workers but leads, instead, to health and community, to life itself: a group of cows, a farmhouse kitchen, a friendship across race, age, and culture, a victory over oppression. Ortiz calls American Indian literature the nation's literature because it unites fierce critique of injustice with deep belief in the power of compassion and love to heal and transform. *Men on the Moon* illustrates the point.

NOTES

1. Critical work on Ortiz's volume of stories does not exist, which is one reason I wish to discuss it. As guest editor Susan Berry Brill de Ramírez points out in her introduction to an excellent 2004 special issue of *SAIL* devoted to Ortiz, his work "has been understudied and underappreciated" ("A Spring Wind Rising . . . Listen. You Can Hear It," *SAIL* 16 [Winter 2004], 7). While most of the essays in this special issue of *SAIL* concentrate on Ortiz's poetry, many nevertheless provide helpful perspectives for readers of *Men on the Moon*. See especially David L. Moore ("'The story goes its own way': Ortiz, Nationalism, and the Oral Poetics of Power"); Tohe ("'It was that Indian': Simon Ortiz, Activist Poet"), Hafen ("'Story Speaks for Us': Centering the Voice of Simon Ortiz"); and Hollrah ("Resistance and Continuance through Cultural Connections in Simon J. Ortiz's *Out There Somewhere*"). Also illuminating though likewise focused on poems is the essay by Fast in *SAIL* in 2005 ("(Re)Claiming America: Ortiz's *After and Before the Lightning*," *SAIL* 17 [Fall 2005]: 27–47). For a social science discussion that refers to Ortiz's story "Men on the Moon," see Young.

2. For the basic tenets of the Environmental Justice Movement as laid down at the famous 1991 First National People of Color Environmental Leadership Summit in Washington, D.C., see the official statement produced at that summit, "Principles of Environmental Justice," reprinted in Hofrichter, *Toxic Struggles: The Theory and Practice of Environmental Justice* (Salt Lake City: University of Utah Press, 2002).

3. See Bullard, *Confronting Environmental Racism: Voices from the Grassroots* (Boston: South End Press, 1993), 7–13; Shiva, *Earth Democracy*; Agyeman, *Sustainable Communities and the Challenge of Environmental Justice* (New York: New York University Press, 2005); Joni Adamson, Mei Mei Evans, and Rachel Stein, eds., *The Environmental Justice Reader: Politics, Poetics, and Pedagogy* (Tucson: University of Arizona Press, 2002); Gedricks, *The New Resource Wars: Native and Environmental Struggles Against Multinational Corporations* (Boston: South End Press, 1993); Girdner and Smith, *Killing Me Softly: Toxic Waste, Corporate Profit, and the Struggle for Environmental Justice* (New York: Monthly Review Press, 2002); Sandler and Pezzullo; Gibson, *Eco-Justice—The Unfinished Journey* (Albany: State University of New York Press, 2004); Washington, Rosier, and Goodall, *Echoes from the Poisoned Well: Global Memories of Environmental Injustice* (Oxford: Lexington Books, 2006).

4. Ortiz, *from Sand Creek*, 77.

5. Only some stories in *Men on the Moon* focus literally in this way on standard environmental justice issues, I should point out, which is meaningful. In Ortiz's work, environmental injustice does not appear separate from all the life issues Indigenous and poor people face. It is part of the whole. Which is also to say: finally, all the stories in this volume have to do with environmental justice. Distinguishing between how human beings relate to the earth and how human beings relate to each other makes no sense from Indigenous points of view. Although my essay singles out certain stories for discussion, it is important to note that everything in the volume is relevant.

6. See, e.g., Helena María Viramontes' well-known contemporary novel about Mexican American migrant workers, *Under the Feet of Jesus* (1996), or the United Farm Workers documentary, *The Wrath of Grapes* (1986).

7. For excellent analytical treatment of this point, see, e.g., Ward Churchill, *Struggle for the Land: Native North American Resistance to Genocide, Ecocide and Colonization* (San Francisco: City Lights, 2002). For excellent discussion of the point in various U.S. literary texts, especially by late nineteenth- and early twentieth-century writers of color, see Myers, *Converging Stories: Race, Ecology, and Environmental Justice in American Literature* (Athens: University of Georgia Press, 2005).

8. In January 2007, a jury found Kerr-McGee guilty of underpaying royalties. In April 2007, a federal judge overruled the verdict. See "Blowing the Whistle," "Kerr-McGee Is Found Liable," and "Oil Whistle-Blower's Lawsuit."

9. See "Silkwood 'Vindicated,'" "Uranium Waste," and "Backfilling Mines."

10. See Drake ("Uranium Mining Boom Echoes in the Radioactive Valley of Ambrosia Lake," *The Center for Land Use Interpretation Newsletter*, Spring 1998), who points out there is no lake (it is only a name) and describes the large,

mostly abandoned area today as "a haunting, debris-strewn landscape, with massive mounds of radioactive tailings" (n.p.).

11. Ortiz makes this connection between the Vietnam War and the Massacre at Sand Creek explicit, of course, in his celebrated volume, *from Sand Creek*.

12. In the current war, although only 19 percent of the U.S. population live in rural areas, 44 percent of the U.S. soldiers in Iraq come from rural places, where high rates of unemployment and poverty lead young people to enlist in the armed services. See "For Veterans In Rural Areas, Care Hard To Reach," *The Boston Globe*, April 29, 2007, section A, 1.

13. On the lethal impact of Kerr-McGee uranium mines on Native workers in the U.S. Southwest, see Spieldoch, "Uranium Is in My Body," *Contemporary Native American Cultural Issues*, Duane Champagne, ed. (Walnut Creek, CA: AltaMira Press, 1999), 307–16. On militarism itself as an environmental and environmental justice issue, see Seager, "Patriarchal Vandalism: Militaries and the Environment," in *Dangerous Intersections: Feminist Perspectives on Population, Environment, and Development*, Jael Silliman and Ynestra King, eds. (Cambridge, MA: South End Press, 1998), who points out: "Militaries are powerful environmental ravagers. . . . The most powerful military contrivances, nuclear and chemical 'capability,' push environmental capability to the limits— past the limits already for some of the radioactive, blighted wastelands created around the world by military testing, dumping, and adventurism" (163). Almost all of those military-created wastelands in the United States, as my earlier reference from Winona LaDuke explains, are on Indigenous lands.

14. Awiakta, *Selu: Seeking the Corn Mother's Wisdom* (Golden, CO: Fulcrum, 1993), 241. Like Vine Deloria's *God Is Red*, this book addresses many of the issues treated by Ortiz, with Awiakta's two poems on facing pages, "Memo to NASA" and "Cherokee Woman on the Moon," especially relevant to Ortiz's volume.

15. Quoted in Jane P. Hafen, "'Story Speaks for Us': Centering the Voice of Simon Ortiz," *SAIL* 16 (Winter 2004): 64.

16. Recent evangelical Christian and liberal Jewish attention to environmental issues may indicate some change in Western values. See, e.g., Jim Wallis, *The Soul of Politics: Beyond "Religious Right" and "Secular Left"* (New York: Harcourt, 1995); James H. Cone, *The Emergence of a Black Theology of Liberation, 1968–1998* (Boston: Beacon Press, 1999); Gibson, *Eco-Justice*; and Michael Lerner, *The Left Hand of God: Taking Back Our Country from the Religious Right* (San Francisco: HarperCollins, 2006). However, caring for the earth out of a monotheistic belief that "God" commands people to do so is very different from the kind of experiential, sacred place-based spiritual values that Deloria, Awiakta, Ortiz, LaDuke, and countless other Native thinkers emphasize.

17. See, e.g., Laurie Anne Whitt, "Cultural Imperialism and the Marketing of Native America," *Contemporary Native American Cultural Issues*; Devon Abbott Mihesuah, *So You Want to Write About Indians? A Guide for Writers, Students, and Scholars* (Lincoln, NE: University of Nebraska Press, 2005); Wendy Rose, "The Great Pretenders: Further Reflections on Whiteshamanism," *The State of Native America: Genocide, Colonization, and Resistance*, M. Annette Jaimes, ed. (Boston: South End Press, 1992), 403–21; Elizabeth Cook-Lynn, *Why I Can't Read Wallace Stegner and Other Essays* (Madison: University of Wisconsin Press, 1996); Philip J. Deloria, *Playing Indian* (New Haven: Yale University Press, 1998); and Andrea Smith, *Conquest: Sexual Violence and American Indian Genocide* (Cambridge, MA: South End Press, 2005), 119–35.

18. *Out There Somewhere*, 69. Significantly, in this passage Ortiz places first among Native heroes the Tewa leader of the successful 1680 Pueblo Revolt against Spanish colonial dominance and enforced Christianity, Popee (also spelled Pope or Popay).

19. The racism and sadism of the Indian boarding schools, genocidally designed, in the famous slogan of Carlisle's founder, Colonel Richard Henry Pratt, to "Kill the Indian, Save the Man," are well documented. See, e.g., Smith, *Conquest*; Debra K. S. Barker, "Kill the Indian, Save the Child: Cultural Genocide and the Boarding School," *American Indian Studies: An Interdisciplinary Approach to Contemporary Issues*, Dale Morrison, ed. (New York: Peter Lang, 1997), 47–68; Churchill, *Kill the Indian, Save the Man: The Genocidal Impact of American Indian Residential Schools* (San Francisco: City Lights, 2004); Ruth Spack, *America's Second Tongue: American Indian Education and the Ownership of English, 1860–1900* (Lincoln: University of Nebraska Press, 2002); and David Wallace Adams, *Education for Extinction: American Indians and the Boarding School Experience, 1875–1928* (Lawrence: University Press of Kansas, 1995).

20. Indigenous people in both Canada and the United States have formed activist reparations and healing projects to address the continuing, devastating effects of the boarding schools on survivors, their families, and communities. See, e.g., The Indian Residential Survivors Society, http://irsss.org, or The Boarding School Healing Project, http://www.boardingschoolhealingproject. org; accessed 2007.

21. Matthew E. Duques, "Revisiting the Regenerative Possibilities of Ortiz," *SAIL* 16 (Winter 2004): 97. Similarly, Tohe observes of Ortiz, "While some of his revelations are hard to take, he avoids descending into cynicism and bitterness. Instead, he reaches for hope, for the continued struggle to survive. His activist poetry converges with the spiritual values of his Aacqu/Acoma upbringing and compassion. Simon, like Ella Deloria, Vine Deloria, Elizabeth Cook-Lynn, and Leslie Marmon Silko, speaks from The People's consciousness for the sake of the land and The People" ("'It was that Indian,'" 55). Likewise Fast states, "Ortiz

demonstrates that survival depends both upon remembering and exposing history, and upon refusing to accept imposed definitions and oppressions. Instead he will uncover the potentially restorative and 'compassionate' possibilities of America, and challenge all of his readers to reclaim and realize them" ("(Re)Claiming America," 31).

22. The name, perhaps a phonetic version of a German name, suggests the demographics of the counties in Pennsylvania we can imagine Quuti walking through in his flight from Carlisle, located in Cumberland County. According to U.S. Census figures for 1880, for example, people born in "the German Empire" followed by people born in Ireland, greatly outnumbered all other immigrants in that and surrounding counties. People from both those places had in many cases fled harsh colonial regimes themselves, which may explain the farmer's welcoming behavior toward Quuti. This fictional immigrant has not yet assimilated.

WORKS CITED

Adams, David Wallace. *Education for Extinction: American Indians and the Boarding School Experience, 1875–1928.* Lawrence: University Press of Kansas, 1995.

Adamson, Joni, Mei Mei Evans, and Rachel Stein, eds. *The Environmental Justice Reader: Politics, Poetics, and Pedagogy.* Tucson: University of Arizona Press, 2002.

Agyeman, Julian. *Sustainable Communities and the Challenge of Environmental Justice.* New York: New York University Press, 2005.

Awiakta, Marilou. *Selu: Seeking the Corn Mother's Wisdom.* Golden, CO: Fulcrum, 1993.

"Backfilling Mines With Uranium Tailings Seen As Disposal Solution." *Chemical Week*, February 28, 1979, 21.

Barker, Debra K. S. "Kill the Indian, Save the Child: Cultural Genocide and the Boarding School." In *American Indian Studies: An Interdisciplinary Approach to Contemporary Issues*, edited by Dale Morrison, 47–68. New York: Peter Lang, 1997.

"Blowing the Whistle on Big Oil." *The New York Times*, December 3, 2006, section 3, 1ff.

Brill de Ramírez, Susan Berry. "A Spring Wind Rising . . . Listen. You Can Hear It." *SAIL* 16 (Winter 2004): 3–7.

Bullard, Robert D. "Introduction." In *Confronting Environmental Racism: Voices from the Grassroots*, edited by Robert D. Bullard, 7–13. Boston: South End Press, 1993.

Churchill, Ward. *Kill the Indian, Save the Man: The Genocidal Impact of American Indian Residential Schools.* San Francisco: City Lights, 2004.

———. *Struggle for the Land: Native North American Resistance to Genocide, Ecocide and Colonization.* San Francisco: City Lights, 2002.

Cone, James H. *The Emergence of a Black Theology of Liberation, 1968–1998.* Boston: Beacon Press, 1999.

Cook-Lynn, Elizabeth. *Why I Can't Read Wallace Stegner and Other Essays.* Madison: University of Wisconsin Press, 1996.

Deloria, Philip J. *Playing Indian.* New Haven: Yale University Press, 1998.

Deloria, Jr., Vine. *God Is Red.* New York: Grosset and Dunlap, 1973.

Drake, Diana. "Uranium Mining Boom Echoes in the Radioactive Valley of Ambrosia Lake." *The Center for Land Use Interpretation Newsletter* (Spring 1998). http://www.clui.org/clui_4_1/lot1/lotlsp98/uran.html (accessed 2007).

Duques, Matthew E. "Revisiting the Regenerative Possibilities of Ortiz." *SAIL* 16 (Winter 2004): 96–98.

Fast, Robin Riley. "(Re)Claiming America: Ortiz's *After and Before the Lightning.*" *SAIL* 17 (Fall 2005): 27–47.

"For Veterans In Rural Areas, Care Hard To Reach." *The Boston Globe*, April 29, 2007, section A, 1.

Gedricks, Al. *The New Resource Wars: Native and Environmental Struggles Against Multinational Corporations.* Boston: South End Press, 1993.

Gibson, William E., ed. *Eco-Justice—The Unfinished Journey.* Albany: State University of New York Press, 2004.

Girdner, Eddie J., and Jack Smith. *Killing Me Softly: Toxic Waste, Corporate Profit, and the Struggle for Environmental Justice.* New York: Monthly Review Press, 2002.

Hafen, P. Jane. "'Story Speaks for Us': Centering the Voice of Simon Ortiz." *SAIL* 16 (Winter 2004): 61–67.

Hofrichter, Richard, ed. *Toxic Struggles: The Theory and Practice of Environmental Justice.* Salt Lake City: University of Utah Press, 2002.

"Kerr-McGee Is Found Liable In Lawsuit Over Oil Royalties." *The New York Times*, January 23, 2007, section 3, 3.

LaDuke, Winona. "A Society Based on Conquest Cannot Be Sustained: Native Peoples and the Environmental Crisis." In *Toxic Struggles: The Theory and Practice of Environmental Justice*, edited by Richard Hofrichter, 98–106. Salt Lake City: University of Utah Press, 2002.

Lerner, Michael. *The Left Hand of God: Taking Back Our Country from the Religious Right.* San Francisco: HarperCollins, 2006.

Mihesuah, Devon Abbott. *So You Want to Write About Indians? A Guide for Writers, Students, and Scholars.* Lincoln: University of Nebraska Press, 2005.

Moore, David L. "'The story goes its own way': Ortiz, Nationalism, and the Oral Poetics of Power." *SAIL* 16 (Winter 2004): 34–46.

Myers, Jeffrey. *Converging Stories: Race, Ecology, and Environmental Justice in American Literature.* Athens: University of Georgia Press, 2005.

"Oil Whistle-Blower's Lawsuit Is Dismissed." *The Denver Post*, April 3, 2007, section C, 2.

Ortiz, Simon. *from Sand Creek: rising in this heart which is our America.* New York: Thunder's Mouth Press, 1981.

———. *Men on the Moon.* Tucson: University of Arizona Press, 1999.

———. *Out There Somewhere.* Tucson: University of Arizona Press, 2002.

———. "Towards a National Indian Literature: Cultural Authenticity in Nationalism." *MELUS* 8 (Summer 1981): 7–12.

Rose, Wendy. "The Great Pretenders: Further Reflections on Whiteshamanism." In *The State of Native America: Genocide, Colonization, and Resistance*, edited by M. Annette Jaimes, 403–21. Boston: South End Press, 1992.

Sandler, Ronald, and Phaedra C. Pezzullo, eds. *Environmental Justice and Environmentalism: The Social Justice Challenge to the Environmental Movement.* Cambridge, MA: MIT Press, 2007.

Seager, Joni. "Patriarchal Vandalism: Militaries and the Environment." In *Dangerous Intersections: Feminist Perspectives on Population, Environment, and Development*, edited by Jael Silliman and Ynestra King. Cambridge, MA: South End Press, 1998.

Shiva, Vandana. *Earth Democracy: Justice, Sustainability, and Peace.* Cambridge, MA: South End Press, 2005.

"Silkwood 'Vindicated.'" *Newsweek*, May 28, 1979, 40.

Smith, Andrea. *Conquest: Sexual Violence and American Indian Genocide.* Cambridge, MA: South End Press, 2005.

Spack, Ruth. *America's Second Tongue: American Indian Education and the Ownership of English, 1860–1900.* Lincoln: University of Nebraska Press, 2002.

Spieldoch, Rachel L. "Uranium Is in My Body." In *Contemporary Native American Cultural Issues*, edited by Duane Champagne, 307–16. Walnut Creek, CA: AltaMira Press, 1999.

Tohe, Laura. "'It was that Indian': Simon Ortiz, Activist Poet." *SAIL* 16 (Winter 2004): 54–56.

Hollrah, Patrice. "Resistance and Continuance through Cultural Connections in Simon J. Ortiz's *Out There Somewhere.*" *SAIL* 16 (Winter 2004): 79–88.

"Uranium Waste As Fertilizer?" *Chemical Week*, October 24, 1979, 43.

Wallis, Jim. *The Soul of Politics: Beyond "Religious Right" and "Secular Left."* New York: Harcourt, 1995.

Washington, Sylvia Hood, Paul C. Rosier, and Heather Goodall, eds. *Echoes from the Poisoned Well: Global Memories of Environmental Injustice.* Oxford: Lexington Books, 2006.

Whitt, Laurie Anne. "Cultural Imperialism and the Marketing of Native America." In *Contemporary Native American Cultural Issues*, edited by Duane Champagne, 169–92. Walnut Creek, CA: AltaMira Press, 1999.

Young, M. Jane. "'Pity the Indians of Outer Space': Native American Views of the Space Program." *Western Folklore* 46 (October 1987): 269–79.

In Open Daring

Risk and Vulnerability in the Poetry of Simon J. Ortiz

Sean Kicummah Teuton

In his 2002 book of poems, *Out There Somewhere*, Simon Ortiz begins "Part One: Margins" by sharing his "Headlands Journal," recorded during a writers' retreat on the West Coast. On Thursday, July 14, at 10:07 a.m., he writes:

> Talk about risk last night. Headlands Center for the Arts is located within federal property managed by the U.S. Park Service and its bureaucratic rules. Which requires Headlands Center artists to abide by the rules. Risk by the rules?
>
> Renee is Mexican Indian, dark skinned.
> I'm risking my reputation, he says.
> And he says about another artist's work,
> That's not risk, that's business!
> What did your people gain, Indian?
> What did your people lose, Indian?
> What is risk? Is there any such thing as risk at all (8–9)?

In his bare, troubled language, Ortiz raises the issue of risk that is far too rarely addressed with the grace, directness, and ethical imperative that pervades virtually every sector of his writing. As a poet, Ortiz is obviously concerned with artistic risk, but he begins his book and journal entry by announcing the stakes of political risk, the federal governmental machinery that sets the "rules" by which the writers must work, or, ridiculously, risk. Beginning thus, Ortiz reminds us that any of our pursuits in Indigenous studies—artistic or intellectual—ultimately involve this kind of risk. For colonial relations dictate our very abilities to risk. One artist says that he is "risking his reputation" and that another's work doesn't qualify as risk but merely as business, artistic work that markets the illusion of risk.

With his daring questions, Ortiz causes us to pause and to consider exactly what it means to risk—as Indigenous people, as intellectuals, as human beings. In his repeated questions that sound like objectifying queries of the colonial naysayer—"What did your people gain, Indian? What did your people lose, Indian?"—the poet begins to focus on his own definition of risk: the willingness to dare to lose with the hope to gain. The control of the seemingly innocuous U.S. Park Service and its bureaucratic rules is, of course, a stand-in for the historical colonial rule of law that justifies then and now the theft of Indigenous lands and restricts Native freedoms, artistic and otherwise. Ortiz starkly pushes his poetic explorations into the underbelly of Manifest Destiny, genocide, and natural resource appropriations: "Risk by the rules?" Located within this stolen land and its arbitrary rules to control its dispossessed, the art enclave could be viewed as a farce. Since good artistic and intellectual ventures rely on the freedom to risk, they can't possibly proceed when their freedom to risk is ruled, and as Ortiz understands profoundly, risk is requisite within any ethical inclination, but only reasonable when volitional.

I linger on this situation to suggest that it might model our present challenge in American Indian studies. For our field to grow, Native literary scholars will have to take risks—but such risks are often greatly restricted by dominating ideas and institutions. Moreover, that risk is not equally distributed. In his journal entry, Ortiz continues:

> What is risk? Is there any such thing as risk at all? . . .
> Good Question.
>
> No. There is nothing at risk.
> There is nothing at risk in this fucked up nation and epoch.
> THEY got it all. And they don't have to risk.
> THEY want us to risk. But for THEM, there is no risk (9).

Here, Ortiz seems to say that there is no risk, yet then clarifies: there is no true risk so long as others—THEY—do not have to share it. Again, our colonial relations determine the very stakes of this risk, for, as Ortiz seems to define it, to risk is to gamble losing something. If the powerful "got it all" and aggressively maintain the rules of risk skewed in their favor, then there is little risk that they will lose this power, ostensibly. If the disempowered must risk, however, they gamble losing what little they have left.

Ortiz later complicates any easy distinction between "us" and "them," but in this moment, he does make two crucial points for scholars: 1) that we must risk because it is central to our very survival; and 2) that all of us do not share the same risk. In the lesser parallel of Native studies, for our discipline to survive, we must risk, and that risk is not equally shared. We should ask, however, what it means truly to risk as scholars in Indigenous studies, and, most crucially, begin to imagine what it would mean to share more equally that risk. For the future of Indigenous studies, I'd like to rethink true risk as a form of *human vulnerability* and shared stakes as *mutual vulnerability*. Awakening to this deepened notion of risk, we scholars can experience the paradox of mutual vulnerability: an unforeseen emotional strength that opens new paths to understanding, thus building Native studies in ways we have yet to imagine. For this view on emotional (and intellectual) risk, I turn again to Ortiz's guidance.

Two days previous to the journal entry above, Tuesday, July 12, 3:45 p.m., Ortiz writes:

> Hold out your hand, I say to Cynthia.
> When I walk up holding out folded sheets of paper.
> And the stones and shells in my hand.
> She smiles. But doesn't hold out her hands.
> Instead she withdraws them, holds them back.
> Tiny hands. Open your hands, I say.
> What is it? she asks. Don't ask, don't be afraid.
> But what is it? she asks. Just open your hands
> And receive what's real. Art. Stones. Shells (8).

Like the best of Ortiz, here he evokes our deepest human emotions embodied in the reluctance of a child or fellow artist to trust in a gift. The "tiny hands" appear defenseless before the quiet command, "Open your hands." The elder teaches Cynthia to trust, to risk opening her hands, with the hope of receiving "what's real," that is, as I've been suggesting, a deeper experience with our knowledge of the world. We readers might find ourselves in Cynthia's place, when the poet approaches us with his poems, "holding out folded sheets of paper." In this exchange, the human vulnerability is quite obvious, but I believe the poet introduces it for this very reason, so that we may come to appreciate, understand, even share the vulnerability offered by the poet himself. In fact, *Out There Somewhere* seems to embrace this openness—at the cost of different risks—to achieve "what's real."

Far from home, the poet is "out there somewhere," vulnerable beyond the safety of his known world and even lost to his relations, if only for the present, in the Acoma saying that the title relates. He seeks other lives at the far reaches of the continent, where some lines of his poetry describe the dizzying vertigo of walking the treacherous coastline, on the margins of what the poet imagines he can know. But such risking demands emotional openness. It's like holding out your hands to someone more powerful than you, largely unaware of what you might receive. In journal entries, perhaps the most vulnerable medium in literature, the poet shares his own vulnerabilities, from bodily weakness to addiction to emotional longings for love or land, holding out his own hands. Yet ask poets why they dare allow this human vulnerability, and they will not say that it is simply their lot to risk so much. Instead, they will likely say that they must risk—and trust to risk—to expand their creative enlightenment.

Indeed, we might approach this view to human vulnerability in the same way that we are learning to value personal experience as a source of knowledge. Theorists have begun to move beyond the poststructuralist impasse that disregards all forms of social mediation as necessarily obstacles to objective knowledge. Instead, as scholars developing what's being called realist theory argue, some forms of mediation, properly interpreted, can actually enable our critical work. Rethinking the risk of vulnerability in this light, those forms of experience that better grow from human vulnerability, such as empathy or even suffering, actually improve our ability to understand literary texts as well as the social world. Such theorists don't view vulnerability as a weakness. Instead, as Minh Nguyen puts it, "it is a source of strength because it lays the groundwork for establishing trust and empathy with others. It does so because our experience of our own vulnerability will more likely guide us to self-reflection and self-examination, to an opening and deepening of our perception of our self" (194).

Perhaps more than most writers, Native poets like Ortiz risk revealing this vulnerability throughout their work, because poetry is finally more personally revealing. My colleague Roberta Hill and I have a friendly disagreement on this question: I tend to feel that poetry is ultimately more emotionally immediate than, say, the novel; the poet's voice is less able to hide in a character like Edgar Bearchild, for example. Though poets run this gambit of vulnerability, readers rarely have the moral character to meet it with their own. Or in Ortiz's words, "THEY want us to risk. But for THEM, there is no risk." I teach *Out There Somewhere* often, and I have found that my students are unwilling to share the stakes. Instead, students often maintain their power in the anonymity that attends withholding their human vulnerability. From this privileged position, they feel entitled to judge the worth or frailty of the poet. For this reason, in exams, I ask students to share the stakes by confronting Ortiz's lines on risk, as they reflect on the risks they themselves have taken in my course. But often such are students; we should consider how scholars might better share the stakes in readings to envision a new Native literary studies.

Let's return to Ortiz's journal entry on risk: "Renee is Mexican Indian, dark skinned. / I'm risking my reputation, he says." I'm sure any number of academics would find that risk of reputation to be a real danger: if the second book takes too many risks, the scholar might not be invited back by that press. But that is only a personal career risk that can often be righted. Of this kind of risk Ortiz declares, "Risk has to be more than personal risk. It has to concern itself with ethical, moral, political, social, historical, spiritual, material issues and questions. Personal risk is the least at stake" (10). In American Indian literary studies, however, scholars risk well beyond the simply personal, in which one's reputation or career dares to suffer. After all, the study of Native literature itself is a risky venture compared to studies in more established and dominant areas, as seen in the number of Native Americanist scholars hired in English departments, the number of books on Indian literature published and where they are published, and even in the number of papers accepted and scheduled primarily at Native Studies conferences. Those scholars who choose to work in American Indian literature display an intellectual vulnerability by this very precondition.

When we consider the more charged debates in our field, most intensify from an admittedly personal risk, but one that resonates boldly for and with others who share a wound, however culturally specific or broadly human. In our studies, I see a willingness to share vulnerability rarely seen elsewhere and, as I have been exploring, such can be viewed as an attempt to open ourselves emotionally and intellectually. From this position of mutual vulnerability, we now have more interpretive media at our service, and thus are better able to imagine the lives of others. This sharing is a struggle for empathy to understand the suffering of others both radically unlike us, yet in a sense indistinguishable from ourselves, in the way that the anthropologist Renato Rosaldo finally understood the Ilongot people's grief through his own, when his wife fell to her death in the field. As a graduate student, I recall following the debate between Elizabeth Cook-Lynn and the late Louis Owens. In a 1996 essay titled "American Indian Intellectualism and the New Indian Story," Cook-Lynn accused self-identified mixed-blood Indian scholars and writers of self-absorbed individualism at the expense of tribal nationalism. Owens responded in 1998 with an entire book titled *Mixedblood Messages*, in which he drew his very strength from a personal family history, when he writes bitterly: "Passing was easy, something I did not really have to think about very much. The hard part was being poor in a small town where people knew everyone. Dirt poor, shit poor, offal poor, embarrassingly poor" (196). Owens's self-disgust in poverty brims in that single statement, and perhaps eventuated his self-destruction. This painful past in fact overwhelms his book, attempting to rebut Cook-Lynn's charge, though I feel he was unsuccessful. In the end, however, I have to say that Owens won the debate. He was willing to share more vulnerability, to spill some blood at the risk of confronting a suppressed past and of being dismissed as a fake Indian.

Other scholars in Native literary studies have risked like poets, offering their vulnerability not to garner sympathy, of course, but to open a path to learning. I'm thinking of Craig Womack's "queer Oklahomo theory," for example, in which Womack infuses his theory with his own personal experience of gay life in Oklahoma to understand Lynn Riggs, as Womack risks exposing his own vulnerability: "Even now, how many Oklahoma Indian guys do I know who, like Riggs, have fled to New York City and San Francisco in hopes of not having to erase themselves any longer?" (278). Other scholars in our field dare to share the stakes by offering their own cultural experiences, however situated, to discover a meeting ground of mutual human vulnerability. Consider, for example, Arnold Krupat's willingness to imagine his Jewish life as a means to understanding Native lives:

"Although the comparison isn't quite exact, still I imagine those cossacks and drunken Russian citizens [who hunted, tormented, beat, and left for dead his grandfather because he was a Jew] as not so very different from Col. John Chivington and his men at Sand Creek . . ." (91).

In his own definition, Ortiz aggressively moves our understanding of risk well beyond the personal to the ethical, spiritual, material. Risks in these areas threaten the loss not only of honor or career—a bad book or even tenure denial—but also the very safety and survival of the communities about which we write. In intellectual work on these areas, a good deal of risk simply—though dangerously—demands our courage in naming domination. How often it is that we are bullied into backing off on our naming! I recall a seminar in graduate school in which my professor corrected my use of the term "genocide" in Native studies; our genocide, she said, was not explicit and systematic. It was rather a "cultural genocide." Even if this were so, what are a people, I replied, without their culture? Under these intimidation tactics, we must write "racial bias" when we really mean to name "racism." We must say "sexism" when we really mean "misogyny." "Homophobia" instead of "homohatred." "Child abuse" for "molestation" and "rape." And "federal trust mismanagement," not the imperialism of U.S. colonial rule. In his journal, Ortiz hazards his own naming when he imagines a sign to replace that posted by the U.S. Park Service. His would read:

ATTENTION LIARS, THIEVES, AND KILLERS

You have stolen enough land and life.
From here on out, you are no longer allowed access.
We claim back our land and life.
Go away.
Do not enter (9).

Why risk naming "what's real"? Because, as Ortiz replies, "Life is at stake." Throughout his writing, Ortiz attempts to raise the stakes, if you will. Entering this kind of risk, the poet explains, is not like

Walking a tightrope. And falling or not falling. Crucifixion.
Car racing. Jumping out of airplanes. Putting stuff in a computer

memory and hoping it'll be there again next time you open up the machine. Spilling your guts out to someone else. Telling someone you love them or not telling someone you love them.

Of these risks, Ortiz says, "Those are important risks but they're selfish and self-centered stuff mainly" (10). To truly risk, the life at stake must be more than our own. It could be the lives of our lovers, our families, but I imagine it must be even more than these. To begin, we must risk with the future of tribal peoples. As most Native creative works stem from specific communities for which we are ultimately accountable, we scholars accept an inherent risk in writing about, and hence defending, some of the poorest places in North America. Such scholars dare to advocate for others, accept leadership roles, and set agendas, as Robert Warrior risks in his recent book *The People and the Word*, where he challenges his Osage community to live up to its democratic principles. And there are other lives at stake, subjugated groups and histories within Indian Country that continue to be silenced simply by our inattention in scholarship in the areas of queerness and disability, African American history and citizenship, disenrollment, and tribal citizen border policing.

No doubt the greatest risk lies with those who cannot speak for themselves—the creatures of our lands. Elsewhere, Ortiz has beseeched, "Fight back, for the sake of the people, for the sake of the land." On this profoundly coterminous future, all of us bear unavoidably shared stakes and mutual vulnerabilities on a planet seemingly bound for destruction despite our cultural differences, the future Leslie Silko's *Ceremony* dared imagine. Even now, when I stand on stage to lecture on treaties or Indian poverty to 350 students, I often find my knees shake, my fearful face flushes, when I must put my culture on trial before those who refuse to share the stakes, to admit their own vulnerability. In such moments, I have learned to remind those who withhold their hands that all of us, despite our backgrounds, share a stake in the future of this land. Reframing our colonial relations in these terms of mutual ecological vulnerability, we can begin to build empathy for the lives of others, discovering that our own incomplete selves are in some way bound to the completion of others. In this final sense, scholars can risk defending the shared planetary lives at stake in the future of Indigenous studies, or as Simon Ortiz humbly calls on us, "to push the matter forward."

WORKS CITED

Cook-Lynn, Elizabeth. "American Indian Intellectualism and the New Indian Story." *American Indian Quarterly* 20 (1996): 57–76.

Krupat, Arnold. *The Turn to the Native: Studies in Criticism and Culture.* Lincoln: University of Nebraska Press, 1996.

Nguyen, Minh T. "'It Matters to Get the Facts Straight': Joy Kogawa, Realism, and Objectivity of Values." In *Reclaiming Identity: Realist Theory and the Predicament of Postmodernism*, edited by Paula M. L. Moya and Michael R. Hames-Garcia, 171–204. Berkeley: University of California Press, 2000.

Ortiz, Simon J. *Out There Somewhere.* Tucson: University of Arizona Press, 2002.

Owens, Louis. *Mixedblood Messages: Literature, Film, Family, Place.* Norman: University of Oklahoma Press, 1998.

Rosaldo, Renato. *Culture and Truth: The Remaking of Social Analysis.* Boston: Beacon, 1989.

Silko, Leslie Marmon. *Ceremony.* New York: Penguin, 1977.

Warrior, Robert. *The People and the Word: Reading Native Nonfiction.* Minneapolis: University of Minnesota Press, 2005.

Womack, Craig S. *Red on Red: Native American Literary Separatism.* Minneapolis: University of Minnesota Press, 1999.

Young Bear, Ray A. *Black Eagle Child: The Facepaint Narratives.* New York: Grove Press, 1998.

Simon Ortiz

The Importance of Childhood

Debbie Reese

"Red Rover, Red Rover, let Angie come over."

"Ne baitsashru!"

Your eyes pass over the letters of the familiar "Red Rover" and the unfamiliar "Ne baitsashru," but I ask you to read those words again, and *hear* the words in the voice of Simon J. Ortiz.

"Red Rover, Red Rover, let Angie come over."

"Ne baitsashru!" (not paginated).

Those words are from Ortiz's book *The Importance of Childhood*, published in 1982 by the Pueblo of Acoma Press. The book is about games Ortiz played as a child. The phrase and game "Red Rover" is familiar to most of us. It has been a popular game of childhood for many generations of Americans. That second phrase "Ne baitsashru!" in the Acoma language of Keres means "Run!" Ortiz's account illustrates an example of how Pueblo people remade something from the outside into something of their own, something that incorporates who we are as Pueblo people. I ask you to hear Ortiz's voice because it is his voice (with the literal and symbolic meanings of that word) that is at the heart of his writing. People who know his voice by way of hearing him read, or by reading his poems and short stories—many of which are about children—may want to take a look at the books he wrote specifically for children. In them is a Pueblo voice speaking to children, trusting their intellect, as he tells them about land, culture, and community.

Ortiz's first children's book, *The People Shall Continue*, was published in 1977 by Children's Book Press. Note the date of publication: 1977. The seventies opened with the occupation of Alcatraz Island. Throughout that decade, American Indians planned and implemented

many political acts of protest against treaty violations and treatment
of American Indians. In May 2008, I spoke with Harriet Rohmer, the
founding publisher of Children's Book Press, about her recollections of
the development of *The People Shall Continue*. In the 1970s, Rohmer was
in San Francisco, helping out at the Native American Survival School.
She wanted to do a book of interviews of Native teens talking about their
lives and their thoughts about the future. This, she thought, would go a
long way to countering the perception that Indians had vanished. She
talked with students, and she talked with school leaders, specifically,
Bill Wahpepah.[1] He expressed concern for the students, saying the raw
qualities of their stories, in print form, might hurt them. He suggested
she get a "university Indian"[2] to do the book, and to that end, he helped
her get in touch with Simon Ortiz, who lived in the Bay Area from 1975
through 1978. When Rohmer met with Ortiz, he talked at length about
survival, and then he began work on the manuscript that would become
The People Shall Continue. It was published in the '70s, during a period
that saw the emergence of multicultural or multiethnic children's literature.[3] Prior to this, children's books were aptly described as "the all white
world of children's books."[4] Characterized as political rather than literary
by Cai,[5] this new body of literature sought to claim space for historically
marginalized groups. Given its content, the book was and is hailed as an
honest history of colonization in North America. Doris Seale, a Santee
Dakota-Cree librarian said, "If you give only one book about Native peoples to your young children, let this be the one."[6] As cofounder of Oyate,
a widely respected Native organization committed to Native peoples and
books about them, Seale commands great influence in the field of children's literature.[7] Her "only one book" recommendation is dead on. In
The People Shall Continue, Ortiz conveys the diversity obscured by the
monolithic term "American Indian." Diversity in creation stories, language, and location. All this is in *The People Shall Continue*. Ortiz begins
the first page in this way:

> Many, many years ago, all things came to be.
> The stars, rocks, plants, rivers, animals.
> Mountains, sun, moon, birds, all things.
> And the People were born.
> Some say, "From the ocean."
> Some say, "From a hollow log."

Some say, "From an opening in the ground."
Some say, "From the mountains."
And the People came to live
in the Northern Mountains and on the Plains,
in the Western Hills and on the Seacoasts,
in the Southern Deserts and in the Canyons,
in the Eastern Woodlands and on the Piedmonts (2).

Eloquently, he gives voice to the many Peoples. He tells us that there is more than one creation story. He acknowledges the presence of Indigenous Peoples throughout the hemisphere, in all directions, each with their respective origins, histories, and beliefs. He privileges no one and no place. And, he tells us, the Peoples knew each other:

The People of the many Nations visited
each other's lands.
The People from the North brought elk meat.
The People from the West gave them fish.
The People from the South brought corn.
The People from the East gave them hides.
When there were arguments,
their leaders would say,
"Let us respect each other.
We will bring you corn and baskets.
You will bring us meat and flint knives.
That way we will live a peaceful life.
We must respect each other, and the animals,
the plants, the land, the universe.
We have much to learn from all the Nations"
     (*The People Shall Continue*, 5).

Note the tone and words with which Ortiz speaks. Succinctly, he conveys the humanity in all of us. He tells the child that people will not always agree, but that we have much to gain by recognizing what we have to offer each other. Without romanticizing Native people and our history, he continues, quietly and gently, preparing the child for the changes to come. Structurally, Ortiz uses a blank line to pace the movement through his next passages:

But one day, something unusual began to happen.

Maybe there was a small change in the wind.
Maybe there was a shift in the stars.
Maybe it was a dream that someone dreamed.
Maybe it was the strange behavior of an animal (7).

He continues, telling us that the People remembered "yellow-skinned men" and "red-haired men" who'd come across the ocean to the Western and Eastern Coasts. Those visitors, he says, did not stay long. "But now," he tells us, "the People began to hear fearful stories" (8) of strange men seeking treasures and slaves and land, men causing destruction among the People. Ortiz names these hurtful men: Spanish. English. Dutch.[8] And he names those who resisted, the names of Native people we revere:

In the West, Popé called warriors from the Pueblo and Apache Nations.
In the East, Tecumseh gathered the Shawnee and the Nations of the Great Lakes, the Appalachians, and the Ohio Valley to fight for their People.
In the Midwest, Black Hawk fought to save the Sauk and Fox Nation.
In the Great Plains, Crazy Horse led the Sioux in the struggle to keep their land.
Osceola in the Southeast, Geronimo in the Southwest, Chief Joseph in the Northwest, Sitting Bull, Captain Jack, all were warriors (12).

How does one, at this point, tell children what happened next? Instead of a feel-good narrative of people living in harmony, Ortiz tells his readers the truth. Many adults feel such truths are beyond the understanding of a young child, but only if we assume that the young reader is not Native. In our communities, our children know these histories. Ortiz knows this, and he does not pull back from the hardships of those years as the People sought to protect their sovereignty:

From the 1500s to the late years of the 1800s,
The People fought for their lives and lands.

In battle after battle, they fought until they grew weak.
Their food supplies were gone, and their warriors were
      killed or imprisoned.
And then the People began to settle
for agreements with the American government (13).

Treaties. Reservations. Promises broken. Government agents. Boarding schools. Relocation. Poverty. Ortiz does not romanticize the People, nor does he use "plight" or "tragic Indian" tropes. Instead, he tells his readers how people use memory and story to continue:

All the time, the People remembered.
Parents told their children,
"You are Shawnee. You are Lakota.
You are Pima. You are Acoma.
You are Tlingit. You are Mohawk.
You are all these Nations of the People."
The People told each other,
"This is the life of our People.
These are the stories and these are the songs.
This is our heritage."
And the children listened (18).

"And the children listened"—a simple, yet powerful statement that conveys his confidence in children and the purpose that storytelling serves in a Native community. In the rest of the book, Ortiz invokes a feeling that Native people felt then and continue to feel. We are the indigenous People of this land. We are still here. We fight for the People, for the Land. And, as Ortiz notes, we are not alone in our fight. On the last page, he speaks to "Black People, Chicano People, Asian People, many White People and others who were kept poor by American wealth and power" (23), telling them we all must care for each other:

We are all one body of People.
We must struggle to share our human lives with each other.
We must fight against those forces
which will take our humanity from us.
We must ensure that life continues.

We must be responsible to that life.
With that humanity and the strength
which comes from our shared responsibility
for this life, the People shall continue (23).

Yes, caring for each other. Survival and well-being depend on caring
for each other, whether that means peoples, tribes, groups, nations
caring for other peoples, tribes, groups, and nations, or simply indi-
viduals caring for each other. Ortiz's second children's book *Blue and
Red*, first published in 1981, explores the latter theme. In the early '80s,
Ortiz conducted writing workshops at Acoma in a project called "Acoma
Partners in Basics." The project, funded by VISTA and directed by Sandra
Simons-Ailes, was designed to develop materials for instructional use
in tribal communities and included establishing a press in the Acomita
Day School. Applying skills he learned at the Southwestern Indian
Polytechnic Institute, Ortiz's nephew, Keith Chino, operated the press.
Books written by participants were published by the Pueblo of Acoma
Press. Among those books is Ortiz's *Blue and Red*.

The title of the book refers to two horses who are brothers. In the
story, Red challenges his older brother Blue to a race, but with more
experience and longer legs, Blue could easily outrun Red, reaching the
top of Horse Mesa first. Instead, Blue slows down to let Red catch up
and lead. As they ran, "They would glance at each other and smile and
laugh as they leaped over fallen logs, stones, and small ravines. Their
manes flew in the wind and caught the sunlight" (not paginated). This
is not a typical race in which there will be a winner and a loser. Blue is
living what he has been taught. More important than winning is being
together, helping his younger brother. Central to Pueblo communities is
collaboration, not competition. That responsibility to community is at
the heart of our survival.

As the horse brothers draw closer to the hill, Blue takes the lead again,
and chooses their path carefully so neither will fall and get hurt. This,
he does, because "Blue had always been told that he must take care of
younger ones" (*Blue and Red*, not paginated). Blue is leader again, but not
with the intent of winning. He knows that being a leader means taking
responsibility for the well-being of those whom one leads. As they race up
the hill, Blue knows that Red is getting tired, and he feels the steepness of
the hill taxing his own strength. He encourages Red: "Run, keep running,

little brother. We're almost to the top of this mountain" (*Blue and Red*, not paginated). Nearing the top, Blue pretends to slip, giving Red time to catch up so they both get to the top of the hill at the same time. Happy, they stand on top together, feeling the wind in their manes.

The caring ethic figures prominently in this story. Blue has been told to take care of younger ones. In the text, Ortiz does not specify who told him this, but given his youth, it is implied that elders in his community have taught him this role. That he listened and does as instructed and that he enjoys the time with Red indicate that he values the teaching as well as his little brother and his community. His care insures the well-being of each of the brothers as they grow in their respective roles as members of the community. In Blue's lessons as older brother, he embodies the responsibility of and for community. And in this way, the community as a whole is strengthened.

Excluding the covers, the book consists of six double-page spreads. The sparse text is on the left, and the illustrations, done by Hilda Aragon[9] (also of Acoma), are on the right. There was a second printing of the book in 1984. The story appeals to a Pueblo reader raised in a Pueblo community, and Aragon's illustrations of the mesa also entice the reader. In text and illustration, *Blue and Red* reflects Pueblo life and values with integrity and accuracy in a way that so few children's books do.[10] And Ortiz's story communicates all this in one slim book. It would be well worth returning this book to print to introduce it to a much broader audience (Pueblo and non-Pueblo, Indigenous and non-Indigenous) than its original Acoma readers.

Ortiz's third children's book and his second book with the Pueblo of Acoma Press is the one with Ortiz's bilingual Keres/English depiction of the children's game Red Rover. *The Importance of Childhood* was first published in 1982. As I read the opening page, I thought of sitting with my parents, aunts and uncles, and grandparents, listening to them talk about their childhoods at Nambé, Ohkay Ówîngeh, and Hopi. The best children's books touch both adult and child readers. A gifted writer, Ortiz took me home with his words, as I sat in my office at the University of Illinois, hundreds of miles from Nambé. This is how the book begins:

> On summer evenings we used to play games way past supper because it was always so warm. Our cousins, clan sisters and brothers, would come down to our home or we would go up to

theirs. These summer days, I hear squeals and laughter and shouts of children the same age as we were years ago.

Our games were usually a variation of "hide and seek." Like "Kick The Can." Or games we learned in Day School, which we would sing and chant. "Little Sally Saucer." "Was it that?" Or "Ring Around the Roses." (We hear children hollering during a baseball game, the ball almost getting lost in the falling summer dark.) Because Day School was so much a part of our daily life and our families and community of Aaqumeh Hanoh was the greater part, we sang, chanted, and shouted our games in Acoma and English languages (*The Importance of Childhood*, not paginated).

The day school that Ortiz refers to is McCartys Day School. He started there when he was six, in 1948. In this volume and elsewhere, Ortiz writes that he liked school. He liked reading, and writing. The story he tells in *The Importance of Childhood* is filled with words in his Keres language and other landmarks and pastimes that Acoma children would recognize as part of their village, for example, hiding by the woodpile or behind the rain barrel when playing hide-and-seek.

Ortiz remembers a painful game that his mother, too, remembers, but neither knows exactly what the point of this game was. Children played the game called "Haa baa chi chi, Haa baa chi chi. Chiii chii" by placing their hands, "one over the others, and fingers pinching the hand below sometimes was pretty painful, like the sting of an ant, and anyone could suddenly jerk their hands away" (not paginated). While I don't remember playing that game at Nambé, I do remember being pinched a lot by my cousins. In Ortiz's game, I imagine a group of children, with each child testing another by pinching the skin on the top of another child's hand, steadily increasing the pressure of that pinch. As they pinched each other, they chanted "Haa baa chi chi, Haa baa chi chi, Diniyacha kqu kqu, Dyuniyacha kqu kqu, Chiii chiii" until someone, unable to stand the pain, pulled his or her hand out, thereby ending the game. While an anthropologist might theorize about the purpose of such a game. Ortiz tells us, simply, the point of that game and many others:

[I]t brought us closer together as children of Diitseyama [McCarty's] and Diichuna [Acomita]; we were reaffirmed as families and clans of our Aaquemah community and people.

The games made us vitally aware of each other. . . . What made the games important was that sense of sharing, cooperation, competition, for the sake of our health and proper social development and recreation. The language used—our words, laughter and delight and activity—is evidence of that creative expressiveness of childhood and growing, and it is what allows us to learn our humanistic heritage deeply and precisely and meaningfully (not paginated).

Words like this are not typically found in a children's book. It is important to remember, however, that Ortiz is speak-writing in a Pueblo way, one that does not patronize children. This passage, especially, marks the "story" he tells as in keeping with the oral tradition. Stories teach.

In the book, one game seems especially rooted in Acoma's ways of being. In Ortiz's Keres language, the game is called "Yaachini tsow winah" which means "kernals [sic] of corn, make a circle." This is how Ortiz describes this game: "You would walk around in a circle, holding each other's hands, and then the person in the middle would give or put something in your hand when the children chanted. The one in the middle would say, 'Du aie mansani' or 'Du aie tsushki eestha,' and we would say, 'Duwaah eh' or scream, 'Ahrreh eh'" (not paginated). The final page in the book lists Acoma expressions "translated into English for our monolingual friends" (not paginated). Using that page, I see that "Du aie mansani" means "Here's an apple" and "Du aie tsushki eestha" means "Here's some wolf wastes." Knowing that, it is easy to understand that the children reply "Dawaah eh" (thank you) for the apple or scream "Ahrreh eh" (yuck) to the wastes!

Throughout *The Importance of Childhood*, Ortiz talks about his mother. This may signal the place of women in Acoma (it is a matrilineal society) or it may simply reflect a warm relationship between Ortiz and his mother. The final page is about her: "Smiling, my mother, who was born in 1903, thought out loud, 'Ahkqu dze eeshkah?,' thinking of games in her childhood, remembering the laughter and delight and activity, remembering the importance of being a child" (not paginated). In English, her thoughts are "Let me think, what else?" This phrase, too, is familiar to me as I recall family gatherings when we tell stories of our childhoods, laughing at the things we did. Whether it is one of my siblings or my mother or someone in her generation who is speaking, we want the laughter and the moment to continue. Invariably, someone says, "What else?" Though *The Importance of Childhood* was written in 1981, the stories within go back to the early 1900s in his mother's childhood. Ortiz closes with "What else?" It is an opening, not an ending. It is the final page of the book, but not the last page that Ortiz would prepare specifically for children. Though many years would pass before Ortiz wrote another book for children, that book embodies all that is important to him. Written in 2004 from the point of view of an elder, it speaks to the importance of childhood and of community.

The Good Rainbow Road/Rawa 'Kashtyaa'tsi Hiyaani is, as Ortiz says in a note inside the book, "a collaborative effort" (not paginated). He had written the story in English and showed it to Beverly Slapin of Oyate.[11] She suggested it be a trilingual book, published in English, Spanish, and a Native tongue. Ortiz had thought of writing a book like that before and was especially pleased that the Spanish translation would be done by Mayan writer, poet, and anthropologist Victor Montejo. In the note, Ortiz says: "I was happy Professor Montejo could do it because I wanted a translation into Spanish by a Native-language speaker who knew at firsthand pertinent matters that have bearing on Spanish language use by Native people in the Americas" (not paginated). Though he does not elaborate on those firsthand matters, Ortiz likely is referring to the complex history and relationships between the Pueblo peoples of the Southwest and the Spanish, who were the first Europeans to come into their midst. Brutal treatment by the Spanish led to the Pueblo Revolt of 1680 by which the Pueblo people successfully drove the Spanish out of Pueblo homelands. Over time, delicate negotiations took place. During the ensuing centuries Pueblo people adapted, rejected, and reworked Spanish influences on Pueblo society, and that negotiation continues to the present day. Slapin introduced Ortiz to Michael Lacapa, an Apache/Tewa/Hopi artist and author, and they began work on the book.[12] Of Lacapa's artwork, Ortiz says, "Michael Lacapa added an important visual dimension to the story. Since stories are abstract language events envisioned in concrete visual terms by the cultural imagination, in a sense the abstract concepts of verbal language can only be communicated by visual artwork" (not paginated). In selecting the Native language, Ortiz chose his Native tongue, Keres. A Keres language consultant from a sister Pueblo provided the translation.

He tells us in the dedication that the book is for his daughter and his grandchildren, "so she and all other children of the earth may always walk the good rainbow road" (not paginated). *The Good Rainbow Road* is the story of two boys charged with helping their people during a drought. In his 2007 essay "Indigenous Language Consciousness: Being, Place, and Sovereignty,"[13] Ortiz says that he has "a mantra of sorts: land, culture, and community" ("Sovereign Bones," 139). That mantra appears explicitly in the opening paragraph of *The Good Rainbow Road*:

> At this time which is four hundred years after the beginning of the European colonization of our Indigenous people, this story is especially for our people who remain as always one with our land, culture, and community. Yes, always the land, culture, and community; always the people sustained with love, compassion, prayer, hope, courage, humility; always a belief in our sacred sovereignty; always the healing belief in ourselves (not paginated).

In this paragraph he gives words to the feelings stirred in the final pages of *The People Shall Continue*. "Always the land, culture, and community. . . . Always the healing belief in ourselves" (not paginated)—a belief that *The People Shall Continue*, that land, that culture, that community, and that healing belief in ourselves and our sovereignty is what *The Good Rainbow Road* is about.

The story begins with a frame, as Ortiz speaks directly to the reader: "We must always look back at the good way our people have lived and the good road they have traveled. We must always look upon the sacred knowledge that has helped our people. Not only must we remember, but we must live the healthy, good ways of tradition and culture. In this way, we will always continue as a strong and healthy people" (not paginated). As in *The Importance of Childhood,* Ortiz speaks directly, teaching the child as he tells the story, trusting the child's ability to gain from a print rendering of the oral tradition of storytelling.

In *The Good Rainbow Road*, a drought has come to the people of the village Haapaahnitse. Life has become hard. An old woman tells the people that they have forgotten that they must ask the Shiwana (spirits of rain and snow) for help. She says that two boys must be carefully chosen to go to the Shiwana. Two brothers, Tsiyah-dzehshi (First One) and Hamahshu-dzehshi (Next One), are selected. They set out on a long and difficult journey, climbing peaks, going into deep canyons, across a vast desert, and to a deep canyon in which lava flows below. First One leaps across, but his younger brother Next One is afraid. Overwhelmed with fear, he sits down, and tears come to his eyes. Though First One calls across to encourage Next One, his words cannot carry over the roar of the lava. Then, he sees someone behind Next One, and calls "Look back! Look behind you!" (not paginated). Next One turns and sees an old woman walking towards the canyon. He realizes she is blind and does not see the chasm of lava. His own fear forgotten, he leaps up. Calling her "Grandmother," he begs her to stop. She thanks him for warning her, and asks why he has been crying. He tells her of the journey and that he is unable to fulfill his task. She says: "Thank you, Grandson, for looking back and seeing me. You saw I am blind and you helped me. It's good too you have told me your fear. I shall help you in turn, beloved grandson. You have an important task to complete" (not paginated). She gives him a stone, telling him to tie it to his arrow and with all his strength, "let it fly" (not paginated). He does so, and, as the arrow arcs over the chasm, a rainbow is formed in its path. That rainbow is a road that has "all the colors of sky and land, all the colors of plant and animal life" (not paginated). The woman tells him to climb the rainbow, to continue his journey.

> The boy turned once more to look back at the steep and rugged mountains and the hot, dry deserts he and First One had traveled, and he thought of the people and the land far beyond the deserts and mountains who needed help. And he looked toward the west, where the Shiwana lived at the horizon. He turned to the old woman then and said, "Thank you for helping me, beloved grandmother, so that I may help the people and the land. I will always remember you." Hamahshu-dzehshi climbed onto the rainbow road and quickly ran on the road high above the canyon of fiery lava and joined his brother, Tsaiyah-dzehshi, and together they journeyed to take the plea of help to the Shiwana for their beloved people and land (not paginated).

In the final frame of the story, Ortiz leaves us with these words: "Yes, it is very important to look back upon the sacred knowledge so that we may live by it in a good and healthy way" (not paginated). "Look back." "Sacred knowledge." Those two phrases appear in the opening pages of the book, and they are in Next One's thoughts as he stands at the cusp of the chasm. Ortiz repeats them again in his closing. Each time he uses them, he couples the phrases with health or survival. He is telling the reader that there is value in one's history, in the sacred knowledge of one's people, that there are lessons there that can help us as we work and play. We need not—should not—perhaps, consume and be consumed with the sparkle of gadgets, with the allure of text messaging that lets us connect with each other at anytime, yet interrupts the natural rhythms of life and the oral tradition which bind us together, which give us the time and space to absorb the sacred knowledge that is key to our well-being.

Though *The Good Rainbow Road* reads like a traditional story, it is not. Ortiz describes it is a "contemporary creative work." In correspondence, he says that he has referenced traditional stories in some of his writing, but he's not retold or translated any of their traditional stories. Whether it is a northern Pueblo like Nambé, or a southern one like Acoma, we share a code to protect sacred knowledge by not revealing it to those outside the community and within it for whom that knowledge is not meant. This protection became necessary when we suffered religious persecution at the hands of the Spanish in the 1600s, and at the turn of the twentieth century, when anthropologists sought to record our ways for academic study. This code is taught to children at a very young age. I recall, for example, my elders saying "Don't go telling your teachers" what we do.

Thus, *The Good Rainbow Road* is not a traditional Acoma story, but it has qualities of traditional stories. As Ortiz explains, it has elements that "are common to and recognizable by the universal human cultural community no matter the ethnic identity or geographic locale" (not paginated). These elements include beliefs in the power of language, and of memory. Both are central to the existence of the human race, and both are at the core of stories all peoples tell. It is memory of what once was (a time of plenty), and what has been forgotten (to ask the Shiwana for help) that sparks the journey of First One and Next One. It is memory of their people that helps Next One climb onto the rainbow road. It is the power of language (a belief in the old woman's words) that creates the road that will lead to the survival of the people. The journey is not easy, but with community members and with care for the community, it is possible.

The People. Children and their games. Red and Blue. First One and Next One. Ortiz says he's been repeating that mantra (of land, culture, and community) for the last ten years. This essay was published in 2007, but I think that mantra has been there much longer. It was present in 1977 in *The People Shall Continue*, and it was there in the early '80s in both *Blue and Red* and *The Importance of Childhood*. As Pueblo people, we are blessed in that our traditional ways are still strong and intact. Is it because we are so rooted, as Ortiz states, in land, culture, and community? While his poetry and short stories are important in their own right, his writing for children demonstrates the reason we continue. It is the importance of children. As I read and reread some of his essays, I see the ideas in *The Importance of Childhood* reflected in his later writings. I see that, again and again, he writes about his Pueblo childhood, how he helped his father add rooms to their home as the family grew. That is the Pueblo way. Children help. Like Ortiz, I was raised in a pueblo, in a house built by adding one room to another as the family grew. And like Ortiz, my childhood was one of helping. Whether it is cutting meat for feast, helping make bread, or mixing mud for adobes, Pueblo children are central to Pueblo life. In our communities, children matter.

In our communities, children have always mattered. Ortiz knows this. It is a sacred knowledge overlooked by scholars, who give short shrift to children and children's books. In American society, in the academy, and in Native studies, the study of children's books has little status. A consequence of this is that our children are inundated by biased, stereotypical, and outright racist books that masquerade as books about American Indians.

Ortiz knows children are sacred. In *The People Shall Continue*, the children listen. In *Blue and Red*, children learn to help other children, and in *The Importance of Childhood*, children learn to play together. In *The Good Rainbow Road*, the survival of our communities is in the hands of children. Yes, Ortiz knows. Children are sacred. And because of children, the People shall continue.

NOTES

Special thanks to Nolan Valdo, librarian at the Acoma Learning Center, Paulita Aguilar, curator at the University of New Mexico Indigenous Nations Library Program, and Karen Strom for helping me obtain copies of books published by the Pueblo of Acoma Press. Thanks, too, to John McKinn (Gila River), Assistant Director of Academic Programming at University of Illinois at Urbana-Champaign's (UIUC) Native American House, for the many academic and laugh-filled conversations we've had during our years together at UIUC.

1. Wahpepah was among the Native people in the Bay Area who worked together on an alternative school of Native children whose families were in the area due to the Relocation Program of that time period. Wahpepah was Sac and Fox. Wilma Mankiller writes briefly about the school in her autobiography, *Mankiller: A Chief and Her People.*

2. By this time, Ortiz had been a student at the University of New Mexico and the University of Iowa. With several successful publications, he was adept at using the printed word to share Native experiences and perspectives. As such, he was well positioned to take on the project.

3. Vine Deloria Jr., Elizabeth Cook-Lynn, Robert Allen Warrior, and other Native scholars state that American Indians are not ethnic peoples. Following their lead, I am calling for the indigenization of children's books by and about American Indians, and, theorizing that American Indians are ill-served by placing us under the multicultural umbrella in teacher-training programs.

4. See Nancy Larrick's September 1965 article of that name in the *Saturday Review.*

5. See Mingshui Cai's *Multicultural Literature for Children and Young Adults* (Greenwood Press, 2002).

6. Her review of the book is in *Through Indian Eyes: The Native Experience in Books for Children,* edited by Beverly Slapin and Doris Seale, first published in 1987. *Through Indian Eyes* is widely regarded as a touchstone volume in the field of children's literature. Slapin would later be involved in the development of Ortiz's *The Good Rainbow Road.*

7. In 2001, Seale received the American Library Association's Equality Award for her life's work.

8. The first Dutch settlement in the Americas was Fort Nassau on Castle Island in the Hudson River, established in 1615.

9. Aragon wrote and illustrated other books, including *Counting Book,* and *Voices of our Elders: Books for our Children.*

10. Elsewhere, I've written about problems in three acclaimed children's books that purport to be Pueblo stories. All three misrepresent Pueblo values and material culture in such egregious ways that many Pueblo libraries do not have the books on their shelves. The three are *Arrow to the Sun* by Gerald McDermott, *Turkey Girl: A Zuni Cinderella* by Penny Pollock, and *Dragonfly's Tale* by Kristina Rodanas.

11. Slapin is the executive director of Oyate. With Seale, she co-edited a second book of essays and reviews of children's books. Published in 2005, *A Broken Flute: The Native Experience in Books for Children* won an American Book Award. Oyate is online at http://www.oyate.org.

12. Lacapa passed away in 2005. In 2007, the Northern Arizona Book Festival established the Michael Lacapa Spirit Prize, an award for a children's book set in the Southwest. Early in my graduate work, I was deeply touched by his *Less than Half, More than Whole*. In that picture book, I saw the power and possibilities in children's books about contemporary American Indians. Books, in other words, that affirm the lives and experiences of Native children today.

13. The essay appears in Eric Gansworth's edited volume, *Sovereign Bones*, published by Nation Books (2007).

WORKS CITED

Cai, Mingshui. *Multicultural Literature for Children and Young Adults*. Westport: Greenwood Press, 2002.

Larrick, Nancy. "The All-White World of Children's Books." *Saturday Review*, September 1965, 63–85.

Ortiz, Simon. *Blue and Red*. Acoma: Pueblo of Acoma Press, 1981.

———. *The Good Rainbow Road: Rawa 'Kashtyaa'tsi Hiyaani*. Tucson: University of Arizona Press, 2004.

———. *The Importance of Childhood*. Acoma: Pueblo of Acoma Press, 1982.

———. "Indigenous Language Consciousness: Being, Place, and Sovereignty." In *Sovereign Bones*, edited by Eric Gansworth, 135–47. New York: Nation Books, 2007.

———. *The People Shall Continue*. Emeryville: Children's Book Press, 1977.

———. Personal interview with author, May 2008.

Slapin, Beverly and Doris Seale. *Through Indian Eyes: The Native Experience in Books for Children*. Berkeley: American Indian Studies Center, 1998.

Learning to Be Human

An Indigenous System of Ethics in the Writing of Simon Ortiz

Elizabeth Archuleta

What does it mean to be human and how does one learn to be human? Rather than assume that all cultures adhere to the same description, one must examine ideas about what it means to be human within specific contexts instead of automatically applying essentialist and ahistorical categories derived from Enlightenment concepts of the autonomous individual. Understanding what it means to be human, in fact, comes from culturally specific constructions of personhood, from the actualities of people's experiences and the worlds in which those experiences occur.[1] Jicarilla Apache philosopher Viola Cordova explains Indigenous notions of personhood and ethics, both from an explicit Indigenous context.[2] Drawing from the philosopher Ludwig Wittgenstein, Cordova demonstrates how improper interpretation can lead to misunderstanding when "the practitioner pulls an idea out of a particular context and attempts to fit it into an idea from within his own cultural context" ("Approaches," 28).[3] She also points to the possibility that literal correlations might not exist, especially with the diversity of Indigenous languages and cultures. Therefore, Cordova challenges philosophers to learn the logics of Indigenous languages and to engage in epistemological studies to begin exploring non-Western philosophies from more culturally sound contexts.

According to Cordova, an Indigenous system of ethics encompasses rules of behavior that teach one to be human, and being human is measured in the ways that we learn to recognize how our actions have consequences beyond ourselves, including the potential to affect others negatively ("Ethics," 177–78). These are lessons I learned early in life.

Although my family has been separated from our traditional community through time and circumstance, my mother instilled in my sisters and me a system of relational ethics. Growing up, we were never allowed to be physically abusive toward one another, so I was shocked when I saw my friends engage in physical altercations with their siblings without consequence. We were even taught to respect the power of words. We could never tell each other, "I hate you!" or call each other names, because we were taught that words have consequences and come back to hurt us as well as those we meant to hurt. Cordova explains that the origins of ethics as a Western philosophical discipline grew out of an awareness that humans exist and live in social environments rather than as isolated individuals. We, as individuals, can choose to live our lives according to the "We-" or the "I-Factor," and the choices individuals make reflect what they consider to be proper behavior either for the individual self or for the larger good of a community. Therefore, Cordova describes ethics as a foundation for codes of conduct by which we, in society, agree to live our lives together harmoniously, and which, ideally, emanate from a concern for communal rather than mere individual survival and well-being ("Ethics," 173). For me, this foundation was laid in the home and during my childhood, and I recognized similar codes of conduct in other Indigenous texts.

A powerful example can be seen in Simon Ortiz's writing, for there he presents an ethic oriented towards the larger good of all, while nevertheless affirming the importance of each person. Ortiz infuses his poetry with such a communal philosophy, presenting examples of what it means to be human from an Acoma Pueblo context. For Ortiz, an Indigenous system of ethics begins with the land and, from there, the relationships that are created and informed by collective values that determine ethical behavior between and among humans and non-humans. Such an ethic creates an environment in which all of creation is recognized, understood, and embraced as an interwoven whole of diverse parts, ideally, to be lived harmoniously. Ortiz's Indigenous philosophy encourages his readers to adopt these values to improve our own interdependent lives and the world in which we live.

What is remarkable in Ortiz's writing is his tenacity in being true to his beliefs, notwithstanding the hyper-individualism of early twenty-first century America, wherein human beings are generally perceived and studied as autonomous individuals who make choices based on their own needs rather than the community's. As Vine Deloria Jr. makes clear, "much of our [non-Indigenous] philosophy, law, and religious thinking continues to make the individual the focus of attention and the starting point for all other analysis" ("Philosophy and the Tribal Peoples," 10). He notes, "[T]he most important differences between tribal peoples' and Western thinking is the concentration in the West on the solitary individual to the exclusion of the group" ("Philosophy and the Tribal Peoples," 10). Additionally, as Cordova explains, choice in Western society is "tied to a set of rewards and punishments," indicating that artificial constraints or threats of punishment are needed to motivate people's adherence to formal and informal laws of social behavior designed to legislate social harmony ("Ethics," 176). As Cordova further elucidates, "[T]he West . . . bases its moral and legal foundations on the *externalization* of law or social behavior"—meaning that "the law that is external is an artificial constraint placed on someone's behavior and enforced through the threat of punishment" ("Ethics," 176, emphasis in original). This contrasts with the Pueblo ethic that Ortiz articulates, or that my mother instilled in me, an ethic that does not require such external enforcement except in extreme cases, but that rather imbues a broader ethical mandate that traditionally was learned early in life. We never feared corporal punishment, because my mother never spanked us. Her warnings about the consequences of practicing hateful actions and words were enough to teach the importance and respect for others, a lesson we internalized.

In contrast to the artificial constraints that motivate autonomous individuals, Cordova claims that Indigenous peoples traditionally have lived their lives according to the We-Factor, a designation that becomes the context by which she as well as Deloria examine personhood. Ethical behavior needs no outward threats if individual lives are lived in accordance with the We-Factor, because "an internal law is one that has been so assimilated into the individuals' character that he is 'a law unto himself'" (Cordova, "Ethics," 176). For Indigenous notions of personhood, Indigenous peoples have internalized relational laws of ethical behavior in their belief that humans are inherently social and want to remain part of a group. Therefore, being human involves interacting with and maintaining social relations with one's community out of a sense of responsibility and obligation rather than fear of punishment. In contrast, choosing isolation means choosing to be something other than human. According to Deloria, individuals who chose to remain separate from society or unattached to anyone could not be trusted: "[V]arious Indian tribes recognized that individuals who had no loyalty to anyone else were exceedingly dangerous to have around" ("Philosophy and the Tribal Peoples," 10). Indeed, punishment for individuals caught violating social codes of conduct came in the form of banishment from one's community, which Deloria describes as a tribe's refusal to recognize the wrongdoer as a functional human, since s/he has demonstrated a severe lack of responsibility to community members and likely will be a danger to others in the future. Therefore the perpetrator is cut off to exercise his or her egocentric self-referentiality as an autonomous individual at a safe distance from the tribal community, without the threat of harm to tribal members (10). Of course, the hoped-for result is that the wrongdoer will gain reflective growth and will change as a consequence of the banishment, but the larger concern is the good of the larger community. Banishment is analogous to what my mother did to us if we fought. She would place us in separate rooms of the house to reflect on our behavior. After one or sometimes two hours, she would bring us all together and have us share with one another what we did wrong, and why it was important to respect one another.

Refusing a wrongdoer the opportunity to engage in relations with others emphasizes the primacy of responsibility and obligation contained in Indigenous notions of personhood, especially since this designation of personhood and the relationships it entails include non-humans whose lives are interconnected with the lives of humans. Traditionally living as integrated members of an interdependent environment, the tribal community extended beyond its human members. Cordova explains that Indigenous peoples' ethical system is more complete and holistic in that their sense of the "We" is non-hierarchical and more inclusive. This includes animals sharing and maintaining relations and feelings of responsibility toward humans. Leslie Marmon Silko (Laguna Pueblo) explains these relations in her work. In particular, she does so through explanations of hunting, describing its ethics as a cooperative relationship between the hunter and the hunted:

The antelope merely consents to return home with the hunter. All phases of the hunt are conducted with love: the love the hunter and the people have for the Antelope People, and the love of the antelope who agree to give up their meat and blood so that human beings will not starve ("Interior and Exterior Landscapes: The Pueblo Migration Stories," 26).

She recognizes the personhood inherent in the antelope and the sacrifice it makes by offering its life for humans. All animals, even domesticated ones, are accorded honor and respect for what they contribute to her peoples' survival. Sheep raised as pets are thanked and reassured in the moments before their death, and "when the hunter brought home a mule deer buck, the deer occupied the place of honor in the house; it lay on the best Navajo blanket with strings of silver and turquoise beads hanging from its neck" ("The People," 85–86). If hunters fail to maintain these relations or proper codes of conduct, the antelope spirits might refuse to share their lives in subsequent years, in effect, withdrawing themselves from humans and refusing to recognize their personhood. Silko explains that a successful hunt would appear to connect an individual with the life of one animal, but "the purpose of the hunt rituals and magic is to make contact with *all* the spirits of the elk" ("Interior and Exterior Landscapes," 29). All lives and spirits are intimately linked, and transgressions can disrupt delicate balances maintained through proper behavior, often celebrated in ritual, prayer, and song.

Like Silko, Ortiz celebrates the interdependencies between all of creation and expresses the non-hierarchical relationships between the people and the land by seeing them as inseparable. Indeed, Ortiz sees this as essential to the well-being of community and also individual well-being. The ethics his poetry conveys recognizes the responsibilities that humans and non-humans bear for each other, not a set of power dynamics where humans have dominion over animals or exercise control over the land:

> The land. The people.
> They are in relation to each other.
> We are in a family with each other.
> The land has worked with us.
> And the people have worked with it. . . .
> The land has given us our life,
> and we must give life back to it
> 　　(*Woven Stone*, 324–25).

The first line of this poem illustrates the non-hierarchical relationship that exists between land and people. Its structure makes an Indigenous system of ethics apparent—the land and the people stand separately, as expressed in the two separate sentences. At the same time, they appear on the same line together as equals who are different. They relate to each other as family, working together and cooperating with one another to survive. Joe Watkins (Choctaw) mirrors this belief when he asserts,

> The relationship between American Indians and the land is multifaceted. It's not one of ownership per se, for we are owned more by the land, tied to it more strongly, than the land is owned by us. We are tied to it by obligations and responsibilities established by our ancestors in times far back, and we pass those obligations on to our children and grandchildren ("Place-meant," 41).

When Ortiz asserts that the people "*must* give life back to [the land]," he echoes Watkins's belief that obligation is a necessary component of an individual's relationship with the land. This Indigenous ethical system recognizes and highlights that being human goes beyond acknowledging what separates us from others or from the rest of creation. Ortiz's poem and Watkins's statement reflect an understanding that humans must engage with the world, recognize and honor that engagement, and acknowledge that we belong to a larger community for which we should exercise certain responsibilities and obligations to ensure the survival and well-being of all. Again, maintaining a relationship with the natural world is a lesson my mother taught us. Each morning she would wake us before sunrise and have us sit in a place where we could watch this daily cycle take place. As the sun rose, we each had to say why we were thankful for another sunrise, another day.

In Ortiz's poetry, humans comprise just one part of the world's natural cycles, with the non-human world contributing to our survival, and these cycles are recognized in ceremonies and through language in prayer and song as well as poetry. Therefore, Ortiz's writing emphasizes humans' responsibility to engage with the world through ritual or celebration that acknowledges, celebrates, and honors those relations. He reiterates these responsibilities in the prologue to his first collection of poetry, *Going for the Rain*, beginning with water, an element that makes life possible in the dry landscape of the desert. His prologue opens with a ritual song concerning two individuals embarking on a journey to bring rain clouds back to the desert. The song's lyrics acknowledge interdependencies between a desert environment, its community, and rain played out in the relationships maintained with the *shiwana*, the sacred spirits called upon to bring rain:

> Let us go again, brother; let us go for the *shiwana*.
> Let us make our prayer songs.
> We will go now. Now we are going.
> We will bring back the *shiwana*.
> They are coming now. Now, they are coming.
> It is flowing. The plants are growing.
> Let us go again, brother; let us go for the *shiwana*
>   (*Woven Stone*, 37).

The word "again" that is echoed in the first and last lines clarifies that the spiritual journey invoking the sacred powers of creation constitutes a ritual process that is needed to occur on a regular basis. To journey again means that one has journeyed in the past and will do so again in the future. Therefore, the song marks a specific moment in time both when the journey takes place and when the rains will come once again to support life in the desert. Ortiz's use of multiple gerunds indicates action in the present tense, keeping everyone focused on and integrated together rather separated from the landscape. Similar to the hunt rituals in which one prepares through prayer and song, the ritual of going for the rain includes components that help humans contact the spirits that bring rain. Humans who journey for the *shiwana* become part of a ritual process based on reciprocal relations that seek to maintain balance, order, and harmony in the physical and spiritual realms.

Ortiz's inclusion of this song additionally emphasizes the importance of oral traditions in connecting humans and the land, illustrating their interdependencies. Because "the landscape sits in the center of Pueblo belief and identity," oral traditions help individuals visualize themselves within stories and within the landscape (Silko, "Interior and Exterior Landscapes," 43). Storytelling, therefore, becomes an important part of forming notions about what it means to be human. Moreover, storytelling is a social practice that involves everyone engaging in and contributing to a ritual coming together of individuals who learn about their place in the world through stories. According to Silko, "traditionally everyone . . . was expected to listen and be able to recall or tell a portion of . . . a narrative account or story. Thus, the remembering and the retelling were a communal process" ("Interior and Exterior Landscapes," 31). The influence of the oral tradition, far from being a relic of the past, is patently present throughout Ortiz's poetry as he demonstrates how storytelling provides a vehicle for teaching, learning, and reinforcing tribal ethics. In other words, we learn philosophies about being human through stories that help us to form deep connections with language, humans, and the land. As Ortiz explains:

> It was the stories and songs which provided the knowledge that I was woven into the intricate web that was my Acoma life. In our garden and our cornfields I learned about the seasons, growth cycles of cultivated plants, what one had to think and feel about the land; and at home I became aware of how we must care for each other: all of this was encompassed in an intricate relationship which had to be maintained in order that life continue
> ("Language," 189).

Language in the form of stories and songs becomes a way to maintain these intricate relationships. Stories and songs contain codes of conduct that influence the people and encourage them to live a certain way. The knowledge contained in stories and songs includes the proper behavior and attitude one must have toward land as well as people. These codes of conduct embody a complex set of relations that must be upheld to ensure human and non-human survival. Interdependencies exist throughout all of creation, and these interdependencies are clearly connected with gifts that contribute to our survival, such as land and rain.

These interdependencies also materialize when Ortiz creates more intimate connections with the land through creation stories. Cordova notes that a complete ethical system "includes not only one's behavior toward other individuals and to the society as a whole but toward the planet which has produced one and upon which one is dependent" ("Ethics," 177). In "The Creation, According to Coyote," Ortiz acknowledges his belief that the land is a sacred and holy place from which humans emerged; the earth as mother consequently established a caring interrelationship with her creatures. The poem portrays Coyote sharing an emergence story about the Acomas' emergence or birth from the land:

You were born when you came
from that body, the earth;
your black head burst from granite,
the ashes cooling,
until it began to rain
(*Woven Stone*, 41).

Our individual identities are created through and linked to our families
and clans, but they are also created through familial relations with the
land, as Ortiz's poem shows. In her description of the Laguna people's
emergence, Silko claims that the event "was an emergence into a precise
cultural identity," but "not until they could find a viable relationship to the
terrain—the physical landscape they found themselves in—could they
emerge" ("Interior and Exterior Landscapes," 36, 38, emphasis in original). Based on this intimate connection with the land, Ortiz portrays our
responsibility as humans to protect it as we would a member of our own
family, because as a member of our larger extended family, it ensures our
own continuance.

Engaging in familial relations with non-humans entails the kind of risk
Sean Teuton's essay explores in Ortiz's writing, because "the life at stake
must be more than our own" ("In Open Daring: Risk and Vulnerability
in the Poetry of Simon J. Ortiz," [314–22] in this volume). Other scholars have recognized Ortiz's courage in promoting a system of relational
ethics. Ecocritic Joni Adamson remarks on the courage it took for Ortiz
to speak out as a voice for the land and against the dominant culture on
social and environmental issues more than twenty years ago, but his commitment to the land, to the environment, and to all of earth is interwoven
with his Acoma Pueblo recognition that in doing so, he is acting to protect a beloved and honored relative (Adamson, "The Challenge of Speaking
First," 60). It is one thing to exemplify the ethics of a tribal community
internally; it is another to steadfastly manifest that ethic within the larger
realm of an America, which is predominantly focused more on the individual and personal consumption. Ortiz portrays this in his poem "Welcome
to America, the Mall," inviting his readers to consider a different ethic (*Out
There Somewhere*, 43). Likewise, Diné writer, Laura Tohe, notes Ortiz's
daring at being

one of the first native writers speaking of border towns, capitalism, exploitation, environmental pollution, and racism. Though they were his words, he spoke powerfully for those of us who were silent. Simon's reading made us feel the power of language, the power of speaking for The People and for the land (Tohe, "'It was that Indian': Simon Ortiz, Activist Poet," 54).

Through his poetry, Ortiz conveys this same sense of responsibility to his readers as well as to his children. He explains that from a young age, children begin to learn their roles in and responsibilities to the world as humans born "from that body, the earth," but to achieve this integration, first their community must encourage the children to take on the task of maintaining these complex sets of relations (*Woven Stone*, 41).

While in the past Indigenous peoples' sense of the We-Factor has embraced equality and inclusivity, children in many Indigenous communities were not considered fully realized members until they passed certain stages in their lives—a process that was supposed to be coherently guided by family, clan, and tribal members.[4] Deloria notes, traditionally, people included the unborn child in their prayers "to establish a family context into which she/he would be born" ("Philosophy and the Tribal Peoples," 10). According to Cordova, full membership comes only after children are mature enough to recognize the needs of others and can conduct themselves according to the community's values. She notes that inclusion into a community through the acknowledgment of one's humanity is what it means to be human in a very specific group ("Ethics," 177). San Juan Pueblo anthropologist Alfonso Ortiz describes this process among the Tewa, specifically through the use of the word *seh t'a*, which is a marker of age as well as maturity and experience. It is, he notes,

> used to distinguish older children from those up to the age of six or seven who have not yet attained the age of reason. Thus, to be not yet *seh t'a* is to be innocent or unknowing. I might sketch the general process of reasoning involved here as follows: to be innocent is to be not yet Tewa; to be not yet Tewa is to be not yet human; and to be not yet human is to be, in this use of the term not entirely out of the realm of spiritual existence (*The Tewa World: Space, Time, Being, and Becoming in a Pueblo Society*, 16).

Alfonso Ortiz describes the process of becoming *seh t'a* as gradual, beginning with rites of passage through which each child goes before becoming recognized as fully human among the Tewa (*The Tewa World*, 30–45). The third rite of passage, called "water pouring," marks a child's transition from non-human to Tewa. The upper age limit at which this third rite of passage occurs is not prescribed, but "children who are less than six years old cannot participate in this transitional rite of passage" (*The Tewa World*, 37).

Simon Ortiz articulates the importance of rites of passage in relation to his own life because at a certain age he could understand the magnitude of his responsibilities as a human being and as a member of his community. In "Always the Stories," he shares a memory from his youth when his community embraced him as a member of Acoma Pueblo, and he understood completely what it means to be human among his people. At the age of twelve, he entered his community's ceremonial chambers to participate in a ceremony that he states embraced the children as members "of the human family, who were now entering a stage of life that required appropriate responsibilities and maturity" ("Always the Stories," 59). In other words, through this ceremony, the elders taught the children that part of being human involved acknowledging one's responsibilities to others. Ortiz recognizes this lesson when he affirms, "The tribal memory remembered specific practices and a philosophy to insure continuity, but it was more than remembrance; there had to be active participation in order to state the belief that life was important" ("Always the Stories," 60). For the Acomas, then, community involvement in ceremonial and everyday life along with their attendant philosophies contributed to survival. Additionally, Ortiz reminds us, survival was not connected to rote memorization and recitation of a belief system but included active participation that demonstrated one lived those beliefs and had internalized them. Once he had gone through the ceremony, Ortiz's community acknowledged that he was human and should perform his responsibilities to family, clan, and community, because these practices have ensured their continuation.

In addition to accepting his responsibilities to his community, Ortiz learns how the land forms a part of his identity because of its presence in their lives. Therefore, being human also means recognizing and valuing the land as an extension of the self in a place Silko describes as having "so little . . . between you and the earth" ("Interior and Exterior Landscapes," 41). This is a lesson a father passes on to his son in "A Story of How a

Wall Stands." The land presents itself as a gift of mud and stone that the Acomas have used to build homes and walls strong enough to last for centuries, even though they support "hundreds of tons of dirt and bones" (*Woven Stone*, 145). The poem's epigraph describes a graveyard wall built on a steep incline, so "it looks like it's about to fall down the incline but will not for a long time" ("A Story of How a Wall Stands," 145). The language the father employs to explain the wall's construction and source of strength also provides lessons about what it means to be Acoma and connected to the land: "'Underneath what looks like loose stone, / there is stone woven together'" ("A Story of How a Wall Stands," 145). The father continues, saying,

> "It is built that carefully,"
> he says, "the mud mixed
> to a certain texture," patiently
> "with the fingers," worked
> in the palm of his hand. So that
> placed between the stones, they hold
> together for a long, long time
>   ("A Story of How a Wall Stands," 145).

We can interpret the adhered stones as symbolic of Acoma individuals who, when held together by the land and community, become powerful and strong. The land becomes a foundation that unites the people and gives them strength to survive even when they seem fragile and close to collapsing. Mud and stones reflect the interconnectedness of creation and community, and in Ortiz's case, they remind him of the creative power derived from the land and people all woven together through participation in their traditions, history, and belief.

In addition to mud's adhesive properties, the land also unites the people through gifts of clay from which the people's storied pottery is created. In oral and written stories, clay is aligned with the sacred, both as part of creation and because it is connected to the Pueblos' creation and emergence. A traditional Cochiti clay narrative explains how the Pueblos came to pottery and explains why it is an important element in their lives:

Itc'tinaku [Thought Woman, Spider Woman] considered how the people should live. She said to herself, "My old father and my

old mother must go down to the people and be Clay (mitsi) Old
Woman and Clay Old Man." In Shipapu she made the old man
and woman into Clay Old Woman and Clay Old Man. The old
woman began to mix the clay with sand and soften it with water.
When she had finished she made it into a ball and wrapped it
in a white manta. She began to coil a pot with her clay, and Clay
Old Man danced beside her singing while she worked. All the
people gathered in the village and watched her all day long. When
she had made her pots so high . . . and the old man was singing
and dancing beside her, he kicked it with his foot and it broke in
many pieces. The old woman picked up his stick and chased him
all around the plaza. She overtook him in the middle of the *kiva*.
They made friends again and she took the broken pot and rolled
it into a ball again. The old man took the post and gave a piece of
it to everybody in the village. They each took it and made pottery
as Clay Old Woman had made it. This was the time they learned
to make pottery. Clay Old Man told them never to forget to
make pottery. Ever since when we do not make pottery these two
masked dancers come with the dance to remind us of the clay they
gave to the people (Benedict, "The Institution of Pottery," 12).

Designing an object from clay celebrates the invitation of Thought
Woman and her parents to humans to use their regenerative powers to
create items from clay analogously as she created humans from clay.[5]
Thought Woman gave humans the power to create in this way when she
placed clay in their hands through her emissaries, Clay Old Man and
Clay Old Woman. The image of Clay Old Woman touching the clay and
mixing it to the right consistency to coil into a pot mirrors the image
of an Acoma father patiently mixing the mud in the palm of his hands
before he builds a wall. Touching and actively participating with the land
in the form of mud or clay reflects an internalized belief about humans'
power and responsibility to remain connected with the sacred, and to
create, to mold, and to live one's life accordingly. As children, my sisters
and I learned to form connections with the land through the gift of food
it offered. Our mother took us out to search for wild strawberries and
asparagus, chokecherries, rose hips, milkweed, watercress, and various
other foodstuffs. She said there was never any need to go hungry if one
learned to live off the land, that the Creator provided all for our survival.

Ortiz's Acoma Pueblo people have been deeply connected to the land through molded clay, both in storied walls that stand the test of time and in the beautiful artistry of his people's well-known pottery. In a poem about his sister's pottery-making, Ortiz shares her connection to clay expressed in motions that emulate the Earth's movements, recalling Silko's statement that little stands between humans and the earth. In his poem, Ortiz explains that she does not see well, yet he marvels at how she is still able to make thin and delicate pots. He describes her skills as having

> ... to do more with a sense of touching
> than with seeing because fingers
> have to know the texture of clay
> and how the pottery is formed from lines
> of shale strata and earth movements.
> The pottery she makes is thin walled
> And has a fragile but definite balance
>   (*Woven Stone*, 129).

Working with clay is a hands-on activity similar to Ortiz's own involvement with the indigenous community on a social, political and spiritual level. The potter's act of creating demonstrates her continued connection to Clay Old Man and Clay Old Woman and her obligation and responsibility to maintain that which they gave her people. Through pottery-making, the people's relationships with clay, earth, and land are renewed and maintained. Santa Clara Pueblo potter Nora Naranjo-Morse describes this relationship as one that "continually fuels [her own] desire to create, and in that desire [she has] found life-giving nourishment" that benefits herself as well as those who experience and appreciate her pottery (*Mud Woman*, 15). By maintaining their physical and spiritual connections with the Earth in these ways, the Pueblo peoples have built and developed strong and enduring cultures that, as Indigenous communities within the larger United States, might appear fragile, but, as Ortiz reminds us, his Acoma people (and indeed all peoples) are balanced and reinvigorated through their pottery and strengthened through their woven stone walls.

Humans' need to engage with the world through ceremonies and activities that connect us with the land extends to our need to engage with other people. Deloria notes, "Through the family, clan, and society there was never a time when an individual Indian was not a part of the cooperative activities of others. It was believed that people are the sum total of their relationships" ("Philosophy and the Tribal Peoples," 10). In the same way that Acoma Pueblo songs and stories taught Ortiz these lessons, his poetry reinforces for his broad range of readers the familial relations that exist between land and humans. The poems "Forming Child" and "To Insure Survival" link the Acoma Pueblo's creation, the ongoing act of childbirth, and the Acoma people's continued relationship with their homeland. Both poems liken humans' formation in and emergence from the Earth's womb to a baby's formation in and emergence from the inner walls of his or her mother's womb (*Woven Stone*, 42). In the poem "To Insure Survival," Ortiz describes his daughter's birth in terms of her emergence into the beauty and colors of creation, inviting his child, Rainy Dawn, to see this relationship and her connection to the landscape of her people:

> You come forth
> the color of a stone cliff
> at dawn,
> changing colors,
> blue to red
> to all the colors of the earth
>   (*Woven Stone*, 48).

Like the "black head" that "burst forth from granite" in Coyote's creation story, Rainy Dawn also emerges resembling the color of stone (*Woven Stone*, 41). Thus, the poetic rendering of her birth is suggestive of the first emergence and alludes to the people's continued survival, as the poem's title "To Insure Survival" states. Just as Ortiz celebrates the birth of his children in poetry, he conveys that the Earth also celebrates their arrival: "the stones with voices, / the plants with bells" all heralding the continuation of harmonious relations between the Earth and the Acomas in the next generation (*Woven Stone*, 46, 49).

Through songs, stories, and ceremonies, families teach children to engage in proper relations with the world and with each other, and Ortiz passes these lessons on to his children and his readers through his poetry. In "Four Poems for A Child Son," he teaches his son the importance of respect for family, for land and creation:

> Respect your mother and father.
> Respect your brothers and sisters.
> Respect your uncles and aunts.
> Respect your land, the beginning.
> Respect what is taught you.
> Respect what you are named.
> Respect the gods.
> Respect yourself
> (*Woven Stone*, 47).

Ortiz's repetition of the word "respect" heightens the emotional impact of exercising reverence for everything—family, geography, learning, the sacred, and oneself—and emphasizes its significance as basic to the laws of social behavior among his people, pointing to respect for people and land as an intertwined value necessary for survival. Throughout Ortiz's poetry, he demonstrates a relational ethics that is inclusive of all parts of creation: human and non-human alike. In this way, he empowers his children as he ends the poem with the declaration, "Everything that is around you / is part of you," a statement from which he includes his people's geographical region as one that has endured through centuries of settlement, including colonization (*Woven Stone*, 47).

Ortiz learned to respect everything around him through rites of passage, ritual celebrations, and lessons handed down in traditional stories. At the same time, he acknowledges that an Indigenous system of ethics continues in the stories that he crafts and relates in his English language poetry and prose: "They would never be lost and finally gone. They would always continue. You can say that in this new language . . . the stories of the People continue. The Acoma stories, culture, way of life, spirituality, and so forth continue on with the use of another language" (Ortiz, "Poetics"). Much as my own Indigenous Mexican-American ancestors learned to do with the Spanish language and our Indigenous *cuentos*, Ortiz's Acoma people have infused English with their Indigenous Acoma perceptions, showing that the worldviews inherent in the Keresan language, for example, are not lost when English is used. Through my mother's teachings, all done in English, my sisters and I learned the importance of respect, responsibility, reciprocity, and relations, meaning my worldview was shaped by an Indigenous system of relational ethics, all in an

urban setting. In his bilingual poems, Ortiz further demonstrates the
linguistic connection through his Keres language ancestry forward into
the language of conquest—English. In "Telling and Showing Her," Ortiz
passes on lessons about relational ethics to his daughter, Sara Marie,
teaching her in his native language and in English that land is life and
that Acoma Pueblo land is part of her life, an Indigenous geography and
relationship that defines not only who she is but also how she is to live:

> *Duwah ya-aie dzah.* This is the dirt.
> *Duwah haatse dzah.* This is the land.
>
> *Duwah sra-ah.* This is ours.
> *Duwah sra-ah haatse.* This is our land.
>
> *How-nu chuutah.* Reach down to it.
> *Pihtya ya-aie.* Touch the dirt.
> *Pihtya haatse.* Touch the land.
>
> *Dyuu tchu-u-tah ya-aie.* Pick up the dirt.
> *Dyuu tchah-yow-uuh haatse.* Pick up the land.
>
> *Ya-aie sru-taie-kquiyah.* Dirt you are holding.
> *Haatse sru-taie-kquiyah.* Land you are carrying.
>
> You are holding your life. You are carrying your life.
> This is what I am showing and telling you
> (*Out There Somewhere*, 66).

Because her people emerged from and have lived for thousands of years
on the land to which her father points, through this powerful bilingual
turn Ortiz articulates the endurance and meaningfulness of kinship ties
to the land. He literally asks the daughter in the poem to touch and hold
the dirt much as did the father who interwove stones to build a wall or a
sister who molds clay as she creates pottery. Ortiz's reiterative emphasis
on the touch of earth invites his readers to consider and to form a physical connection to place that comes from intimate association and tactile
sensation.[6] As Ortiz demonstrates in his poetic craft, through language

and story, one can create a physical connection to place even when one leaves home, so he teaches his daughter to connect with the landscapes in which she resides by connecting with the land.

Communicating the realities of alienation and disconnection, Ortiz offers other poems that emphasize the importance of maintaining relationships to land wherever one happens to reside. He articulates the experiences of being away from home, lost in cold and foreign landscapes where deep and vital connections to land are impeded by the speed and concrete of urban America. In time, Ortiz, his narrators, and ideally his readers, too, come to realize that life requires that one remain connected to one's environment to maintain an Indigenous sense of connection to land and people—a connection that urban living threatens to destroy. Living in an urban landscape, my mother knew the significance of maintaining a connection to the land, so we would often drive up to Cottonwood Canyon close to sunset to reflect on the end of a day that we had earlier greeted. Those Wasatch Mountains and their grandeur inspired awe in me. Their size humbled me, but their beauty earned my respect. As we did in the morning, we would express why we were thankful for the day and what lessons it brought us. These moments of self-reflection were easier when we were surrounded by aspen, pine, and the smell of earth.

Traveling away from a landscape that possesses "red and brown land, / sage, and when it rains, / it smells like piñon" (*Woven Stone*, 97), Ortiz writes of encountering a "blinding city" and colorless "streets gray with cement / and glaring glass" (*Woven Stone*, 76). Landing at an airport and emerging from a plane, he depicts an asphalt and steel maze without horizons, distinct landforms, or other familiar geographic structures to mark one's way. The power of a person's integral balance that comes from a life lived in community with the land can be seen in the remembered grounding of a familiar and beloved mountain:

> It occurs to me again
> that wherever I have been,
> I have never seen a Mountain
> that has stood so clearly
> in my mind; when I have needed
> to envision my home, when loneliness
> for myself has over come me,

the Mountain has occurred
(*Woven Stone*, 128).

The mountain of which he speaks is Kaweshtima, the mountain on the
northern horizon of *Aacqu*, the Keresan name for Acoma. This is Mount
Taylor, just north of Grants, New Mexico, west of Laguna Pueblo and
at the northern edge of Acoma Pueblo lands. This is also the centering
mountain of Leslie Marmon Silko's novel *Ceremony*. In Ortiz's poem, he
conveys how the mountain, even when he is far from home, can nourish
his soul and remind him that there is always a landscape that can help
him define and locate his proper place in the world.

In his more recent collection *Out There Somewhere*, Ortiz admits
that most of his life has been spent "out there somewhere" away from
home in distant places where a remembered Indigenous system of ethics
facilitates ways of relating to land and place regardless of where one
might be. The lessons of an Indigenous land ethic from Acoma come
through Ortiz's poetry in the form of rain clouds, plants, stone, mud,
and clay. They also come through in mountains. A deep relationship
with Kaweshtima provides the orientation that enables Ortiz to connect deeply, too, with other mountains. In "Look to the Mountain" and
"Mountains All Around," he recognizes and acknowledges other sacred
mountains in Tucson, Arizona, reminders that other landscapes can be
embraced within the inclusiveness of his Indigenous code of ethics (*Out
There Somewhere*, 87):[7]

> All around the sacred mountains
> that enclose Tucson, all around.
> Whenever I need to locate myself
> I look for the mountains I know.
> It doesn't matter where I am
> I look for mountains I know
> (*Out There Somewhere*, 89).

Ortiz acknowledges the struggles necessary to give form and substance
to things that appear to be alien, and he returns to the father's analogy of
using the earth to build a strong foundation. Throughout his work, Ortiz
affirms an inclusively relational system of ethics by which he lives his life,
and it provides him with the hope that life will endure—a hope that is

particularly poignant in the writing of a man whose people have endured five centuries of external colonization that continues today.

In perceiving the land as embodying a code of ethics as Ortiz does, we are constantly reminded about our responsibilities to move in harmony with the natural processes of the world. Ortiz equates being human with "being real in a real world," which means "loving and respecting" one's self, others, and all of creation (*Woven Stone*, 32). He notes, "This I believe has always been the true and real vision of Indigenous People of the Americas: to love, respect, and be responsible to ourselves and others, and to behold with passion and awe the wonders and bounty and beauty of creation and the world around us" (*Woven Stone*, 32). Whether it is Ortiz's own Indigenous Acoma Pueblo people who still live on their ancestral homelands, or whether it is my own Indigenous Mexican-American peoples, so many of whom live away from our Yaqui, Aztec, or other tribal lands, the relational ethic that Ortiz explores in his poetic craft presents an Indigenous vision of an interconnected world that is valuable to all his readers. I value Ortiz's work, because his voice is familiar. His words and lessons are mirrored in my mother's voice, the woman who taught me to be human.

NOTES

1. For a discussion of other Indigenous writers who incorporate notions of personhood and intersubjective relations, see Susan Berry Brill de Ramírez, *Contemporary American Indian Literatures and the Oral Tradition* (Tucson: University of Arizona Press, 1999), especially pp. 117–26.

2. While Cordova generalizes between Indigenous and the West in her discussion on ethics, she does so to show the contrasting features of Indigenous and western philosophies. To note tribal differences, one must contextualize ethics within tribes.

3. Cordova opens her article with Wittgenstein's critique of James Frazer's *Golden Bough* in "Remarks on Frazer's *Golden Bough*" in James Klagge and Alfred Nordmann, *Philisophical Occasions: 1912–1951*. 131–33. Here, Wittgenstein accuses Frazer of being unable to pull himself out of the context of being an English man. Frazer misinterprets the rituals of the indigenes he objectifies as "other"; Wittgenstein's point is that similar rituals exist within English culture, but Frazer's lack of cultural grounding in his scholarship prevents him from recognizing ordinary and familiar practices, which he misrepresents as exotic and primitive. Thus, Wittgenstein shows that Frazer is unable to understand the notions he tries to explain.

4. It is important to note that these traditional ideals have not always been maintained because of the negative impacts of colonization, urbanization, and modernization.

5. Nora Naranjo-Morse's *Mud Woman: Poems from the Clay* (Tucson: University of Arizona Press, 1992) speaks about the spiritual and ritual process of collecting, processing, and working with clay.

6. Kenneth Roemer's "A 'Touching Man' Brings Aacqu Close" explores the tactile imagery in Ortiz's poetry. *Studies in American Indian Literatures* 16, no. 4 (2004): 68–78.

7. For more on Indigenous ethics that reside in the land, see Keith H. Basso's *Wisdom Sits in Places: Landscape and Language among the Western Apache* (University of New Mexico Press, 1996).

WORKS CITED

Adamson, Joni. "The Challenge of Speaking First." *Studies in American Indian Literature* 16, no. 4 (2004): 57–60.

Benedict, Ruth. "The Institution of Pottery." Tales of the Cochiti Indians in *Bulletin of the Bureau of American Ethnology* 98. Washington, D.C., 1931.

Cordova, Viola. "Ethics: The We and the I." In *American Indian Thought: Philosophical Essays*, edited by Anne Waters, 177–78. Malden: Blackwell Publishing, 2004.

———. "Approaches to Native American Philosophy." In *American Indian Thought: Philosophical Essays*, edited by Anne Waters, 27–33. Malden: Blackwell Publishing, 2004.

Deloria, Vine, Jr. "Philosophy and the Tribal Peoples." In *American Indian Thought: Philosophical Essays*, edited by Anne Waters, 3–11. Malden: Blackwell Publishing, 2004.

Naranjo-Morse, Nora. *Mud Woman: Poems from the Clay*. Tucson: University of Arizona Press, 1992.

Ortiz, Alfonso. *The Tewa World: Space, Time, Being, and Becoming in a Pueblo Society*. Chicago: The University of Chicago Press, 1969.

Ortiz, Simon. "Always the Stories: A Brief History and Thoughts on My Writing." In *Coyote Was Here*, edited by Bo Schöler, 57–69. Aarhus, Denmark: SEKLOS/University of Aarhus Press, 1984.

———. "The Language We Know." In *I Tell You Now: Autobiographical Essays by Native American Writers*, edited by Brian Swann and Arnold Krupat, 187–94. Lincoln: University of Nebraska Press, 1987.

———. *Woven Stone*. Tucson: University of Arizona Press, 1992.

———. *Out There Somewhere*. Tucson: University of Arizona Press, 2002.

———. *Poetics and Politics.* Edited by Larry Evers. Tucson: University of Arizona, 1992. http://www.coh.arizona.edu/english/poetics/ortiz/ortiz.html (accessed September 3, 2007).

Silko, Leslie Marmon. "Interior and Exterior Landscapes: The Pueblo Migration Stories." In *Yellow Woman and a Beauty of the Spirit*, 25–47. New York: Simon & Schuster, 1996.

———. "Language and Literature from a Pueblo Indian Perspective." In *Yellow Woman and a Beauty of the Spirit*, 48–59. New York: Simon & Schuster, 1996.

———. "The People and the Land ARE Inseparable." In *Yellow Woman and a Beauty of the Spirit*, 85–91. New York: Simon & Schuster, 1996.

Tohe, Laura. "'It was that Indian': Simon Ortiz, Activist Poet." *Studies in American Indian Literature* 16, no. 4 (2004): 54–56.

Watkins, Joe. "Place-meant." *The American Indian Quarterly* 25, no. 1 (2001): 41–45.

Wittgenstein, Judwig. "Remarks on Frazer's Golden Bough." In *Philosophical Occasions*: 1912–1951, edited by James Klagge and Alfred Nordmann, 131–33. Indianapolis: Hackett, 1993.

Simon J. Ortiz's Powerful Poetic Resistance

A Review Essay of A Good Journey *and*
Fight Back: For the Sake of the People,
For the Sake of the Land *by Simon J. Ortiz*

Geary Hobson

A Good Journey by Simon J. Ortiz (Turtle Island Foundation: Berkeley, California, 1977). 165 pages. $6.95 paper; and *Fight Back: For the Sake of the People, For the Sake of the Land* by Simon J. Ortiz (Albuquerque, New Mexico: Institute for Native American Development, Native American Studies, University of New Mexico, 1980). 75 pages. (Both books are reprinted in *Woven Stone* [Tucson: University of Arizona Press, 1992].)

A Good Journey is the second collection of poems by Simon J. Ortiz, not including the slim chapbooks that appeared with little notice several years ago.[1] Partly because of the chapbooks, but largely because his poetic voice is so unique, Ortiz has been recognized for the past ten years, especially in Indian circles all across the nation, as possibly the best contemporary Native American poet. After several years of delayed action, Harper & Row finally issued Ortiz's first full-size book of poems, *Going for the Rain*, in 1976 and it received enthusiastic response from readers and critics alike. Now *A Good Journey*, published by Turtle Island Foundation and at 165 pages, it, like the 112-page *Going for the Rain*, is a remarkably substantial book of poems, both in size and content, and one that should do much in establishing Ortiz as not only the major contemporary Indian poet but as a major American poet as well.

Most reviews of books by contemporary Native American writers seem to focus almost exclusively on the writers' concern and attachment to his or her cultural heritage. While Simon J. Ortiz is certainly concerned with his particular Acoma Pueblo Indian heritage, and mirrors his tribe's history and present-day circumstances in almost every line of his work, it would be a disservice to overlook his contribution as a remarkably incisive critic of contemporary society, both in the Indian as well as the non-Indian world. For instance, few poets writing today seem as deeply concerned with environmental issues than Ortiz. In "For Our Brothers: Blue Jay, Gold Finch, Flicker, Squirrel," the poet presents a series of elegies for each of these birds and animals, killed by passing motorists and soon lying dead at the side of the highway. The poem contains a subtitle, or explanatory note, which reads: "Who perished lately in this most unnecessary war, saw them lying off the side of a state road in southwest Colorado," and the poet tells us in the first line "they all loved life / And suddenly, / It just stopped for them." While the poem is an anguished indictment of the senseless killing of animals and birds because of our haste and carelessness, it is also an apology, and a prayer, for what is being made of modern life: "Well, I'm sorry for the mess. / I'll try to do what I can / To prevent this sort of thing / Because, Gold Finch, goddamnit, / The same thing is happening to us (129–30)."

The indictment continues even more harshly in the long poem which derives its title from an April 1974 editorial comment in the *Albuquerque Journal* as "the State's claim that it seeks in no way to deprive Indians / of their rightful share of water, but only to define that / share, falls on deaf ears." And fall on deaf ears it should indeed, since anyone at all familiar with American Indian history knows that this was the primary purpose expressed in most of the old hastily concluded treaties with various Indian tribes—not to "take" the land and resources, but to "define the boundaries." Of course, the process of defining necessarily entailed land cessions. An aspect of this is seen in the poem entitled "Right of Way":

> The elder people at home do not understand
> . . .
> You tell them, "The State wants right of way.
> It will get right of way."
> . . .
> They ask, "What is right of way?"

You say, "The State wants to go through
your land. The State wants your land."
They ask, "The Americans want my land?"
You say, "Yes, my beloved Grandfather."
They ask, "I already gave them some land."
You say, "Yes, Grandmother, that's true.
Now, they want more, to widen their highway."
They ask again and again, "This right of way
that the Americans want, does this mean
They want all our land?"
. . .
There is silence because you can't explain
and you don't want to . . . (137).

As modern American life presses irrevocably upon the Indian world,
the poet in "Long House Valley Poem" observes the contrast:

Power line over the Mountain,
toward Phoenix, toward Denver,
toward Los Angeles, toward Las Vegas,
carrying our mother away.
. . .
The Yei
and hogans and the People
and roadside flowers
and cornfields and the sage
and the valley peace,
They are almost gone (109).

Lately, quite a few non-Indian poets are writing "Coyote" poems,
using the quintessential trickster figure of Western Indian tribes as the
principal symbolic character. It is refreshing to read Ortiz's poems about
Coyote, in which the persona of Coyote is seen in the most authentic way
possible and not merely as a convenient literary symbol culled from textbooks and other second-rate poems. Coyote, in Ortiz's poems, is a natural part of the daily life of the Acoma people, like breakfast or morning
sunrise. In "Telling About Coyote," the poet says: " . . . you know, Coyote /
is in the origin and all the way / through . . . he's the cause / of the trouble,

the hard times / that things have . . ." (15). Yet he is part of the good times, too, and the stories; and he is always leaving and returning:

> O yes, last time . . .
> when was it,
> I saw him somewhere
> Between Muskogee and Tulsa . . .
>   . . .
> He'll be back. Don't worry.
> He'll be back (17–18).

It should be added that Ortiz will be back, too. Like Coyote, he's too good a storyteller—and a poet—to stay away for too long. Indeed, Ortiz's subsequent and even more powerful collection *Fight Back: For the Sake of the People, For the Sake of the Land* was published a few years later by the Institute for Native American Development. INAD was established in 1979 as a research component of the Native American Studies program of the University of New Mexico. Ortiz, recently employed by the program as a literature instructor, allowed the Institute to publish his combination poetry/prose manuscript as the first installment of their new publishing venue. In 1980, *Fight Back* thus became volume one, number one of the INAD Literary Journal.

As both *A Good Journey* and *Fight Back* demonstrate, there are few poets so truly bardic or as deeply politically committed as Ortiz, and the poems of *Fight Back* reiterate these qualities many times over. By the very title, Ortiz exhorts not only his fellow Pueblo Indians in New Mexico to begin resisting the continuation of cultural and economic exploitation of themselves and their homeland, but for all Indians everywhere—indeed, the call is for all economically oppressed peoples everywhere—to begin the needed processes of reversal through active resistance. In an inauguratory poem entitled "Mid-America Prayer," Ortiz writes:

> Standing again
> with all things
> that have been in the past
> that are in the present,
> and that will be in the future
> we acknowledge ourselves

to be in a relationship that is responsible
and proper, that is loving and compassionate,
for the sake of the land and all people;
   . . . we ask in all sincerity, for hope, courage, peace,
strength, vision, unity and continuance (1).

As subsequent poems begin to feature references to "mine super-
intendents," "uranium boom business," "cave-ins," "Atomic Energy
Commission," "yellowcake," "Ambrosia Lake," and "Jackpile," the reader
immediately realizes that Ortiz is describing an all-too-real Indian world
of which few non-Indian people have only the slightest bit of knowledge.
Ortiz is addressing the shameless exploitation of Acoma and Laguna
Pueblo lands through the several varieties of uranium mining that are
devastating the area. Several poems relate the lives of Acoma men who
went to work in the mines, such as "Kay's Story," in which an Indian miner
tells of an "Okie" Indian worker named Lacey who is killed in a cable
foul-up in Primary Crusher (one of the stages of ore processing), and of
workers named Herb, Art, Wiley and the author himself who "rode car
pool" and worked the same shift in "The First Hard Core."
   A long, twenty-seven-page poem, with several alternating prose passages, entitled "No More Sacrifices," is (except for the postscript poem,
"A New Story") the concluding statement of the author about the energy
corporations' raping of the Southwestern landscape (47–73). In the nar-
ration and description of the short history of the outside mining companies, it is scathing in its indictment of Kerr-McGee and Anaconda with
their immediate short-term emoluments to local Indian people in the
form of wages, but long-lasting and deadly in its after-effects. The massive increase of Indian deaths by cancer and other respiratory diseases,
and the denuded, uglified landscape left after pit mining, the poet says,
far outweigh any beneficial means as put forth by the mining industry. As well, "No More Sacrifices" is also a briefly rendered tribal history of Aacqu, or Aacqumeh Hanoh, of the Acoma Pueblo people. While
the "U.S. and New Mexico maps and tourists bureaus do not know the
Aacqumeh Hanoh's name for the local community [McCartys, where
the poet was raised] . . . ," he tells us that it is "Deetzeyamah–The North
Door . . . ," names that "do not appear anywhere except in the people's
hearts and souls and history and oral tradition, and in their love" (47).
This detailed process of establishing the people, and their names for

themselves and their land, is in stark contrast to the mining company officials who live far off and away from the places they are defiling, and who will live out their entire lives without the least clue of their soulless-ness and emptiness.

In "To Change in a Good Way," a friendship between two couples— a Laguna one and white one from Oklahoma—stresses that the mining industry also exacts a heavy toll on whites as well as Indians. Both men are miners and both know the hard work and the dubious future in store for them. In "What I Mean," a young Acoma miner named Agee is mys-teriously killed after trying unsuccessfully to start a union (37–40). "The First Hard Core" unveils the racism that often exists in the mines— whites versus Indians, Indians versus Mexicans, and all sorts of interre-lated permutations (15–17). *Fight Back* is one of the first explicitly political works by a contemporary Native American writer. Ortiz reminds us that, for modern-day Indian people, the term "post-colonial" is nonsense for peoples still living under the yoke of the Euro-American colonization of Indian lands and nations. Indigenous peoples worldwide are perhaps the most pervasively and extensively colonized, exploited, and oppressed, and this is especially so throughout the western hemisphere. In both *A Good Journey* and *Fight Back*, Ortiz gives poetic voice to this legacy and the continuing survivance of Native peoples.

EDITORS' NOTE

1. Geary Hobson's review of Ortiz's earlier volumes articulates the particular distinctiveness of his poetry during the early years of its appearance. Originally written in 1979 and 1980, the review places Ortiz's poetry within its historical moment and speaks the excitement that Ortiz's person and voice created almost thirty years ago. The section of this review that focuses on *A Good Journey* was first published in *Western American Literature* in 1979.

WORK CITED

Hobson, Geary. "Review: *A Good Journey.*" *Western American Literature* 14, no. 1 (Spring 1979): 77–78.

Ways of Telling an Historical Event

Lawrence Evers

Do you see what happens when the imagination
is superimposed upon the historical event?
It becomes a story. The whole piece becomes
more deeply invested with meaning.
　　—N. Scott Momaday, "The Man Made of Words"

On Good Friday in 1952 New Mexico state trooper Nash Garcia was killed and burned in his patrol car twenty miles from McCartys, New Mexico, deep in the Acoma reservation, and the following Monday two Acoma brothers, William and Gabriel Felipe, were arrested and charged with the murder. From the outset the killing stirred imaginations. William Felipe's confession printed on the front page of the *Albuquerque Journal* appeared a forced and inadequate explanation for the charred pile of bones and St. Christopher medal pictured sensationally above on the same page. Motive was the most persistent question in press coverage, the long hearings and trial, through the final psychiatric testimony in the case which gained the brothers a reduced sentence of life imprisonment early in 1953. The press, the court, the psychiatrists all looked for meaning in the event before they allowed it to sink into some slight chapter in the history of New Mexico. The small meanings they found were colored by the expectations of their professions and the majority community which they shared, and it remained for two Pueblo writers, in fictions published some twenty years after, to turn that small line segment of history into circles of form.

This essay was originally published as "The Killing of a New Mexico State Trooper: Ways of Telling an Historical Event," in *Critical Essays on Native American Literature*, ed. Andrew Wiget (Boston: G. K. Hall, 1985), 246–61.

As fictions, Leslie Silko's "Tony's Story" and Simon Ortiz's "The Killing of a State Cop" have been noticed and praised.[1] Their editor writes: "It is interesting, and perhaps noteworthy, that two stories in this volume, by two different authors, deal with this same theme of violence and death of the white intruder" (Rosen, _The Man to Send Rain Clouds_, xi). The similarities of the stories are remarkable, all the more so against the background of N. Scott Momaday's _House Made of Dawn_. And it was initially an attempt to understand the relations of these imaginative accounts which took me back to examine the records of the case on which they were based.[2] Records of _United States v. William R. Felipe and Gabriel Felipe_ help us to see the role of the individual imagination in the creation of fiction, but they are of interest in their own right as well. They preserve an intriguing variety of perspectives on a single event.

I

The barest account for the events of Friday, April 11, 1952, comes to us through confessions wrung by the F.B.I. agents from the Felipes early in the morning of April 14 (Plaintiff's Exhibits 10, 16). Both William, thirty-two at the time of the killings, and Gabriel, twenty-eight, were born at Acomita, New Mexico, where they were living then—William with his wife, Gabriel with his mother and step-father, Mariano Vicente. According to Gabriel's confession, the brothers borrowed their step-father's pickup, bought two pints of Tokay wine at Los Ritos bar on Highway 66, and drove with their 30–30s north of Acoma toward Mount Taylor to hunt deer the morning of the killing. After an eerie hunt, William returned with a small deer, put it on the floor in the cab, and they returned to Los Ritos to buy sandwiches and more wine. There they turned west to Grants. It was about 2:00 p.m.

> We headed west on Highway 66 and I was driving. We had driven
> about 10 miles west from Los Ritos when I saw Nash Garcia parked
> in his state patrol car beside the highway. We drove on west about
> one mile and decided we had better not go to Grants with the deer
> in the pickup. William had deer blood on his pants so we decided
> to go home instead of going to Grants. I turned around and headed
> east on Highway 66, and I was driving about 65 or 70 miles per hour
> when we passed Nash Garcia still parked beside the highway. Garcia

honked at us when we passed, and I stepped on the gas. And when we were about 1/2 mile east of where we passed Garcia, William looked back and said, "that patrol is following us." I looked and could see the state police car in the mirror. I drove on east to the McCarty road and turned south on McCarty road. Garcia followed us at a high rate of speed for about 7 or 8 miles, and I told William that Nash Garcia was the patrol chasing us and that he was the son-of-a-bitch that had put me in jail for drunk driving and for us to ambush Garcia and kill him. William said, "O.K., let's kill him, but not here as this is not a good place to ambush him." We drove on about five miles with Garcia following us until we came up to a hill which had rocks and trees on it, and I said to William, "This is it." I drove the pickup off the road toward the hill and hid it behind a cedar tree. William jumped out of the pickup, took a 30–30 rifle and ran into the ditch about 15 feet from the pickup. Just as Garcia yelled, "I give up. Don't shoot," Garcia opened the car door and stepped out of his car and fell beside his car (Plaintiff's Exhibit 16, 4–7).

Loading the body into the patrol car, the brothers drove deeper into the backcountry, hid it in a grove of piñons, and returned to spend the night at their mother's home. In the morning, Gabriel, carrying Garcia's revolver in his suitcase, went to Albuquerque with his mother and step-father. William returned to the hidden patrol car, piled the front seat with dry cedar, and set the wood on fire. The following evening—Easter Sunday—he was arrested at Acomita. Gabriel remained free another day until, ironically, he was arrested on the streets of Albuquerque by a cousin of Garcia's.

The circumstances under which these confessions were obtained were questionable, as their very language suggests, a matter to which I shall return. However, in terms of the above reconstruction, the central motivation for the killing was clearly an old grudge given circumstantial intensity by alcohol and guilt at poaching a deer. Later in a November 11, 1952, statement given to psychiatrist Robert Navarre, Gabriel recalled the source of the grudge. He had been working for the railroad near Lincoln, Kansas, and had returned home.

All of us Acoma Indians come home. I went to Grants to pick up a mattress, I got drunk, and I sit in a car with three other Indian

boys. A patrolman come to where we were parked on the side of
the street. This is the same patrolman I got in trouble with later
[Garcia]. He asked us what we were doing. We say, "nothing." He
say "drinking?" We say, "no." He search us and find bottle. He
arrest us for drunk driving. This patrol always bothers Indians. We
were by road, not driving (not paginated).[3]

Garcia's prior record with Indians in general and Gabriel in particular was of scant interest to the Albuquerque press as they rushed to
report the sensational killing and eulogize the first officer slain in the line
of duty in the state. Garcia, it was reported, had been a popular officer in
Grants, and in the pages of the *Albuquerque Journal* and *Star* his stature
grew. He entered law enforcement as a deputy sheriff in Albuquerque,
joining the state police force about eight years before the killing. Garcia
advanced to the rank of Captain and for a time was in charge of state
police detachments in the Santa Fe area. Ben Chavez, an Albuquerque
city patrolman, former neighbor, and friend of Garcia, praised him to the
Albuquerque Journal: "When Nash was made Captain in 1948, he won it
through merit. He was one of the best men in the district. A good man,
a sincere man, faithful to his superiors, he believed in police work as a
profession" ("Laud Slain Officer," 1). The remark punctuated two large
pictures on the same front page which bore the caption:

Held in ambush killing—Willie Felipe shows State Police Chief Joe
Roach the remains of Patrolman Nash Garcia near Grants. Roach
lowers his head and chokes back tears as he views the ashes—all
that was left of his fellow officer when Garcia was shot down in a
hail of bullets and then burned.

Garcia seems to have come to Grants in exile, though, after being
demoted to patrolman. His brother Pete blamed the demotion on politics and jealousy and recalled that Garcia "was broken hearted when he
was demoted and transferred two years ago" ("Job Came First," 13). Yet the
press was mute about the circumstances surrounding the demotion and
transfer, focusing rather on such comments from Garcia's superior office
as "He didn't have a chance to use his gun. They shot him down like a dog"
("Nash Garcia," 1). On April 15, a front page picture in the *Albuquerque
Journal* showed Garcia with two small children. The caption read: "Nash

was their grandfather and hero." On April 17, the papers reported a hero's funeral for Garcia. His bronze casket approached the church in a 1300 car procession while fifty uniformed state policemen and thirty city policemen and sheriff's deputies gave the final salute. "Hushed citizens along the street removed their hats at the passing of the bier," and "the crowd at the church overflowed onto the front steps" ("Laud Slain Officer," 1). Joseph Montoya spoke at the graveside as the State of New Mexico buried a hero.

Heroes are not created idly. More often than not, they come to being to serve some political cause. So too in this case, though the emotional force generated by the death and memory of Nash Garcia, "godfather and hero," diffused in surprising directions. Sixties liberals might predict lynch mobs and a rebirth of Kit Carson style Indian control programs. But response was not so clear cut, a reflection of wavering federal Indian policy of the time. Indians were viewed with increased regard then, we recall, following their dramatic performances in World War II. Navajo was our unbreakable secret code. Ira Hayes toured the country with a Medal of Honor. William Felipe, in fact, had been awarded a Bronze Star. And federal efforts to reward Indians with admission to the urban splendors of the fifties through relocation programs were well underway. Yet Indians remained wards. "I have lived with them. I know them. They are children," said one prospective juror during jury selection for the Garcia case (*U.S. v. Felipe et al.*, 40.) More consistently in the documents of the case the brothers and all Indians are called "boys." They are viewed as possessing a kind of cultural immaturity, so that in assigning responsibility for the killing, the press looked not to the Felipes but rather to those who influenced them, their legal guardians.

Alcohol provided a convenient focus for the search. Early reports of the killing give the bottles of Tokay a special prominence, and liquor is clearly blamed for the act. Even "the grim-faced residents of Grants—where Garcia was well-liked—put part of the blame upon persons who sell liquor to the Indians" (*Albuquerque Star*, April 19, 1952, 1). Accordingly, one of Governor Edwin L. Mechem's first responses to the case was to call State Liquor Director Elfego Baca onto the carpet. And Baca responded quickly. On April 18 charges were filed against Nepomucena Sanchez, owner of El Cerritos Bar, for allegedly selling liquor to the Felipes. Manuel Ortiz, operator of La Mesita Bar in the same area, was also charged with bootlegging liquor to Indians as similar investigations spread throughout the state.

The political uses of the murder went well beyond a shakeup in the state liquor commission, however. The *Albuquerque Journal* editorialized in an early news story on the case: "Garcia's brutal slaying flung a challenge at federal and state law enforcement. It boils down to what the officers will do about the problem in Northwestern New Mexico with its complicated troubles of Indian lands and white cities" ("Laud Slain Officer," 1). The problem, of course, derived from the peculiar legal topography of the reservation border area where a checkerboard of federal, state, private, and Indian allotment lands created jurisdiction troubles. Properly, federal officers had jurisdiction over federal and federal trust lands, while state officers (like Nash Garcia) reigned on state and private lands. Customary agreements with tribal officials (in this case, the governor of Acoma Pueblo) allowed state officers to respect or ignore the boundaries as convenience dictated. In any case, the "challenge" posed by the press displaced any racial tensions generated by the murder with bureaucratic ones. Governor Mechem suggested that Bureau of Indian Affairs law enforcement efforts "have been nil," and righteously replaced Garcia with two men (*Albuquerque Star*, April 19, 1952, 10). Federal officials reacted defensively and in kind. The memory of a heroic Garcia, the need to find influences that made the "boys" go wrong, and a flurry of political bickering suppressed any attempt by the press to deal with the more complex cultural aspects of the case.

II

The trial of the two brothers opened September 22, 1952, at Santa Fe with the Honorable Carl A. Hatch, U.S. District Judge, presiding in open court. U.S. Attorney Maurice Sanchez represented the government; Albuquerque attorneys Phillip Dunleavy and A. T. Hannett—himself a former governor of the state—represented the Felipes. Prior press treatments of the killing were felt in the courtroom. While a number of prospective jurors were excluded because they objected to the death penalty, each of the twelve Anglo males seated admitted freely to having followed the case in area newspapers. Judge Hatch repeatedly overruled Dunleavy's objections to this knowledge as prejudicial. When jury selection was complete, Hatch summarized: "All the jurors stated that they could and would lay aside anything they had read and decide the case solely upon the evidence" (*U.S. v. Felipe et al.*, 96).

In all, the evidence presented at the trial from which the jurors were charged to decide the case bore striking resemblance to the newspaper accounts they were instructed to disregard. The prosecution labored to tell the events of the killing with gruesome realism. At one point Sanchez introduced a movie taken from a patrol car following the chase route that led to the scene of the killing, as he attempted to paint the crime as "the blackest in the history of the state" (*U.S. v. Felipe et al.*, 221). Despite a few sensational remarks of their own and despite frequent objections, the defense brought a weary fatalism to the trial, echoing the apologetic motivations proffered in the Albuquerque newspapers.[4] The brothers had killed Garcia, admitted Dunleavy, but they did so possessing a "very low grade intelligence" and under the influence of alcohol. Therefore they were not responsible for their actions; they were temporarily insane.

To establish patterns of alcohol use and the level of William's intelligence, Dunleavy called not only expert professional testimony but also members of the family. He probed William's war record at length, as a key defense strategy appears to have been to establish the profound change service in the war had on him. Pabilita Vicente, William's mother, testified that "when he came back, he was a changed boy. I could not understand that he was so different, that his behavior wasn't good. . . . And it seemed like he learned that [to drink alcohol] in the army" (*U.S. v. Felipe et al.*, 362). Mariano Vicente, William's stepfather, similarly testified to a "tremendous change" on his return from the war (*U.S. v. Felipe et al.*, 368).

William himself recalled that he was reluctant to go into the Army: "I was called by the draftboard and I didn't want to join the Army, and they had a little time in hunting me. But I finally got into the service when they found me" (*U.S. v. Felipe et al.*, 380).[5] Once inducted, William served the Infantry in the 37th Division well. His service earned him a Bronze Star awarded April 28, 1944, for meritorious service at Bougainville, Solomon Islands. The citation, introduced as evidence at the trial, reads in part:

> Throughout enemy attack PFC Felipe was a gunner in a light machine gun squad. His pillbox bore the brunt of the enemy's small arms and automatic fire, and was only fifty yards from the nearest enemy held pillbox. PFC Felipe manned his gun throughout the entire battle, delivering steady and murderous fire throughout. He refused all offers of relief. Later he volunteered on ammunition and food carrying parties over a route through open

trenches and was subject to enemy sniper and knee mortar fire
(*U.S. v. Felipe et al.*, not paginated).[6]

Discharged in October of 1945, William reenlisted within a year to serve
as a truck driver. A superior noted on his papers: "likes Army, and would
like to make it a career" (*U.S. v. Felipe et al.*, not paginated).

Yet a distinguished warrior does not make a distinguished truck
driver. Following his reenlistment, questions were raised about William's
ability to serve in his new role. In March of 1947 he was discharged for
"inaptness." It was on this "inapt" image that the defense rested its case,
coupling it with a final attempt to shift accountability to the brothers'
guardians: "The real criminal was the bootlegger who gave these boys
the liquor" (*U.S. v. Felipe et al.*, 167). The whole of the defense argument
was ruled irrelevant by Judge Hatch. In his instructions to the jury, Hatch
ordered them not to consider drunkenness or mental ability as factors in
determining temporary insanity, and the jury quickly found the brothers
guilty of first degree murder. On October 17, 1952, Hatch sentenced them
to die in the electric chair in Santa Fe.

III

In an effort to substantiate an appeal, the defense had the Felipes transferred to the United States Department of Justice Medical Center in
Springfield, Missouri, for psychiatric examinations, and it was there that
a deeper cultural context for the killing began to unfold. One of the first
matters the federal psychiatrists reviewed were the confessions I have
quoted. Dr. George Devereux wrote of the confessions:

> It is absolutely certain that this inmate [William] is materially
> unable to understand many of the words contained in his
> confession and the long sentences it contains. Regardless
> of whether the confessions are true or not, he signed a
> document which he did not understand as to content, and
> whose significance for his fate he was unable to evaluate
> properly (Devereux "William Felipe," 4).

Trained in both anthropology and psychiatry, Devereux was unusually
qualified to examine the brothers, and he pushed beyond the particular

problem of the confessions to larger linguistic and cultural consider-
ations which had been ignored in the trial.[7] He pointed out that one had
to know Acoma culture to understand what the brothers meant by any
given English word, thereby questioning the validity of previous testing
of William: "To us a Bear paw is just a bear paw. To him this expression,
which, I understand, appears in one of his Rorschach tests, has a special
meaning: bear paws are used in Acoma curing rituals. If he says 'mother,'
he can mean either his mother or his mother's sister, etc" (Devereux,
"William Felipe," 4).

But more directly related to the killing, argued Devereux, were the
brothers' dreams and witch beliefs. He diagnosed Gabriel as a psycho-
path, one who compensated for a sense of inadequacy in fantasy through
persecutory ideas of "being misunderstood," "picked on," and "envied."
Gabriel was convinced that people envied him for his large flocks of
sheep and therefore sought to harm him by gossip and by witchcraft.
This, Devereux notes, is an "abnormal attitude for an Acoma Indian" in
one important respect: Gabriel's feeling that witches had to be dealt with
privately, instead of calling in one of the Acoma medicine societies who
are supposed to deal with such matters. Gabriel, for example, told stories
of his uncle's behavior that he considered normal:

> His uncle saw one night a large and a small fox—the latter being
> the "guardian" of the large fox—attack his flock. The uncle pursued
> them, and found two witches in human shape who had beside
> them foxskins, showing that they had just resumed human shape.
> (*Real* transformation, not just casting off a foxskin is meant.) They
> pleaded to be let off, but the uncle shot them.
>
> His uncle saw three deer: one male, two female, whose actions
> suggested that they were witches. He pursued them and when
> he saw them in human shape, despite their pleas, he shot them
> ("Gabriel Felipe," 1).

These actions Gabriel considered natural, whereas, according to
Devereux, a normal Acoma would have called in a medicine society: "The
normal Acoma considers witchcraft a public matter. This inmate considered it a private grievance" ("Gabriel Felipe," 1). In addition to regular
persecution dreams Gabriel told Devereux that he was bothered by hearing whistling sounds at night that were not heard by others: "although he

was somewhat vague at this point, he seemed to say that ghosts converse by whistling" ("Gabriel Felipe," 3). In view of these factors and his entire examination, Devereux concludes his report on Gabriel with an inferential reconstruction of his state of mind during the killing:

> The evening before [the offense], the inmate was frightened by the ominous hooting of owls—birds of ill omen in Acoma culture. He was also quite drunk. During the hunt [the morning of the killing] he saw at thirty yards a large antlered deer—shot at it—thought he hit it, but the deer disappeared. When he went to the spot he saw no tracks, although he is a good tracker. This suggested to him—quite frighteningly—that he had had an experience with a witch-deer. . . . The pursuit itself [by Garcia] startled and frightened him a great deal, since being pursued is one of his principal nightmares. It is interesting to note that although they had out-distanced the police car, they stopped. One of Gabriel's nightmares is that of being pursued and being unable to get away and, for reasons of internal, neurotic motivation, [*sic*] *could* not get away. By the time he stopped the pickup . . . he was temporarily insane ("Gabriel Felipe," 5).

As in his examination of Gabriel, Devereux argued that William Felipe was psychotic on the basis of his transformations of cultural beliefs about witchcraft into private, personal, and paranoiac ideas.[8] People on the Acoma reservation hated and envied him and caused him trouble by witchery. "Sent" illness (witchcraft) killed his child. Fox-witches tore out the throat of several of his sheep but did not eat them. Like Gabriel, he believed that his maternal uncle had trouble with three witch-deer, and that the morning of Garcia's killing, Gabriel shot at a witch-deer. But Devereux shows that William's problems were more deeply entwined with the psychological history of his family. In a December 16, 1952, statement, William spoke poignantly of the return of an elder brother from the service:

> He lost his heart. The Indian doctors went out and brought his heart back and he was supposed to swallow it and chew it, but my brother chewed it and he did not get any better. The Indian doctors burned special weeds and my brother swallowed the

smoke and then he was supposed to throw up his bad heart and bad spirits and feel better. The Indian doctors did this four times in four days, but he did not get better and he died in the state hospital in Colorado (Navarre, 2).

William believed that his natural father Santiago Felipe, who had died some years before of a fall from a cliff, appeared to his maternal aunt and his sister with the top of his body transformed into a mountain lion, and that the aunt caused his father to die by supernatural means. William told Devereux that he knew this because when the corpse of his father was found in the cleft of a rock, he had an "old hole" in his side which had been plugged (not paginated).

William believed that the killing of Garcia was not an act of free will, but the result of having been witched. He had recurring anxiety dreams that he had had a terrible dream of being pushed off a cliff. He considered this dream to be an omen of something terrible to happen.[9] Devereux recreated what did happen in William's mind on April 11, 1952, as follows:

Each human being has a touchy point little related to reality. In this case of this man being pursued was about the worst thing that could happen to him, especially when it came on top of an anxiety dream and an encounter with a witch-deer—and under the influence of alcohol. On top of all this, he was pursued by a *black car*, which he related to the ominous black car which he had hallucinated sometime earlier near a salt lake. At this time the patient was in a state of *insane fear*, to such an extent that he is convinced that the black car was *flying* after him. (I carefully ascertained that he meant "flying" literally, and not in the sense of "going fast.") to the inmate this pursuit was a witch experience, triggering off temporary insanity. In reply to what he saw when he aimed, looking down the barrel, he replied, in obvious confusion "Something black—just a black car—something black." When asked the color of the trooper's uniform he hesitated and had great trouble recalling that it was black. As far as the inmate knows now, he shot simply at something black: a black car which pursued him ("William Felipe," 6).

In sum, Devereux argued in his report to the court that previous legal tellings of the killing were culturally blind, as they ignored the compelling psychic factors which moved the Felipes to kill Nash Garcia. He cautioned that while Indian beliefs are sometimes mistaken for delusions, in this case the danger was the reverse: that the delusional character of Indian beliefs, as held by the Felipes, might be mistaken for "normal" Acoma belief. The degree and manner of the brothers' witch beliefs marked them as psychotic rather than cultural in character.

Devereux's report was offered to Judge Hatch in an effort to obtain another trial for the Felipes. The new evidence of a supernatural context for the murder gained the Felipes not a second trial but a final headline and a reduced sentence ("'Delusions of Witchcraft,'" 8). On March 3, 1953, Judge Hatch spared them the electric chair and sent them to prison for life.

IV

Writers of fiction and storytellers are united in their need to imagine historical events. Even as the pages of the *Albuquerque Journal* yellowed and the Felipe brothers' trial record slipped into the federal storage center in Denver, memories of the Nash Garcia case lived in rumor along Highway 66. The rumors solidified into a legendary image of Garcia very different from the journalistic image I have reviewed. Leslie Silko recalls:

> This one rumor was that he hated Indians and that he'd been transferred to the Laguna area from near Cuba or Santa Fe because his superiors already knew he was psychotic about Indians. Another story was that his own family admitted that there was something haywire with him, and he got what was coming to him.[10]

In a recent visit to Laguna-Acoma High School, Silko found that well over half the children in her audience were aware of this image of Garcia. Five years old when the Felipe brothers were sent to prison, what Silko knows of the case is based on these tellings of the killing she heard as she grew up at Laguna. This rumor image of an Indian-hating Garcia is evident in "Tony's Story," as are the bare bones of the event that we have viewed in newspaper accounts and the trial record: the returned veteran, the wine, the chase, the 30–30, the burning of the body. Throughout it is clear that Silko has very consciously shaped the event in her own mold.

A parched summer landscape is integral to Silko's design, and she shifts the time of the action from early spring to San Lorenzo Day late in summer. From the opening of the story, life on the reservation withers as the pueblo awaits overdue summer rains. But it is only as the brutal state trooper appears behind him on the highway that Antonio Sousea "knew why the drought had come that summer (Silko in Rosen, *The Man to Send Rain Clouds*, 73). In the story's climactic scene Antonio is moved to act on that recognition, and shoots the trooper. The sand soaks up the trooper's blood even as it had Leon's on the carnival grounds in the opening scene of the story: "The tumbleweeds and tall yellow grass were sprayed with glossy, bright blood. He was on his back, and the sand between his legs and along his left side was soaking up the dark, heavy blood—it had not rained for a long time, and even the tumbleweeds were dying" (77). As the trooper and his car burn, the story closes with rain clouds gathering in the west.

Silko also shapes her characters carefully. The Felipe brothers of fact become types no less a pair for their lack of a blood relation. Tony is the younger, yet a traditionalist, deferential even in his final action. Leon is aggressive, a war veteran. He talks too loudly, shakes hands like a white man, and drinks boldly in defiance of the whiteman's law. In conflict with the trooper, Leon holds to his "rights" and "letters to the BIA" for support; Tony to old Teofilo's stories and chants and arrowheads. As the "he" becomes an "it" for Tony, the trooper remains a "big Bastard" and a "state cop" to the end for Leon. Similarly, the historic Nash Garcia undergoes a transformation to become the state cop in "Tony's Story." Silko draws him as purely symbolic as the albino in N. Scott Momaday's *House Made of Dawn*. Like the albino, the state cop hides behind prominent dark glasses and speaks in a high pitched voice. And like the albino he is perceived as a witch.

The witch perception lies at the very center of Silko's telling of the event, giving it an eerie likeness to the Devereux report. The presence of the big cop lingers with Tony as he returns from the San Lorenzo Day carnival:

> Stillness breathed around me, and I wanted to run from the feeling behind me in the dark; the stories about witches ran with me. That night I had a dream—the big cop was pointing a long bone at me—they always use human bones, and the whiteness flashed silver in the moonlight where he stood. He didn't have a human face—only little, round, white-rimmed eyes on a black ceremonial mask (72).

Later when Tony looks at the cop he sees only "the dark image of a man" which he avoids, remembering his parents' caution "not to look into the masked dancer's eyes because they would grab me, and my eyes would not stop" (73–74). Pursued by the cop in the final scene, Tony must look at the cop and his eyes do not stop until the cop's body is in flames. Disposal of the witch-cop by burning is one of the few supernatural motifs Silko uses which Devereux does not mention in his analysis of Willie Felipe. Just as Willie Felipe has ominous dreams which foreshadow the killing of Garcia, so too Tony. As Felipe felt pursued by a black object and saw only a black object when he shot, so too Tony doesn't remember aiming and kills not a cop but a witch in a "strange form." But Silko was unaware of the Devereux report until well after publication of the story, and despite similarities, the two accounts of the killing are profoundly different. As I have noted, Devereux interpreted the Felipes' witch beliefs as aberrant by Acoma standards, as evidence of their psychosis. Linking the witch motif with the drought setting, Silko creates a psychological and cultural context in which Tony is drawn irreversibly to the killing. Tony's witch perception gives evidence of the persistence of cultural belief. By force of characterization and setting, Silko casts the act which rises from the belief in an affirmative tone.

V

If Leslie Silko's telling of the event gives form to Devereux's psychological telling, Simon Ortiz's "The Killing of a State Cop" does the same for journalistic accounts. Twelve years old at the time of the killing and a resident of the reservation on which it occurred, Ortiz's experience with the event was more immediate than Silko's. Accordingly, his story is more faithful to the "facts" of the case. "The Killing of a State Cop" reflects the rumored image of Garcia, but not to the exclusion of the tone of journalistic accounts. In fact, Ortiz's description of the murder of Luis Baca rivals the tellings of the *Albuquerque Journal* and prosecutor Sanchez in its graphic detail. He emphasizes the deliberate fashion in which the brothers lured Baca to the murder scene and evokes a sort of pathos for Baca as he dies: "He called something like he was crying. 'Compadre,' he said. He held up his right hand and reached to us" (107).

But while Ortiz describes the murder with a chilling realism, like Silko he shapes our reaction to it through his art. One example of this is the way in which he handles motivation. As in newspaper and trial accounts, blame for the killing is most explicitly placed on the wine Felipe drank and the craziness it created in him. Yet Ortiz's Felipe recognizes that in some fey sense Baca *wanted* to die:

> Aiee, I can see stupidity in a man. Sometimes even my own. I can see a man's drunkenness making him do crazy things. And Luis Baca, a very stupid son-of-a-bitch, was more than I could see. He wanted to die. And I, because I was drunken and *muy loco* like a Mexican friend I had from Nogales used to say about me when we would play with the whores in Korea and Tokyo, wanted to make him die (106).

The psychological bond between Felipe and Baca suggested here is given a faint supernatural tone by other details in the story. Felipe sees the same disguised fear in Antonio while they wait to ambush Baca as when they "were kids and he used to pretend not to be scared of rattlesnakes" (107). After they shoot, Baca's car continues on in a preternatural way.

A key device Ortiz uses to mitigate our response to the killing is point of view. The story is told by a young Acoma who like Ortiz was twelve years old at the time of the killing. Felipe brothered the narrator. He took him hunting and fishing and shared his plans with him. More importantly, Felipe told the boy stories and, as a story, the telling of the killing was special for Felipe wanted the narrator "to remember what he said always" (101). Felipe's purpose in telling the killing to the boy was clearly didactic: "[Felipe] told me I better learn to be something more than him, a guy who would probably die in the electric chair up at Santa Fe" (103).

Ortiz uses the boy's comments on Felipe to frame his story much as Silko uses setting to frame hers. The boy's opening comments give depth to the "inapt" Felipe of press and legal tellings at the same time they place the killing in another political context entirely: "That was one trouble with him [Felipe]. He was always thinking about what other people could do to you. Not the people around our place, the Indians, but other people" (101). The remark turns the paranoia assigned the brothers by Devereux into too deep a concern with oppression. Baca's Indian-hating becomes but an explicit and extreme case of a more general and constant pressure, a case answered by an extreme act.

But Ortiz does not let us off so easily. The narrator's closing comments reveal that fact and fiction are blurred in his mind. Did the murder happen or was it but another of Felipe's stories? Even after his parents confirm the story's reality—perhaps the more so—the boy is left with a feeling of vague hopelessness. Appropriately, the narrator's initial response to this malaise is vaguely Christian: "Every night, for quite a while, I prayed a rosary or something for him" (108). The veneer of Christian hope gives little solace, and it is finally the telling of the story itself which is the narrator's best response to his experience with Felipe not as a polemic or an apology, but as a culturally sensitive documentary.

VI

There is one other imaginative account which may be based in part on the Nash Garcia case. N. Scott Momaday has on occasion remarked that portions of the plot of his novel *House Made of Dawn* were loosely based on an actual case history.[11] He recalls reading of a young Indian who when brought to trial for murdering a man testified that he killed the man because he was a witch. Witch murders have occurred periodically throughout the history of the American Southwest and only a speculative link may be made between the newspaper account Momaday noticed and reports on the supernatural aspects of the Garcia case.[12] Nonetheless, links between Momaday's novel and the case are provocative.

Springfield psychiatrist Robert Navarre's "Report of Neuropsychiatric Examination of William Felipe" contains the following summary of Felipe's psychic history:

After his discharge he returned to his old life on the Acoma Reservation. The patient was now no longer contented with his old life. . . . He became quite restless and frequently had an urge to leave the reservation, and "go someplace." He became increasingly irritable and found it difficult to control himself. He had difficulty sleeping at night, had nightmares about his Army experiences, and relived his experiences during which artillery shells and mortar shells hit the ground very close to him. At night he would shake and tremble when he heard a sudden noise. His heart would beat fast, his hands would shake, he would develop twitching of his eyes and lips, he would have difficulty in getting his breath, and would sweat all over and feel chilly. At night he would awake suddenly: "It feels like somebody is standing there right beside me, right behind me and I start to get scared after that." He would then have great difficulty in going back to sleep. He became apprehensive of some impending disaster, and had a strong urge to do something about this, but did not know what to do. He had dreams in which snakes tried to kill him. . . . The only relief that he was able to obtain from all these difficulties was from drinking alcohol (3–4).

The report reads as a summary of Abel's return to Walatowa after World War II in *House Made of Dawn*. The dreamlike memory of combat and a mysterious threatening presence come together for him at the end of Part One of that novel when he kills an albino who he perceives as a snake-witch outside a bar.[13] Momaday turns in the rest of the novel from perspective to perspective to give us glimpses of the motivation of that act. Abel himself views the act as simple: "A man kills such an enemy if he can" (95). Father Olguin, curate at Walatowa, argues at Abel's trial "that in his own mind it was not a man he killed, but something like an evil spirit," and adds: "I believe that this man was moved to do what he did by an act of imagination so compelling as to be inconceivable to us" (94). The court responds to Olguin with facts: "He committed a brutal and premeditated act which we have no choice but to call by its right name" (94). But the cultural enigma posed by the murder is most memorably expressed in the novel by Tosamah, Kiowa Priest of the Sun, in a typically sardonic burst:

And do you know what he said? I mean, do you have an *idea* what that cat said? A *snake*, he said. He killed a goddam *snake*! *The corpus delicti*, see, *he threatened to turn himself into a snake*, for crissake, and rattle around a little bit. Now ain't that something, though? Can you *imagine* what went on at that trial? There was this longhair, see, cold sober, of sound mind, and the goddam judge looking on, and the prosecutor trying to talk sense to that poor degenerate Indian: "Tell us about it, man. Give it to us straight." "Well, you honors, it was this way, see? I cut me up a little snake meat out there in the sand." Christ, man, that must have been our finest hour, better than Little Bighorn. That little no-count cat must have had the whole Jesus scheme right in the palm of his hand. Think of it! *What's-His-Name v. United States.* I mean, where's the legal precedent man? When you stop to think about it, due process is a hell of remedy for snakebite (136).

Like Silko and Ortiz, Momaday, through Tosamah, makes painfully visible the tension between the "facts" and the illusive cultural realities in a single murder case. But Momaday makes explicit what is only implied in the short stories. The murder typifies life at the friction point between cultures.

In a tantalizing forward to his fictionalized account of a Chicago murder, *Compulsion,* Meyer Levin proposes that certain crimes become emblems for the era in which they occur. Dostoevsky's *Crime and Punishment* evokes the "feverish soul-searching" of nineteenth-century Russia, *An American Tragedy* the "sociological thinking" of Dreiser's America (ix). Similarly, my colleague John Hallowell suggests that *"In Cold Blood* exemplifies the meaningless crime that has become symptomatic of America in the last decade" (*Between Fact and Fiction,* 2). From a more restricted vantage, journalistic, legal and psychiatric records, taken together with the imaginative accounts of Silko, Ortiz, and Momaday, refract the killing of Nash Garcia in a varicolored emblem of post-war Indian relations.

Postscript February 15, 2008

"The Killing of a State Cop" is now available in Simon J. Ortiz, *Men on the Moon: Collected Short Stories* (Tucson: University of Arizona Press, 1999), 79–86. "Tony's Story" is available in Leslie Marmon Silko, *Storyteller* (New York: Seaver Books, 1981), 123–29. Both stories are reprinted in the very useful anthology, *Nothing But the Truth: An Anthology of Native American Literature* (Upper Saddle River, NJ: Prentice Hall, 2001), edited by John L. Purdy and James Ruppert.

I first read this paper on October 23, 1976, at the annual convention of the Rocky Mountain Modern Language Association in Santa Fe, New Mexico. It was published in Andrew Wiget, ed., *Critical Essays on Native American Literature* (Boston: G. K. Hall, 1985), 246–61, and in the *Wicazo Sa Review* 1 (1985), 17–25, then reprinted in Helen Jaskoski, *Leslie Marmon Silko: A Study of the Short Fiction* (New York: Twayne, 1998),

128–42. I have made some small corrections and editorial changes for this reprinting.

Dennis Hoilman published an article, "The Ethnic Imagination: A Case History," *The Canadian Journal of Native Studies* V, 2 (1985), 167–75, that uses many of the same court documents to interpret the stories of Ortiz and Silko. Among subsequent readings, Brewster E. Fitz, "Undermining Narrative Stereotypes in Simon Ortiz's 'The Killing of a State Cop,'" *MELUS* 28.2 (Summer 2003), 105–20, is notable. He argues that the story is "a retold 'confession' of the conflicted, suicidal 'stupidity and 'craziness' in persons from two cultural groups, Pueblo and Mexican, both marginalized to different degrees by dominant Anglo-European culture." Eric Cheyfitz, "The (Post) Colonial Construction of Indian Country: U.S. American Indian Literatures and Federal Indian Law," in *The Columbia Guide to American Indian Literatures of the United States Since 1945* (New York: Columbia University Press, 2006) 1–126, calls attention directly and exactly to shifting federal policies and evolving legal precedents in Indian Country as he gives a very compelling reading of the killing of the albino in *House Made of Dawn*, as well as of key scenes from other works of American Indian literature. At this juncture, I believe the most illuminating consideration of the actions of the Felipe brothers is Simon J. Ortiz's own in "Our Homeland, A National Sacrifice Area," which is the final section of *Fight Back: For the Sake of the People, For the Sake of the Land*, originally published as a separate monograph, republished in *Woven Stone* (Tucson: University of Arizona Press, 1992), 332–65.

"Teller of Stories: An Interview with Leslie Marmon Silko" by James C. Work and Pattie Cowell, *Colorado State Review*, New Series, VIII, 2 (Spring-Summer 1981), 68–79, contains some reflections by Leslie Silko on "Tony's Story" as a response to the "first assignment" in a creative writing class. Silko talks about knowing the story from family and community tradition and how, after I sent her the materials from the court documents, she felt "chills" as she compared the story she had imagined independently to the one Devereux developed in his analysis. She defers respectfully to Simon J. Ortiz, who knew "a great deal more" about the case, and locates her knowledge in oral tradition. In "Language and Literature from a Pueblo Indian Perspective," in *English Literature: Opening Up the Canon* (Baltimore: The Johns Hopkins University Press, 1981), she gives an account of visiting the high school in the Laguna-Acoma area and finding that "almost all" the students in the class she met had heard stories about the Felipe brothers and the killing of the state policeman. She recognizes this as powerful evidence of the persistence of oral traditions and "the story and the feeling of the story" (68–69). She has retold this visit a number of times, perhaps most powerfully and movingly in "Memory and Promise: Leslie Marmon Silko's Story," Laurie Mellas, *Mirage: The University of New Mexico Alumni Association* (Spring 2006), 10–16. The "heroic" image of Nash Garcia persists on the New Mexico State Police Association Web site, http://www.nmstatepoliceassoc.org/garcia.html, on which the following information is provided: "One of the brothers served 19 years in prison and the other served 20 years for the murder." The release of the Felipe brothers, thus, seems to have come about the same time as the publication of the two short stories.

NOTES

1. The stories were published in Kenneth Rosen, ed., *The Man to Send Rain Clouds: Contemporary Stories by American Indians* (New York: Viking, 1974). Two notable reviews of the book are Peter G. Beidler's, published in the *Arizona Quarterly* 30 (1974), 357–59, and Mick McAllister's in the *American Indian Quarterly* 1 (1974), 210–11.

2. I should like to acknowledge the help of my students Kathleen Cohill, Glenn D. Michaels, and Marlene Hoskie in gathering information on the case. Ann Neff in the Office of the Clerk, United States District Court, District of New Mexico, kindly arranged to have the file of *United States v. William R. Felipe and Gabriel Felipe* transferred from the Federal Records Center in Denver, Colorado, to United States District Court in Tucson for my review. The file includes transcripts of the trial, the court's correspondence regarding the case, and many of the exhibits introduced, which include the Felipes' confessions, reports of their psychiatric examinations, photos of the scene of the killing, and other materials.

3. Gabriel Felipe's driver's license was revoked February 1, 1952, following his conviction January 25, 1952, for driving while intoxicated.

4. For example, Dunleavy to Captain White, head of the New Mexico state police: "Are you familiar with the fact that less than two years ago the chief of the state police was convicted of putting a bicycle lock on the testicles of an accused person?" (*U.S. v Felipe et al.*, 168).

5. Compare Ortiz's "Kaiser and the War" (47–60).

6. Citations of military documents are from copies introduced as evidence at the trial.

7. One of Devereux's best-known contributions in the area is *Reality and Dream: Psychotherapy of a Plains Indian* (New York: International Universities Press, 1951).

8. Unless otherwise noted, the following material is taken from Devereux's "Summary Psychiatric Evaluation of William Felipe."

9. ". . . we must remember that his father was found dead in a cleft rock, after having fallen from a cliff. . . . Falling into a cleft rock also occurs in a rather terrible contest in one of the chief Acoma myths." Devereux, "Summary Psychiatric Evaluation of William Felipe," 3.

10. Leslie Marmon Silko, personal communication, March 30, 1976, Laguna, New Mexico.

11. N. Scott Momaday, personal communication, October 18, 1971, Omaha, Nebraska.

12. See Marc Simmons, *Witchcraft in the Southwest: Spanish and Indian Supernaturalism on the Rio Grande* (Flagstaff: Northland Press, 1974).

13. For a more extended treatment of the significance of the albino, see my essay "Words and Place: A Reading of *House Made of Dawn*," *Western American Literature* 11 (1977), 296–320.

WORKS CITED

Albuquerque Star, April 18, 1952, 24.

Albuquerque Star, April 19, 1952, 1, 10.

Beidler, Peter G. *Arizona Quarterly* 30 (1974): 357–59.

"'Delusions of Witchcraft' Cited in New Psychiatric Report on Felipe Brothers." *Albuquerque Journal*, February 27, 1953, 8.

Devereux, George. *Reality and Dream: Psychotherapy of a Plains Indian.* New York: International Universities Press, 1951.

———. "Summary Psychiatric Evaluation of Gabriel Felipe." Federal Criminal Medical Center, Springfield, Missouri, December 26, 1952. Filed as part of a Motion for New Trial by the defense, file stamped January 6, 1953.

———. "Summary Psychiatric Evaluation of William Felipe." Federal Criminal Medical Center, Springfield, Missouri, December 26, 1952. Filed as part of a Motion for New Trial by the defense, file stamped January 6, 1953.

Evers, Lawrence. "Words and Place: A Reading of *House Made of Dawn*." *Western American Literature* 11 (1977): 296–320.

Hallowell, John. *Between Fact and Fiction: The New Journalism and the Nonfiction Novel.* Chapel Hill: University of North Carolina Press, 1976.

"Job Came First." *Albuquerque Journal*, April 16, 1952, 13.

"Laud Slain Officer." *Albuquerque Journal*, April 15, 1952, 1.

Levin, Meyer. *Compulsion.* New York: Simon and Schuster, 1956.

McAllister, Mick. *American Indian Quarterly* 1 (1974): 210–11.

Momaday, N. Scott. *House Made of Dawn.* New York: New American Library, 1969.

———. Personal communication, October 18, 1971.

"Nash Garcia is Ambushed." *Albuquerque Journal*, April 1952, 1.

Navarre, Robert, "Report of Neuropsychiatric Examination of William Felipe." *United States v. William R. Felipe and Gabriel Felipe.*

"Nash Phillip Garcia." New Mexico State Police Association. http://www. nmstatepoliceassoc.org/garcia.html (accessed November 2008).

Ortiz, Simon. "Kaiser and the War." In *The Man to Send Rain Clouds: Contemporary Stories by American Indians*, edited by Kenneth Rosen, 47–60. New York: Viking, 1974.

Plaintiff's Exhibits 10 and 16. *U.S. v. William R. Felipe and Gabriel Felipe.*

Rosen Kenneth, ed. *The Man to Send Rain Clouds: Contemporary Stories by American Indians.* New York: Viking, 1974.

Silko, Leslie Marmon. Personal communication, March 30, 1976.

———. "Tony's Story." In *The Man to Send Rain Clouds: Contemporary Stories by American Indians*, edited by Kenneth Rosen, 69–78. New York: Viking, 1974.

Simmons, Marc. *Witchcraft in the Southwest: Spanish and Indian Supernaturalism on the Rio Grande.* Flagstaff: Northland Press, 1974.

United States v. William R. Felipe and Gabriel Felipe: Transcript of All Open Court Proceedings. United States District Court for the District of New Mexico. Criminal Docket No. 16902, 400–401.

Epilogue

Simon J. Ortiz—Wali wathon pa-ke pai

Robert Warrior

"Wali wathon pa-ke pai." That's the Osage way of saying that the people around the drum are singing pretty songs. It reminds me of one of my relatives, Arita Jump, who had the bench she sat on at the Pawhuska dance arbor placed in what she thought was the best spot where she could sit and listen to our dance songs, especially on the first afternoon, Thursday, when she thought the singers sang both slowly and prettily. I sometimes sat with Arita on that bench, and I learned pretty quickly that she was there to listen and watch, not to chit-chat.

Back then, I didn't know how to say "wali wathon pa-ke pai." I learned that sentence in a class in the Osage Nation Language Program, in which I was a student for five semesters before I took my current job at the University of Illinois. "Wali wathon pa-ke pai" came to mind one day when I was dancing, not at Pawhuska, but at one of the other Osage districts, my home district of Grayhorse, when I was searching for something to say to others who were learning wazhazhe i-e (our name for our language). It is a phrase that helped me express in wazhazhe i-e the depth and significance of what I was thinking and what I was feeling as we as Osage people took care of our dance, our drum, and our songs.

Simon Ortiz, an Indigenous writer who is fluent in his Native Acoma/ Keres language, was often on my mind as I drove the three hours between Norman, Oklahoma and Pawhuska for my weekly language classes. No other intellectual encouraged me in my studies of wazhazhe i-e more than Simon, and his published work on the importance of Indigenous languages helped me crystallize my own sense of how and why what I was learning was important.

As I drove and tried to do my homework, one passage from Simon's work came often to mind. In a 1977 booklet on language, perception, and song reprinted in this volume, he mentions a young Navajo, or Diné, woman who related to him her frustration at learning her birthright language, saying, "I can't seem to hear the parts of it" (*Song, Poetry and Language*, 2). Responding by describing how his home community of Acoma Pueblo regards spoken language "with a sense of completeness," Ortiz goes on to say, "And I meant that a word is not spoken in any separate parts, that is, with reference to linguistic structure, technique of diction, nuance of sound, tonal quality, inflection, etc. Words are spoken as complete words" (2).

Ortiz then relates how he himself had asked his father about certain Acoma words, saying, "What does that word break down to? . . . And he has looked at me with exasperated—slightly pained—expression on his face, wondering what I mean. And he tells me, 'It doesn't break down into anything'" (2). This, for Ortiz, who was saying it in an essay published three decades ago, is more than a neat, romantic story about incommensurability. It was part of a larger theory he was articulating about the intricate relationship between language, perception, experience, and expression. That is, for Ortiz in 1977, language not only expresses our experiences, but is itself an experience. Thirty years later, I found myself involved in the same dynamics, and I was thankful to have Simon Ortiz's words and wisdom to help me. It was my sitting with Arita Jump and listening to a drum and its singers and watching the dancers and dancing myself that I came to really understand the depth of my Osage language. As I danced and thought to myself "Wali wathon pa-ke pai," these words conveyed the weight of a twenty-first-century Osage man dancing in community, in ancestry, in tribal history and beauty, forward in our continuance. In this way, I heard Ortiz teaching us the importance of language in its wholeness.

As I finished reading this collection of writings by Simon Ortiz, Evelina Zuni Lucero, Susan Berry Brill de Ramírez, Greg Cajete, Ralph Salisbury, David Dunaway, Kimberly Roppolo, Leslie Marmon Silko, Gwen Griffin, Joy Harjo, Laura Tohe, Kate Shanley, Esther Belin, Roger Dunsmore, Kimberly Blaeser, David Moore, Sophia Cantave, Jeff Berglund, Elizabeth Ammons, Sean Kicummah Teuton, Debbie Reese, Elizabeth Archuleta, Geary Hobson, and Lawrence Evers, I thought to myself, "Wali wathon pa-ke pai," and thanked Simon Ortiz for helping me find the gift of my own language, which I have taken to calling my birthright language, that helps me express my appreciation. I hope other readers agree that these writers, especially Simon, are singing pretty songs.

About a year before I started taking classes in wazhazhe i-e, Simon Ortiz came to the University of Oklahoma as a distinguished lecturer. I was then teaching at Oklahoma and had arranged Simon's visit, so I had the good pleasure of taking him from place to place on his itinerary, or making sure whomever was charged with doing so got him where he was supposed to be.

For Simon's second afternoon, I blocked out lunch and a couple of hours afterward for him to spend with Geary and Barbara Hobson, old friends from Albuquerque in the 1970s who had since come to OU. After lunch with both of them, Simon sat in Geary's office where the two of them talked until the next event on the schedule later in the afternoon. Geary was to bring Simon to Monnett Hall on the North Oval of the OU campus a few minutes before Simon's appearance there, so I waited on a bench outside to make sure everything happened as planned.

Soon, I saw Simon and Geary walking toward Monnett. As they came closer, I found myself admiring their old friendship and the familiarity they seemed to be enjoying. They could have been any two men making their way across campus, but I marveled at the depth of meaning their friendship represented and how this short journey represented a much longer journey that had begun years before. Watching them, I thought of Albuquerque in the 1970s and how it became a crossroads that changed the landscape of what we now know as Native literature. Simon's published work as a poet, short story writer, and essayist, of course, is incredible, and Geary has written more than his share, as well. But I was thinking more of the dozens of writers these men had published in their important anthologies, how many scores they had encouraged and mentored, how many hundreds they had influenced, how many thousands had listened to them, and how many thousands more had read their work. Wending their way to Simon's next event, they looked to me satisfied, and I would guess even more that they were each happy to be able to talk about their lives and their work with someone who had seen it all unfold without the gauzes and screens of history.

As they got close enough to hear me, I stood and said something like, "I wish I had a camera. I would love to have a picture of you two old friends walking here together." Simon smiled and replied, "You already do." And indeed, I do have that picture and will treasure it as I do so many other memories of Simon Ortiz.

Looking at all the different things so many people have had to say about Simon's work in these pages, I am thankful that we have all taken the time to honor this great writer in a way that he has deserved for a long time. There's so much good and deep analysis of specific aspects of Simon's work here, but I think it's important to say here at the end that our work in these pages is just a short journey in what has been a long, beautiful trek. I, for one, feel fortunate to be part of the journey.

It's remarkable company we're in here. I keep marveling at the web of influence and relationships—can you believe that Joy Harjo actually says that Simon gave her the gift of poetry? Or that Leslie Silko credits Simon with helping her come to an understanding that she could be a writer? We're in the stratosphere here, and I think it's worth remembering at the close of this volume that we transcend into it and fly through it because of the power of the work. Simon is so gracious to so many, it's worth remembering that we have been fortunate to tag along. Maybe one or several of us will learn to fly so high on our own, but most of us are just along for the ride.

As much as anything, though, as I consider the pieces gathered here, I keep thinking that there's so much more to say. That's the point, though, about Simon's work. There is so much more to say, and Simon, this volume's editors, the writers, critics, readers, and listeners won't stop saying those things anytime soon. We may only just now be comprehending it, but these poems, stories, and essays of Simon Ortiz's that he has been writing and we have been reading and teaching are going to continue as surely as the Indigenous people Simon has written about, and their communities, and the lands upon which they live, will continue. As much or more than any Indigenous writer, Simon has managed to link the things he writes to our continuance as peoples. And so we continue, to use a term that Simon has defined for us so complexly. We continue.

What I hope readers, writers, and critics in the future experience in the work of Simon Ortiz is the same wonder that I do. Around the time Simon visited OU, I taught a graduate seminar that traced his writing from the earliest chapbooks to the present. What struck me week by week was how, whether in turns of phrase, developments in plots, images, or consistency across genres, time, and forms, Ortiz found so many ways to astonish me as a reader. Just think of the way he writes about being a devoted father who teaches his young son about the realities of colonialism in one poem, the way he evinces both the idea of a community sharing in his recipe for really good chili, and a lonely political vigil with Rex the dog near Fort Lewis College in another, or the way he demonstrates the possibility of emotional and spiritual solidarity between a Pueblo man and a white Oklahoman who labor together in a mine in the short story "To Change in a Good Way."

Then think about that woman on the street in "I Tell You Now." Many Indigenous writers cower at accusations that their work is irrelevant to Indigenous communities, but Simon insists on communicating with this woman through his poem as if it's the most natural thing to do. Or think about the countless children who have learned an alternative to what it means to be Indigenous from *The People Will Continue* or *The Good Rainbow Road*. Then there's the voluminous nonfiction, from the essays about language to the searing latest work on trauma and memory.

Having read from that early work to the present, I could only posit that Ortiz has managed to do so much because of the depth of his honesty. "Grief memorizes this grass" is the incredibly focused first image in the body of *from Sand Creek*. Contrast that subjectivity with the hazy consciousness of the man passing out on the floor in the middle of the night in "The Wisconsin Horse." Now add to the picture the non-judgmental yet incisive comments about overcoming alcohol addiction in Simon's introduction to *Woven Stone* and subsequent writings. Failure, recovery, and victory pale before the sheer honesty of the arc between the 1970s and now.

Beyond all these things that Simon has written, there's so much more, and my hope for his readers is that they will glimpse in his work all the different ways he has participated in the complex and changing Indigenous world. He has done important work as an editor, for instance, not just in *Earth Power Coming* and *Speaking for the Generations* and *Beyond the Reach of Time and Change*, but also his work on the *Treaty Council News* and the National Indian Youth Council's *ABC: Americans Before Columbus* back in the 1970s. He wrote and published bilingual books for kids at Jemez Pueblo and has contributed to innumerable books, journals, and other publication efforts. He is also a veteran of the United States Armed Forces, has worked as a miner, attended the first Convocation of American Indian Scholars, and has had a distinguished career as a college professor.

For Simon's reading at Oklahoma in 2005, I asked the brothers of Sigma Nu Alpha Gamma (also known as the Society of Native American Gentleman, or SNAG) to welcome him with some songs at their fraternity drum. The reading was at 7 p.m., but I asked them to start a little early. As the standing-room only crowd gathered in the Oklahoma Memorial Union, the men of SNAG sang, filling all three floors of the Union with their steady beats and glorious voices. Later, right before he read, SNAG sang an honor song for Simon. It was really cool.

Most readings are just readings—the same sorts of people gathering to hear the same sorts of fiction or poetry in the same sorts of places. Simon, though, drew an incredible array of people from on and off campus—including people he hadn't seen since the 1970s who somehow managed to hear about the event—and he drew us all into his singular world of language, history, and perception. And, at least on that night, he did a little singing of his own to complement the drum.

I was sad to see it end and wanted to hear more. The same is true here. It seems like we all ought to keep going until we have managed to more thoroughly and completely say what needs to be said about Simon and his work. But then I close my eyes and bring a picture to mind of that night—the words, the music, and the people. And it continues. Thanks, Simon, for that picture and for all that you've done to help me value it. Back then, I didn't know how to say in my birthright language how well you have done in all your work to make so many things possible for so many of us. Now I do.

Tha-le wa-zho-e, my friend. Tha-le wa-zho-e.

CONTRIBUTORS

Elizabeth Ammons is Harriet H. Fay Professor of Literature at Tufts University. She is the author of *Edith Wharton's Argument with America* (1980) and *Conflicting Stories: American Women Writers at the Turn into the Twentieth Century* (1991) as well as numerous essays, and she has edited several volumes, including *Short Fiction by Black Women, 1900–1920* (1991) and *Harriet Beecher Stowe's "Uncle Tom's Cabin": A Casebook* (2007). She teaches courses on environmental justice and on Native American writers and is currently working on a book about activism and American literature.

Elizabeth Archuleta (Yaqui) teaches in Arizona State University's Women and Gender Studies program. She has published articles in *Wicazo Sa Review, SAIL, American Indian Quarterly, New Mexico Historical Review, Indigenous Peoples' Journal of Law, Culture & Resistance*, and has a forthcoming essay in the edited collection, *The National Museum of the American Indian: Critical Conversations*. She is a 2008–2009 Ford Diversity Postdoctoral Fellowship recipient and received the Gilberto Espinosa Prize for Best Article, 2007 from *New Mexico Historical Review*.

Esther Belin, a writer and two-dimensional artist, teaches in the Writing Program at Fort Lewis College. In 2000, she won the American Book Award for her first book of poetry, *From the Belly of My Beauty* (University of Arizona Press). She lives in Durango, Colorado, about two hours from her tribal homeland.

Jeff Berglund is an Associate Professor of English at Northern Arizona University. He is the author of *Cannibal Fictions: American Explorations of Colonialism, Race, Gender, and Sexuality* (2006) and other works published in *Studies in American Indian Literature, American Indian Quarterly, Camera Obscura,* and *Studies in American Fiction.* He was the recipient of an NEH grant for his forthcoming project *Remembering the Long Walk to Hwééldi: Diné (Navajo) Memorial Histories.*

Kimberly Blaeser, a professor at University of Wisconsin–Milwaukee, teaches creative writing and Native American literature. Her publications include three books of poetry: *Trailing You* (1994), winner of the first book award from the Native Writers' Circle of the Americas, *Absentee Indians and Other Poems* (2002), and *Apprenticed to Justice* (2007). Her scholarly study, *Gerald Vizenor: Writing in the Oral Tradition* (1996), was the first native-written book-length study of an Indigenous author. Of Anishinaabe ancestry and an enrolled member of the Minnesota Chippewa Tribe who grew up on the White Earth Reservation, Blaeser is also the editor of *Stories Migrating Home: A Collection of Anishinaabe Prose* (1999) and *Traces in Blood, Bone, and Stone: Contemporary Ojibwe Poetry* (2006). Blaeser's poetry, short fiction, and personal essays have been widely anthologized. Her recent scholarly publications include "Cannons and Canonization: American Indian Poetries Through Autonomy, Colonization, Nationalism, and Decolonization" in *The Columbia Guide to American Indian Literatures of the United States.* She is currently at work on a verbal and material collage tentatively titled *Tinctures of a Family Tree.*

Susan Berry Brill de Ramírez is Caterpillar, Inc., Professor of English at Bradley University where she teaches Native American literatures, environmental literatures, ecocomposition, folklore, and literary criticism and theory. She is the author of *Wittgenstein and Critical Theory* (1995), *Contemporary American Indian Literatures and the Oral Tradition* (1999), *Native American Life-History Narratives: Colonial and Postcolonial Navajo Ethnography* (2007) and many scholarly essays. She is completing a monograph on Native American women's ethnography and is coediting a volume on orality in Native American and medieval literatures. She is currently exploring the concepts of the conversive and "geographies of belonging" in Indigenous and diasporic literatures.

Gregory Cajete is a Tewa Indian from Santa Clara Pueblo, New Mexico, whose work is dedicated to honoring the foundations of Indigenous knowledge in education. Cajete has written five books: *Look to the Mountain: An Ecology of Indigenous Education* (1994); *Ignite the Sparkle: An Indigenous Science Education Curriculum Model* (1999); *Spirit of the Game: Indigenous Wellsprings* (2004); *A People's Ecology: Explorations in Sustainable Living;* and *Native Science: Natural Laws of Interdependence* (1999 and 2000). He has served as a New Mexico Humanities scholar in ethno-botany of Northern New Mexico and as a member of the New Mexico Arts Commission. In addition, he has lectured at colleges and universities in the U.S., Canada, Mexico, New Zealand, Italy, Japan, and Russia. Currently, he is Director of Native American Studies and an Associate Professor in the Division of Language, Literacy and Socio-cultural Studies in the College of Education at the University of New Mexico.

Sophia Cantave is a doctoral student in the graduate program in English and American literature at Tufts University. Her essay "Who Gets to Create the Lasting Images? The Problem of Black Representation in *Uncle Tom's Cabin*" appeared in the MLA volume *Approaches to Teaching Stowe's Uncle Tom's Cabin* (2000) and is reprinted in the Oxford University Press volume, *Harriet Beecher Stowe's Uncle Tom's Cabin: A Casebook* (2007). She has presented conference papers on various topics and is currently finishing her dissertation on W. E. B. Du Bois, Zora Neale Hurston, and the idea of a Black Diaspora.

David Dunaway, author of half a dozen volumes of biography and history, is Professor of English at the University of New Mexico. Awarded the first PhD in American Studies from Berkeley, Dunaway specializes in the presentation of literature and history on public radio and television in such national series as *Writing the Southwest* (www.unm.edu/~wrtgsw), *Aldous Huxley's Brave New Worlds*, and *Across The Tracks: A Route 66 Story* (www.unm.edu/~rt66). His newest radio series is with Pete Seeger: How Can I Keep From Singing (www.peteseeger.org). Dunaway's Web site is www.davidkdunaway.com.

Roger Dunsmore retired in 2003 after forty years teaching in the Humanities and Wilderness Programs at the University of Montana. His

Earth's Mind: Essays in Native Literature was published by the University of New Mexico Press in 1997. A selection from his third volume of poems, *Tiger Hill: China Poems* (Camphorweed Press, 2002), won an Individual Artists Fellowship from the Montana Arts Council in 2001. He has twice been short-listed to the governor for the position of Montana Poet Laureate. He currently teaches literature and writing at the University of Montana Western in Dillon.

Lawrence Evers is a professor in the English Department at the University of Arizona, where he holds a joint appointment with American Indian Studies. His work includes *Yaqui Deer Song/Maso Bwikam: A Native American Poetry* (1987), co-authored with Felipe S. Molina, *Hiakim: The Yaqui Homeland* (1992), co-authored with Felipe S. Molina, *Home Places* (1995), co-edited with Ofelia Zepeda, and *Native American Oral Traditions* (2001), co-edited with Barre Toelken. "The Elders' Truth: A Yaqui Sermon," an article he co-authored with Felipe S. Molina, won the Spicer Award for the best article in the *Journal of the Southwest* in 1992. Evers has consistently provided leadership for the growth and development of American Indian Studies at the University of Arizona for over two decades.

Gwen Westerman Griffin is an enrolled member of the Sisseton Wahpeton Dakota Oyate. An award-winning artist, she has shown her work at the Northern Plains Indian Art Market and the Heard Museum Guild Indian Fair and Market, as well as in installations at Ancient Traders Gallery and The Minneapolis Foundation in Minneapolis, Minnesota. Her new book of poetry, *Follow the Blackbirds*, is forthcoming from Michigan State University Press. She is currently Professor of English at Minnesota State University, Mankato, and the Director of the Native American Literature Symposium.

Joy Harjo was born in Tulsa, Oklahoma, and is a member of the Mvskoke (Creek) Nation. Her seven books of poetry include *She Had Some Horses*, *The Woman Who Fell From the Sky*, and *How We Became Human, New and Selected Poems*. Her poetry has garnered many awards, including a Lila Wallace-Reader's Digest Award, the New Mexico Governor's Award for Excellence in the Arts, the Lifetime Achievement Award from the Native Writers Circle of the Americas; and the William Carlos Williams

Award from the Poetry Society of America. She has released three award-winning CDs of original music and performances: *Letter from the End of the Twentieth Century, Native Joy for Real,* and *She Had Some Horses.* A song from her forthcoming CD, *Winding through the Milky Way,* just won a New Mexico Music Award. She has received the Eagle Spirit Achievement Award for overall contributions in the arts from the American Indian Film Festival. She performs internationally solo and with her band Joy Harjo and the Arrow Dynamics Band, in which she sings and plays saxophone and flutes, and premiered a preview of her one-woman show, *Wings of Night Sky, Wings of Morning Light* at the Public Theater in New York City in December 2007. She co-wrote the signature film of the National Museum of the American Indian, *A Thousand Roads.* She is a founding board member of the Native Arts and Cultures Foundation. Harjo writes a column, "Comings and Goings," for her tribal newspaper, the *Muscogee Nation News.* She lives in Honolulu, Hawai'i, where she is a member of the Hui Nalu Canoe Club.

Geary Hobson (Cherokee-Arkansas Quapaw) teaches at the University of Oklahoma. He is the author of *The Last of the Ofos* (2000), a novel, *Deer Hunting and Other Poems* (1990), and *Plain of Jars and Other Stories* (forthcoming), as well as the editor of *The Remembered Earth: An Anthology of Contemporary Native American Literature* (1979).

Evelina Zuni Lucero, Isleta/Ohkay Owingeh Pueblo, is the chair of the creative writing department at the Institute of American Indian Arts. She is author of *Night Star, Morning Star* (2000), which won the 1999 First Book Award for Fiction from the Native Writers Circle of the Americas. Lucero received a 2007 residency at the Mabel Dodge Luhan House in Taos, New Mexico, a residency at the Hedgebrook Women Authoring Change program at Widhbey Island in June 2006 and was a Civitella Ranieri Fellow at the Civitella Ranieri International Artist Center in Umbertide, Italy, in 2004. She is working on a second novel, *Silicon Coyote,* in which the reservation casino becomes the point of intersection of history, myth, and imagination.

David L. Moore is a professor of English at the University of Montana. His fields of research and teaching at graduate and undergraduate levels include cross-cultural American Studies, Native American literatures,

Western American literatures, Peace Studies, Baha'i Studies, literature and the environment, and ecocritical and dialogical literary theory. He has taught previously at the University of South Dakota, Salish Kootenai College, University of Washington, and Cornell University. His book, *"That Dream Shall Have a Name": Native Americans Rewriting America,* is forthcoming from University of Nebraska Press. He lives with his family in Missoula, Montana (http://www.cas.umt.edu/english/faculty/moore.htm).

Simon J. Ortiz (Acoma Pueblo) is a poet, fiction writer, essayist, and storyteller. He has received many awards, including the "Returning the Gift" Lifetime Achievement Award, WESTLAF Lifetime Achievement Award, the New Mexico Governor's Award for Excellence in Art, and awards from the National Endowment of the Arts, the Lila Wallace—Reader's Digest Fund, Lannan Foundation's Artists in Residence. He is currently a Professor at Arizona State University, Department of English and American Indian Studies.

Debbie Reese is tribally enrolled at Nambe Pueblo. Raised at Nambe, Reese taught at Native schools in New Mexico and Oklahoma prior to undertaking doctoral study and a faculty appointment in American Indian Studies at the University of Illinois. Her research publications cross three disciplines: education, library school, and American Indian studies. She also publishes a widely read blog, "American Indians in Children's Literature" (www.americanindiansinchildrensliterature.blogspot.com).

Kimberly Roppolo, of Cherokee, Choctaw, and Creek descent, is a visiting assistant professor of Native Studies at the University of Oklahoma and the National Director of Wordcraft Circle of Native Writers and Storytellers. She has published poems in many journals and anthologies such as *Red Ink, Studies in American Indian Literatures, Native Realities, Frontiers: A Journal of Women's Studies, CCTE Studies,* MariJo Moore's *Birthed from Scorched Hearts: Women Respond to War,* Robert Bensen's *Children of the Dragonfly,* Geary Hobson and Janet McAdams's *The People Who Stayed Behind: Southeastern Indian Writing After the Removal,* and Gloria E. Anzaldúa and AnaLouise Keating's *This Bridge We Call Home: Radical Visions for Transformation.* She is the proud mother of three.

Ralph Salisbury's *Blind Pumper at the Well,* published by Salt Press in January 2008, is his ninth book of poems. His third book of short fiction, *The Indian Who Bombed Berlin,* will be published by Michigan State University Press in fall 2008. *Light from a Bullet Hole, Poems New and Selected* will be published by Silverfish in early 2009. His work has been published by *Greenfield Review, Poetry, The New Yorker, Northwest Review, Ploughshares,* and other journals. He has won a Chapelbrook Award, a Rockefeller Bellagio Award, and four Senior Fulbright Awards.

Kathryn W. Shanley (Assiniboine), Professor of the Native American Studies Department at the University of Montana and Special Assistant to the Provost on Native American and Indigenous Education, has published widely in the field of Native American literary criticism on issues of representation of Native American people in popular culture as well as about authors such as James Welch, Maria Campbell, Leslie Marmon Silko, Linda Hogan, Thomas King, and N. Scott Momaday. She has edited *Native American Literature: Boundaries and Sovereignties* (Delta, 2001) and an issue of *SAIL* as a tribute to James Welch.

Leslie Marmon Silko (Laguna Pueblo) is the author of novels, short stories, poetry, and essays: *Laguna Woman* (1973), *Ceremony* (1977), *Storyteller* (1981), *Almanac of the Dead* (1991), *Sacred Water* (1993), *Yellow Woman* and a *Beauty of the Spirit* (1996), and *Gardens in the Dunes* (1998). Her many awards include the Lifetime Achievement Award from the Native Writers Circle of the Americas, the National Endowment for the Arts, the Pushcart Prize for Poetry, and a MacArthur Foundation Fellowship. She recently completed a novella, *Ocean Story,* and is also working on a memoir, *Turquoise Ledge,* and a novel, *Blue Sevens.* She lives at the end of the road in the Tucson Mountains with seven dogs and ten parrots.

Sean Kicummah Teuton (Cherokee) is Associate Professor of English and American Indian Studies at the University of Wisconsin-Madison. Teuton is the author of *Red Land, Red Power: Grounding Knowledge in the American Indian Novel* (2008). He is at work on a second book on human rights and Native diplomacy titled "Cities of Refuge: American Indian Literary Internationalism," a project that has received the Woodrow

Wilson National Fellowship and the Katrin H. Lamon Fellowship at the School of American Research.

Laura Tohe is Diné (Navajo). She teaches in the English Department at Arizona State University. She wrote *Making Friends with Water* and the award-winning *No Parole Today*. She co-edited *Sister Nations: Native American Women Writers on Community*. She writes poetry, essays, short fiction, children's plays, and most recently, a commissioned libretto that has been produced in Canada, Europe, and the U.S.

Robert Warrior (Osage) is the co-author, most recently, of *American Indian Literary Nationalism* with Jace Weaver and Craig Womack (2006). He is Director of the American Indian Studies Program and Professor of American Indian Studies and English at the University of Illinois at Urbana-Champaign.

INDEX

CPSIA information can be obtained
at www.ICGtesting.com
Printed in the USA
LVHW070840270623
750890LV00001B/33